Battle for Stalingrad

Titles of Related Interest

Adragna	ON GUARD FOR VICTORY: MILITARY DOCTRINE AND BALLISTIC MISSILE DEFENSE IN THE USSR
Baxter	THE SOVIET WAY OF WARFARE
Bellamy	RED GOD OF WAR: SOVIET ARTILLERY & ROCKET FORCES
Gareev	M.V. FRUNZE, MILITARY THEORIST
Hemsley	SOVIET TROOP CONTROL
Laffin	BRASSEY'S BATTLES: 3500 YEARS OF CONFLICT, CAMPAIGNS AND WARS FROM A–Z
Messenger	HITLER'S GLADIATOR: THE LIFE AND TIMES OF SS-OBERSTGRUPPENFUEHRER AND GENERAL DER WAFFEN–SS SEP DIETRICH
Mikheyev	THE SOVIET PERSPECTIVE ON THE STRATEGIC DEFENSE INITIATIVE
Niepold	THE BATTLE FOR WHITE RUSSIA: THE DESTRUCTION OF ARMY GROUP CENTRE JUNE 1944
Parrish	BATTLE FOR MOSCOW: THE 1942 SOVIET GENERAL STAFF STUDY
Simpkin	RED ARMOUR

Related Periodicals*

Armed Forces Journal International

Defense Analysis

Specimen copies available upon request

Battle for Stalingrad

THE 1943 SOVIET GENERAL STAFF STUDY

Edited by

LOUIS C. ROTUNDO

PERGAMON-BRASSEY'S
International Defense Publishers, Inc.

Washington · New York · London · Oxford
Beijing · Frankfurt · São Paulo · Sydney · Tokyo · Toronto

USA (Editorial)	Pergamon-Brassey's International Defense Publishers, Inc, 8000 Westpark Drive, Fourth Floor, McLean, Virginia 22102, U.S.A.
(Orders)	Pergamon Press Inc, Maxwell House, Fairview Park, Elsmford, New York 10523, U.S.A.
UK (Editorial)	Brassey's Defence Publishers Ltd, 24 Gray's Inn Road, London WC1X 8HR, England
(Orders)	Brassey's Defence Publishers Ltd, Headington Hill Hall, Oxford OX3 0BW, England
PEOPLE'S REPUBLIC OF CHINA	Pergamon Press, Room 4037, Qianmen Hotel, Beijing, People's Republic of China
FEDERAL REPUBLIC OF GERMANY	Pergamon Press GmbH, Hammerweg 6, D-6242 Kronberg, Federal Republic of Germany
BRAZIL	Pergamon Editora Ltda, Rua Eça de Queiros, 346, CEP 04011, Paraiso, São Paulo, Brazil
AUSTRALIA	Pergamon-Brassey's Defence Publishers Pty Ltd, P.O. Box 544, Potts Point, N.S.W. 2011, Australia.
JAPAN	Pergamon Press, 5th Floor, Matsuoka Central Building, 1-7-1 Nishishinjuku, Shinjuku-ku, Tokyo 160, Japan
CANADA	Pergamon Press Canada Ltd, Suite No. 271, 253 College Street, Toronto, Ontario, Canada M5T 1R5

Copyright © 1989 Pergamon-Brassey's International Defense Publishers, Inc.

First edition 1989

Library of Congress Cataloging in Publication Data
Battle for Stalingrad: the 1943 Soviet General Staff study/edited by Louis C. Rotundo. – 1st ed.
p. cm.
Translation of unpublished manuscript: Sbornik materialov po izucheniiu opyta voiny. No. 6.
1. Stalingrad, Battle of, 1942–1943. I. Rotundo, Louis C.
II. Soviet Union. Raboche-Krest ianskaia Krasnaia Armiia.
General ñyi shtab. III. Title: Sbornik materialov po izucheniiu opyta voiny. No. 6.
D764.3.S7B33 1989   940.54′2–dc19   88–23503

Battle Library Cataloguing in Publication Data
Battle for Stalingrad: the 1943 Soviet
General Staff study.
1. World War 2. Battle of Stalingrad
I. Rotundo, Louis C.
940.54′21

ISBN 0–08–035974–4

Printed in Great Britain by BPCC Wheatons Ltd, Exeter

Contents

EDITOR'S INTRODUCTION   1

PREFACE   10

1. **Defeat of the German Troops at Stalingrad**   12

2. **The German Stalingrad Group**   21
   Operational Plans of the Germans in 1942   21
   The German Stalingrad Group and its "Liquidation"   26
   General Conclusions   37

3. **Battle for Stalingrad**   41
   The General Situation   41
   Operations on the Distant Approaches to Stalingrad   45
   The Battles on the Immediate Approaches to Stalingrad   54
   *Offensive Operations of the Stalingrad (Don) Front
   (September–October, 1942)*   59
   General Conclusions   63

4. **Flank Attacks of the Red Army in the
   Battle of Stalingrad**   69
   Enemy Grouping about November 19, 1942   69
   *Plan of Operations for the Encirclement of the Enemy Group
   at Stalingrad*   71
   *The Course of Operations for the Encirclement of the
   Stalingrad Group of Germans*   79
   Conclusions   89

5. **Action of the Mobile Group of the 5th Tank Army in a Breakthrough** 96

Conditions Under Which the Mobile Troops are Committed into a Breach 96
Missions of the 5th Tank Army and the Planning of the Operation 101
The Course of Operations and Actions of the Tank Corps in the Breakthrough 104
General Conclusions 110

6. **The Kotelnikovo Operation** 114

General Situation at the Beginning of the Operation 114
The Offensive of the Kotelnikovo Group of the Enemy 117
Offensive of the 2nd Guards Army and the 51st Army 124
General Conclusions 129

7. **Liquidation of the Encircled Stalingrad Group of the Enemy** 134

The Stalingrad Group of the Enemy (Its Composition and Its Intentions about January 10, 1943) 134
Preparation of the Operation on the Don Front 140
Summary, Conclusions, and Deductions 152

8. **Cavalry in the Offensive Operations Around Stalingrad** 159

Operations of the 8th Cavalry Corps 161
Operations of the 3rd Guards Cavalry Corps 168
Operations of the 4th Cavalry Corps 177
Conclusions Pertaining to the Strategic Employment of Cavalry 189
General Conclusions 196

9. **Artillery in the Offensive Operations at Stalingrad** 199

Operations of the Artillery of the Southwestern Front 199
Operations of the Artillery of the Don Front 210
Operations of the Artillery of the Stalingrad Front 217
Brief Conclusions 226

10. Action of the Army Air Forces in the Battle for Stalingrad 229

Operations of Aviation in the Period of the Withdrawal of Our Troops and the Defense of Stalingrad 230

Operations of Aviation in the Period of the Destruction of the Stalingrad Group of the Enemy 242

11. Adequate Provision of Engineer Means in the Operations of the Stalingrad Front 258

Missions and Plans for Providing Adequate Engineer Works 258

Work of the Engineer Units in the Preparatory Period of the Operation 263

Work of the Engineer Troops in the Period of the Operation 271

Command of the Engineer Troops 276

General Conclusions 279

12. Work of the Road Units at Stalingrad 281

The Don Front 281

The Stalingrad Front 285

13. Means of Antiaircraft Defense in the Fight for Stalingrad 288

Operations of the Aviation of the Enemy 289

Tactical Employment of the Means of Antiaircraft Defense 293

Command of Antiaircraft Defense 305

Conclusions 307

14. Editor's Appendix 311

ABOUT THE EDITOR 326

NAME INDEX 327

SUBJECT INDEX 329

Editor's Introduction

Of the major battles of the German–Soviet war of 1941–45, perhaps the most well-known in Western historiography is the struggle for the city of Stalingrad. The results of that summer through winter campaign on the Volga have been portrayed many times as a significant turning point in the course of World War II. As a result, the Stalingrad battle has received a great deal of attention, not only from German and American writers but also logically from the Soviet side where the heroic struggle marks the beginning of the long road of liberation for the occupied parts of the Soviet Union.[1] This analysis of the battle began even before the end of the war.

As World War II progressed, the Soviet General Staff quickly discerned the need to formalize the learning process for assimilating combat experiences. As a result, in 1942 the General Staff initially organized a special section within its Operations Division to collect and disseminate the practical lessons learned through Soviet combat operations during the war. In 1944, due to the constantly increasing workload, the General Staff expanded the section to become the Department for the Use of War Experience led by Major General P.P. Vechnyi. Under Vechnyi's guidance, a total of 26 consecutive studies—from the first in 1942 to no.26 in 1948—were prepared and issued under the common title of *Sbornik materialov po izucheniiu opyta voiny* (*Collection of Materials for the Study of War Experiences*). The material, aimed primarily at senior officers and command personnel, was designed as an information tool and an instructional publication. The present volume, *The Battle for Stalingrad*, was prepared and issued as study no.6 in 1943.

As would be expected in commemoration of so outstanding a victory, Soviet literature on the battle of Stalingrad has been quite detailed and continues to present a varying image of the actual campaign. These writings reflect not only the heroism of the troops but the strategic and operational decisions that led to the final destruction of the German 6th Army. The available Soviet material falls roughly into three groups: the memoirs of the participants, the scholarly studies and official histories, and the collection of archival material. In some respects these writings, having appeared at different times, mirror the rise and fall of military and political reputations. To a degree, they reflect the petty jealousies and continued animosities of many of the commanders involved as well as the then-*current* political truths. However, with those understandings aside, the available significant literature help present the campaign as a more complete picture than was possible with the primarily German sources available shortly after the war.

Of the major participants in the battle for Stalingrad that were in a position to discuss the planning and execution of the major decisions, only a handful of individuals have left memoirs reflecting the significant decisions relating to the 1942 defensive struggles in the southern Soviet Union and the decisive November counteroffensive. At the highest level, J.V. Stalin never left any written documents that could accord with the detailed analysis necessary to study the battle. Similarly, N.S. Khrushchev has left memoirs of the battle, but they form only a small, but nonetheless important, source of information on command decisions.[2] Another potential primary source of information, G.M. Malenkov, in his role as Stalin's representative at the front, left no authoritative work. Thus, by default, the best and most authoritative work remains that by Marshal of the Soviet Union G.K. Zhukov.

Zhukov's two-volume *Reminiscences and Reflections* provides a detailed look at the inner workings of the Soviet High Command as well as most of the important decisions that went into the major operations of the war.[3] Zhukov however, was a prolific writer and these official two volumes must be supplemented by the numerous articles that he wrote for various other publications. Zhukov's memoirs, appearing late in the 1960s and a later edition appearing in 1974, provide an especially clear insight into the Stalingrad decisionmaking for the long-planned counteroffensive. As deputy to the supreme commander, Zhukov more than most had access to the relevant actors and could authoritatively discuss the elements that went into the final decisions. Also, Zhukov served as overall director and was admirably positioned to discuss his role in the key September counterattacks on the Don land-bridge north of Stalingrad. Zhukov's memoirs however, remain as one personal account and should only be read in conjunction with the equally important remembrances of Marshal of the Soviet Union A.M. Vasilevskii. Vasilevskii's book, *A Lifelong Cause*, unfortunately is somewhat unfulfilling, since it is designed for general readership. However, the numerous articles written by this former Chief of the General Staff nicely supplement the official directives and insights that are missing from the book.[4] In his remembrances, Vasilevskii is basically supportive of Zhukov's version of the planning phase of the Stalingrad campaign. Additionally, as the High Command

(*Stavka*) representative on the scene, Vasilevskii participated in most of the important operational decisions that occurred after the initial breakthrough. His insights help give the battle a more complete image than is found in the Zhukov memoirs, since Zhukov was not present for the actual counteroffensive.

Finally, there is the memoir of the Chief Marshal of Artillery N.N. Voronov who served also as representative of the High Command during the battle and coordinated the reduction of the Stalingrad pocket. His book, entitled *Na sluzhbe voennoi*, although quite informative, is full of philosophical contradictions and factual omissions.[5] For example, although the work was published under Khrushchev and is certainly critical of Stalin in some sections, it also contains praise for the Supreme Commander and his leadership. Likewise although the overall depth of coverage of events is good, it neglects or skims over other important battles. With regard to Stalingrad, the coverage is mixed at best. Yet as a major participant, his writings deserve attention simply for his additional personal insights.

Regarding air operations, A.A. Novikov, the Air Force commander wrote no authoritative memoirs on Stalingrad, and the other collected works on air operations are discussed in the editor's notes to chapter 10 of this study.

Of the three involved Front commanders, later Marshal of the Soviet Union A.I. Eremenko has provided the most information. In his early and somewhat controversial work, *Stalingrad*, Eremenko discussed his role as the responsible commander during the defensive fighting and the subsequent counteroffensive phases.[6] Although quite detailed in battle narrative, its controversy arose over Eremenko's claim, advanced during the Khrushchev years, to be the author of the counteroffensive plan. Both Zhukov and Vasilevskii decisively refute this claim in their memoirs; however, the various Front Commanders' degree of participation in the evolution of the document makes room for some pride of authorship with regard to the finished version.

A second commander, later Marshal of the Soviet Union, K.K. Rokossovskii, in *A Soldier's Duty*, depicted his role in the reduction of the Stalingrad pocket.[7] However, it is in this memoir that the complications arising from various Front commanders' absences from the main decisionmaking in Moscow becomes painfully apparent. Rokossovskii's memoir reads as if he were a distant observer at Stalingrad, even regarding those decisions in which he was a major participant. Another example of this problem can be found in the volume by Lieutenant General of Artillery V.I. Kazakov, the artillery commander who served with Rokossovskii. Entitled *Ne perelome*, this gritty combat narrative serves notice that this is not a work of strategic insights.[8] However, his comments (pp. 126–128) on the lack of coordination in the various arms of service within the Red Army provide a welcome addition to the information provided in this General Staff study.

Finally, perhaps the best report would have come from the Southwestern Front Commander, Colonel General N.F. Vatutin. As a major participant in the battle and a former Deputy Chief of the General Staff, Vatutin was a rapidly rising star in the Soviet command echelon. Unfortunately, Vatutin was killed in 1944 and left no published record for historians. A recently published authoritative biography is lacking in such details.[9]

Of the relevant Army commanders, most were experienced combat soldiers but generally were too junior in rank to have had a hand in the strategic decisionmaking of the Stalingrad campaign. Operationally, however, their contributions were substantial. Of the written memoirs, the reader is directed to those of P.I. Batov, A.A. Grechko, S.S. Biriuzov, V.I. Chuikov, N.I. Krylov, D.D. Leliushenko, K.S. Moskalenko, and A.S. Zhadov.[10]

Another source of information on the battle of Stalingrad may be found in the many scholarly studies published by various Soviet military and civilian historians. First are the official histories of the war of which five major studies have been published by the Soviet government since 1960. Initially released during the Khrushchev years was the six-volume _Istoriia velikoi otechstvennoi voiny Sovetskogo Soiuza, 1941–1945._[11] Due to the various biases in the initial work and the removal of Khrushchev, a new one-volume edition entitled _Velikaia otechestvennaia voiny Sovetskogo Soiuza, 1941–1945; kratkaia istoriia_ made its appearance.[12] The new volume provided additional details about the war and corrected some of the more obvious references to the role of Khrushchev, which had been stressed in the original six-volume work. A somewhat later release was the detailed _50 Let vooruzhennykh sil SSSR_, which focused on military information to the exclusion of the political and economic material found in the previous studies.[13] Finally, starting in the mid 1970s, the USSR simultaneously released the twelve-volume study of the entire war, _Istoriia vtoroi mirovoi voiny_, and the eight-volume _Sovetskaia voennaia entsiklopediia._[14] Both provided an enormous amount of factual data that had not previously appeared. This material allowed the struggle on the Volga to be seen in a new light, not necessarily the one portrayed in the accompanying text of the two works.

Specific analysis of the Stalingrad campaign has produced numerous works about the battle. Of these, perhaps the best starting point is the outstanding volume prepared by a military historians' collective under the authorship of Marshal Rokossovskii. Entitled _Velikaia pobeda na Volge_, it features a detailed campaign analysis written in a matter-of-fact style.[15] The companion volume of maps is simply the best available visual analysis of the many shifting stages of the battles near Stalingrad.

However, the Rokossovskii edition should be examined along with the best overall strategic study prepared by A.M. Samsonov. in his superbly detailed *Stalingradskaia bitva*, Samsonov provides the quality of scholarship that is expected of superior historians.[16] In its various permutations and editions, it ranks as the best Soviet analysis of the strategic campaign. Complete with archival material and many previously unpublished directives and correspondence, it presents the Soviet insider's view of the battle. The detailed appendix and the excellent maps provide additional information for the serious student.

Another important study is *Stalingradskaia epopeia*, edited by Samsonov, with an introduction by Marshal M.V. Zakharov, the Chief of the General Staff.[17] The study contains a series of detailed military articles written by the various participants in the battle. The authors provide new archival material and additional operational details. Another extensive collection of articles presented in the volume *Bitva za Stalingrad*[18] covers familiar ground, with some authors providing additional information. A similar study is the work *Dvesti ognennikh dnei* with its collection of author-participant remembrances.[19] Additional material on the battle may be found in the official history of the Volga Military District *Krasnoznamennii Privolzhskii* and the authoritative *World War II, Decisive Battles of the Soviet Army*. The authors' collective in both cases sought to provide new information or interpretive analysis.[20]

The final source of Soviet information on the battle of Stalingrad may be the various articles published in *Voenno istoricheskii zhurnal*. Specifically, three articles stand out as sources of factual data on the campaign: "Kontrnastuplenie pod Stalingradom v tsifrakh (Operatsiia 'Uran')," "K 30-letiiu Stalingradskoi bitvy," and "Likvidatsiia okruzhennoi gruppirovki (Operatsiia 'Koltso' v tsifrakh)." Further remembrances are also available, including "Razgrom ital'iankoi ekspeditsionnoi armii na Sovetsko–Germanskom fronte."[21]

The actual course of the summer–fall campaign and the subsequent decisive winter counteroffensive are quite sufficiently covered in the above-referenced texts. Any attempt to discuss the campaign fully in this introduction of course, would be inadequate. However, the nature of this particular study does lend itself to a few additional remarks with reference to the overall strategic situation in the summer of 1942 and the changes in the balance of power by the fall.

During the spring of 1942, the Nazi forces in the USSR were rebuilt, and new reinforcements were obtained from Germany's allies. Simultaneously, the Soviet Union launched a series of counterattacks designed to retain the initiative and upset the German's ability to resume the offensive

Battle for Stalingrad

TABLE 1. *Soviet Reserves in 1942*

	April	May	June	July	August	Sept.	Oct.	Nov.	Dec.
Combined arms armies	2	2	7	10	6	3	5	5	5
Tank armies	—	—	1	1	2	1	1	1	1
Air armies	—	—	—	—	3	3	—	—	—
Rifle division	24	10	40	62	23	18	17	27	14
Rifle brigade	5	14	—	4	1	16	7	6	4
Cavalry division	3	4	3	3	—	—	2	—	—
Independent tank & Mechanized corps	—	1	3	5	2	3	4	5	6
Aviation corps	—	—	—	—	—	—	3	4	2
Aviation division	—	—	1	1	11	10	1	4	8
Independent aviation Brigades	3	3	3	3	1	1	—	—	—
Independent aviation Regiments	37	33	34	32	13	24	12	10	9

Source: *Istoriia Vtoroi Mirovoi Voiny* (*IVMV*), vol. 5, p. 324, Table 18.

in the summer. The sweeping German counterattacks and the crushing offensive in the Crimea totally upset the Soviet's calculations for retaining the initiative. A measured decision to stand on the strategic defensive was adopted. Those Soviet reserves that were available were deployed to meet what was anticipated to be the main German attack toward Moscow (more on this misconception is in the body of the study). As a result, when the German attacks came along the Voronezh axis of operations instead of the Orel direction, the Soviet forces were caught off balance and undermanned on the axis of main operations. This lack of Soviet strength led the German High Command toward erroneous conclusions as to the nature of the true balance of forces. A better picture is seen in Table 1:

This availability of troops provided Stalin with the means to continually allocate fresh forces to the main theater of operations. Between July 23 and October 1, the southern wing of the Soviet front received a total of 55 rifle divisions, 9 rifle and 30 tank brigades, 7 tank corps, and substantial numbers of draft replacements.[22] Additionally, from October to November, a further 25 rifle and 9 cavalry divisions, 6 tank and mechanized corps, and a large number of artillery formations were provided to prepare for the counteroffensive. This strengthening of forces was far in excess of the quality and quantity of forces being provided to Army Group "B" and was possible because of two significant points. First, by the end of September 1942, Moscow had reached the conclusion that the main German thrusts in the south had been contained and the Nazi Army was locked into a grinding battle of attrition. Neither side seemed capable of forcing a decision with the troops currently available; however, this was the impression that the Soviet High Command was deliberately trying to foster by deception. As seen in Table 2, Soviet

TABLE 2. *Deployment of Soviet Forces on November 19, 1942*[1]

From/To	Fronts	Km	Men[2]	Guns/Mortars[3]	Tanks	Aircraft[4]
Barents	Karelian	1,550	340	3,941	220	177
Sea to	7th Sep.	25	5.6	5.1	3.0	5.8
Ladoga	Army					
Ladoga	Leningrad	1,160	1,232	16,435	1,089	277
to	Volkhov	19	20.4	21.3	14.8	9.1
Kholm	Northwestern					
Kholm	Kalinin	1,050	1,890	24,682	3,375	1,170
to	Western	17	31.4	32.0	45.9	38.6
Bolkhov[5]	Moscow DZ[6]					
Bolkhov	Bryansk	550	644	7,834	884	225
to Nova	Voronezh	9	10.7	10.1	12.0	7.4
Kalitv						
Novo Kalitv	Southwestern	850	1,103	15,501	1,463	928
to	Don	14	18.4	20.1	19.9	30.6
Astrakhan	Stalingrad					
		1,000	816	8,797	319	255
————	Northern Caucasus	16	13.5	11.4	4.4	8.5
Total		6,160	6.030	77,180	7,350	3,032

1. The upper number is a total; the lower number is the total expressed as a percent of the theoretical 100.
2. Expressed in thousands. Without the troops of the *PVO* or the VMF.
3. Without the anti-aircraft guns or 50 mm mortars.
4. Aircraft as of November 1, 1942 without the long-range bombers, (ADD).
5. Near Orel.
6. Moscow Defense Zone.
Source: *IVMV*, v. 6, p. 35, Table 4.

forces along the entire front were already significantly stronger than Germany's troops, and when compared to the available reserves for both sides, this picture reveals how far the balance had already tipped against Hitler.

This image brings up a second significant point: the rapid recovery of Soviet industrial strength and the concurrent lag in German production, when coupled with the continuing German difficulties with manpower and the Soviets' ability to provide new soldiers, allowed Stalin to contemplate a sweeping series of offensives. The coming attacks would destroy not only the German 6th Army at Stalingrad but would crack the siege of Leningrad, crush the German position at Velikiye Luki, and push the German army back toward the Ukraine. In summation, the *existing* change in the balance of strength would radically alter the military situation.

The instructional value for the contemporary reader of *The Battle for Stalingrad: The 1943 Soviet General Staff Study* can be found in its terse operational analysis of the key points of the campaign. The Red Army appears in this narrative devoid of its present-day rhetorical trappings. At this point, the beginning of its long string of successes, the Red Army can be viewed with both its promise of things to come and its shortcomings of 1942. Phrases that rarely appear in today's written histories are seen in this study: blame for failures is apportioned, and guidelines for future efforts are outlined. In short, the present study is a thorough operational analysis with significant tactical instructions on one of the most important campaigns of the war. As such, it deserves its place in the contemporary literature on World War II.

A Note on Style

The translation from the Soviet original was prepared by the U.S. government and is currently in the possession of the U.S. Military History Institute. My thanks to that organization for the use of the original. I also attempted to check the present copy against the Soviet-language edition in the possession of the National Archives. Further changes have been made from the translation copy to clarify the choice of expressions and the spellings of the various locations since the original Soviet edition, having been a collected work, exhibits numerous variations in expression and spelling. I have standardized these divergences and superimposed the Library of Congress transliteration scheme on the U.S.-translated copy. Also, I added additional words (that is, *rifle* or *cavalry* has been repeated with unit numbers) to assist the reader in identifying the proper military units. Additional phrases, such as *infantry*, have been replaced with the term *rifle troops* for Soviet forces. *Panzer* has been added to German/Rumanian designations for armored formations, while *tank* has been retained to identify Soviet formations. Thus, while the flow of the work has been altered to ease its understanding for the reader, no major changes in the meaning of the work have been made.

Regrettably, the maps that appear in this volume are not the ones that were originally issued. Neither the translation copy nor the Soviet original in the National Archives contain the maps, or sketches issued in 1943. The maps that do appear in the text are from the various sources as noted. As always in the translated edition, the serious scholar is directed to the Soviet original at the National Archives for the final content.

Editor's Notes

1. The best source of information on Soviet military books on World War II is the two-volume work by Michael Parrish, *The U.S.S.R. in World War II*, (New York: Garland Publishing, 1981). This annotated bibliography is an indispensable tool for the serious scholar of Soviet military affairs.
2. N. Khrushchev, *Khrushchev Remembers* S. Talbott, ed, and trans. (Boston: Little, Brown and Co., 1970).
3. The Zhukov two-volume edition was translated and issued in Moscow by Progress Publishers in 1985.
4. The Vasilevskii memoir was translated and issued in Moscow by Progress Publishers in 1981.

5. Published in Moscow by *Voenizdat* in 1963.
6. Published in Moscow by *Voenizdat* in 1961.
7. Translated and published in Moscow by Progress Publishers in 1985.
8. Published in Moscow by *Voenizdat* in 1962.
9. In Zakharov, *General Armii N.F. Vatutin* (Moscow: Voenizdat, 1985).
10. For Batov, *V polkhodokh i boiakh* (Moscow: Voenizdat, 1962); for Grechko, *Godgi voini* (Moscow: Voenizdat, 1976); for Biriuzov, who served as chief of staff of 2nd Guards Army, *Surovye gody* (Moscow: Nauka, 1966); for Chuikov, *Nachalo puti* (Moscow: Voenizdat, 1959) and *Gvardeitsy Stalingrada idut na zapad* (Moscow: Sovetskaia Rossiia, 1972); for Krylov, who served as chief of staff of the 62nd Army, *Stalingradskii rubezh* (Moscow: Voenizdat, 1979); for Leliushenko, *Moskva–Stalingrad–Berlin–Praga* (Moscow: Nauka, 1971); for Moskalenko, *Na iugo-zapadnom napravlenni* (Moscow: *Nauka*, 1969); and for Zhadov, *Chetyre goda voiny* (Moscow: *Voenizdat*, 1978).
11. P.N. Pospelov, ed., (Moscow: Voenizdat, 1960–1964). Hereafter *IVOVSS*.
12. P.N. Pospelov, ed., (Moscow: Voenizdat, 1965).
13. M.V. Zakharov, ed., (Moscow: *Voenizdat*, 1968).
14. A.A. Grechko, ed., (Moscow: *Voenizdat*, 1973–1982). Hereafter *IVMV*. The encyclopedia, *Sovetskaia voennaia entsiklopediia* in eight volumes, was published in Moscow by *Voenizdat* between 1976–80.
15. Published in Moscow by *Voenizdat* in 1965.
16. Published in Moscow by *Nauka* in 1968.
17. Published in Moscow by *Nauka* in 1968.
18. Published in Volgograd by *Nizhne-Volzhskoe kn. izd.* in 1969.
19. Published in Moscow by *Voenizdat* in 1968. An English-language edition is available under the title *200 Days of Fire* (Moscow: Progress Publishers, 1970).
20. For the Military District history, G.A. Gromov, ed. (Moscow: Voenizdat, 1984); for the "Decisive Battles," V.V. Larionov, et. al. (Moscow: Progress Publishers, 1984).
21. In order of mention, the *VIZ* articles appear in No. 3, 1968, pp.64–76; No. 11, 1972, pp. 20–77; No. 2, 1973, pp.34–66; and No. 4, 1968, pp.44–54. This is not to ignore the excellent articles presented in other Soviet periodical journals. However, *VIZ* is where the more specific military materials are presented.
22. *IVMV*, vol. 5, p. 194 and vol. 6, p. 33.

Materials for the Study of the War Experience
Number 6
(Battle of Stalingrad, July 1942–2 February, 1943)

General Staff of the Red Army
Military Publishing House of the People's Commissariat of Defense
(Moscow, 1943)

Preface

The sixth issue of *Collection of Materials for the Study of the War Experience* was devoted to the battle of Stalingrad, ending in the encirclement and defeat of a large group of German forces.

The outline of the events of the Great Patriotic War, included in this *Collection*, embraces the period from the beginning of the advance of the German forces from the line of the Severnaia Donetz River in July 1942 up until the annihilation and capture of the remainder of the 6th German Army of Field Marshal von Paulus in the area of Stalingrad on February 2, 1943. Such an arrangement makes it possible to follow in general outlines the course of the campaign of 1942 and to dwell in detail on its concluding stage, the offensive operation of the Southwestern, Don, and Stalingrad Fronts.

The materials of this *Collection* are not military–historical accounts of the fighting for Stalingrad. In the *Collection*, we have given a provisional summary and conclusion dealing with the problems of the operational employment of the different branches of the Army, the plan of the operations, command and supply of troops in the largest offensive operation of the Red Army.

The contents of the *Collection* are of great importance for commanding personnel and for commissioned and noncommissioned personnel. For the purposes of a broader and more thorough study of the military experience of the Stalingrad battle, we have greatly enlarged this edition of the *Collection*, attached maps of the areas of combat actions, and revised the estimate of the distribution of editions in such a way as to place the *Collection* in the hands of commanders of divisions and brigades and of other corresponding persons of the commanding personnel of the other branches of the service.

References to the contents of *Collection* and questions should be sent to the Department for the Utilization of the War Experience of the General Staff of the Red Army.

In working up the materials contained in the present *Collection* the following persons have participated:[1]

Lieutenant General of Engineer Troops M. P. Vorobev,

Major General of Aviation N. A. Zhuravlev,

Major General A. A. Martianov,

Major General L. V. Onianov,

Major General of Artillery F. A. Samsonov,

Major General N. A. Talenskii,

and Major General of the Tank Troops M. L. Cherniavskii.

Colonels: A. P. Alekseev, F. G. Barskii, F. D. Vorobev, I. E. Gromov, P. G. Esaulov, N. M. Zamiatin, G. V. Litvinov, M. R. Mazalov, A. P. Penchevskii, V. P. Peshekhontsev, M. V. Savin, S. N. Sevrugov, V. D. Utkin, and A. D. Tsirlin.

Lieutenant Colonels: Z. S. Alshits, S. A. Vladimirov, and N. G. Pavlenko.

Responsible Editor
Major General P. P. Vechnyi.

Editor's Note

1. A select biography appears in the appendix to this volume.

This modest overview of the campaign sets the stage for the more detailed chapters to follow. Of note are the details of forces utilized to attack, the not so subtle jab at the lack of a Second Front, and the matter-of-fact tone of the narrative. The belief that victory unfolded based on a deliberate and well-executed plan has already taken its place in Soviet literature—Ed.

1

Defeat of the German Troops at Stalingrad

As an example of modern battle, with all of its complexities and varieties of form, the battle for Stalingrad is of exceptional importance. The final stage of this gigantic battle is the classic unsurpassed example of a present-day "Cannae," an example of an operation carried out with the determined purpose of surrounding and completely destroying a large enemy group.

The battle of Stalingrad, in duration, number of troops engaged in it, and also in the varied character of their combat actions in the different stages, is an intricate complex of several large operations. These include

the defensive battle, lasting from July 17 to November 19, 1942;
the blow of the Red Army and the encirclement of the Stalingrad group of Germans in the period from November 19–30, 1942;
the offensive operations carried out for the purpose of encircling and liquidating the German group at Stalingrad, November–December 1942; and
operation for the annihilation of the encircled German–Fascist troops at Stalingrad from January 10 – February 2, 1943.

Circumstances Preceding the Battle

As a result of our losing some hard-fought battles in June 1942, the German forces, by a strong attack from the area of Kursk–Kharkov, succeeded in breaking through in the area of contact between the Briansk and Southwestern Fronts in the general direction toward Staryi-Oskol and Voronezh.

After defeats in the battles at Voronezh, where the offensive of the enemy was stopped by the stubborn defense of the troops of the Voronezh Front, the German-Fascist command directed the main blow of its southern group along the right banks of the Don toward Stalingrad.[1]

The main purpose of the German advance in the summer of 1942 was to bypass Moscow toward the east, to cut it off from the Volga and the Ural rear, and then attack it.[2] In the calculations of the German High Command, Stalingrad as a strategic point connecting our armies in the north and in the south, occupied an important place, and the capture of the city would facilitate to a considerable extent the execution of their plan as a whole. Wishing to control this important strategic center as quickly as possible, the German High Command planned to capture Stalingrad on July 25.

The right wing of the troops of the Southwestern Front, ripped in two by the tank battering ram of the German 1st and 4th Panzer Armies, fought some heavy battles and then crossed the Don River on the Boguchar–Serafimovich sector. The left wing, however, while conducting delaying actions, withdrew to the southeast, after joining up with the South Front. As a result of this, the routes to the Don Bend and Stalingrad were open for the advance of the enemy.

In the middle of July, a large group, made up of the enemy's 4th Panzer and 6th Panzer Armies, moved into the Don Bend in the area of Bokovskaia, Morozovskii, Millerovo, and Kantemirovka. Stalingrad and the Volga were seriously menaced. It was necessary to take immediate measures for protecting the vital arteries of our country connecting the center of the Soviet Union with the Caucasus.

It was not possible to employ the troops of the Southwestern Front for protecting the Volga and Stalingrad, because getting them ready after the long retreat, carried out under difficult conditions, required a great deal of time. For covering Stalingrad, however, it was necessary not only to quickly organize a defense on a front of over 400 kilometers, but also to prepare operational reserves sufficiently strong to hold the enemy moving toward the Volga and capable of inflicting upon him a decisive defeat. For this purpose it was necessary to gain time and hold the space in the great Don Bend to the west of Stalingrad.

The Defensive Battle

The first stage of this battle embraced the period from July 17 to August 17 and included the battles on the distant approaches to Stalingrad. During this period, the troops of the Stalingrad Front, and later those of the Stalingrad and Southeastern Fronts, fought some hard defensive battles on the west banks of the Don River and southwest of Stalingrad before withdrawing to Stalingrad's outer defensive line along the Myshkova River.

The second stage of the defensive battle embraced the period of the battles on the immediate approaches to Stalingrad from August 17 up to September 2. It was characterized by the hard fighting of our troops with the group of the enemy, breaking through to the Volga north of Stalingrad in the area of Erzovka-Rynok on August 23, and also with the troops of the enemy taking the offensive from the region of Kalach and along the railroad from Salsk to Kotelnikovo. In the course of these battles, the enemy tried to seize Stalingrad by concentric blows from the west and southwest. The stage closed with the withdrawal of our troops to the inside lines of defense of the Stalingrad fortified area.

The third stage embraced the battle for the inside lines of the Stalingrad fortified area. It ended on September 13 when the enemy succeeded in breaking through our defenses and marching directly to the city.

The fourth, and last stage of the defensive battle lasts from September 14 to November 19. During this period there was fierce and continuous street fighting for Stalingrad.

In the battles on the immediate approaches to Stalingrad a part of the forces of the Stalingrad front (1st Guards, 63rd, and 61st Armies) seized a bridgehead on the right bank of the Don River, in the area southwest of Serafimovich, Perekopka, Shukhin (exclusive) Sirotinskaia. Simultaneously, the northern group of the Stalingrad Front conducted an offensive from the area of Kuzmichi for the purpose of parrying the blow of the enemy group breaking through to the Volga.

Even though these offensive operations did not result in great victories, they still diverted a part of the enemy forces and thus helped Stalingrad to hold out.[3]

The Blow of the Red Army and the Encirclement of the Stalingrad Group of the Enemy

The operations on the distant approaches to Stalingrad cannot be regarded in isolation from the successive stages of the general battle of the campaign of 1942 for the encirclement and the destruction of the Stalingrad group of German–Fascist forces.

The task of our troops in the defensive battle was not only to stop the advancing German troops but also to create favorable conditions for a subsequent general attack for the purpose of smashing and destroying the German group breaking through to the Volga.

It is only with this understanding of the task of the defensive battle that it becomes clear why the *Stavka Verkhovnovo Glavno Komandovaniya* (*Stavka*), continually insisted on the protection of Stalingrad at all costs, on holding and broadening the bridgeheads on the right bank of the Don in its middle course and south of Stalingrad.[4]

The idea of concentric attack against the German troops advancing against Stalingrad, made from the middle course of the Don and from the area of the interlake defiles south of Stalingrad, was conceived in the very beginning of the period of the defensive operation. However, *Stavka* and the General Staff started the immediate planning of this operation in the second half of September. On October 4, a representative of *Stavka*, Marshal of the Soviet Union G. K. Zhukov, with the command of the various fronts, held a special conference devoted to the problems of preparing for the approaching offensive.[5]

The purpose of the offensive operation was the encirclement and subsequent destruction of the entire hostile group breaking through to Stalingrad. As conceived, the aim of the operation was, first, to defeat the flank groups of the enemy defending themselves on the middle course of the Don and south of Stalingrad, with a subsequent enveloping movement for surrounding the main German group in the area of Stalingrad.

This offensive operation was a strategic operation of three Fronts: Southwestern, Don, and Stalingrad.

In keeping with the adopted plan, in the period from October through the first half of November, we concentrated additional forces and means and also carried out a regrouping within the fronts and armies. From the reserves of the *Stavka*, we assigned the following reinforcements to the Southwestern Front: 4 rifle divisions, 2 tank corps, 3 tank regiments, a cavalry corps, 13 army artillery regiments, 7 army and 6 Guards Mortar regiments. In addition to this, the Southwestern Front was given the following from the Don Front: 3 rifle divisions, a tank corps, a cavalry corps, 11 artillery regiments, and 2 Guards Mortar regiments. The Stalingrad Front received 2 rifle divisions, a cavalry corps, a tank brigade, 6 mechanized brigades, 12 tank regiments, and 6 army artillery regiments.

The concentration of such a large number of troops and equipment involved great difficulties due to the limited number of railroads (one for each front) and their lack of carrying capacity due to the constant attacks by enemy airplanes.

We encountered special difficulties in the shifting of troops arriving for the Stalingrad Front on the right bank of the Volga. The troops crossing the Volga were subjected to continued aerial and artillery bombardment by the enemy. Because of the ice drifts, which had already started, the crossings sometimes took five hours and more, while ordinarily it would take 40 to 50 minutes.

In carrying out the concentration and regrouping operations, excellent as a rule only at night, we took every possible precautionary measure to ensure secrecy. As a result of this the enemy was unable to discover the concentration of our shock groups.

In strict accordance with the plan of *Stavka* the offensive of the Southwestern Front and of the right flank of the Don Front began on November 19 and that of the Stalingrad Front on November 20. By the close of the first day of the operation, we had broken through the defenses of the enemy on the sectors of advance of the shock troops, and by November 23 the operational encirclement of the German group at Stalingrad had been completed. The mobile formations of the Southwestern and the Stalingrad Fronts had reached the Don River north and south of Kalach, while the rifle troop echelons of the Stalingrad Front had reached the line of the rivers Chervlenaia and Karpovka.

In the period November 24–30, we fought battles the general purpose of which was the contraction of the right of encirclement and the conversion of the operational encirclement into a tactical encirclement. In the steel ring of our troops, 22 enemy divisions with a great amount of equipment were caught in an area of about 1,450 square kilometers capable of being bombarded from any direction by our long-range field artillery.

Before passing to a determined attack, our troops on the separate sectors of the front carried out only local operations, limited in scope, for the seizure of lines advantageous from a tactical standpoint, for the purpose of improving our jump-off positions for the approaching offensive, and for harassing and wearing down the encircled enemy.

The Providing of Operational Security for the Encirclement and Destruction of the Stalingrad Group of Germans

In organizing the November offensive, *Stavka* paid special attention to the matter of reliable operational security. It was clear that the German High Command would try with all of its strength and means to reestablish the situation, after remedying the situation caused by the breakthroughs on the front effected by our troops. At the same time, *Stavka* took into account the fact that in case of the success of our offensive and encirclement of the basic grouping of the Germans west of Stalingrad, the enemy would undertake a number of determined measures for the liberation of the encircled troops, by blows of mobile groups from the outside. Usually, as the experience of the preceding operations had proved, the Germans executed flank attacks for this purpose. We anticipated the possible directions of enemy attacks and concentrated the necessary reserves in these sectors.

The operational security of the initial period of our November offensive was carried out by the advance of strong screening forces made up of a cavalry corps and a number of rifle formations on the rivers Kislia and Chir for protecting the right flank of the shock group of the Southwestern Front, and by the attack of the right flank army (65th) of the Don Front for covering the left flank of the shock group. The security of the open left flank of the Stalingrad Front was provided by moving units of the 51st Army and 4th Cavalry Corps in the direction of Kotelnikovo. However, when the enemy—after giving up his local counterattacks, which were repulsed by our covering troops—started at the beginning of December to organize some strong groups in the areas of Tormosin and Kotelnikovo for breaking through to the encircled 6th Army, the *Stavka* changed its method of operational security. In the period December 16–30, the right wing of the Southwestern Front carried out a great new offensive operation for the purpose of smashing the 8th Italian and 3rd Rumanian armies and the liquidation of all the groups created by the German–Fascist command.[6] As a result of this operation, the thickness of the layers separating the encircled group from the line of the outer front increased to 300 kilometers, due to which further attempts of the enemy to break through to his enclosed group became practically useless.

LIQUIDATION OF THE GERMAN GROUP SURROUNDED AT STALINGRAD

From January 10 to February 2, 1943, the troops of the Don Front carried out the final operations of the Stalingrad battle—liquidation of the 6th German Army, surrounded at Stalingrad.[7]

As a result of the first stage of the operation, our troops captured the western part of the territory of the ring of encirclement and the enemy was thrown back to the east bank of the Rossoshka River.

By January 17, as a result of the successful carrying out of the second stage of the operation, the enemy was thrown back to the former inside line of the Stalingrad fortified area.

On January 26, our troops broke through into the city, cutting the encircled German group into two parts, a northern group and a southern group.

On January 31, we captured the southern group together with its commander, Field Marshal von Paulus, and on February 2 the northern group also capitulated. This completed the liquidation of the enemy group surrounded at Stalingrad.

Conclusion

The smashing of the Stalingrad group of Germans is a great strategic victory by the *Stavka* of the Red Army. The strategic plan of the *Stavka* included the following: the carrying out of a number of defensive operations aimed at harassing and weakening the enemy; the gaining of the time necessary for gathering the forces and equipment for the subsequent passage to a determined offensive; the achievement of an offensive in the form of flank blows, executed by an operational encirclement of the enemy; the security of the operations aimed at smashing the German group encircled at Stalingrad; and the utter defeat of the encircled German forces.

The defensive battle was carried out in the period when the general situation toward the south—in view of the absence of a Second Front in Europe—was developing in a manner extremely unfavorable for us.[8]

A striking expression of the strategic foresight at this stage is the skillful and expedient combination of defensive and offensive actions, in particular, the cooperation between the troops of the Don and Stalingrad Fronts during the fighting for Stalingrad, and also the exceptional expediency, firmness, and perseverance in the matter of making available and utilizing the strategic reserves. In spite of the serious situations that developed at times and our tactical failures, the basic strategic reserves were not scattered but were saved for the decisive moment when we passed to a general offensive.

We were most fortunate in the selection of the precise time for passing to a general offensive. The attack of the enemy had run into a blind alley, and the offensive power of his army had been sharply reduced. Then, too, the fighting power of his units, in particular the Rumanian and Italian, had also been considerably lowered. The German High Command felt that a period had set in when, due to climatic and meteorological conditions, there was no possibility of large-scale offensive operations and that the winter campaign of 1942–43 was practically over. This was determined in view of the fact that the Germans did not take any steps to provide security for their front which, stretching as it did over a great arc between the Don and Volga, was in an extremely unfavorable situation from the point of view of defense.

The selection of the direction of the main blow was made on the basis of a careful analysis of the grouping of the enemy, taking into account its advantages and disadvantages and especially its defenses. The attacks of the Red Army on the enemy were highly successful because they were made suddenly and unexpectedly against the weakest and most vulnerable parts of the front, bring our troops by the shortest route into the rear of the enemy and astride his communications.

The taking of timely measures for security of the offensive against attempts of the enemy to disrupt it and flexible and timely changes from one method of operational security to another at the various stages of the operations all made possible a successful and victorious conclusion of our offensives and doomed to failure all the countermeasures of the German command.

The concluding stage of the battle of Stalingrad—the smashing, destruction, and capture of the 6th German Army, well supplied with all kinds of modern equipment—will go down in the history of warfare as one of the most brilliant pages of the history of the Great Patriotic War. History does not record a single other case when the surrounded army was completely liquidated, with not a single one of its soldiers escaping from the ring of encirclement, and when all the weapons and equipment of this army fell to the victor as spoils of war.[9]

A distinguishing characteristic of the successful operation in the annihilation of the Stalingrad group of Germans is the fact that the encirclement was carried out by our armies shifting from the defensive to the offensive in a manner entirely unexpected by the enemy. The brilliant victory was won as a result of the fact that our army had previous experience in modern warfare.

The battle of Stalingrad showed the growth and the excellent preparation of the command cadre of the Red Army and the stubborness and excellent military training of the troops.

There can be no doubt that only the correct strategy of the command of the Red Army and the flexible tactics of our commanders-executors could lead to such an outstanding event as the encirclement and liquidation at Stalingrad of the large elite army of Germans numbering 330,000.[*]

Finally, the battle of Stalingrad showed in an exceptionally graphic manner the weakness of German strategy and its organic defects. Starting from the criminal assumptions of their policy, the German High Command undertook a risky campaign against Stalingrad. Ignoring the changes in the situation and in the relative strength of the opposing forces taking place in the course of the battle, the German High Command tried, at any price, to win some tactical victories. The initial tactical victories of the German Army, which were not based on the possibilities of its strategy, led in the end to a failure of the plans of the German High Command in the campaign of 1942.

Our victory at Stalingrad inspired still greater confidence in the power of the Red Army and the skill of its commanders, raising to a still greater height the prestige of the Soviet Union and the Red Army among our allies and all the freedom-loving peoples of the world fighting against German fascism.

Editor's Notes

1. The Soviets did not realize then, and sometimes do not acknowledge today, that the German drive down the Don was by plan. The struggle for Voronezh, while heroic in individual

*Order of the Supreme High Command, No. 95, February 23, 1943.

terms, was not the decisive focal point of the campaign. Indeed the tragic mishandling and destruction of the original 5th Tank Army under Major General A. I. Lizukov could just as easily prompt German claims of victory in this sector. See vol. 2 of F. Halder's *The Halder Diaries*, 2 vols. trans. (Boulder, CO: Westview, 1976), p.344. Von Bock's delay in releasing forces toward the south was harshly criticized by Halder (pp. 341–342).

2. The Soviet error over the final German objectives was repeated quite often during Stalin's lifetime to explain the mistake in deployment of the early summer. This error was acknowledged by the publication of *IVOVSS*. A thorough review of this issue is found in Earl Ziemke, "Operation Kreml," *Parameters* (March 1979): 72–83. The Soviet miscalculation was also helped by the intelligence being received by Moscow from its agents in Western Europe. Although many of the reports were quite accurate, the ambiguous nature of the possible interpretations served only to allow confusing interpretations. See Sandor Rado, *Codename Dora* (translated), (London: Abelard, 1979). The problem over the misinterpretation of the "Kreml" cover plan is still active. A. Samsanov, interviewed in *Argumenti i Fakti* No. 19, 1987, p. 2, still complained that the German deception operation was not being acknowledged as a success.

3. See Zhukov, vol. 2, p. 98. "I can state with full responsibility that but for the persistent counterattacks of the Stalingrad Front and the systematic air strikes, Stalingrad might have endured something far worse."

4. The *Stavka* was the highest organization for the guidance of the Soviet Armed Forces during the war. Originally formed in June 1941 as the *Stavka Glavnovo Kommandovaniia*, by August it had changed into the present configuration. The *Stavka* reported to the *Gosudarstvennii Komitet Oboroni* (GKO), the State Defense Committee, chaired by J. V. Stalin. Always few in number, the *Stavka's* original members were: Stalin, V. Molotov, Marshals S. Timoshenko, K. Voroshilov, and S. Budenni, General of the Army G. Zhukov, and Admiral N. Kuznetsov. Later, Marshal B. Shaposhnikov was added, and when he retired due to health reasons, Colonel General A. Vasilevskii was appointed. The latter two individuals were appointed in their successive capacities as Chief of the General Staff.

5. The need for an intermediate level of command between the *Stavka* and the field commands led to the use of special representatives of the *Stavka*. The initial prototype of this arrangement occurred in the first days of the war with the dispatch of selected officers to the various Fronts to clarify and oversee the operations of the commanders on the spot. At the time of Stalingrad, *Stavka's* representatives on the scene were Zhukov, Vasilevskii, and Colonel General of Artillery N. Voronov. At this time, Zhukov also served as the Deputy to the Supreme Commander, a rank created especially for him. Although the original text indicated Zhukov's rank as that of a Marshal, at the time of the battle he was still a General of the Army.

6. This was Operation Saturn. See Y. Plotnikov and V. Safronov, "Razgrom 8-i Ital'ianovskoi armii v operatsii Malii Saturn (Dekabr' 1942)" in *Voenno istoricheskii zhurnal* No. 12, 1982.

7. This was Operation "Koltso" (Ring). See Chapter 7 of this study.

8. See as an example of contemporary comments on the situation, O. Rzheshevskii, *World War II, Myths and the Realities* (Moscow: Progress, 1984), p. 128.

9. Total German losses are hard to pinpoint. An excellent summary may be found in M. Kehrig, *Stalingrad* (Stuttgart: Deutsche Verlags-Anstalt, 1974), pp. 671–72. (Hereafter, Kehrig, *Stalingrad*).

The plans for the German offensive had been prepared as far back as fall 1941. At that time the operations toward the Caucasus were suspended until the return of better weather. The strategic question of whether Germany should attempt another offensive or remain on the strategic defensive until its strength had been rebuilt was a little debated issue. Hitler still needed a knockout blow against the USSR and the 1942 time period was the last opportunity before the resurging strength of Great Britain and the arrival of American forces in the European theater of operations would significantly alter the strategic picture—Ed.

2

The German Stalingrad Group

Operational Plans of the Germans in 1942

The German High Command, after the defeats suffered in the winter of 1941–1942, began preparations for their famous spring offensive of 1942, widely propagandized by the German press for the purpose of maintaining the morale of the German people and the army.

This was the preparation for the second period of the war of 1942, which Comrade Stalin, in his report of November 6, 1942, characterized in the following manner:

> The second period was the summer period, when the German–Fascist forces, taking advantage of the absence of a Second Front in Europe, gathered all their available reserves, broke through the front in a southwest direction, and, having the initiative in their hands, advanced in places, in five months, up to 500 kilometers.*

The preparation for the spring offensive of 1942 put an enormous

---

*Report of the Chairman of the State Defense Committee, Comrade Stalin, *Pravda*, No. 311 (9082) of November 7, 1942.

21

strain upon the German military economy and army. For strengthening the Eastern Front there were organized three new Panzer divisions (22nd, 23rd, 24th) and preparations were made for the dispatch of as many as 10 new infantry divisions. In addition to this, for providing replacements for the badly mauled units on the Eastern Front, replacements were thrown in to the number of 500,000 men.[1]

Such a heavy strain was the direct result of the first period of the war, because even then the German High Command, for the stabilization of the Eastern Front only in the central direction, was forced to throw in 25 divisions from its strategic reserves, in addition to marching battalions.

The chief aim of the German offensive of 1942, in accordance with what Comrade Stalin found, was

> to bypass Moscow to the east, cut it off from the Volga and Ural rear areas and then attack it. The advance of the Germans in a southern direction, toward the oil field, had as its secondary aim not so much the seizure of the oil fields as it did the drawing away of our main reserves to the south and the weakening of the Moscow Front, in order in this way to increase the chances of success in the attack against Moscow. This in reality also explains the fact that the main group of the German forces is not in the south now but in the area around Orel and Stalingrad.[2]

On October 1, 1942, on the Stalingrad Front in the area of Sadovoe, we took from a dead German officer of the General Staff a map giving the schematic plan of the offensive of the enemy. This document confirmed the prediction of the *Stavka* of the Red Army concerning the plans of the Germans for the summer campaign of 1942.[3]

In accordance with this plan, the German troops were to move into the following areas:

Borisoglebsk	July 5–10	Salsk	August 1
Povorino–Stalingrad	July 25	Uralsk	September 1
Saratov	August 5–10	Novrossiisk	August 15
Kuibyshev	August 10–15	Baku	September 20–25

This plan, on the basis of the most charitable evaluation represents a gross miscalculation on the part of the General Staff of the German Army and shows the failure of its intelligence. In reality, it is the most striking indication of the recklessness of German strategy. The plan of the German High Command shows in a graphic manner a number of things: impudence and swaggering on the part of the Germans, their absolute failure to understand the enemy in the second year of the war, as well as their monstrous and stupid underestimation of the strength of the Red Army and the power of its country as a whole.

The notes on the back of this same map show the strategic intentions of the German High Command (we give here a correct translation of them):

1. Forces for breaking communications in the northern sector.
2. Forces for the progressive encirclement of Moscow.
3. Maximum concentration of forces in the south.
4. The idea of maneuver on the offensive: the capture of the ports of Murmansk and Astrakhan; Leningrad and Moscow will not be taken by an offensive; the attack will move from the area of Orel; to surround Moscow; to surround the army between the Donetz and the Don. After the fall of Rostov the attack should move toward Novorossiisk, the Caucasus, Baku.

The development of the operations in the spring of 1942 fully confirmed attempts to carry out this plan.

For the protection of its sea communications between the Crimea and Rumania and for the purpose of coordinating the attack against the Caucasus through the Taman Peninsula, the troops of the German 11th Army, on May 8, 1942, started an offensive in the Crimea. In this same month and on into the first half of June, the German 1st Panzer and 6th Armies and the 6th Rumanian Army Corps carried out three local operations for reaching the Oskol River on the sector Kupiansk-Izum, having as their purpose the driving out of our troops of the Southwestern Front, whose offensive in May created a direct threat to Kharkov. Under cover of these local operations, the German High Command completed preparations for a decisive attack in the direction of Voronezh.

The main efforts of the German General Staff were directed toward a maximum concentration of forces on the south sector of the front (from Orel to Taganrod) for the purpose of carrying out a "progressive encirclement of Moscow." Starting from this basic mission, the operational organization of the armies was to correspond to the idea of the maneuver. However, the Germans desisted from an attack from the area of Orel, feeling that such an attack would not have sufficient depth for the operational maneuver, and they shifted it to the area of Kursk. By such a method the Germans evidently intended to effect a closer cooperation with their Stalingrad group and to shorten the distance to the point (Saratov) where they intended to join the efforts of the main blows of both groups.

The German High Command intended to effect the gradual and steady accumulation of forces both for the attack toward Voronezh and that against Stalingrad as it was proportionally able to replace the German troops on the Don River by Rumanian, Hungarian, and Italian troops. The bringing in of the armies of the three allies of Germany (the 3rd Rumanian, 2nd Hungarian, and 8th Italian) afforded considerable relief to enemy troops on the southern sector of the Eastern Front, making it possible subsequently to relieve the German divisions of the 2nd Army for the defense of Voronezh from the north and east, the 4th Panzer and 6th Armies for an attack against Stalingrad, and the 1st Panzer Army and 17th Army for an attack against the Caucasus.

For breaking the contact between the forces in the north sector of the Eastern front, that is, between Volkhov and the Northwestern Fronts the Germans intended to use their 11th Army, the divisions of which, after being provided again with replacements (after the enormous losses sustained in the Crimea), started in August to move into the area of Viritsa, Tosno, and Mga.[4] But this offensive was not to materialize. The passage to the offensive of the units of the Volkhov Front prevented this offensive, and the divisions of the 11th Army were drawn into battle by units and subsequently suffered irreparable losses on several occasions. The plan for the capture of Murmansk failed in exactly the same way. For strengthening, the 20th Army Germany intended to use the 3rd, 5th and 7th Mountain Divisions, but even after the first two divisions were on their way to Finland, the German High Command ordered them to turn against the Volkhov Front.

The strategic and operational organization of the German Army in the spring of 1942 was the following:

In keeping with the plan of the campaign of 1942, the German Army was deployed in four groups of armies (Fronts), instead of three as in 1941. The armed forces of the Eastern Front consisted of 16 armies (of these 13 were German), counting the separate 20th Army operating against the Karelian Front, which the Germans chose to designate as the "Lapland" Army.

For the offensive operations in the southeast direction, the German High Command concentrated from Kirsk to Taganrog eight armies (of these five were German) and the 6th Rumanian Army Corps; the total in this group was 91 divisions, including 10 tank divisions.[5]

The considerations that caused the German High Command to create two groups of armies (Fronts) for the southern sector of the Eastern Front were of a strategic nature, namely, the encirclement of Moscow from the east. By dividing the southern group there were created two lettered groups of armies (Army Group "A" and Army Group "B").

Consequently, in accordance with the plan of the summer campaign of 1942, two army groups (Northern and Central) were to pin down our forces, and the other two army groups, "A" and "B," were to serve as shock fronts. When Army Group "B" reached the Don River between Voronezh and Boguchar it was assigned the further mission of advancing against Stalingrad, with a subsequent change of direction toward the north along the Volga River. Before the capture of Stalingrad, the armies of the allies of Germany were to serve as a defensive force along the Don

River to pin down our units from Voronezh and Kletskaia. This mission was assigned to the 2nd Hungarian, 8th Italian, and 3rd Rumanian Armies.

Whereas, the "B" group of armies were to reach the Volga in the area of Stalingrad; the southern, or "A" group of armies, were to carry out a mission that was secondary, namely, to carry out an offensive against the northern Caucasus.

The makeup and grouping of the troops of the enemy on the Eastern Front by July 1, 1942 were the following:

Groups of Armies (Fronts)	Armies	Number of Divisions (Brigades)	Remarks
Murmansk direction and Karelian Front	20th Army North Army Karelian Army	38	In this number: *German* 14 *Finnish* 24
North Group of Armies (General Kuechler)[1]	16th Army 18th Army	35	Of these: one *Spanish* infantry div. and one *Estonian* infantry brigade
Central Group of Armies (General Klugge)[2]	4th Army 9th Army 2nd & 3rd Panzer Armies	79	In this number: 65 infantry divs., 5 motorized divs., 9 Panzer divs.
South Group of Armies "B" (General Bock)	2nd Army 6th Army 4th Panzer Army 2nd Hungarian Army 6th Rumanian Corps	71	In this number: *Hungarian* 10 inf. brigades, 1 cavalry brigade; *Rumanian* 5 inf. divs., 1 Panzer div., 1 cavalry brigade; *Italian* 1 inf. div.
South Group of Armies "A" (General List)	17th Army 11th Army 1st Panzer Army 3rd Rumanian Army 8th Italian Army	43	In this number: *Rumanians* 4 inf. divs., 1 motorized div., 4 cavalry brigades, 2 inf. brigades; *Italian* 3 inf. divs; *Slovak* 2 motorized divs.

1. The four "Generals" were in fact all Field Marshals.
2. Von Kluge's name was misspelled in the original—Ed.

The total number of divisions and brigades was 266. Of this number: Infantry had 198; Panzer, 22; motorized, 19; infantry brigades, 18; and cavalry brigades, 9.[6]

After the departure of the 6th Army and the 4th Panzer Army in the Stalingrad direction (a change of direction from the front Chertkovo-Millerovo) the 3rd Rumanian and eight Italian Armies became a part of the "B" group of armies. Rumanian divisions formerly with the 11th Army in the Crimea were formed into the 4th Rumanian Army, which had in its makeup a cavalry corps and a mountain-infantry corps, and was placed under the command of Army Group "A."

As before, the basic *strategic* directions of the German armies and the armies of Germany's allies were the Leningrad, North Caucasus, Voronezh, and Stalingrad directions, which were formed in the course of operations and acquired significance as *main* directions, in view of the general strategic missions of bypassing Moscow on the east.

In keeping with these operations, the strategic deployment of the armies of the enemy was also changed. In the Voronezh direction, between Belgorod and Kharkov, there were concentrated the 4th Panzer Army, the 2nd Army provided with seven new divisions as replacements, and the 2nd Hungarian Army and units of the 6th Army. The staff of the 4th Panzer Army was shifted from the Viazma direction from the central group of General von Kluge. This Panzer Army had in its makeup the 9th, 11th, 3rd, 23rd, 22nd, and 24th Panzer Divisions. In the area of Slavyansk there were concentrated units of the 1st Panzer Army (13, 14, and 16 Panzer Divisions) and in the operational depths in the Donbass there were concentrated the 8th Italian and the 3rd Rumanian Armies.

After reaching the Don River at Voronezh and Ostrogozhsk and encountering the irresistible defense of the Red Army on the east bank of the Don, the main part of the forces of the 4th Panzer Army—made up of the 3rd, 22nd, 23rd, and 24th Panzer Divisions and the 6th Army —turned and moved south along the Don River in the direction of Chertkovo and Millerovo.

Here, evidently, the Germans intended to carry out the point of the plan "to encircle the army between the Donets and the Don." The 1st Panzer Army and the 17th Army were to cooperate in this plan by a frontal offensive from the region of Slaviansk. The 2nd Army, reinforced by the 9th and 11th Panzer Divisions, were assigned the mission of covering the left flank of Army Group "B."[7]

Though they started the offensive on June 28, the German troops were not able to reach the Don Bend until August 8.

The German Stalingrad Group and Its "Liquidation"

The Group on the Approaches to Stalingrad

After the stubborn August battles the 6th German Army—under the command of Colonel General Paulus and made up of the 8th, 11th, and 51st Army Corps; the 14th Panzer Corps; with units of the 79th, 113th,

376th, 100th, Jaegar, 305th, 384th, 389th, 76th, 44th, 295th, and 71st Infantry Divisions; the 16th and 22nd Panzer Divisions; and the 3rd and 60th Motorized Divisions—reached the Don Bend by August 18, 1942, on the line of Serafimovich, Kletskaia (exclusive), Kremenskaia, Sirotinskaia, (excluded), Kalach, and Nizhne–Chirskaia (sketch 3). While covering his left flank and the rear of the 6th Army on a line west of Serafimovich with units of the 8th Italian Army, the enemy began preparations for forcing the Don River.

On August 18, the leading units of the 384th and 389th Infantry Divisions, with a strength up to two infantry regiments and under cover of the fire of as many as 50 guns, 100 mortars, and air units operating in groups of 20 to 30 airplanes—succeeded in forging the Don River on the sector Trekhostrovskaia-Akimovskii and in fortifying themselves on its eastern bank. On August 23, while still holding the captured bridgehead and with the mass support of air units, the enemy broke through our frontline defenses on the sector Vertiachii-Peskovatka. Exploiting his gains with units of the 14th Panzer Corps (the 16th Panzer Division, 3rd and 60th Motorized Divisions), the enemy moved into the area of Erzovka (north of Stalingrad). By bringing into battle his infantry and tank echelons, the enemy succeeded in repelling the counterattacks of our units and in fortifying himself on the line: north of Vertiachii, south of Kotluban Station Akatovka.

At the same time, the 4th Panzer Army, under the command of General Hoth— made up of the 48th Panzer Corps (14th and 24th Panzer Divisions, 29th Motorized Division), the 4th Army Corps (supposedly the 94th, the 297th, and 371st Infantry Divisions), the Rumanian 6th Army Corps (1st, 2nd, 4th and 20th Infantry Divisions)—moving from Kotelnikovo, carried out the main attack in the general direction of Krasnoarmeisk. By August 18, units of 6th Rumanian Army Corps and the 4th Panzer Army reached the line Aksai River—Abganerovo Station-Plodovitoe. Between August 18 and 23, the enemy, continuing his fierce attacks and suffering at the same time heavy losses (on August 20–22 alone, 127 tanks and over 2,000 men were killed or wounded in the Krasnoarmeisk direction) reached the region to the west of Bolshoi Chapurnikii-Trudolubie-Tsatsa.

Failing in his efforts to exploit his gains in the direction of Krasnoarmeisk, the enemy carried out a regrouping of the 14th and 24th Panzer Divisions in the area of Vasilevka-Kapkinskii, and on August 29 started an offensive from this region to the north. On August 30, the enemy succeeded, with mobile leading units, in capturing Nariman and with a part of his forces crossed to the northeast bank of the Chervlenaia River. On August 31, up to two regiments of motorized infantry with 80 tanks (supposedly units of the 24th Panzer Division), forced the Chervlenaia River in the region of Novyi Rogachik, and reached Pitomnik. At the same time, up to two motorized regiments with 80 tanks (supposedly units of the 14th Panzer Division), after breaking through our defenses on the sector Tsybenko-Varvarovka. advanced some distance in a northeast direction.

The Battle on the Near Approaches and the Storming of Stalingrad

After creating a superiority of forces, especially in tanks and airplanes (over 500 tanks and up to 600 airplanes), the enemy—with units of the 389th, 295th, 305th, 76th, 71st, 94th, 297th, and 371st Infantry Divisions; 24th and 14th Panzer Divisions; 29th motorized Division; and the 20th, 1st, 2nd, and 4th Rumanian Infantry Divisions—by September 10, as a result of fierce fighting in which he suffered heavy losses, reached Gorodishche, Razguliaevka, Elshanka, Elkhi, Andreevka, Tundutovo, Dubovyi Ovrag, and Semkin.

After securing the left flank of his main offensive group with units of the 14th Panzer and 8th Army Corps on the line of Nizhne-Gnilovskii —south of Kotluban, Kuzmichi, and Akatovka—on September 10, with the main forces of the 4th Panzer and 6th Army—up to 9 infantry, 3 tank, and 3 motorized divisions with units of reinforcements—and with mass support of the *Luftwaffe*, the enemy started the assault against Stalingrad.

After the enemy reached the Volga on the sector of Tsentralnaia Pristan, the mouth of the Tsaritsa River, and Kuporosnoe, the center of the military actions were shifted to the areas of the Stalingrad Tractor Plant, the Barrikady, and Krasnii Oktiabr. In spite of a preponderant superiority in forces, the calculations of the enemy for the capture of Stalingrad were completely upset. The battle was prolonged until November. In the course of the battles, the enemy, suffering irreplaceable losses without any decisive victories, was forced to reinforce the Stalingrad direction by taking a number of divisions (the 79th and the 100th Jaegar) from other sectors of the front. In addition to this, the field units were reinforced by combat engineers, construction battalions, tanks, and artillery.

During the time of the battles on the distant and near approaches to the city and in the city itself, the enemy had lost by November 20, on the basis of approximate data, about 200,000 killed and wounded, over 1,000 guns of various calibers, over 1,400 mortars, about 4,300 machine guns, and about 1,500 tanks knocked out, burned, destroyed, or captured.

THE GROUPING OF THE ENEMY BEFORE THE BEGINNING OF OUR COUNTEROFFENSIVE

About November 19, the left flank of the 6th German Army was protected by the 3rd Rumanian Army (brought up in September from the rear of the zone of operations), consisting of the 1st Army Corps (7th, 11th, Infantry Divisions), the 2nd Army Corps (9th and 14th Infantry Divisions), the 5th Army Corps (5th and 6th Infantry Divisions), the 4th Army Corps (13th Infantry Division and 1st Cavalry Division), and having in reserve the 7th Cavalry Division in the area of Blinovskii, the 1st Rumanian Panzer Division in the area of Perelazovskii, and two infantry regiments of the 15th Infantry Division in the area of Selivanov.[8]

The 3rd Rumanian Army was on the defensive on the line of (exclusive) Veshenskaia, Yagodnyi, Bolshoie, Bobrovskii, and Kletskaia. The general combat and numerical makeup of the 3rd Rumanian Army (according to available data, which still requires filling out in detail) was as follows: about 100,000 men, up to 6,000 machine guns and weapons of various calibers amounting to 1,300, 1,100 to 1,200 mortars, and 130 tanks.

On the front (exclusive) Kletskaia, Sirotinskaia, Nizhne-Gnilovskii, Kuzmichi, Akatovka, Stalingrad, and Elkhi, the following continued to operate: 6th Army (11th, 8th, 51st Army Corps); 14th Panzer Corps; 4th Panzer Army (4th Army Corps and 48th Panzer Corps); having in their composition the 376th, 44th, 384th, 76th, 113th, 94th, 389th, 305th, 79th, and 100th Jaegar; 295th, 371st, 71st, and 297th Infantry Divisions; the 60th, 3rd, 29th Motorized Divisions; and the 16th, 14th, and 24th Panzer Divisions. In addition to this, the 22nd Panzer Division was supposedly in reserve in the region of Verkhne-Buzinovka.

The right flank of the 4th Panzer Army was covered by the 6th Rumanian Corps—made up of the 20th, 2nd, 18th, 1st, and 4th Infantry Division—and the 5th and 8th Cavalry Divisions, which defended themselves on the line Andreevka-Tsatsa-Khanata.

By this time, the enemy had on the front from Veshenskaia up to Khanata a total of 38 divisions, including the following: 27 infantry, 3 motorized, 5 Panzer, and 3 cavalry. The character of the actions of the enemy in continuing the attack against Stalingrad and the intensified construction of defensive installations on other sectors of the front) indicated that he was trying to get complete possession of the city and simultaneously prepare defensive positions for winter on the other occupied sectors.

The Actions of the Enemy in the Period of Our Counter-attack[9]

During November 18–20, units of the 3rd Rumanian Army were subjected to attacks by our forces. By numerous counterattacks of regimental and divisional reserves in combination with a stubborn defense on the front edge, they tried to prevent a breakthrough of the tactical zone on the sectors of the 9th and 14th Rumanian Infantry

Divisions and units of the 13th and 15th Rumanian Infantry Divisions. As a result of battles lasting for two days the enemy was thrown back in the direction of Station Seniutkin.

On November 20, the enemy threw into the battle, from the area southeast of Station Seniutkin, up to 80 tanks of the German 22nd Panzer Division, which, in a meeting engagement, suffered heavy losses and were thrown back in the direction of Perelazovskii.[10] Toward the end of November 20, the defensive zone of the enemy in the direction of Bolshoi was breached on a front of 15 to 20 kilometers and to a depth of 20 to 25 kilometers. In the course of the battle, the 14th Rumanian Infantry Division and the 36th Infantry Regiment of the 9th Rumanian Infantry Division were completely smashed.

In the direction of Kletskaia, the enemy threw into battle two regiments of the 15th Rumanian Infantry Division, which were in the army reserve, and on the 20th of November from the region of Verkhne-Buzinovka, he threw in the units of the German 14th Panzer Division.[11] As a result of the battles in this direction on November 19–20, the following were defeated: the 89th Infantry Regiment of the 13th Rumanian Infantry Division, the 12th Infantry Regiment of the 15th Rumanian Infantry Division. The German 14th Panzer Division also suffered considerable losses. The defense of the enemy in this sector was also breached to a depth of 16 to 17 kilometers over a front of 15 to 18 kilometers.

On November 21, the enemy committed to battle the 7th Rumanian Cavalry and 1st Rumanian Panzer Divisions from the area of Korotkovskii for the purpose of delivering a flank blow, but after stubborn tank engagements, they were defeated and driven back in the southeastern direction.

Toward the close of November 22, our units operating in the directions from Kletskaia toward Verkhne–Cherenskii and from Station Seniutkin toward Perelazovskii joined up—after having completed the encirclement of the 4th and 5th Army corps of the enemy—in the areas of Verkhne-–Fomikhinskii, Verkhne–Cherenskii, Verkhne–Solomakhovskii, Raspopinskaia, and Bazkovskii. The enemy's attempts to escape the encirclement were unsuccessful. During the nights of November 22–23, large groups made up of the 4th and the 5th Army Corps began to surrender. Among those captured were commanders of the 5th and 6th Rumanian Infantry Divisions, Generals Lasker and Mazarini together with their staffs, and 4,000 soldiers and officers.

After unsuccessful efforts to break out of the encirclement, units of the 4th and 5th Army Corps, following negotiations during the nights of the 23rd to the 24th of November, ceased resistance and surrendered with their commander, Brigadier General Stenesku. The total number of troops surrendering from the encircled group amounted to about 20,000 men. Of these there were one general, 10 colonels, and up to 200 senior officers belonging to the 5th, 6th, 13th, and 15th Rumanian Infantry Divisions.

As a result of the battles of November 23–24, the organized resistance of the enemy on the Pronin–Manoilin–Verkhne–Buzinovka line was broken. South and east of Kletskaia, units of the 1st Rumanian Cavalry Division and units of the 376th German Infantry Division were driven from the line Malye Iarki-Blizhnaia Perekopka, and the German 3rd Motorized and 14th Panzer Divisions threw away their equipment and armaments and withdrew in the direction of Bolshenabatovskii-Kalach.

Around November 24, for covering the flank of the 8th Italian Army in the region of Bokovskaia, the enemy tranferred units of the 29th Army Corps (62nd and 294th Infantry Divisions) from other sectors of the front.

By November 29, the enemy on the sector of the breakthrough was driven back to the line: Gorbatovskii, Chernyshevskaia, western bank of the Chir River, Oblivskaia Surovikino Rychkovskii, and the Don River.

To sum up, we will say that in the course of 5 or 6 days, in the battles in this sector of the front, we routed the 3rd Rumanian Army and defeated the 14th and 22nd German Panzer Divisions and the 62nd and the 294th German Infantry Divisions. On the basis of incomplete data, the enemy lost 34,000 killed and wounded men between November 19–30. The following were destroyed: over 500 machine guns, about 570 guns, over 100 tanks, and 174 airplanes. Captured: more than 31,000 rifles, about 3,100 machine guns, 1,000 guns, 234 tanks, 139 airplanes, and 54,250 soldiers and officers of the enemy.[12]

From November 20–30, on the right flank of the 4th Panzer Army we shattered units of the 6th Rumanian Army Corps (20th, 2nd, 18th, and 1st Infantry Divisions). Of the 8th Cavalry Division, the small groups left of them threw away their weapons and fled in panic toward the west and the southwest. By the end of November, the enemy had succeeded in making a stand on the Elkhi-Tsybenko line, and farther along the railroad (which was being restored) up to Prodboi, the south edge of Voroshilov Camp, and Marinovka. In the Kotelnikovo direction the enemy was driven from Liapichev and Logovsk, and the remnants of the defeated units offered resistance on the line of Verkhne–Kurmoiarskaia, Zakharov, Pimen–Cherni, and Vershin–Sal.

In the course of the battles in this sector November 20–30, the following were captured: 9,750 soldiers and officers, and in military equipment: 11 airplanes, 281 tanks, 130 mortars, 514 machine guns, and 650 guns of various calibers. Soldiers and officers of the enemy killed: 28,300; destroyed: 103 airplanes, 343 tanks, 584 machine guns, 172 weapons, and 190 mortars.

By November 24, the 6th Army and units of the 4th Panzer Army were encircled operationally as a result of the movement of our mobile units from the northwest into the area of Kalach and from the southeast into the Krivomuzginskaia—Sovetskii area. The remains of the flank groups of the enemy, continuing their withdrawal under the attacks of our troops, were thrown back to the following line by December 12: Gorbatovskii, Chernushevskaia, and farther along the western bank of the Chir River, Oblivskaia, Surovikino, Nizhne–Chirskaia, Verkhne–Kurmoiarskaia, Zakharov, Pimen–Cherni, Sharnutovskii, and Vershin–Sal.

In the region west of Stalingrad 20 German and two Rumanian divisions were completely surrounded and squeezed in an iron ring by the enveloping movement of our forces.

Hence, during the period of the battles from November 19 to December 20, northwest and southwest of Stalingrad, the following were defeated: 1st, 2nd, 5th, 6th, 9th, 13th, 14th, 15th, 18th, and 20th Rumanian Infantry Divisions; 1st and 7th Rumanian cavalry and 1st Rumanian Panzer Divisions; 44th, 376th, and 384th German Infantry and 22nd German Panzer Divisions. The 4th, 7th, and 11th Rumanian Infantry Divisions, as well as the 14th German Panzer and 29th German Motorized Divisions suffered considerable losses. The total losses of the enemy in these battles, according to data that is not yet complete, were more than 90,000 soldiers and officers killed and wounded; and over 70,000 captured. During this same period, we destroyed about 1,000 guns of different calibers, up to 600 tanks, and over 600 airplanes. We captured 150 airplanes, more than 1,000 tanks, and about 2,200 guns of various calibers.

Action of the Kotelnikovo Group of the Enemy

For the purpose of rendering assistance to the troops encircled west of Stalingrad, the German High Command quickly created the following:

in the area of Kotelnikovo, a motorized–mechanized group consisting of the 6th Panzer Division, transferred from France, and the 17th Panzer Division, shifted from the North Caucasus area. In addition to this, the 4th Infantry Division, the 5th and 8th Rumanian Cavalry Division, and the remains of the 18th Rumanian Infantry Division were in this area;

in the areas of Tormosin, Nizhne–Chirskaia, and Oblivskaia, a group consisting of the German 11th Panzer Division—redeployed from the Western Front—7th Luftwaffe Field Division, 336th Infantry Division, and nine separate battalions.

On December 12, the enemy started an offensive with a motorized–mechanized group from the regions of Kotelnikovo and Pimen–Cherni, along the railroad Kotelnikovo to Station Zhutovo. This offensive exerted pressure upon our units. By December 20, the 17th, 6th, and 23rd Panzer divisions reached the line of the Myshkova River.

By the operations of our forces in the period from December 22–30, the enemy was beaten and thrown back into the area southwest of Kotelnikovo. In the course of the battles we routed the 4th Rumanian Infantry Division and the 5th and 8th Rumanian Cavalry Divisions. The 16th, 17th, and 23rd German Panzer Divisions suffered heavy losses. According to data that is incomplete, the enemy lost in killed and wounded more than 12,000 men, and more than 4,000 soldiers and officers were captured.

THE SITUATION OF THE ENCIRCLED ENEMY BY JANUARY 10, 1943

Before the beginning of the general offensive of the Red Army units for the destruction of the encircled Stalingrad group of the enemy, 22 divisions of the 6th Army and of the 4th Panzer Army were completely encircled. The total makeup of the encircled troops of the enemy is shown in the table below.

The enemy units in the make up of four army corps and one Panzer corps on the defensive were as follows:[13]
14th Panzer Corps (29th and 3rd Motorized Divisions, 14th Panzer Division, and 376th Infantry Division), on the line to (exclusive Tsibenko, Rogachik, Marinovka, Dmitrievka, Kazachii, and Kurgan;
8th Army Corps (384th, 44th, 76th and 113th Infantry Divisions) on the (exclusive) Kazachii Kurgan-Zapadnovka sector and the eastern slopes of Elevation 143.8 (west of Kuzmichi);
11th Army Corps (60th Motorized Division, 16th and 24th Panzer Divisions, and 94th Infantry Division) on the line of Elevation 143.8, Kuzmichi, and the southwest edge of position Spartakovka;
51st Army Corps (389th, 305th, 79th, and 100th Jaegar, 295th and 71st Infantry Division) on the sector Position Spartakovka (exclusive) Kuporosnoe;
4th Army Corps (371st and 297th German Infantry Divisions, 20th Rumanian Infantry Division, 1st Rumanian Cavalry Division) on the Kuporosnoe Elkhi-Tsybenko sector.

At the beginning of the general offensive (January 10, 1943), the numerical strength of the German Stalingrad group was 190,000 men, from the total strength of 330,000 surrounded on November 23, 1942. We must note that the reconnaissance units of the Front, making use of the information furnished by prisoners concerning the losses in their units, made an error in their calculations and in the evaluation of the numerical strength of the surrounded enemy group. According to the data of the Intelligence section of the staff of the Don Front, the numerical strength of this group by January 10, 1943 was as follows:

Branch of The Army	Total	Number of Formations and Units	Remarks
Infantry divisions	15	44th, 71st, 76th, 79th, 94th, 100th 113th, 295th, 297th, 305th, 371st 384th, 389th, 376th—German 20th—Rumanian	384 Disbanded
Motorized divisions	3	3rd, 29th, 60th	
Panzer divisions	3	14th, 16th, 24th	
Cavalry divisions	1	1st Rumanian	
Artillery regiments of reinforcement	7	42nd, 44th, 46th, 59th, 61st, 65th, 72nd	General Head-quarters Reserves
Assault gun battalions	1	243rd	
Artillery battalions	7	1/97th Art. Reg., 43rd, 639th, 733rd, 856th, 861st	General Head-quarters Reserves
Mortar regiments of six-barreled mortars	2	2nd, 51st	General Head-quarters Reserves
Antiaircraft battalions	6	9th, 12th, 25th, 30th, 37th, 91st	From various regiments
Independent Engineer battalions	9	45th, 71st, 294th, 336th, 652nd, 672nd, 685th, 501st	The number of one unit was not ascertained.
Independent construction battalions	4	21st, 40th, 540th, 539th	
Independent signal regiments	2	6th, 594th	
Artillery spotter battalions	2	7th, 28th for operations and procedures	
Bridge columns and other service units	—		Numbers not ascertained

75,550 men, 1,997 weapons of various calibers, 366 mortars, 6,881 machine guns, 34,730 submachine guns, 245 tanks. The final makeup of the surrounded group was determined accurately by a comparison of the losses, war booty, and prisoners of the enemy, with statements, and so on, of Colonel von Kulovsky, the 1st "General Quartermaster" of the staff of the 6th German Army.

THE ACTIONS OF THE STALINGRAD GROUP OF THE ENEMY
DURING THE PERIOD OF ITS ENCIRCLEMENT

Before the beginning of the general offensive of the units of the Red Army, the encircled group organized five or six mobile shock detachments of motorized infantry, tanks, and artillery, having a strength of 500 to 600 men; the strength of each detachment varied from a company to a battalion, with 10 to 15 tanks, and 10 to 15 close-support guns attached. The missions of these detachments were to carry out counterattacks for the purpose of recovering lost positions. In addition to the detachments, local reserves were made ready in the directions of our most probable attack, also varying in strength from a company to a battalion, the purpose of which was to hold the positions captured in counterattacks.

In the period of the advance of the units of the Red Army, the enemy offered a stubborn resistance, having recourse to local counterattacks with small units varying in strength from a company up to a battalion with a small number of tanks.

All the measures of the Germans for the organization of the defense under conditions of complete encirclement amounted to conservation of the combat power and stability of the troops. The Rumanian units, which were not very reliable, were disbanded and mixed in with the Germans. The separate units of the auxiliary branches of the service and all unnecessary rear units and institutions were disbanded, and their personnel placed in combat units as soon as they could be spared.

Every effort was made to maintain the morale and stability of the personnel of the encircled Army by promising fresh reinforcements, frightening the men with cruel tortures if they surrendered, shooting all those who tried to surrender, and liberally rewarding and promoting those distinguishing themselves.

A careful check was made immediately of all the supplies. The food ration, ammunition, and fuel rations were reduced; judging from intercepted radio messages, every unit was to have a ten-day reserve of food that was not to be touched.

The supplying of the encircled forces was carried out by transport planes. One of the captured documents of January 5, 1943 read: "Up until this time, 4,180 tons of freight have been delivered into the fortress [evidently in the area of the encirclement] by 2,515 airplanes." Consequently, 60 to 65 airplanes delivered each day on an average of 100 tons of supplies. The minimum daily food requirement was 50 tons, and the amount of fuel delivered was 30 to 50 tons. Hence, very little ammunition was supplied, and the enemy, after expending the supplies on hand, was forced to decrease the intensity of its fire from day to day.[14]

Prisoners of war and Colonel von Kulovsky said that all the supplies that the troops had received since November 23 had been delivered by airplanes. Up until January 15, an average of 80 transport planes came into the ring of encirclement (the maximum number in good weather was 150 airplanes). The food rations for the encircled personnel were fixed as follows: *from December 8, 1942,* bread, 350 grams; fats, 80 grams; meat, 100 grams; *from December 24,* bread, 200 grams; fats, 30 grams; meat, 50 grams; *from January 25, 1943,* bread, 120 grams. *By January 10,* not a single horse was left in the area of the encirclement.

Before the capture of the Pitomnik locality by units of the Red Army, the encircled troops received 50 to 60 tons of fuel a day. Then the ration was reduced to 4.5 to 5 tons, and the number of airplanes dropped to five to 10 a day. With the capture of Ezhovki, one half of the supplies delivered by airplanes and released on parachutes was lost in the snow.

By concentrating all efforts on holding the dominating lines of the locality, the enemy shifted his main efforts to counterattacks and maneuvers by the most stable units.

The leaflets dropped by our airplanes exerted their influence on the morale of the enemy troops.

On January 22, the capture of Voroponovo made a breach in the inner circle of the Stalingrad fortifications. The personnel of the encircled German Army still hoped to find protection from the cold in Stalingrad. Fearing the disintegration and collapse of the units, the enemy, while still offering stubborn resistance, retreated to the city ring of fortifications. The destroyed city of Stalingrad caused disillusion among those who hoped to find warmth in it. After the loss of space and the airfields, the supply situation of the encircled enemy grew worse. Under the influence of cold, hunger, and the hopelessness of the situation, even the officer personnel now saw clearly how senseless it was to continue the resistance.

On January 26, the city line of fortification was breached in the area of Mamaev Kurgan, and the enemy group was split into two parts. The commander of the 297th Infantry Division surrendered with all of his staff and what was left of his division. During the night of January 26–27, a parlementaire of the enemy, in the name of the Commander of the Army, asked to start negotiations for surrender, but the next morning von Paulus refused to enter into negotiations.

Our units, operating against the southern group of the enemy, destroyed the centers of resistance in street battles, occupied quarter after quarter tightening its ring, surrounded the staff of the 6th German Army on January 31 and captured it with Field Marshal von Paulus and all the rest of this group.

The northern group, consisting of more than 30,000 men, continued to resist and refused to capitulate. However, the bombardment of the fortified positions with powerful artillery almost at point-blank range from open positions made the leaders of this group more compliant. On the night between February 1–2, the General of the northern group of the enemy prepared a systematic surrender of the troops, and on February 2, this group, numbering 33,000, surrendered.[15]

The General Results of the Operation

The operations for the encirclement and destruction of the Stalingrad group of the enemy ended on February 2, 1943 with a complete victory for the Red Army.

Between January 10 and February 2, 1943, the 6th Army and parts of the 4th Panzer Army of the enemy, consisting of the units and formations listed in the table on page 34 were wiped out, killed, or captured. During this period, more than 100,000 soldiers and officers of the enemy were killed, and 130,000 were captured. Of this number, 24 were generals and more than 4,000 were officers. In the period of the general offensive alone during the operations for the liquidation of the encircled Stalingrad group, we captured the following war materials: 744 airplanes; 1,666 tanks; 5,572 guns; 1,312 mortars; 12,701 machine guns; 156,987 rifles; 10,722 motor vehicles; 10,679 motorcycles; 811 tractors, prime movers, and combat vehicle carriers; 696 radio sets; 137 various kinds of dumps; and many other kinds of military equipment.

General Conclusions

The tactical victories of the German Army and its allies, won as a result of the summer offensive of 1942, were considerably reduced by the destruction of the 6th Army and the main forces of the 4th Panzer Army at Stalingrad. The German High Command recognized very well that the occupation of the North Caucasus could be assured only by a firm hold on the region of Stalingrad. In attempting to achieve this goal, the Germans displayed exceptional obstinacy, bordering on stupidity. As a result of the annihilation of the Stalingrad group the whole winter campaign of 1942–1943 ended in a failure.

Due to the results achieved by the offensive of the troops fighting on the Transcaucasus Front and the necessity of protecting the withdrawal of Army Group "A" of General List from the North Caucasus—chiefly the latter—the Stalingrad group of 330,000 soldiers and officers was sacrificed. The Germans succeeded in avoiding a catastrophe for the army of General List by a stubborn defense of the eastern approaches to the Taman Peninsula.[16]

The hopes that the Germans pinned on a stubborn defense of the area of Stalingrad, which would protect the withdrawal of its troops retreating from the Caucasus through Rostov under the blows of the Red Army, did not materialize. The counteroffensives of the 6th, 17th and 23rd German Panzer Divisions in the Kotelnikovo direction had two purposes: to open a route of escape for the encircled German Stalingrad group and to facilitate the withdrawal of the Germans from the north Caucasus through Rostov. Neither of these purposes was achieved due to the complete failure of the Kotelnikovo operation. The perspicacious foresight of the *Stavka* frustrated the plans of the German High Command. The most stubborn fights, having a decisive influence on the outcome of this great battle, terminated in a complete victory for the Red Army, the throwing of the enemy beyond the Manychskii Canal, and the capture of Salsk and Rostov.

By losing the 6th Army and the 4th Panzer Army, the enemy did not improve the situation of the armies in the North Caucasus. With the movement of our troops into the area of Kishchevskaia, the German armies in the Caucasus were isolated from the Rostov group and thrown back toward the Taman Peninsula.

As each day went by, the front moved farther and farther away from the group surrounded at Stalingrad. As the shots were fired farther and farther away, hope for aid from the outside gradually faded, and finally the decisive assault of the victorious Red Army completed the liquidation of the once haughty and supercilious victors of the German Stalingrad group.

Before the summer offensive of 1942, the 6th Army, 1st Panzer Army, the 17th Army, the Italian Expeditionary Corps, and 6th Rumanian Corps occupied a front from Kharkov up to Taganrog. The Red Army, which started its offensive on November 19, 1942, again reached approximately this same line by the rout and destruction of the enemy.

On October 14, 1942, Hitler issued to the German Army an order No. 420817/42:

The preparations for the winter campaign are now in full swing. The second Russian winter finds us ready and better prepared. The Russians, whose strength has been considerably reduced, as a result of the recent battles, can no longer bring into battle in the course of the winter 1942–43 such forces as they did in the past winter campaign. Whatever happens we cannot have a winter that will be any harder or more difficult.

To this order he added the following postscript:

The final winter line of the defense runs as follows: Army Group "B": Yashkul (200 km west of Astrakhan) along the elevation to the north of the Volga, Stalingrad—present front of the 6th Army, 8th Italian Army, 2nd Hungarian Army, and 2nd Germany Army.

How greatly mistaken was the command of the German Army. The winter of 1942–43 was much harder and more difficult than the previous winter. The Germans considered the previous winter to be unsurpassable for severity. How would they appraise this winter? All the armies enumerated in the postscript to the order of Hitler were either destroyed or completely routed, and to these we must also add the 4th Panzer Army, the 3rd Rumanian Army, the 1st Panzer Army, and the 17th Army.

The resistance of the units of the Red Army at Stalingrad forced the enemy command to try to fascinate its soldiers with the economic importance of Stalingrad and the advantages that those seeking plunder might count on.

This "encouraging" order was issued by the High Command of the Army Group on September 11, 1942.

The Commander in Chief of the Army Group issued the following order:

The troops of the 4th Panzer and the 6th Army have already shown in the 3 weeks' battle for Stalingrad a readiness for action which far exceeds the ordinary, and they have also displayed a remarkable offensive spirit under difficult combat conditions. I express thanks and gratitude for these extraordinary achievements. Now the problem is to hold out until the final capture of Stalingrad and with this complete the defeat of the enemy. Signed, Von Weichs.

The commander of the 6th Army, in making this order, considered it necessary to add:

In keeping with the order of the Supreme Command I again order that you bring to the knowledge of the troops the proclamation of Stalin on September 8, 1942, to explain to them still further the economic importance of Stalingrad explained in the new communications, so that each soldier on the Stalingrad front will clearly understand what great significance the loss of Stalingrad has for the Russians. Such knowledge will have an encouraging effect upon the troops and will make clear to them the importance of the victory which we are fighting for and which we expect to win soon. Signed, Paulus, Commander in Chief of the 6th Army. Ia/Ic No. 3349/42. Secret.

The adventurous strategy of the German–Fascist leaders collapsed at Stalingrad.

This strategy was opposed by the Stalin strategy, the basis of which is Bolshevik organization and the genius of our great strategist Comrade Stalin, who is unsurpassed in our epoch.

Editor's Notes

1. For an excellent discussion of German efforts to repair the damage of the 1941 campaign see Burkhart Muller–Hillebrand, *Das Heer, 1939–1945* Band III (Frankfurt/Main: E.S. Mittler & Sons, 1969), pp. 45–71. In English, see Albert Seaton *The German Army, 1933–1945* (New York: Meridian Press, 1985), pp. 188–90.
2. The overall scope of German operations were governed by Directive No. 41 issued in April 1942. The two primary operations regarding the Stalingrad battle were for a consolidation of the position of Army Group South, and then an offensive toward Voronezh/Stalingrad and the Caucasus. The oil resources of the Caucasus appear as the primary objective although the stated intention is to destroy all remaining Soviet war potential—a task not covered without an occupation of Moscow and the area of the Urals.

3. This was not the first clue given to Soviet intelligence. The unfortunate case of Major Reichel, the chief of operations of 23rd Panzer Division, who was killed in June 1942 while carrying detailed plans of the first phase of the summer campaign is an excellent example of the availability of information on German objectives and timetables.

4. In fact, Halder complained of just the opposite on June 29, 1942. While indicating that the 11th Army was the only major German reserve force in the east, he stated that it could not be rebuilt and that each division would remain 2,000–3,000 men understrength. See Franz Halder, *The Halder Diaries*, 2 vols., translated, (Boulder: Westview Press, 1976), vol. 2, p. 337.

5. Actual strength was 68 German divisions including 9 Panzer and 6 Motorized. The allies of Germany contributed an additional 50 so-called divisions since many were not up to divisional size.

6. The problem was that the impressive increase in divisional totals hid a very vexing problem. The German Army in the East was short of establishment by 650,000. See Muller–Hillebrand, *Das Heer*, p. 65.

7. In actuality, 9th and 11th Panzer Divisions were released to Army Group Center for offensive operations to consolidate German positions.

8. In reality, the 1st Rumanian Panzer Division was still working up when the Soviet breakthrough occurred. Nominally a powerful formation with 108 tanks; in actuality it contained only 21 modern (Mark III) tanks and another 87 obsolete (Czech T-35) models with only a 37 mm gun, a weapon hopelessly inadequate against Soviet armor. It did however, have a strong flak detachment including 17 88 mm guns. See the National Archives, Captured German Records, series T–314, Roll 1160, Frames 000183 and 000192. Hereafter National Archives German Records.

9. Soviet strength on the Stalingrad direction on November 19 was;

	Soviet	German	Ratio
Men	1,103,000	1,011,500	1,1:1
Guns/Mortars	15,501	10,290	1,5:1
Tanks/SP Guns	1,463	675	2,2:1
Combat Aircraft	1,350	1,216	1,1:1

Source: *IVMV*, vol. 6, p. 35, Table 5.

10. Unfortunately, this is a case, all too common in this work. of more tanks attacking than are available to the Germans. This is to be expected of a document prepared in wartime from official reports. For example, on November 18, 1942, the 22nd Panzer Division only possessed 40 tanks, and by November 20, they were down to 31 tanks. See National Archives German Records T–314, Roll 1160, Frames 000192 and 000274.

11. This 14th Panzer Division was, in reality, a battle group of the division. Total strength on November 18, 1942, was only 36 tanks. See National Archives, German Records: T–314, Roll 1160, Frame 000192.

12. On November 27, 1942, the 22nd Panzer Division was down to only 16 tanks, and on November 28, the 1st Rumanian Panzer contained only 3 tanks. See National Archives, German Records: T–314, Roll 1160, Frames 000414 and 000443.

13. In actuality this listing misses the 9th Flank Division.

14. In fact, what was needed, according to 6th Army, was 750 tons per day. See Albert Seaton *The Russo–German War, 1941–45* (New York: Praegar, 1970), p. 321.

15. The commander of the northern group was Lieutenant General W. von Seidlitz-Kurzbach.

16. Field Marshal List was no longer in command of Army Group "A." He had been superseded by Hitler's personal command through the existing headquarters staff.

The crushing German victory in the May battles around Kharkov left the defending Soviet forces exhausted and understrength. Coupled with the Stavka mistake in placing the Red Army's existing reserve forces around Orel, the Nazi divisions on the southern axis of the frontline had an excellent balance of strength to open the summer 1942 campaign. This chapter details the belated Soviet efforts to correct the strategic error of the initial Soviet dispositions and the subsequent efforts to slow and then halt the German drive west of Stalingrad. Although Soviet forces fought in tenacious defense of the successive defense lines, the final Soviet successes of August and September in stopping the German troops lay as much with the inadequacy of German logistics as with the confusing decisions of Stavka—Ed.

3

Battle for Stalingrad August–October 1942

The General Situation

For carrying out their strategic plan for enveloping Moscow from the east and isolating it from the Urals and the Volga rear areas, the German High Command, toward the summer of 1942, deployed large forces of German–Fascist troops in the southern sector of the Eastern Front. Between Kursk and Taganrog eight armies were concentrated (of these five were German): the 3rd Rumanian, 8th Italian, 2nd Hungarian Armies, and the 6th Rumanian Army Corps. In all, this group had 91 divisions, including 10 Panzer divisions. The enemy Panzer divisions, combined into the German 1st and 4th Panzer Armies, played an important role in the summer campaign of 1942.

After the breakthrough of the defenses at the junction of the Briansk and Southwestern Fronts, the German 1st and 4th Panzer Armies moved into the operational depths of the dispositions of our troops and, in the

41

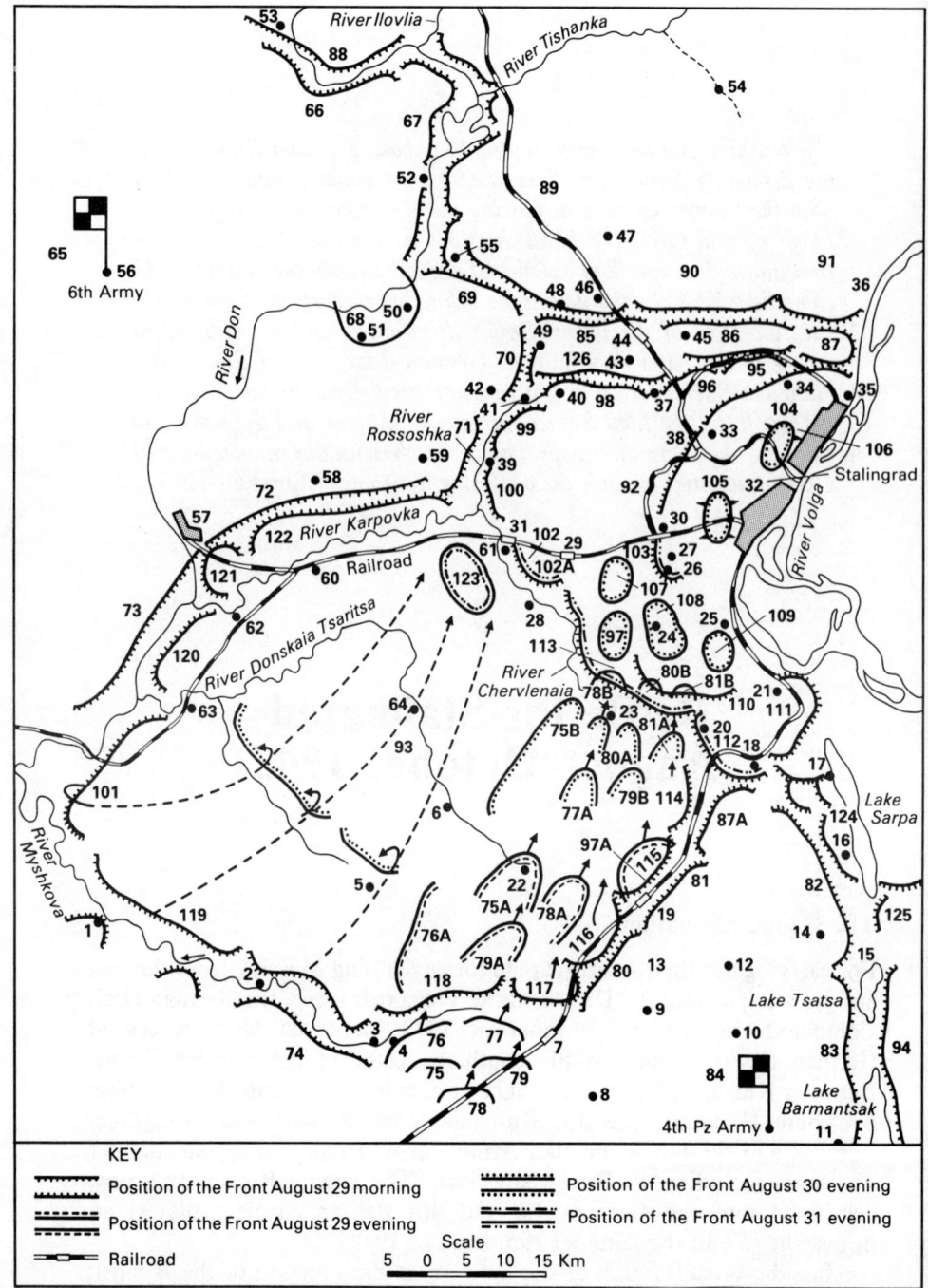

KEY

▨▨▨▨ Position of the Front August 29 morning

▨▨▨▨ Position of the Front August 30 evening

▰▰▰▰ Position of the Front August 29 evening

▰▰▰▰ Position of the Front August 31 evening

▭━▭ Railroad

Scale

5 0 5 10 15 Km

Source: Basic Data from K.K. Rokossovskii, *Velikiye pobeda na Volge* (Moskva: Voenizdat, 1965), Map 14.

Map One
"Combat Operations of the 64th Army on the Inner and Middle Fortified Positions"

Cities
1. Shebalinskii
2. Gromoslavka
3. Vasilevka
4. Kapkinskii
5. State Farm Krep
6. Verkhne-Tsaritsynskii
7. Abganerovo Station
8. Abganerovo
9. State Farm No. 2
10. Plodovitoie
11. Tunditovo
12. Tinguta
13. State Farm No. 3
14. State Farm Privolzhskii
15. Trydoliubie
16. Dubovyi Ovrag
17. Bolshe Chapurniki
18. Solianka
19. Tinguta Station
20. Ivanovka
21. Krasnoarmiesk
22. Zety
23. Nariman
24. Elkhi
25. Beketovka
26. Staro-Dubovka
27. Peschanka
28. Rakotino
29. Basargino Siding
30. Alekseevka
31. Karpovka Station
32. Stalingrad
33. Gorodishche
34. Orlovka
35. Rynok
36. Erzovka
37. Novaia Nadezhda
38. Gumrak Station
39. Novo-Alekseevskii
40. Bolshaia Rossoshka
41. Zapadnovka
42. State Farm No. 1
43. Borodkin
44. Siding 564km
45. Kuzmichi
46. Samofalovka
47. State Farm Kotluban
48. Kotluban
49. State Farm Borodkin
50. Vertiachii
51. Peskovatka
52. Trekhostrovskaia
53. Sirotinskaia
54. Sadki

55. delete
56. Osinovka
57. Kalach
58. Illarionovskii
59. Dmitrievka
60. Sovetskii
61. Novy Rogachik
62. Kolpachki
63. Liapachev
64. Buzinovka

German Units
65. 6th Army Headquarters
66. 41st Infantry Division
67. 305th Infantry Division
68. 389th Infantry Division
69. 384th Infantry Division
70. 76th Infantry Division
71. 295th Infantry Division
72. 71st Infantry Division
73. Units of the 71st Infantry Division
74. 1st Rumanian Infantry Division
75. 24th Panzer Division
75A. 24th Panzer Division
75B. 24th Panzer Division
76. 2nd Rumanian Infantry Division
76A. 2nd Rumanian Infantry Division
77. 20th Rumanian Infantry Division
77A. 20th Rumanina Infantry Division
78. Units of the 29th Motorized Division
78A. Units of the 29th Motorized Division
78B. Units of the 29th Motorized Division
79. 14th Panzer Division
79A. 14th Panzer Division
79B. 14th Panzer Division
80. 297th Infantry Division
80A. 297th Infantry Division
80B. 297th Infantry Division
81. 371st Infantry Division
81A. 371st Infantry Division
81B. 371st Infantry Division
82. Units of the 29th Motorized Division
83. 4th Rumanian Infantry Division
84. 4th Panzer Army Headquarters
85. 60th Motorized Division
86. 3rd Motorized Division
87. 16th Panzer Division
87A. 94th Infantry Division

Soviet Units
88. 21st Army area of operations
89. 4th Tank Army area of operations
90. 1st Guards Army area of operations
91. 66th Army area of operations
92. 62nd Army area of operations

93. 64th Army area of operations
94. 51st Army area of operations
95. 2nd Tank Corps
96. 23rd Tank Corps
97. 13th Mechanized (Tank) Corps
97A. 13th Mechanized (Tank) Corps
98. 187th Rifle Division
99. 196th Rifle Division
100. 33rd Guards Rifle Division
101. 118th Guards Rifle Division
102. 157th Independent Artillery Battalion
102A. 160th Independent Artillery Battalion
103. 20th Engineer Brigade
104. 10th *NKVD* Rifle Division
105. 78th Tank Brigade
106. 26th Tank Brigade
107. 204th Rifle Division
108. 29th Rifle Division
109. 138th Rifle Division
110. 36th Guards Rifle Division
111. 244th Rifle Division

112. 422nd Rifle Division
113. 38th Rifle Division
114. 154th Motorized Rifle Brigade, 138th Motorized Rifle Brigade, 20th Motorized Rifle Brigade.
115. 204th Rifle Division
116. 138th Rifle Division
117. 29th Rifle Division
118. 126th Rifle Division
119. 157th Rifle Division
120. Units of the 112th Rifle Division
121. 20th Motorized Rifle Brigade
122. 112th Rifle Division and 131st Rifle Division
123. 66th Motorized Rifle Brigade and 157th Rifle Division
124. 38th Motorized Rifle Brigade and 15th Guards Rifle Division
125. 198th Rifle Regiment and 26th Guards Rifle Division
126. 35th Guards Rifle Division

Source: Basic Data from K.K. Rokossovskii, *Velikiye pobeda na Volge* (Moskva: Voenizdat, 1965), map 14.

first half of July 1942, developed an attack from the Rossosh-Starobelsk line in a south–southeast direction.

The troops of the Southwestern Front, split up and disorganized by the enemy Panzer group, withdrew a portion of its forces beyond the Don River to the Boguchar-Serafimovich sector and with the remainder, joined the Southern Front and conducted a holding battle with the pursuing mobile forces of the enemy.

About July 14 the troops of the right wing of the Southern Front fought on the line of Pronskii, Nizhne–Astakhov, Kashary, Millerovo, and Belovodsk. About this time, up to four Panzer and one motorized German divisions came into the Millerovo–Degtevo–Meshkov area, aiming at Kamensk Shakhtinskii, for the purpose of cutting off the route of withdrawal of the troops of the Southern Front that were west of the Severnaia Donets River. One Panzer and one motorized division moved into the Morozovskii area and farther on to Tsymlianskaia.

Simultaneously two Panzer divisions and one motorized division moved from the line Starobelsk, Lisichansk, in an easterly direction. Following them and also moving toward the east were the infantry formations of the 6th German Army and the Rumanian 3rd Army. During the middle of July, the main efforts of the Germans were directed at the capture of Rostov. After this, we had to suppose that the main operational efforts of the enemy would be shifted into the area of Stalingrad, the capture of which was an integral part of the plan by the German High Command for the capture of Moscow from the east.

Under such conditions the organizing of the troops of the Southwestern Front required considerable time and effort. It was not possible to commit these troops for covering the approaches to Stalingrad. For covering Stalingrad it would have been necessary to establish a front of over 400 kilometers and to assemble in this direction operational reserves capable not only of holding the enemy breaking through to the Volga but also of defeating him. In order to carry out this mission, it was necessary to gain time and to hold the area in the large bend of the Don River west of Stalingrad.

About July 10, 1942, the newly created Stalingrad Front, consisting of the 62nd and 63rd Armies and a part of the troops of the Southwestern Front—which had been moved behind the Don River and put in the 21st Army—had the mission of holding the line along the Don River from Babka up to Serafimovich and farther to the south—Kletskaia, Kalmykov, Surovikino, Suvorovskii—to protect the concentration in the area northwest and the operational reserves west of Stalingrad.[1]

The left wing of the Stalingrad Front touched the 51st Army of the North Caucasus Front, which was on the defensive along the lower course of the Don River on the front of Verkhne–Kurmoiarskaia, Titov, Semikarakorskaia, Bataysk.

Operations on the Distant Approaches to Stalingrad

By July 15, the troops of the Stalingrad Front had taken up defensive positions as follows:

The 63rd Army (four rifle divisions) covered the communications northwest of Stalingrad, having assumed the defensive on a front extending a distance of 250 kilometers along the Don River from Babka up to the mouth of the Medveditsi River. There were no reserves.

The 21st Army took up positions on the line from the mouth of the Medveditsi River up to the mouth of the Ilovlia River with the mission of protecting the junction between the 63rd and the 62nd Army.[2]

The mission of the 62nd Army (six rifle divisions) was to cover the shortest route to Stalingrad from the west by firmly holding the line of Kletskaia, Evstratovskii, Kalmykov, Slepikhin, and Suvorovskii, creating the greatest density on the Evstratovskii–Slepikhin sector. With the approach of the 64th Army, transported from the region of Tula, the aim was to divide the front of the 62nd Army's defense between the 62nd and 64th Armies with a junction in the area of Slepikhin.[3] The 62nd Army assumed the defensive on the line pointed out above, having five rifle divisions in the first echelon and one rifle division in reserve, in the area of Gureev and Popov No. 1.

For assuming the defensive in the depths in the area of Stalingrad, there were concentrated two naval brigades and cadets from eight rifle schools from the North Caucasus. At the same time, work was started on a large scale for the construction of concentric defense lines covering Stalingrad. The outer line of defense, with a length of 400 kilometers, was placed on the Gornaia Proleika-Bolshe Ivanovka-Krasnoiarskii line on the south along the east banks of the Ilovlia, Don, and Myshkovo rivers, Station Abganerovo, Lake Tsatsa, and Raigorod. The middle line of defense was on the Pichuga-Station Kotluban-Karpovka line, along the Chervlenaia River, Station Tundutovo, and Svetlyi Yar. The inner defense line was on the line Orlovka, Station Gumrak, Alekseevka, Beketovka, and Krasnoarmeisk [see map 2—Ed.].

As subsequent experience showed, such a system of concentrically constructed defense lines on fronts stretching over long distances did not prove to be effective, because the object to be defended was far away and the system lost its stability when broken through in one place. The creation of a fixed system of intermediate lines and switch positions, making possible the maneuver of reserves in depth for delivering counterattacks, is more effective for a stable defense. A system of concentric lines on the immediate approaches to the object defended would certainly be effective.

The line occupied by the 62nd Army met the requirements for defense. The enemy approaches were taken into account over a great depth. In the rear up to the Don River, there were two lines suitable for defense. The weakness was that there were localities accessible for tanks over almost the whole front of the defenses.

Being stretched out on a line, the Army did not have sufficient forces and equipment for creating the proper density of defense and a reliable depth. In addition to this, a considerable part of the strength of the Army (up to 25 percent) was assigned to leading detachments upon orders of the Front Commander.

The leading detachments, consisting of a reinforced battalion up to a reinforced regiment, were to move to the Chir and the Tsymla Rivers with the mission of destroying the leading enemy units. Though they were sent to a distance of 40–60 kilometers from the forward edge of the main line of defense, the leading detachments were not provided with a sufficient amount of mobile equipment. There was no planning or cooperation between the detachments on the front, and there was no cooperation in depth between the leading detachments and the leading divisions sending them out. In July 18–19, these detachments engaged the enemy's mobile units and were defeated one by one, and a large part of them were surrounded, without any opportunity to break out to the main forces. These, in turn, could not help the leading units, however much they wished to do so, without direct detriment to the execution of their own basic mission.

Hence, even before the beginning of the decisive battles on the main

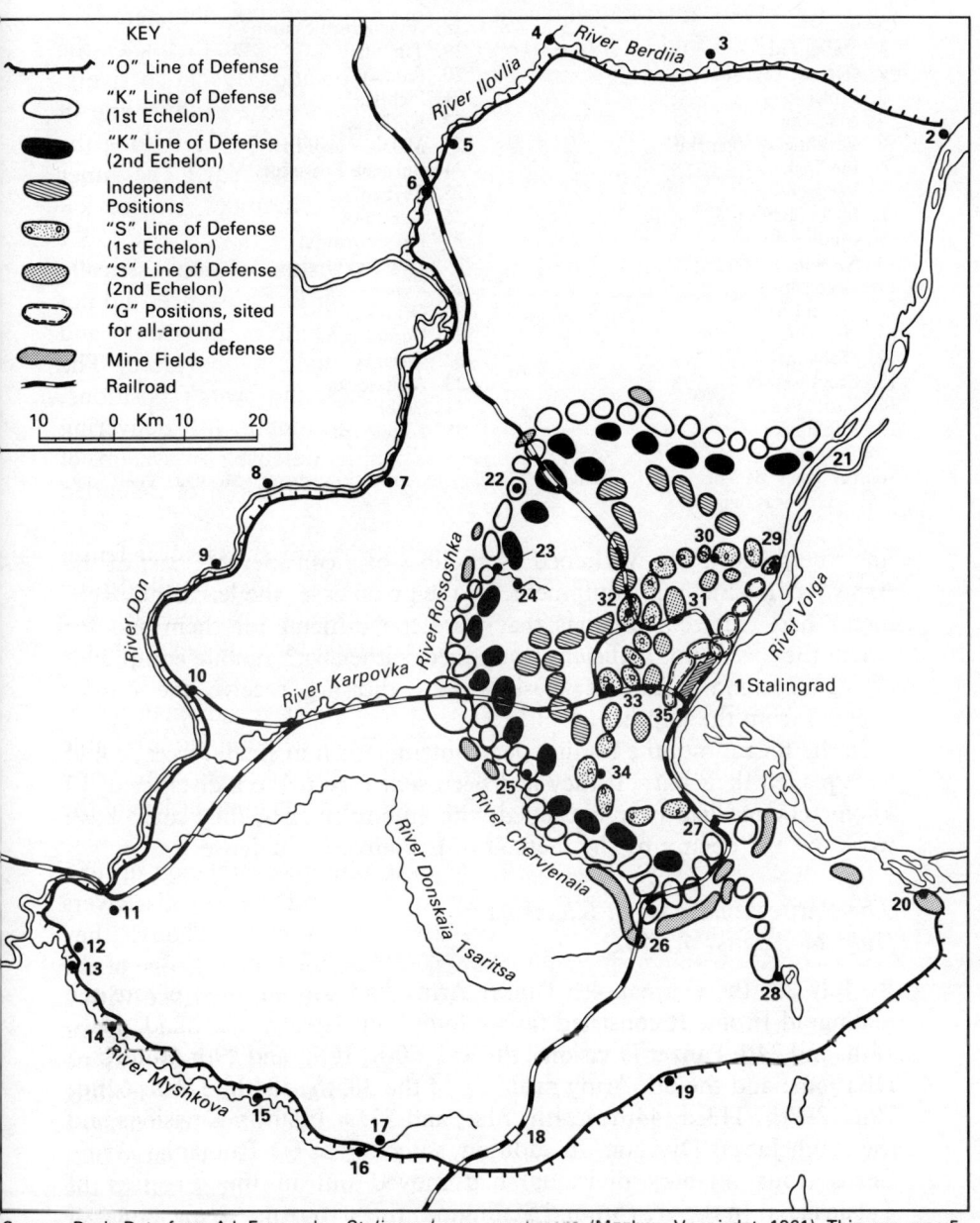

KEY

"O" Line of Defense

"K" Line of Defense (1st Echelon)

"K" Line of Defense (2nd Echelon)

Independent Positions

"S" Line of Defense (1st Echelon)

"S" Line of Defense (2nd Echelon)

"G" Positions, sited for all-around defense

Mine Fields

Railroad

10   0   Km 10   20

River Berdiia

River Ilovlia

River Rossoshka

River Don

River Karpovka

River Volga

1 Stalingrad

River Chervlenaia

River Donskaia Tsaritsa

River Myshkova

Source: Basic Data from A.I. Eremenko, *Stalingrad* map supplement, (Moskva: Voenizdat, 1961). This was map 5.

Map Two
"The Fortified Lines Prepared to Defend Stalingrad"

Cities
1. Stalingrad
2. Gornaia Proleika
3. Proleiskaia
4. Alikovka
5. Verkhne Peschanskii
6. Ilovlinskaia
7. Vertiachii
8. Malonabatovskii
9. Golubinskii
10. Kalach
11. Logovskii
12. Ermokhinskii
13. Demkin
14. Shabalinskii
15. Gromoslavka
16. Vasil'evka
17. Kapkinskii

18. Abganerovo Station
19. Tinguta
20. Raigorod
21. Pichuga
22. Kotluban'
23. Malaia Rossoshka
24. Bolshaia Rossashka
25. Tsybenko
26. Tundutovo
27. Krasnoarmeisk
28. Dubovyi Ovrag
29. Rynok
30. Orlovka
31. Gorodishche
32. Gumrak
33. Alekseevka
34. Elkhi
35. Kuporosnoe

Source: Basic data from A.I. Eremenko, *Stalingrad*, map supplement (Moskva: Voenizdat, 1961). This was map 5.

line, the defense was weakened by the loss of a considerable part of the Army's personnel and equipment. In the given case, the leading detachments had received missions that were too difficult for them and for which they were not sufficiently supplied, either with mobile equipment or signal communications; besides they did not receive the proper support from the depths.

In the meantime, the leading detachments, even in small forces, could have played their part. If they had been sent forward to a distance of 15 kilometers and had been equipped with entanglements, they could have worn out the enemy by the method of maneuvering defense.

The Battle Southeast of Kletskaia
(July 24–August 6, 1942)

By July 23, the German 4th Panzer Army had concentrated before the Stalingrad Front. It consisted (as we found out later) of the 22nd, 14th, 16th, and 24th Panzer Divisions; the 3rd, 60th, 16th, and 29th Motorized Divisions; and the 6th Army made up of the 305th, 384th, 376th, 62nd, 79th, 297th, 113rd, 44th, 294th, 71st, and 271st Infantry Divisions and the 100th Jaeger Division. In addition, some of the 6th Rumanian Army Corps (four infantry divisions) had moved out in the direction of Tatsinskaia. In the area around Stalingrad, there were operating a total of four Panzer, four motorized, and 16 or 17 infantry divisions.

In the main, the infantry formations of the enemy completed their concentration on the Chir River in the areas of Bokovskaia, Chernysheskaia, and Pokrovskii. Up to four infantry divisions assumed the defensive on a broad front opposite the 63rd Army to protect the main group from the north.

The Panzer and motorized divisions of the Panzer Army were grouped in the following order: two Panzer and three motorized divisions (the 22nd and 16th Panzer Divisions; 3rd, 60th, and 29th Motorized Divisions) were concentrated southwest of Kletskaia. Two Panzer divisions and one motorized division (24th and 14th Panzer Divisions and the 16th Motorized Division) were concentrated in the area of Tsymlianskaia.

The troops of the Stalingrad Front assumed the offensive on the former grouping. The 64th Army was transported by railroad. After detraining, parts of the Army moved out to assume the defensive on the line of Surovikino, Novomaksimovskii, and Verkhne-Kurmoiarskaia. In the area of Stalingrad, the remainder of the 57th Army assembled for assuming the defensive on the inside line of defense. The 1st and 4th Tank Armies started to form up in the area of Stalingrad on July 24.[4]

On the morning of July 24, enemy tank formations started an offensive against the 62nd Army from the Verkhne–Cherenskii-Perelazovskii front in the direction of Verkhne-Buzinovka. At the same time, the enemy began active operations in the area of Tsymlianskaia against the 51st Army of the North Caucasus Front.

Of the 150 enemy tanks that attacked the 33rd Guards Rifle Division of the 62nd Army, 35 were knocked out, and 30 succeeded in wedging into the defensive depths of the Division. The Commander of the 62nd Army concentrated against the sector of the breakthrough all his tanks, the Guards' Mortar units, the destroyer antitank regiments, and also his reserve, the 184th Rifle Division.

For action against the enemy's motorized–mechanized forces, we concentrated the main part of our air units of the Front and a part of the reserve air units of the *Stavka*. The measures taken enabled us to localize the breakthrough, and thus the efforts of the enemy to exploit his victory were unsuccessful.

The battles in the areas of Kletskaia, Verkhne-Buzinovka, and Manoilin were fierce and prolonged. The enemy tried to widen the gap by throwing in fresh forces. We opposed the enemy with the 1st and 4th Tank armies, which had not yet finished forming up and were committed with units of the 21st Army in the area of Kletskaia, and units of the right flank of the 62nd Army.

By the beginning of August, the enemy had wedged into the defense on the sector of Kletskaia, Ventsy, Naidenov, Golubinskkaia, Lipologovskii, and Manoilin. All attempts by the command of the Stalingrad Front to cut off this wedge by an advance of the 21st Army from the north in cooperation with the 62nd and 4th Tank Armies were unsuccessful, even though the forces and equipment at the given time were sufficient.[5]

The basic weakness of the counterattacks was in their poor planning. The counterattacks were carried out hastily, without taking into account reconnaissance data and without organized cooperation on the front between the armies and between the divisions in the armies. Each branch of the service operated by itself. The time for the preparation of the operation was determined in part by the number of hours necessary for writing the field order and delivering it to the army staff.

With such planning of the counteroffensive, success was out of the question; the units suffered heavy losses, and the attack was stopped. Oftentimes the tactical formation and direction of the attacks adopted at the beginning of the operation remained unchanged during almost all the length of the battles, which lasted sometimes for more than a week. And this gave the enemy an opportunity to concentrate a maximum of forces and means in the directions most threatened and to repel the attacks successfully.

The operation southeast of Kletskaia again confirmed the truth that numerical superiority alone does not decide the outcome of battle and that victory is achieved chiefly as a result of intelligent combat planning.

THE SITUATION SOUTHWEST OF STALINGRAD
(JULY 29–AUGUST 10, 1943)

By the end of July, the enemy had concentrated in the Tsymlianskaia-Nikolaevskaia region two Panzer, one motorized, and two or three infantry divisions and had seized a bridgehead on the south banks of the Don River in the areas of Krasnovarskaia, Log, Boguchary, Kholodnyi, Oblivnoi, and Nesmeionovka. The 6th Rumanian Army Corps moved to the Don River on the Olkhouski and Nizhne-Kurmoiarskaia front. On the left wing of the Stalingrad Front, there was a threat from Tsymlianskaia, where the enemy had started to press the units of the 51st Army of the North Caucasus Front that had assumed the defensive on a wide front.[6]

Four divisions and two naval rifle brigades of the 64th Army had assumed the defensive on the line of Surovikino, Staromaksimovskii, Rychkovskii, Gorodskoi, and Verkhne-Kurmoiarskaia, over a distance of 100 kilometers.[7] The maximum density of the Army was on the line of the Chir River, where the efforts of the German infantry to move into the area of Kalach from the southwest had been repulsed.

On August 1, the mobile units of the enemy broke through the front of the 51st Army and, having thrown back the units of the 138th and 157th Rifle Divisions toward the northeast, continued to develop the gains in the general direction toward Dubovskoe, Kotelnikovo, and Abganerovo. For covering Stalingrad from the southwest, we created the operational group of General Chuikov, composed of units of the 51st Army (178th and 157th Rifle Divisions) falling back to the Stalingrad Front, the 15th Naval Rifle Brigade, and the 29th Rifle Division of the 64th Army (which by August 4 had assumed the defensive along the Aksai River on the Chausovskii-Klykov front). On the southwestern front of the external Stalingrad fortified line, the following were on the defensive: three rifle regiments of cadets, two Fortified Regions, and units of the 208th and 126th Rifle Divisions.

Division of the Fronts

By August 7, the following situation had developed on the Stalingrad Front. The enemy motorized–mechanized group had reached the Don River north of Kalach, threatening encirclement of the 62nd Army's units that were west of the Don River. Up to four enemy infantry divisions carried out an attack in the Novomaksimovskii-Kalach direction, with the mission of closing the ring of encirclement around the 62nd Army west of the Don River.[8] In the direction of Kalach, the following were operating: up to three motorized, two Panzer, and up to ten infantry divisions; and the approach of three infantry divisions had been observed.

Southwest of Stalingrad, two Panzer and five or six infantry divisions, attacking along the Kotelnikovo-Stalingrad railroad, came up to the outer ring of the Stalingrad fortified area on the Kapkinskii-Abganerovo sector and broke through the defense with tanks in the direction of Plodovitoe and Station Tinguta.

The troops of the Stalingrad Front were conducting a fierce defensive battle under a very serious situation. The lack of railway communications limited the possibility of a rapid concentration of reserves. The divisions were unloaded and committed to battle by units, by regiments, and by battalions. The rear establishments of the divisions were still being transported by railway, while the forward units were already obliged to carry on heavy fighting. There was no tactical control of troops and there were no means or time for planning it.

The staffs of the 62nd and 64th Armies, each directing not less than ten—or even more—formations, naturally were not able to handle all of them, and the control of troops was often interrupted. Under the already complicated situation, this led to a sad state of affairs. Beginning on August 7, for purpose of more organized control, *Stavka* divided the Stalingrad Front into two fronts—the Stalingrad Front and the Southeastern Front.[9] The line of demarcation between the Fronts was fixed as follows: Morozovskii, Verkhne-Chirskaia, and Stalingrad (the latter exclusive for the Southeastern Front).

The Stalingrad Front was given the mission of destroying the enemy, which had broken through to the Don River north of Kalach, and, having reestablished the situation at the junction of the 62nd and 21st Armies, to cover Stalingrad securely from the northwest and west. The Front was made up of the 63rd, 21st, and 4th Tank and 62nd Armies; they were in the following positions:

1. The *63rd Army*, made up of six rifle divisions in an unchanged group, carried out its previous mission.

2. The *21st Army*, on the Serafimovich-Kletskaia front, having a length of 50 kilometers, occupied a favorable flank position with respect to the enemy, but without any reinforcements, it was not capable of taking the offensive. In the next few days the Army was to receive three fresh new divisions. Upon the approach of these divisions, the Army was to make a vigorous attack against the rear of the enemy group that had broken through.

3. Made up of three rifle divisions and 80 tanks, the *4th Tank Army* occupied a front of 50 kilometers—Malye Iarki, Ventsy, and Verkhne-Golubaia—was in a favorable position with respect to the enemy, and, in cooperation with the 21st Army and after receiving replacements, could represent a serious threat to the enemy.

4. The *62nd Army*, made up of four complete and four weakened rifle divisions and 30 tanks, was on the defensive on a front of 130 kilometers—Lipologovskii, Plesistovskii, Roginovskii, Surovikino, Rychkovskii, it was half encircled from the northeast and south, thus the ability of the Army to conduct active operations was very much limited.

For rendering assistance to the 62nd Army, the Front Commander decided to assume the offensive on the morning of August 8 with units of the 4th Tank and 21st Armies, but this hurriedly planned offensive did not produce any positive results and did not render the desired assistance to the 62nd Army.

The enemy, firmly covering himself from the north and northwest, continued to tighten the ring around the 62nd Army and, as early as the end of August 8, had reached the crossings on the Don at Kalach from the north and southwest. In the period August 8–10, the 62nd Army carried on some heavy fighting with the onrushing enemy. With heavy losses in men and equipment, the 62nd Army crossed to the east bank of the Don River, where it assumed the defensive on the Peskovatka-Kalach-Liapichev front.

The Southeastern Front—made up of the 64th Army (five rifle divisions and one tank brigade), the 51st Army (the remains of five rifle divisions, one cavalry division, and two tank brigades without equipment), and 57th Army (five rifle divisions)—was given the mission of preventing the enemy from breaking through the south front of the outside ring of the Stalingrad fortified area and reaching the Volga south of Stalingrad. The Armies also had to prepare a counterattack for smashing the main group of the enemy in the direction of Kotelnikovo.

By the close of August 8, the situation on the front was the following:

the 64th Army defended the Logovskii-Ermokhinskii line on toward the east along the north bank of the Myshkova River, Station Abganerovo, Privolzhskii State Farm, and Raigorod. The leading detachments were on the east bank of the Don River and on the Aksai River. On the left flank of the army on the Generalovskii-Aksai line, units of the 6th Rumanian Army Corps were operating. In the direction northeast of Abganerovo, two Panzer and two infantry divisions of the enemy made persistent but unsuccessful attacks against the center of the army.

The 51st Army, while conducting a holding battle, withdrew from Zimovnikov to the Shebalin-Kupriianov-Grabbevskaia line. The Army was numerically weak; the divisions had 200 to 300 bayonets and separate guns. The 57th Army, also being low in numbers, assumed the defensive on the line of the inner ring of the Stalingrad fortified area.

Conclusions

As a result of fierce battles lasting three days, the shock group of the enemy operating in the Kalach direction succeeded in advancing 60 kilometers and in reaching the Don River, but it suffered heavy losses. In the main, the units of the Stalingrad Front carried out their mission and gained time for the concentration of reserves in the area of Stalingrad. The success of the mission was assured by the concentration of forces and equipment in the main direction, making it possible for the defenders to create strong shock groups and to strike powerful counterblows against the enemy, forcing him to shift from the offensive to the defensive and at the same time to suffer heavy losses.

The success of the counterattacks would have been more decisive if they had been better directed and had there been closer cooperation between the branches of the service.

The poor training of the tank crews, the units, and the formations had an adverse effect upon operational success. On the field of battle, the tanks did not maneuver; they moved to the attack at a low rate of speed, often stopping and conducting fire from a stationary position, resulting in heavy losses.

The dividing of the Stalingrad Front into two Fronts—the Stalingrad Front and the Southeastern Front—complicated somewhat the control of troops. In the course of hard fighting, the Fronts had to divide between themselves the troops, aviation, means of reinforcement, special units, and the rear establishments. The result was that in many cases both Fronts either regarded one and the same formation as their own, or the unit or establishment was not claimed by either Front. By August 10 the situation had been corrected somewhat by placing the command of both Fronts in the hands of one person, the Commander of the Southeastern Front.

The Battles on the Immediate Approaches to Stalingrad

The Battle for the Sirotinskaia Base of Operations (August 15–30, 1942)

Upon reaching the Don River on the Malogolubaia-Kalach front and farther south, the enemy regrouped toward the north and concentrated in the region of Osinovka, Malogolubaia, Sukhanoviskii up to two Panzer, two motorized, and two or three infantry divisions, and in the Srednii-Ventsi-Platonov area up to three infantry divisions.

On the morning of August 15, the enemy assumed the offensive against the 4th Tank Army, defending itself along the line of Malo-Kletskii, Oskinskii, and Bolshenabatovskii. After hard battles lasting for three days, the units of the 4th Tank Army were shifted to the east bank of the Don River on the Sirotinskaia-Malonabatovskii front. The withdrawal of the 4th Tank Army placed under attack the 1st Guards Army, which was beginning a concentration for a counterattack in the areas of Kremenskaia, Logovskii, Sirotinskaia; two divisions suffered heavy losses.

To defeat the main group of the enemy assembled in the bend of the Don River southeast of Kletskaia, and to recover the base of operations lost by the 4th Tank Army, the following operation was planned.

1. Up to four rifle divisions of the left flank of the 63rd Army and of the right flank of the 21st Army made an attack in the direction of Ust-Khoperskii and Perelazovskii, and threatening communications of the enemy.

2. The 1st Guards Army with three rifle divisions and 80 tanks via an attack against Oskinskii from the Kremenskaia-Novogrigorevskaia region reached the Logovskii-Ventsy-Golubaia River line.

3. The 62nd Army, with two right-flank rifle divisions and in cooperation with the 1st Guards Army, made an attack from the Vertyachii-Peskovatka region against Oskinskii.

The troops' readiness for attack was set for August 20–21. The preparations for the counterattack were made under complicated conditions. The enemy, continuing active operations, forged the Don River in the areas of Nizhne-Gerasimov and Vertiachii and tried to widen his base of operations on the left bank of the Don River.

The 1st Guards Army, not having received the means of reinforcement planned by the staff of the Stalingrad Front, assumed the offensive on August 22 with three rifle divisions and 20 tanks and without the support of aviation. The available artillery was not provided with ammunition.

By August 30, as a result of the operation carried out, certain victories were won on the sector of the 63rd and 21st Armies, where we defeated units of the 2nd and 9th Italian Infantry Divisions and where we seized a base of operations on the right bank of the Don River southwest of Serafimovich. Units of the 1st Guards Army widened the base of operations somewhat by moving up to the line of Perekopka, Shokhin, (exclusive) Sirotinskaia. The right flank of the 62nd Army was disrupted by the enemy, who broke through in the area of Vertiachii in the direction of Stalingrad.

The Breakthrough of the Enemy Southwest of Stalingrad

The offensive actions of the center of the Stalingrad Front did not have any serious effect upon the operational situation, because they were carried out with the participation of limited forces and equipment in a short period of time and with inadequate organization.

By the end of August, the enemy, with six Italian divisions of the 8th Army, assumed the defensive on the right bank of the Don River on the Novo-Kalitva and (exclusive) Serafimovich Front.

On the Serafimovich-Kletskaia-Sirotinskaia Front, units of the 79th, 113th, 376th, and 305th Infantry Divisions were on the defensive, covering the main group of the German 6th Army from the north. This group was assembled in the region of Trekhostrovskaia, Golubinskii, and Verkhne-Golubaia and was made up of the German 16th and 22nd Panzer Divisions, the 3rd and 60th Motorized Divisions, the 100th Jaegar Division, and the 384th, 389th, 294th, 76th, and 44th Infantry Divisions. A total of ten divisions were concentrated on a front of about 35 kilometers.

South of the Don River, on the Golubinskii-Kalach-Podtikhov line, up to two German infantry divisions had assumed the defensive on a wide front. South of Stalingrad, the enemy concentrated a shock group—the 4th Panzer Army, consisting of the German 14th and 24th Panzer; 29th Motorized; 94th, 295th, 371st, and 297th Infantry Divisions; and, on the line of the Myshkova River, the 1st, 2nd, 4th, 20th, and 17th Infantry Divisions of the 6th Rumanian Army Corps. Hence, in the second half of August, the enemy held an enveloping position with respect the left-wing troops of the Stalingrad Front and with respect to all the troops of the Southeastern Front. It was clear that the enemy intended to attack from the northwest Trekhostrovskaia-Vertiachii region and from the south from the Tingula and Plodovitoe areas and to join up in the region of Stalingrad, after having encircled the main body of its defending troops.

The Defensive Battle of the Southeastern Front (August 17–23, 1942)

After having concentrated its shock group, the German 4th Panzer Army started its attack on August 17 in the general direction of Plodovitoe and Krasnoarmeisk.

The commander of the Southeastern Front, having left on the 60-kilometer Logovskii-Gromoslavka-Vasilevka Front the 66th Motorized Rifle Brigade, the 157th Rifle Division (numerically weak), and two cadet regiments, then concentrated his main forces of the 64th Army in the Tebektenerovka-Station Abganerovo region. The defense of the strip east of Tinguta and Ivanovka was left to units of the 57th Army.

The enemy attacks were parried by blows of powerful mobile fire groups made up of Guards Mortar units, field and antitank artillery. Under their attacks and those of aviation, the offensive of the enemy, carried out between August 17–23, did not have any considerable success. By taking very heavy losses in personnel and tanks, the enemy advanced on the narrow sector of the main blow to a depth of not more than 6 to 7 kilometers; only on one sector did the enemy break through to a greater depth. With a 100 tanks the enemy broke through from Privolzhskii State Farm and advanced by August 23 into the area of Elevation 118 to a distance of 15 kilometers; but the enemy Panzer group was not able to exploit this success.

After exhausting the offensive possibilities of the troops in the given operation, the enemy stopped the offensive and on August 24 began to bring up reserves to carry out a regrouping in preparation for a new attack.

The troops of the Southeastern Front successfully carried out the operation of wearing out the enemy. In stubborn defensive battles we prepared favorable conditions for passing to a counterattack, but the absence of sufficient reserves made it impossible to do this.

The successful defense was the result of correctly evaluating the intentions of the enemy, timely regrouping of forces in the threatened direction, and, by means of troops taken from secondary sectors, creating lines of defense echeloned in the tactical depth. The successes of the defense were due in no small degree to the active operations of the troops, which struck damaging blows at the enemy by numerous counterattacks. The decisive role was played by the concentrated attacks of powerful fire groups of Guards Mortars and artillery at the most threatening enemy group at the given moment. Enemy tanks also suffered heavy losses in the minefields.

THE BATTLE OF THE STALINGRAD FRONT, AUGUST 23–30, 1942

On August 23, the German 16th Panzer, 60th, and 3rd Motorized Divisions, with powerful support of aviation, broke through the front at the junctionof the 4th Tank and 62nd Armies in the area of Vertiachii. Developing their successes, they broke through the front to the northern edge of Stalingrad, reaching the area of Erzovka, Rynok, and Orlovka.

The troops intended for assuming the defensive on the middle ring of the Stalingrad fortified area west of Stalingrad had just arrived by railroad and were unloaded in the area of Station Log and farther north. The 87th and 315th Rifle Divisions were surprised by the enemy on the march and suffered heavy losses.

The city line of defense was occupied for defense by units of the NKVD.[10] Two tank corps were concentrated in the area of Stalingrad. For the defense of the city, we stopped four rifle brigades that were on their way to the Caucasus.

From August 23 to August 25, the troops of the Front carried on some heavy fighting to destroy the advancing group of the enemy and close up the breach on the Station Kotluban-Bolshaia Rossoshka Front. The left-flank divisions of the 4th Tank Army, together with the right-flank division of the 62nd Army, carried out the task of closing the gap and reached the area of Samofalovka (4th Tank Army) and 2 or 3 kilometers to the north of Bolshaia Rossoshka (the 35th Guards Rifle Division of the 62nd Army) at the end of August 25, thus contracting in this way the front of the breakthrough to 4 kilometers.

On August 26 we decided to commit the 23rd Tank Corps to close the breach in a definitive manner; then, with the approach of the two tank corps that were expected, to smash the enemy who had broken through; and to restore the situation.[11]

With the approach of the enemy to the Volga north of Stalingrad, the front of our troops was cut into two parts. The enemy, assuming the offensive north of Kalach, tried to widen the gap, and at the same time, the 4th Panzer Army resumed active operations to try to reach Stalingrad from the south.

The staffs of the Stalingrad and Southeastern Fronts were in the area of Stalingrad, and this made the control of the northern group's forces of the Stalingrad Front more difficult. In the area of Ivanovka, we organized a temporary control post, at which were stationed the Chief of Staff of the Front and the Deputy Commander of the Front, but they did not have any means of control. In the meantime, new divisions and tank corps had arrived. It was necessary to assemble forces for active operations and prepare an attack against the enemy group breaking through from the north.

The counterattack of the troops of the Stalingrad Front—carried out in August 26–29 from the area of Stalingrad in a northern/northeastern direction and from the north, from the area of Kuzmichi in a southeastern direction—and the flank attacks of the 4th Tank and 62nd Armies, did not have any decisive results. The enemy was able to bring up reserves and to organize a solid defense with a front on the north on the Akatovka-Kuzmichi-Borodin-Kislov line and with a front on the south on the Vinnovka-Spartakovets-Konnaia line north of Bolshaia Rossoshka. The subsequent operations of the enemy were aimed at widening the breakthrough in a southeastern direction.

On the morning of August 29, the enemy's 4th Panzer Army started a determined attack directed along the railroad of Abganerovo-Stalingrad. Not having any success to the east of the railroad, the enemy moved to the middle defense ring in the area of Nariman (Plantator).

In order to prevent the encirclement of the 62nd Army, which had come to form a part of the Southeastern Front, and the 64th Army and to create a denser defense on the approaches to Stalingrad, on the night of August 31, units of those armies were withdrawn to the main line of defense in Rynok, Orlovka, Novaia Nedezhda, Malaia Rososhka, and (exclusive) Karpovka. In the Aleksandrovka-Pitomnik area, they had the following in reserve: two rifle divisions and a tank brigade.

The organized withdrawal of the troops to a new line did not succeed, because the enemy, exploiting his success, broke through the defensive front on the Varvarovkii line, and advancing toward the north, reached the areas of Basargino and Vagodniv on September 1. In this way the enemy succeeded in forcing the troops of the Southeastern Front to withdraw to the inner ring, on the line of Rynok, Novaia Nadezhda, Gonchara Farmlet, Alekseevka, Elkhi, and Ivanovka.

Conclusions

The breakthrough of the enemy on August 23 into the area Vertiachii and his approach on the same day to Stalingrad was made possible because our defense in this direction was not echeloned and had no reserves in the tactical depths.

The counterattacks of the northern group were not successful because of inadequate troop control, which was based on chance personal visits to the units by liaison officers of the commander of this group. Besides, no plans were made for supplying the groups with material; the units fought without fuel and with only a small quantity of ammunition.

The locations of the staffs of both fronts in Stalingrad were not entirely appropriate and complicated their control of the troops of the Stalingrad Front after the Germans' breakthrough to Stalingrad and contributed to a considerable degree to the failures of the counterattacking troops.

The withdrawal of the troops of the Southeastern Front to the middle defense ring was started with a delay of one or two days. In the end, the effort to hold the space while fighting for a limited base of operations had an adverse effect upon the defense. If the troops from the secondary sectors had been withdrawn to a more narrow front on the middle defense ring and if this withdrawal had been carried out in time, the defense would have been organized beforehand and would have had a sufficient density to stop the enemy.

A timely decision to withdraw was also especially important because each of the staffs of the Army, with limited means of control at its disposal, had immediately under it up to ten large units, and the timely transmission of that decision to the troops under such conditions was extremely difficult.

Subsequent operations of the Southeastern Front in the course of September, October, and the first half of November were aimed at causing the attrition of the personnel and equipment of the enemy in the area of Stalingrad and at crushing his offensive power. In the stubborn, hard-fought defensive battles with extensive employment of counter-attacks and counterblows, the troops at the front—under complicated conditions of communications with the rear across the Volga that was under the fire of the enemy ground troops and aircraft and cut off in isolated centers of defense—carried out their mission in an honorable manner. The successful defense of the city was made possible by the tenacity of the troops and the continuous supply of the front both with reserves and with all kinds of materials. Holding Stalingrad was also made possible by the active operations of the troops of the Stalingrad Front in the northwestern part of the city.

Offensive Operations of the Stalingrad (Don) Front (September–October 1942)

Toward August 30, the German 4th Panzer Army and the 6th Army, while covering themselves to the northwest of Stalingrad, utilized their combined force to exert great pressure against the troops defending the city to the west and southwest. The troops of the Southeastern Front needed time to organize the system of defenses for the city and for the units continuing to withdraw under enemy attacks. For that purpose, the troops of the Stalingrad Front were assigned to assist the Southeastern Front by striking the flank and rear of the main group of the enemy advancing against Stalingrad.

On August 29, the 1st Guards Army, advancing for this purpose northwest of Sirotinskaia, received orders to pass to the defensive. The field command of the 1st Guards Army, after having transferred its troops to the 21st Army, was to establish itself by the morning of September 1 in the area of Sadkii at a distance of over 50 kilometers from the front line to meet the troops of the 24th Army (five rifle divisions) and the 66th Army (six rifle divisions), which was to reach the Ilovlinskaia-Sadki-Dubovka line by September 3.[12]

The 63rd and 21st armies were given the mission of firmly holding the occupied line and of preventing the advance of the enemy toward the northeast. The 4th Tank Army, defending the Piatidesiatinskii-Station Panshino-Station Kotluban line covered the concentration and deployment of the 245th and 66th Armies. Beginning the morning of September 2, in conjunction with the left flank of the 1st Guards Army, the 4th Tank Army was to strike a secondary blow in a southwesterly direction for the purpose of screening the right flank of the 1st Guards Army as it moved forward.

The 1st Guards Army, made up of seven rifle divisions and three tank corps, had the following mission: by means of an attack on September 2 in the direction of Grachi and Gorodishche, they were to break through the defenses of the enemy northwest of Stalingrad and smash the enemy group in the city.

By the close of September 3, the 24th Army was to deploy its main forces on the Pervomaisk-Sadki Front to assume the offensive on the morning of September 5 along the front line of Kislov and Grachi toward Dmitrieevka; to smash the enemy in the region of Vertiachii, Bolshaia Rossoshka, and Illarionovskii; and by the close of September 8, to reach the line of Riumino-Krasnoiarskii and Karpovka.

Toward the close of September 3, the 66th Army was to approach the Sadki-Peskovatka line with its main forces to assume the offensive, beginning with the morning of September 5, along the front line of Grachi and Erzovka and toward Gorodishche and Peschanka.

The concentration and all the preparations for the offensive of the 1st Guards Army took place under very difficult conditions. For two to three days, it was necessary to assemble troops that were still in movement and that had been expected toward the end of September 2. The tanks and rifle troop units arrived without fuel and means of transportation. There was a danger that the attack intended for September 2 would be delayed because the units did not have time to move to the jump–off position and to bring up fuel and ammunition.

In view of the threatening situation developing in the area of Stalingrad, the troops of the 1st Guards Army, while having no reinforcing artillery or antiaircraft defense and without sufficient preparation, assumed the offensive on September 3 to distract the enemy forces at Stalingrad. On September 5 we committed to battle the troops of the 24th and 66th armies, which had not yet had time to complete their concentration, did not have sufficient artillery, and had not been able to organize their offensive in the proper manner because their divisions went into battle immediately after the completion of a 50-kilometer march.[13]

Such piecemeal commitment of an army into battle, without means of reinforcement, without knowledge of the enemy defense system, and without the proper general preparation, did not give the expected results. Fierce battles continued up to September 7. Even though we did not succeed in effecting a breakthrough, the attack from the north forced the enemy to remove a part of his troops from the area below Stalingrad and to throw all of his aviation against the attacking groups. The pressure against Stalingrad was somewhat relieved and the troops of the Southeastern Front were given a short breathing spell and an opportunity to improve their defenses.

Between September 9 to 13, after a regrouping, the offensive of the Front continued with the same results. Without interrupting the active operations with separate detachments, on September 13 the troops started to prepare a new offensive intended to begin on September 18. At a time when the troops were conducting active operations, reserves continued to arrive, and a large operation was prepared to deliver a decisive blow against the enemy Stalingrad grouping. The beginning of the decisive offensive was set for September 18 utilizing the following operational forces:

● The 1st Guards Army was made up of nine rifle divisions, three tank corps, three tank brigades, nine reinforcement artillery regiments, six Guards Mortar regiments, and eight Guards Mortar battalions. These forces made their attack toward Gumrak, along an 18-kilometer front running from Elevation 100.0 to the ruins at point 564. The Army was arranged in three echelons. The first echelon included five rifle divisions, a tank corps, three tank brigades, and all means of reinforcement; the second echelon, three rifle divisions and one tank corps; and the third echelon, one rifle division and one tank corps, the latter held in reserve and at the disposal of the Commander of the Army. The rifle troops were to follow the tanks, while the tanks of the second echelon were assigned to exploit the breakthrough.

● The 24th Army, made up of four rifle divisions, two tank brigades, four reinforcement artillery regiments, three Guards Mortar regiments, and one mortar regiment attacked toward Gorodishche along a six-kilometer front from the ruins at point 564 to Kuzmichi. The Army was arranged in two echelons: the first echelon had two rifle divisions, two tank brigades, and all means of reinforcements and the second echelon, two rifle divisions.

● On the 24th Army's left wing, the 66th Army, with its three right flank divisions, protected the left flank of the 24th Army. Concurrently, the 4th Tank, 63rd, and 21st Armies defended a front of 480 kilometers.

The total forces in the breakthrough echelon of the 24-kilometer front were seven rifle divisions, five tank brigades, and one tank corps; in the second echelon, the total was five rifle divisions, and one tank corps; and in the third echelon, one rifle division.

The tactical results of the offensive beginning about September 26 were insignificant. But, in the holding of Stalingrad, the operation exerted a great influence. The enemy, having suffered heavy losses, was forced to bring up reserves from the area of Stalingrad and at the same time to concentrate German divisions that were replaced on the middle course of the Don River by Rumanian units. The enemy air attacks against the city were reduced because the main part of his aviation was thrown against the units attacking on the Stalingrad Front. But, in the end, this operational success was achieved at the price of great loss of life.

From September 30 the Stalingrad Front was renamed the *Don Front*. The troops of the Don Front started preparations for a new offensive operation. Up to October 20, the troops of the Front carried on active operations of a local character, improving their positions in the area of Kletskaia and on the left wing. In the period from October 20 to 25, another unsuccessful attempt to break through to Stalingrad was made by the left wing. As a result of the operations carried out at Stalingrad, the enemy was held and his troops exhausted. The offensive possibilities of the enemy had weakened considerably. On October 28 we again formed a Southwestern Front, which had in its composition the 63th and 21st Armies from the Don Front. The final period of the Stalingrad epic was at hand—the preparation for the encirclement and destruction of all groups of the enemy at Stalingrad.

Conclusions

Great masses of troops and military equipment were employed in the offensive operations of the Stalingrad Front in September and October. Since they were assembled simultaneously and prepared for battle, these forces were able to strike a crushing blow at the enemy. But the following factors influencing the outcome of all the operations enumerated were identical for each separate instance.

1. The troops were committed to battle unit by unit, without sufficient reinforcements and equipment. By the time the reinforcements arrived, the rifle troops, having suffered losses, were exhausted and had low morale, feeling helpless in the face of the destructive fire of the enemy defenses, saturated with weapons and enemy aviation and operating with impunity.

2. The troops went into battle without knowing the enemy's system of defense. Reconnaissance was conducted in a superficial manner. Often there was no observation of the battlefield. As a result of insufficient study of the enemy's defenses, his line of combat was frequently taken for the forward edge of the main zone of defense. During the period of artillery preparation, shells were fired into vacant areas. When the rifle troops advanced to the attack, they had to go a great distance to reach a system of enemy defenses that had not yet been neutralized.

3. The arrangement of the rifle troops' combat formations as well as the units of combined arms in several echelons in depth resulted in the deployment of the troops on too narrow a front. With a front of 1 to 2 kilometers to the division, a very small part of the fire means of the rifle

troops participated in battle. The main body of the rifle troops was inactive on the battlefield and, at the same time, suffered heavy losses from enemy air and artillery attacks.

4. There was no cooperation between the rifle troops, tanks, artillery, and aviation. Each branch of service operated for itself. The tanks went into battle without artillery support or air cover. The rifle troops expected the artillery and tanks to neutralize the enemy fire system in an effective manner, did not use their own weapons, and were not sufficiently trained. The artillery conducted zone fire. Aimed fire was made difficult by a lack of knowledge of enemy defense and the difference of observation posts from the combat formations of infantry. Questions of cooperation were worked out on the basis of maps. In a steppe locality, poor in reference points, there were cases of confusion, mix-ups, and even clashes among our own troops. Signal communications between adjacent units on the front and signal communications for cooperation were absent as a rule.

In addition to the fact that the staffs did not yet have sufficient cohesion and were not provided with means of signal communications, there was insufficient time for planning of the battle because of the situation and, sometimes, because of the excessive haste of the old commanders.

5. The tank formations did not have sufficient cohesion; the crews were not trained. On the battlefield, the tanks did not maneuver but rather conducted fire from a stationary position or moved at a slow rate of speed and so forth. The results were heavy losses in tanks. On an average, the tank corps conserved its ability to conduct battle for two or three days. The lack of aviation cover and the poor organization for the repair of materials often had a serious effect upon the combat ability of the tank units.[14]

6. None of the errors in the organization for battle, in the actions of the branches of service, and in the utilization of the material escaped the attention of the high command in the course of battle. The troops as well, in conducting battle, learned to correct their errors.

On the basis of the experience of the Stalingrad battles, generalized orders of the People's Commissar of Defense Nos. 306 and 325, the troops prepared for the approaching decisive battles. The results of this preparation showed in the great victories won by the Red Army in the battles of winter campaign of 1942–43.

General Conclusions

1. The large-scale defensive battle of the Red Army for the area of Stalingrad, which lasted four months, demonstrated most clearly not only the ability of modern defense to withstand the pressure of attack of large military masses equipped with powerful means of attack, but also the

ability of the defense to crush the offense and completely smash the attackers.

As a result of the fierce battles, great losses were inflicted upon the enemy. The offensive power of his troops was undetermined, but he still moved into Stalingrad, reached the Volga, and, while holding the Stalingrad base of operations, was able to assemble forces for the further development of his success.

The complete smashing of the enemy was made possible only by the transition of the Red Army to a decisive offensive, and this was logically carried out by the complete destruction of the German 4th Panzer and 6th armies.

2. Passive defense, based only on a system of fire, even with powerful fortifications, is impractical. Present-day means of attack are able to overcome such a defense, though it would be at the price of heavy losses.

Active defense—combining a system of fire based on a locality equipped from an engineering standpoint, with counterattacks by strong reserves, and sufficiently enveloped in depth (multizone)—is fully able to inflict heavy losses upon superior forces of the enemy and defeat his offensive.

3. The proper disposition of reserves in the area of the strategic objective makes the timely establishment of a new front line possible, when necessitated by the destruction of the old line and by the advance of the enemy into the maneuvering space. The timely establishment of the front line by the 62nd and 63rd Armies made possible the holding of the base of operations on the approaches to Stalingrad and the concentration of reserves from other distant places.

4. The enemy tried to break through the front of the defense in the main directions on sectors having a width of 10 to 15 kilometers, using strong motorized–mechanized groups, and cooperating with large forces of combat aviation. A carefully planned system of antitank defenses and the presence of large reserves of antitank means, chiefly artillery, provided a stable defense in the direction of the main blow. The combat formations, conducting the battle in the main direction, should be covered by sufficient means of antiaircraft defense, even if this is at the expense of the means of antiaircraft defense taken from secondary sectors. Since it is difficult to determine beforehand the direction in which the enemy will strike his main blow, the command should be ready to maneuver his antitank reserves and antiaircraft forces.

5. The success of the defense depends upon the outcome of combat in the tactical zone. The breakthrough into the tactical depths of the defense by the enemy threatens the encircled troops of the defense and destroys the stability of the defense. The strategic reserves of the defenders should be ready to liquidate the enemy breaking through into the tactical zone.

Garrisons, prepared for conducting battles of long duration under encirclement and tying down enemy forces, cooperate with these counterattacks of the reserves and hold up the development of the enemy success. For supplying the encircled garrisons in the centers of resistance, we should prepare beforehand reserve supplies of ammunition and food. In addition, the command should have ready at hand reserves of air transport for supplying the encircled garrisons with reserves and with everything necessary for battle.

6. The basis of the organization of the locality for defense by engineering work should be the idea of defensive operation. We cannot say this about the engineering preparations of Stalingrad. The system of fortified concentric lines with their center in Stalingrad and their flanks resting on the Volga River, as well as the absence of switch lines, did not meet the requirements of an active defense.

The lines prepared in the depth of the defense should be occupied by permanent garrisons, constituting the skeleton of a defense. Experience shows that the enemy mobile units breaking through into the depths anticipate those troops of the defense in moving to the rear lines. If these lines are not occupied by troops for defense, the enemy will use them for closing the ring of encirclement or for protecting himself from possible counterattacks, just as happened in the enemy breakthrough of the defense northwest of Stalingrad on August 23.

7. Counterattacks are possible for drawing away the enemy forces from the direction most threatened at the given moment for the purpose of striking a certain group of the enemy. In all cases, the counterattacks should be carried out in sufficient force. The cooperation of the Stalingrad and Don Fronts was built up on position defense on the one front and offensive action on the other front.

In the final accounting, the offensive operations of the Don Front exerted an influence on the holding of Stalingrad by drawing away the forces of the enemy from the objective that he was trying to reach, but the decisive aim was not achieved because of the absence of proper organization of the operation.

8. The counter preparation—organized with powerful fire groups of artillery and Guards Mortar units by attacks against concentrations of tanks, infantry, and artillery fire positions in the direction of the main enemy blow—inflicted heavy losses upon the enemy and, many times, broke up his offensive for several days.

9. The extensively developed network of command posts in the defense organization assured the stability of command during critical situations.

From this point of view, the placing of two combat commands—the Stalingrad and the Southeastern Fronts—in Stalingrad was not advantageous. The course of events showed this very clearly when, after the breakthrough of the defenses by the enemy on August 23, the troops defending Stalingrad were cut into two parts. In the direction from which there should have been an immediate counterattack (north of Stalingrad), there was no one to organize the attack. The large units of the northern group, operating while isolated, had no success and the enemy was able to bring up his reserves and fortify himself. If the staff of one of the Fronts had been present in the area of concentration of the reserves, the situation would have been more favorable for the organization of a counterattack.

10. If, under the conditions of a stable front, the staffs of armies are not in a position to exercise direct command of the numerous army divisions, then under the complicated conditions developing as a result of the enemy's breakthrough of the front and the battles in the depth of the defense, the stability of command is quickly disrupted.

Corps command or in extreme cases temporary tactical groups, provided with the necessary signal communications, greatly simplify and facilitate the command of troops, making the command more stable.

11. In the battle of Stalingrad, we discovered weaknesses in the command of troops and their combat training. The study of the numerous battles and operations, the elimination of mistakes, and the discovery of errors made possible further successful actions by our troops in the winter campaigns of 1942–1943.

12. The experience gained in the battle of Stalingrad and the offensive operations carried out by the Southwestern, Don, and Stalingrad (Southern) Fronts should be studied thoroughly and in an all around manner by the commands, staffs, and troops of the Red Army.

Editor's Notes

1. The 62nd Army was activated in July from the 7th Reserve Army. Its commander was Major General V. Ia. Kolpakchi. The 63rd Army was also activated in July from the 5th Reserve Army; its commander was Lieutenant General V. I. Kuznetsov. These reserves were well-equipped with antitank (AT) weapons. The 63rd Army had 390 AT guns and 2,100 AT rifles. The 62nd Army had 530 AT guns and 1,900 AT rifles. See Rokossovskii, *Velikaia pobeda na Volge*, p. 42.
2. The 21st Army was commanded by Major General A. I. Danilov. Its units were reformed from the remnants of the disbanded Southwestern Front.
3. The 64th Army was activated in July from the 1st Reserve Army (first formation). Its commander was Lieutenant General V. I. Chuikov. The 64th Army also was well-supplied with anti–armor weapons, with 414 AT guns and 1,760 AT rifles.
4. The 1st Tank Army was formed from the base of the battered 38th Army. Its commander was Major General K. S. Moskalenko. The Army formed up in late July in the area around Manoilin. It consisted of the 13th and 28th Tank Corps and other units with a total of 301 tanks. Of these, 139 were light and the rest were T-34s. See K. Moskalenko *Na yugozapadnom napravlenie* vol.1 (Moscow: *Voenizdat*, 1969), p. 267. At the time of commitment to battle, however, it was not fully concentrated. Its real strength was only 160 tanks and one rifle division. See *IVOVSS* vol. 2, p. 429.
   The 4th Tank Army was formed on the remnants of the 28th Army; its commander was Major General V. D. Kruchenkin. At the time of commitment to battle, it was not fully formed. Its total strength was only one tank corps (80 tanks) and one rifle division.
5. This is an interesting statement, given later attempts to indicate the shortages and

disorganization on the Soviet side of the line. Perhaps even more revealing is the statement by Marshal K. K. Rokossovskii made in the authoritative postwar study *Velikaia pobeda na Volge,* (p. 90):

Having correctly evaluated the intentions of the Nazis on the southern wing of the Soviet–German front after the breakthrough, the *Stavka* made gross miscalculations in the measures carried out directed at elimination of the enemy breakthrough. *Stavka* hadn't calculated all of the advantages which the enemy possessed in the Stalingrad direction in comparison with ours. There wasn't calculated the time needed to concentrate new forces, capable of organizationally meeting the enemy and giving him a rebuff. In connection with this, there was not actually determined the limits for concentration and deployment of the troops being advanced at Stalingrad. In the decisions of *Stavka* and the General Staff, desire prevailed over possibilities. The directives and orders issued to the troops did not correspond to the situation which developed at the front. In connection with this, troops were introduced into battle on the run, disorganized and subjected to destruction by units. In addition to everything, they substituted for the front commanders, depriving them of the possibility to operate independently in connection with the actual situation being developed. This was also practiced by the front commanders in relation to their subordinates.

6. The 51st Army was under the command of the Deputy Commander Major General T. K. Kolomiets in the absence of the ailing Commander Major General N. I. Trufanov. A history of the 51st Army may be found in S. Sarkis'ian, *51-ia armiia* (Moscow: Voenizdat, 1983).

7. Naval rifle (infantry) brigades were ordinary Soviet rifle brigades that originally had drawn a percentage of its strength from the various fleets. Senior naval officers originally occupied many command positions when the brigades were first formed. See V. Shlomin, *"Dvadstat' piat morskikh strelkovich,"* Voenno istoricheskii zhurnal No. 7, 1970.

8. Kolpakchi's Army had been roughly handled by Paulus, and as a result the *Stavka* chose to replace him at the end of July with Lieutenant General A. I. Lopatin.

9. The order of August 5 divided the Stalingrad Front into the following: the *Stalingrad Front*—Commander, Lieutenant General V. N. Gordov; Political Member, N. S. Khrushchev; Chief of Staff, Major General D. N. Nikishev; and the *Southeastern Front*—Commander, Colonel General A.I. Eremenko; Political Member, Brigade Commissar V. M. Laiok until August 13 and then N. S. Khrushchev; and Chief of Staff, Major General G. F. Zakharov. On August 12, the *Stavka* assigned Colonel General A. M. Vasilevskii, Chief of the General Staff, to be its representative on the scene and to coordinate the activities of the two fronts. On August 13, *Stavka* appointed Eremenko to command both fronts with Gordov as his Deputy for Stalingrad Front and Lieutenant General F. I. Goliikov as Deputy for Southeastern Front. Interestingly, Khrushchev did not have a military rank at this time. He became a lieutenant general in 1943.

10. The commander of the garrison in the city was Colonel A. A. Saraev. He was the commander of the 10th NKVD Division.

11. The commander of the 23rd Tank Corps, until August 30, was Major General of Tank Troops A. M. Khasin. Until October 16, it was Major General of Tank Troops A. F. Popov; until November 29, Colonel V. V. Koshelev; and after that date, Major General of Tank Troops E.G. Pushkin.

12. The decision to commit more of *Stavka*'s reserve forces was made on August 27 at a meeting at the Kremlin. The purpose of the reinforcements was outlined by Stalin in a briefing for Zhukov. The 1st Guards Army (created in August from the 2nd Reserve Army) was under the command of Moskalenko since the deactivation of 1st Tank Army. The commander of the 66th Army (8th Reserve Army) was Lieutenant General R. Ia. Malinovskii. The commander of the 24th Army (9th Reserve Army) until October 1, was Major General D. T. Kozlov; after that date, it was Major General I. V. Galinin. Neither of the latter two armies had high combat value, being composed mostly of average men with little training, according to *IVOVSS* vol. 2, p. 438.

13. Zhukov conducted this battle under constant pressure from Stalin who feared Stalingrad would fall during the period of preparation. See Zhukov, *Reminiscences and Reflections*, vol. 2, pp. 89–90. See also Samsanov, *Stalingradskaia epopeia*, pp. 160–161 in regard to Zhukov's lengthy request to cease the piecemeal and destructive attacks that Stalin was demanding of the three armies.

14. Zhukov reported to Stalin that the counterattack by the three armies on the Don landbridge north of Stalingrad was disrupted by constant enemy air attacks. See Zhukov, vol. 2, p. 89.

The crushing flank attacks of the Red Army in November 1942 were designed to fall on the weakest part of the Nazi front—that occupied by the Rumanian 3rd and 4th armies. The premise of the operation was that the previous controlled fighting in Stalingrad had drawn in the German reserves and worn them down. The present offensive thus would find only allied formations, thereby allowing a quick and deep penetration to facilitate an encirclement of the German troops. The plan worked far beyond the most optimistic expectations—Ed.

4

Flank Attacks of the Red Army in the Battle of Stalingrad

Enemy Grouping about November 19, 1942

In the course of September, October, and more than half of November 1942, units of the German 4th Panzer and 6th Armies carried on some hard fighting for the capture of Stalingrad, suffering heavy losses in personnel and equipment. The enemy reserves, coming from the rear, were scarcely sufficient for supplying the replacements for the divisions, which had been bled white, and for maintaining their combat capacity on a level sufficient for carrying on the offensive operations.

As a result of the active operations of the troops of the Don Front in September and October 1942, in the direction of Kuzmichi and Gorodishche, a real threat was created to the immediate rear of the Stalingrad group of the enemy, and the German command was obliged to draw back in this direction the divisions that were previously on the defensive in the middle course of the Don River on the Boguchar-Kletskaia Front. In place of the German units taken from the defensive positions on the middle course of the Don River, the Nazi High Command employed units of the 3rd Rumanian and 8th Italian Armies brought up from the rear. On the right wing of the Stalingrad group south of Stalingrad, five Rumanian infantry divisions and two Rumanian cavalry divisions in defensive positions on the line of Andreevka, Dubovyi Ovrag, and Sadovoe protected the basic group of the Germans from the southeast.[1]

Made up exclusively of elite German units, the shock group's shifting of its center of gravity into the area immediately contiguous to Stalingrad (in addition to being helpful in the direct mission of capturing Stalingrad) was also in complete harmony with the further intentions of the German High Command; that is, to develop the success after the capture of Stalingrad along the Volga River toward the north.

Toward November 19, 1942, the enemy was grouped as follows: on the south bank of the Don River, on the Krasno-Orekhovoe Front (northwest of Boguchar), and Veshenskaia.Defensive positions were occupied by the 2nd and 35th Army Corps of the 8th Italian Army and the 29th German Army Corps. For greater stability of defense in the given direction, the German Units were mixed with the Italians. The Germans evidently feared an attack in the Boguchar direction and did not have much confidence in the stability of their Italian allies.

Great hope was pinned on the Rumanians. The 3rd Rumanian Army was given all of the zone from Nizhne-Kalinskii (Semenovskii) up to Malye Iarkovskii (15 kilometers northeast of Kletskaia). The following were on the defensive in this zone: *1st Army Corps* (7th and 11th Infantry Divisions) on the Semenovskii, Krivskoi, and Iagodnyi fronts; *2nd Army Corps* (9th and 14th Infantry Divisions) on the (exclusive) Iagodnyi, Bolshoi (exclusive), and Verkhne-Fomikhinshii fronts; *5th Army Corps* (5th and 6th Infantry Divisions) on the Verkhne-Fomikhinshii, Bazkovskii, and Raspopinskaia lines; and *4th Army Corps* (13th and 15th Infantry Divisions and the 1st Cavalry Division) on the Raspopinskaia (exclusive) and Malye Iarkovskii line.

On the average, a division occupied 15 kilometers of defense front. Up until this time, the Rumanian and Italian divisions had not participated in large operations and were at full strength.

On the front of Malye Iarkovskii (exclusive), Sirotinskaia, Trekhostrovskaia, Kuzmichi, and Akatovka, the German 376th, 44th, 384th, 76th and 113rd Infantry Divisions, the 60th and 3rd Motorized, and 16th Panzer Divisions were deployed on the defensive. Attacking in the area immediately adjacent to Stalingrad on a front of 30 kilometers, about 14 German divisions were deployed (94th, 305th, 389th, 79th, 100th Jaegar; 295th, 71st, and 371st Infantry; 3rd and 29th Motorized; 14th and 24th Panzer Divisions; and a number of independent regiments and battalions).

The total strength of the Stalingrad group of Germans, as we later ascertained, amounted to 330,000 men, armed to the teeth with the most powerful weapons. The 1,666 tanks, 5,762 guns, over 1,300 mortars, and 12,701 machine guns, captured as a result of the smashing of this single group—not counting heavy losses sustained before this on the distant and close approaches to the city—indicated clearly the strength of the enemy concentrated for the capture of Stalingrad.[2]

The 6th Rumanian Army Corps (2nd, 18th, 20th, 1st, and 4th Infantry Divisions) and 4th Cavalry Corps (5th and 8th Cavalry Divisions) were on the defensive on the front of Andreevka, Dubovyi Ovrag and Sadovoe.

However, we should note that the enemy, after having created a sufficient density of defense on the flanks of his Stalingrad group, did not have in his depth of defense (extending to the zone of army reserves) any strong strategic reserves. Thus, in the Boguchar direction, where the Army expected our attack first, the enemy had in the depths of his tactical defense about three infantry divisions and, in his depth of defense, he had two infantry divisions. In the Serafimovich direction, the enemy had as tactical reserves one cavalry and about one infantry division. In the depth of his defense, the enemy had in this direction, one Panzer division (Perelazovkii) and about one infantry division in Chernyshevskaia, the number of which was not determined.

Several days before our offensive, the enemy shifted into the area of Verkhne–Buzinovka one Panzer division and the remains of a second Panzer division.[3] In the Krasnoarmeisk direction, a motorized division was brought up to serve as a operational reserve.

The most vulnerable places in the operational disposition of the Stalingrad group of the enemy were the flanks, which were protected by the less stable Rumanian units and created favorable conditions for carrying out the encirclement of the main German group.

The heroic defense of Stalingrad by the Red Army units and the great losses sustained in the hard battles on the approaches to the city and within in weakened the offensive capacity of the Germans. Toward the end of October and in November, the pauses between the operations for the capture of the city became longer and longer. The operations themselves were carried out in short convulsive jerks lasting two or three days. The critical situation of the enemy was felt when the troops were clearly no longer able to carry out the duties assigned to them.

All of this together created favorable conditions for striking a decisive counterblow against the elite groups of the enemy, which had already been bled white but were still attacking. The operations of the Don and Stalingrad Fronts in the period preceding the offensive against the Stalingrad group of Germans are given in the article entitled "Battle for Stalingrad."

Plan of Operations for the Encirclement of the Enemy Group at Stalingrad

At the end of October 1942, the *Stavka* of the Red Army started carrying out the final part of the Stalingrad epic, namely, the destruction of the enemy group at Stalingrad [see map 3—Ed.].[4]

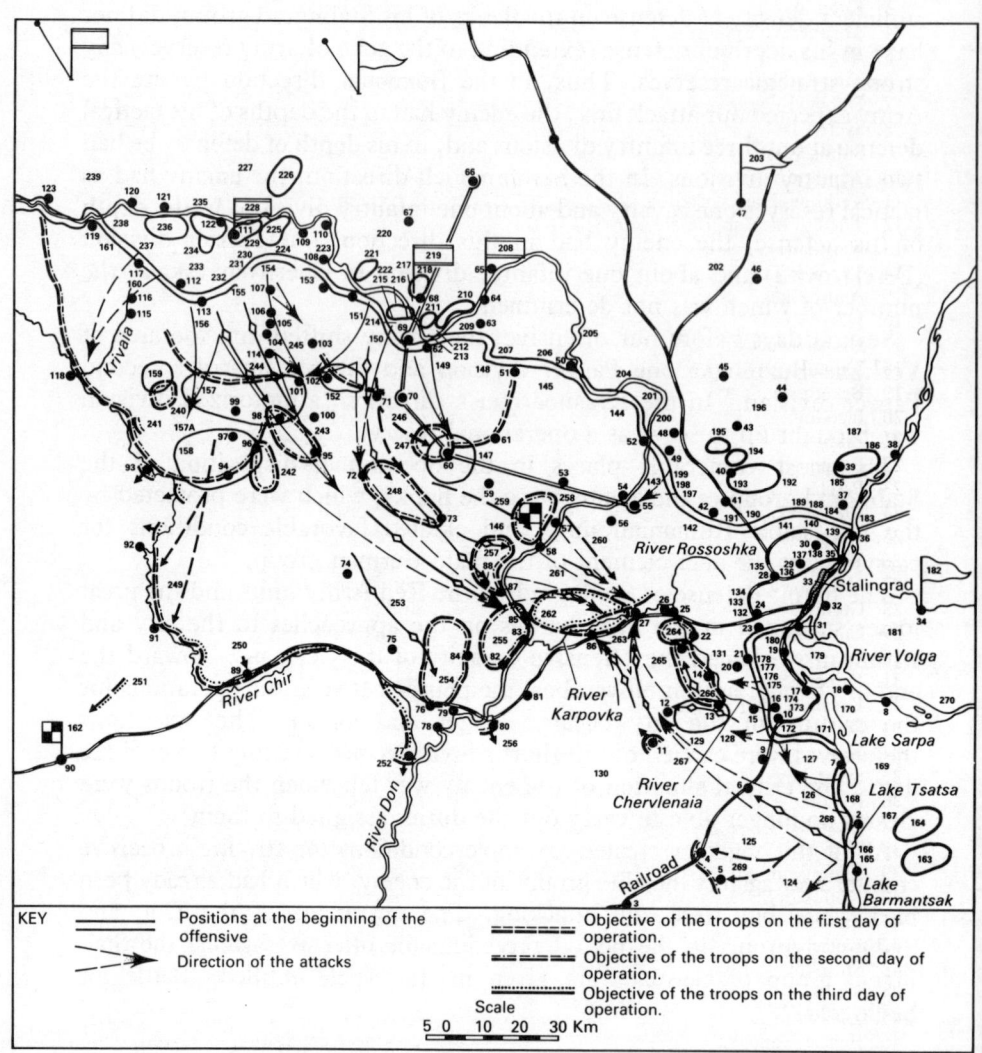

KEY

	Positions at the beginning of the offensive		Objective of the troops on the first day of operation.
	Direction of the attacks		Objective of the troops on the second day of operation.
			Objective of the troops on the third day of operation.

Scale

5 0   10   20   30 Km

Source: K.K. Rokossovskii, *Velikiye pobeda na Volge,* Map 20.

Map Three
"The Planned Counterattack for the Soviet Forces near Stalingrad"

Cities
1. Semkin
2. Tsatsa
3. Kotelnikovo
4. Abganerovo Station
5. Abganerovo
6. Tinguta Station
7. Dubovyi Ovrag
8. Svetlyi Iar
9. Siding Koshary
10. Tundutovo
11. Verkhne-Tsaritsynskii
12. The 8th of March State Farm
13. Nariman
14. Varvarovka
15. Andreevka
16. Ivanovka
17. Krasnoarmeisk
18. Tatianka
19. Beketovka
20. Iagodnyi
21. Elkhi
22. Peschanyi
23. Peschanka
24. Alekseevka
25. Karpovskaia
26. Karpovka
27. Marinovka
28. Gumrak
29. Gorodishche
30. Orlovka
31. Kuporosnoe
32. Krasnaia Sloboda
33. Stalingrad
34. Krasnyi Sad
35. Spartakovka
36. Rynok
37. Erzovka
38. Dubovka
39. Zheltukhin
40. Kotluban State Farm
41. Samofalovka
42. Kotluban
43. Shirokov
44. Sadki
45. Zavarykin
46. Bolshe Ivanovka
47. Solodcha
48. Kachalinskaia
49. Verkhne-Gnilovskii
50. Sirotkinskaia
51. Blizhniaia Perekopka
52. Trekhostrovskaia
53. Evlampievskii
54. omitted
55. Vertiachii
56. Peskovatka
57. Malogolubaia
58. Golubinskii
59. Osinovka
60. Verkhne-Buzinovka
61. Oskinskii
62. Melo-Kletskii
63. Perekopka
64. Perekopskaia
65. Akimovskii
66. Golubinskii
67. omitted
68. Orlopskii
69. Kletskaia
70. Tsimlovskii
71. Vlasov
72. Maniolin
73. Maiorovskii
74. Lobakinskii
75. Surovikino
76. Novomaksimovskii
77. Nizhne-Chirskaia
78. Verkhne-Chirskii
79. Rychkovskii
80. Lozhki Station
81. Liapichev
82. Piatiizbianskii
83. Kumovka
84. State Farm No. 8
85. Kalach
86. Sovetskii
87. Rubezhnyi
88. Lozhki
89. Oblivskaia
90. Morozovskii
91. Artemov
92. Ust-Griaznovskii
93. Chernyshevskaia
94. Kalach-Kurtlan
95. Zotovskii
96. Lipovskii
97. Malaia Donshinka
98. Perelazovskii
99. Bolshaia Donshinka
100. Osinovka
101. Verkhne-Cherenskii
102. Ivanushevskii
103. Golovskii
104. Korotkovskii
105. Sredne-Tsaritsynskii
106. Karagichev
107. Verkhne-Fomikhinskii
108. Bobrovskii
109. Zatonskii

110. Sarafimovich
111. Iabushenskii
112. State Farm No. 4
113. Bolshoi
114. Zhirkovskii
115. Gorbatovskii
116. Dubovskoi
117. Iagodnyi
118. Bokovskaia
119. Rybnyi
120. Elanskaia
121. Elanskii
122. Ust-Khoperskaia
123. Veshenskaia

Units
Soviet
163. 4th Mechanized Corps
164. 4th Cavalry Corps
165. 302nd Rifle Division
166. 126th Rifle Division
167. 51st Army (as in area of Deployment, not headquarters)
168. 15th Guards Rifle Division
169. 57th Army (same as above)
170. 13th Mechanized Corps
171. 143rd Rifle Division
172. 422nd Rifle Division
173. 169th Rifle Division
174. 38th Rifle Division
175. 157th Rifle Division
176. 204th Rifle Division
177. 29th Rifle Division
178. 66th Naval Infantry Brigade
179. 64th Army (as in area of Deployment, not headquarters)
180. 7th Rifle Corps
181. 62nd Army (Deployed in Stalingrad) including the 13, 37, 39th Guards Rifle Divisions; 45th, 95th, 112th, 138th, 193rd, 284th, 308th Rifle Divisions; 32nd, 115th, 124th, 149th, 160th, 42nd Rifle Brigades.
182. Stalingrad Front Headquarters
183. 99th Rifle Division
184. 116th Rifle Division
185. 64th Rifle Division
186. 299th Rifle Division
187. 66th Army (as in area of Deployment, not headquarters)
188. 226th Rifle Division
189. 343rd Rifle Division
190. 260th Rifle Division
191. 173rd Rifle Division
192. 233rd Rifle Division
193. 273rd Rifle Division
194. 84th Rifle Division
195. 16th Tank Corps

196. 24th Army (as in area of Deployment, not headquarters)
197. 298th Rifle Division
198. 49th Rifle Division
199. 214th Rifle Division
200. 120th Rifle Division
201. 24th Rifle Division
202. Don Front (area of operations)
203. Don Front Headquarters
204. 4th Guards Rifle Division
205. 65th Army (as in area of Deployment, not headquarters)
206. 40th Guards Rifle Division
207. 23rd Rifle Division
208. 65th Army Headquarters
209. 321st Rifle Division
210. 258th Rifle Division
211. 252nd Rifle Division
212. 304th Rifle Division
213. 27th Guards Rifle Division
214. 76th Rifle Division
215. 293rd Rifle Division
216. 4th Tank Corps
217. 277th Rifle Division
218. 3rd Guards Cavalry Corps
219. 21st Army Headquarters
220. 21st Army (as in area of Deployment, not headquarters)
221. 333rd Rifle Division
222. 63rd Rifle Division
223. 96th Rifle Division
224. One rifle regiment from the 346th Rifle Division
225. 26th Tank Corps
226. 346th Rifle Division less one regiment
227. 5th Tank Army (as in area of Deployment, not headquarters)
228. 5th Tank Army Headquarters
229. 159th Rifle Division
230. 124th Rifle Division
231. 119th Rifle Division
232. 47th Guards Rifle Division
233. 14th Guards Rifle Division
234. 8th Motorcycle Regiment
235. 1st Tank Corps
236. 8th Cavalry Corps
237. 203rd Rifle Division
238. 278th Rifle Division
239. 197th Rifle Division
240. 8th Cavalry Corps
241. Advanced detachment of the 8th Cavalry Corps
242. 1st Tank Corps
243. 26th Tank Corps
244. 1st Tank Corps
245. 26th Tank Corps
246. 3rd Guards Cavalry Corps
247. 3rd Guards Cavalry Corps

248. 4th Tank Corps
249. 8th Cavalry Corps
250. Advanced detachment of the Motorcycle Regiment and divisions of the 5th Tank Army
251. Advanced detachment
252. Advanced detachment of the 1st Tank Corps
253. 1st Tank Corps
254. 1st Tank Corps
255. 26th Tank Corps
256. Advanced detachment of the 1st Tank Corps
257. 4th Tank Corps
258. 3rd Guards Cavalry Corps
259. 3rd Guards Cavalry Corps
260. 3rd Guards Cavalry Corps
261. 4th Tank Corps
262. 26th Tank Corps
263. 4th Tank Corps / the second day
264. 13th Mechanized Corps*
265. 13th Mechanized Corps / the first day
266. 13th Mechanized Corps / the first day
267. 4th Mechanized Corps / the first day
268. 4th Mechanized Corps
269. 4th Cavalry Corps / the second day
270. Stalingrad Front area of operations
**** the solid double bars are the Front boundaries of operations

German
124. 1st Rumanian Infantry Division
125. 6th Rumanian Army Corps
126. 18th Rumanian Infantry Division
127. 2nd Rumanian Infantry Division
128. 20th Rumanian Infantry Division
129. 29th Motorized Division
130. 4th Panzer Army
131. 297th Infantry Division
132. 71st Infantry Division 371st Infantry Division
133. 100 Jaeger Infantry Division 295th Infantry Division
134. 79th Infantry Division 24th Panzer Division
135. Units of the 14th Panzer Division
136. 305th Infantry Division
137. 389th Infantry Division
138. 94th Infantry Division
139. 16th Panzer Division
140. 3rd Motorized Division
141. 60th Motorized Division
142. 113th Infantry Division
143. 76th Infantry Division
144. 384th Infantry Division
145. 44th Infantry Division
146. 6th Army Headquarters
147. Units of the 14th Panzer Division
148. 376th Infantry Division
149. 1st Rumanian Cavalry Division
150. 1st Regiment of the 15th Rumanian Infantry Division
151. 13th Rumanian Infantry Division
152. 2/3 Regiments of the 15th Rumanian Infantry Division
153. 6th Rumanian Infantry Division
154. 5th Rumanian Infantry Division
155. 14th Rumanian Infantry Division
156. 9th Rumanian Infantry Division
157. 1st Rumanian Panzer Division
157A. 48th Panzer Corps
158. 22nd Panzer Division
159. 7th Rumanian Cavalry Division
160. 1st Rumanian Infantry Division
161. 7th Rumanian Infantry Division
162. 3rd Rumanian Army Headquarters

Source: K. K. Rokossovskii, *Vellklye pobeda na Volge*, Map 29.

An outstanding characteristic of this operation was, first of all, the fact that it was the concluding stage of active defense and was carried out against a powerful offensive group of the enemy that had set for itself some far-reaching tasks. The purposes of the operation were by active operations to tie down the Stalingrad group of Germans on the front and the immediate flanks; then to strike a decisive blow against the covering armies stretched out in defense (3rd Rumanian Army and 6th Rumanian Army Corps) in order to move into the depths of the strategic rear of the Germans; and to effectively encircle first their mobile units, then the large formations of combined arms of the main forces of the Stalingrad group.

In keeping with the purpose of the operation, the Don Front, for convenience of command, was divided on October 29 into the Southwestern Front and the Don Front.[5] The cooperation between the Fronts consisted of having the shock groups of the Southwestern Front and the right flank of the Don Front attack west of the Don River from the north in the direction of Kalach, cutting off and encircling from the west the Stalingrad group of the enemy.

The mission of the troops of the Stalingrad Front was the following: by a blow south of Stalingrad in the general direction of Kalach, to join up with the troops of the Southwestern Front at Kalach; to complete the encirclement of the Stalingrad group of Germans from the south and southwest; and then, together with the troops of the Don Front, to destroy this group of the enemy.

A part of the forces of the Southwestern Front protected the operation from the west and southwest by an attack against Bokovskaia, Chernyshevskaia, and Oblivskaia. The Stalingrad Front protected the operation from the south by sending a part of its forces into the area of Abganerovo and then to the Nizhne-Chirskaia and Kotelnikovo line.

The Southwestern Front

The forces of the Southwestern Front struck their main blow with the 5th Tank and 21st armies from the line of Bolshoi, Verkhne-Fomikhinshii, Raspopinskaia, and Kletskaia in a general direction toward Perelazovskii and Kalach.

A secondary blow for the purpose of protecting the 5th Tank Army from the west was made by three rifle divisions of the 63rd Army from the line of (exclusive) Rybyi and Otdelenie State Farm (five kilometers west of Kotovskii) in the general direction of Yagodnyi and Bokovskaia.

The 5th Tank Army attacked on a front of 32 kilometers with a force of six rifle divisions, two tank corps, one cavalry corps, five howitzer artillery regiments, four gun artillery regiments, eight destroyer antitank regiments, four mortar regiments, four Guard Mortar regiments, one battalion of M-30s, and one PVO division of antiaircraft defense.[6]

The combat formation of the 5th Tank Army was arranged in the following manner. In the first echelon of the Army, there were four rifle divisions with means of reinforcement. In the second echelon of the Army, there were two rifle divisions, two tank corps, and a cavalry corps, that were to go into the breakthrough prepared by the combined arms units of the first echelon.

In the direction of the main blow, the breakthrough of the defense zone of the enemy was carried out by three rifle divisions on a front of 10 kilometers with an artillery density of 35 to 50 guns per 1 kilometer of front. In the direction of the secondary attack, one rifle division, with an artillery of 12 to 14 guns to the kilometer, attacked on a front of 12 kilometers.

The 1st and 26th Tank Corps, after the rifle troops had achieved the breakthrough, exploited their success by an attack in the direction of Perelazovskii-Kalach. where they were to establish contact with the mobile group of the Stalingrad Front.

For protection of the action of the tank corps from the southwest, a cavalry corps followed the tank units with the mission of seizing the most important centers of defense of the enemy on the Chir River. They were to hold these centers until the approach of the rifle units of the Army, whose mission it was to establish a solid defense on the Bokovskaia, Chernyshevskaia, Oblivskaia, and Surovikino fronts.

The total depth of the operation was as follows: for tank formations, about 130 kilometers; for rifle troops, about 35 to 100 kilometers.

The 21st Army—consisting of six rifle divisions, one tank and one cavalry corps, three independent tank regiments, two howitzer and four "gun" artillery regiments, six mortar regiments (including three regiments of Guard Mortars), one battalion of M-30s, six destroyer–antitank artillery regiments, and four PVO artillery regiments of antiaircraft defense—attacked on a front of 40 kilometers in the general direction of Zakharov, Verkhne-Buzinovka, and Golubinskii.[7]

In the first echelon, the attack was carried out by four rifle divisions, and in the second echelon by two rifle divisions, one tank, and one cavalry corps. In the main direction of the major blow, the defensive zone of the enemy was broken through by three rifle divisions on a front of 12 kilometers with an artillery density of about 40 guns to a kilometer of front.

In the secondary direction, an attack was made by one rifle division, one regiment of which was on the defensive on a front of 22 kilometers, and two regiments made an attack on a front of 3 kilometers.

The mobile group (tank and cavalry corps) had as missions to destroy, together with the rifle troops, the units of the 2nd and 5th Rumanian Corps. After developing the offensive in the general direction toward Sukhanovskii, Golubinskii, the mobile group in cooperation with the right wing of the Don Front, attempted to gain the rear of the German group to the west of the Don, cutting off its route of escape to the main Stalingrad group of the enemy. Upon reaching the Don River, the 21st Army became operationally subordinate to the Don Front.

The average rate of advance planned for the troops of the Southwestern Front was as follows: for tank corps, 50 kilometers a day; for rifle troops, in the main direction (first day of battle), up to 20 kilometers.

The Don Front

After occupying a central position, the troops of the Don Front, in cooperation with the 21st Army of the Southwestern Front, broke through with their right wing, the defensive zone of the enemy in the area southwest of Kletskaia, delivering the main blow in the direction

Mukovninskii and Vertiachii, and with their center in the direction of Station Panshino-Vertiachii.

The missions of the troops of the Don Front were to encircle the enemy group, consisting of four infantry divisions and one cavalry division, that were in defensive positions west of the Don River, and to cut them off from Stalingrad.

The 65th Army, with five rifle divisions and two tank brigades, made an attack on a front of 20 kilometers in the direction of Kletskaia and Mukovninskii.[8]

The 24th Army made an attack in the direction of Vertiachii for the purpose of preventing the enemy group on the right side of the Don from crossing the Don River at Vertichii and Peskovatka. The Army was to make its attack simultaneously with the arrival of the 65th Army at the Don.[9]

The Stalingrad Front

In conducting active military operations in the area of Stalingrad, the troops of the Front made their main attack with forces of the 57th and 51st Armies from the Ivanovka, Tundutovo, and Semkin areas with the mission of smashing the units of the 6th Rumanian Army Corps and, in cooperation with the troops of the Southwestern Front, of encircling the German Stalingrad group.[10] In view of the smaller depth of the attack (50 to 90 kilometers) and for the purpose of facilitating cooperation of the Fronts as to time, the Stalingrad Front started its offensive one day later than the Southwestern Front.

The 62nd Army, made up of 11 rifle divisions and five rifle brigades, reinforced by one tank brigade and by three gun artillery regiments, and three tank destroyer regiments, was assigned the mission of holding firmly the positions occupied on the eastern edge of Stalingrad.[11]

Subsequently, with the breakthrough of enemy defenses, the 57th and 51st Armies and the troops of the 62nd Army were, by a determined offensive, to prevent the enemy from removing from the front units operating in the area of Stalingrad and to mop up the town. For support of the 62nd Army, we detailed a combat artillery group operating from the eastern bank of the Volga.

The 64th Army, while providing a rigid defense on its right flank, made an attack on its left flank with three rifle divisions and two tank brigades in the direction of Gavrilovka, providing security for the operations of the 57th Army on the north after the commitment in the breakthrough of the 13th Mechanized Corps and outflanking the Stalingrad group of the enemy from the southwest along the Chervlenaia River.[12]

The 57th Army with two rifle divisions and one rifle brigade broke through the defenses of the enemy on a front of 8 kilometers, and by committing into the breech the 13th Mechanized Corps, enveloped the enemy from the west and southwest. By a simultaneous attack with one rifle brigade toward the south, in cooperation with the right flank division of the 51st Army, it surrounded units of the 2nd Rumanian Infantry Division to the west of Dubovyi Ovrag.

The 13th Mechanized Corps, by a determined movement in the direction of Chervlenyi, Blinnikov, and Rokotino was to reach the areas of Tsybenko, Novyi Rogachick, and Karpovka, cutting off the withdrawal of the enemy toward the southwest.

By a thrust toward Plodovitoe, the 51st Army, with two rifle divisions, covered the commitment into the breakthrough of the 4th Mechanized Corps and of the 4th Cavalry Corps. By an attack with one rifle division from the north of Lake Tsatsam in cooperation with units of the 57th Army, they encircled the enemy to the west of Dubovyi Ovrag. Subsequently, the 51st Army, with a part of its forces, reached the Karpovka-Sovetskii Front and with another part (three rifle divisions, 4th Cavalry Corps) protected the main group of the Front from possible enemy attacks from the direction of Nizhne-Chirskaia and Kotelnikovo.

The 4th Mechanized Corps, after moving into the breakthrough on the sector Lake Tsatsa, Semkin reached the Karpovka-Sovetskii line by a rapid thrust in the direction of Plodovitoe, Zety and, with the mobile units of the Southwestern Front, jointly closed the ring of encirclement around the Stalingrad group of the enemy.

While carrying out a rigid defense of Astrakhan, the 28th Army—with a shock group made up of one rifle division, one rifle brigade, and one tank brigade—was to smash the opposing enemy (16th Motorized) and seize the area of Elista.[13]

The Course of Operations for the Encirclement of the Stalingrad Group of Germans

The Southwestern Front

At 8:50 on November 19, 1942, after an artillery preparation lasting one hour and twenty minutes, the troops of the Front started the decisive offensive [see map 4—Ed.]. On the first day, they broke through the strongly fortified defense zone of the enemy, surmounting the barbed-wire entanglements and mine fields. After repelling repeated counter attacks of the tactical reserves of the enemy, toward the end of the day the units reached the Staro–Seniukin and Srredne–Tsaritsynskii line, advancing and fighting 20 to 25 kilometers in the main direction. The 5th Tank Army, after smashing units of the Rumanian 9th and 14th Infantry and one regiment of the 5th Rumanian Infantry Division, advanced 20 to 22 kilometers, thus completing the mission of the day.

Toward 2:00 P.M., the front of the enemy defenses was breached over all the tactical depth, and the mobile group of the Army—consisting of

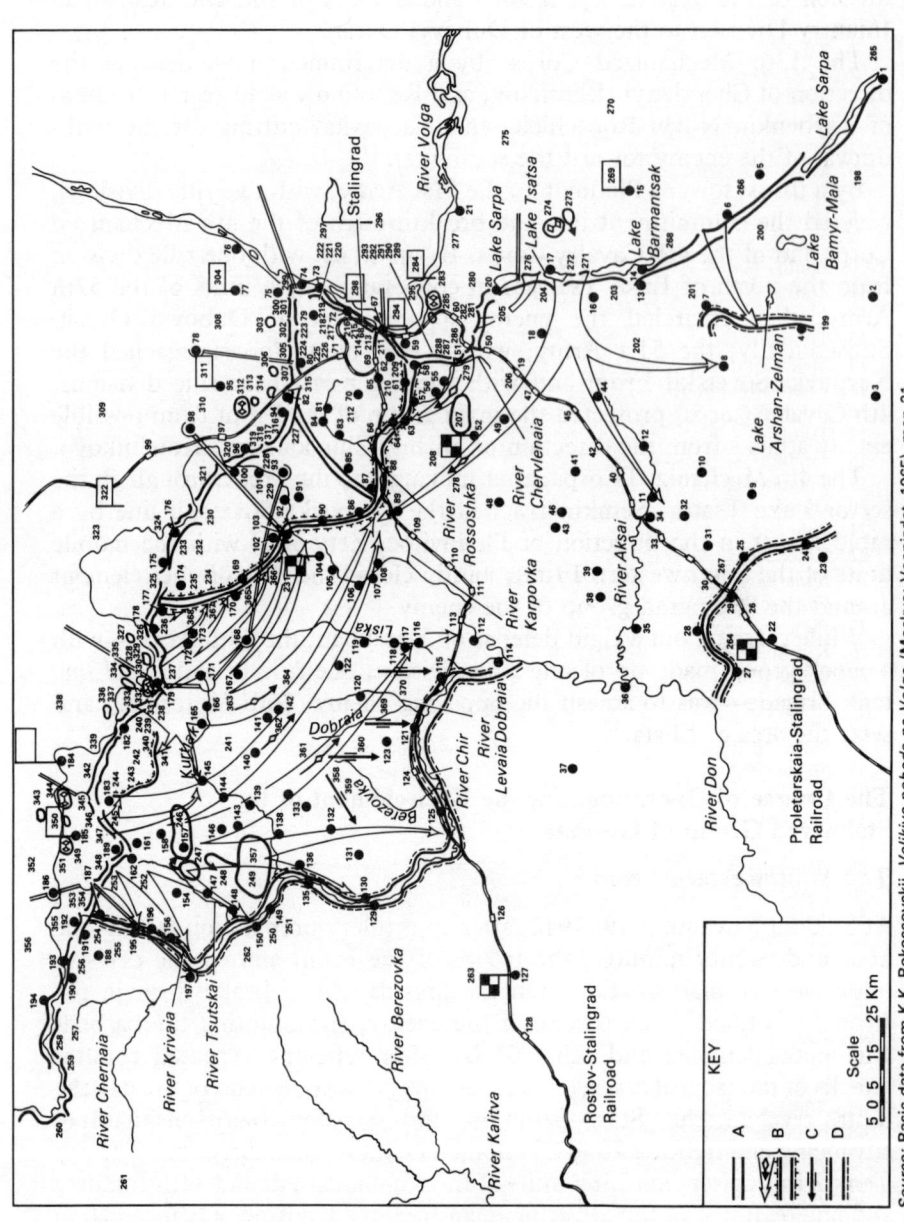

Source: Basic data from K.K. Rokossovskii, *Velikiye pobeda na Volge* (Moskva: Voenizdat, 1965), map 21.

Map Four
"The Activities of Soviet Forces During the November Counteroffensive"

Cities
1. Khazyk
2. Ketchenery
3. Kiselevka
4. Obilnoe
5. Batrak
6. Magdyn Khyduk
7. Sadovoe
8. Umantsevo
9. Sharnutovskii
10. Zhutov No. 2
11. Zhutov No. 1
12. Aksai
13. Tundutovo
14. Malye Derbety
15. Khair-Khuduk
16. Zakharov
17. Tsatsa
18. Tinguta
19. Tinguta Station
20. Dubovyi Ovrag
21. Raigorod
22. Kotelnikovo
23. Budarka
24. Poperechnyi
25. Pimen-Cherni
26. Kurmoiarskii
27. Pokhlebin
28. Verkhne-Iablochnyi
29. Gremiachii
30. Siding 161km
31. Nebykov
32. Chelikov
33. Siding 140km
34. Krugliakov
35. Generalovskii
36. Suvorovskii
37. Tormosin
38. The "8th of March"
39. Verkhne-Kumskii
40. Gnilioaksaiskii
41. Kapkinskii
42. Kapkinskii Station
43. Gromoslavka
44. Abganerovo
45. Abganerovo Station
46. Ivanovka
47. Siding 74km.
48. Eriko-Krepinskii
49. Zety
50. Siding 55km.
51. Tundutovo Station
52. Verkhne-Tsaritsynskii
53. Buzinovka
54. Varvarovka
55. Nariman
56. Gavrilovka
57. Tsybenko
58. Elkhi
59. Beketovka
60. Chapurniki Station
61. Popov
62. Peschanka
63. Rakotino
64. Bereslavskii
65. Basargino
66. Karpovskaia Station
67. Kuporosnoe
68. Stalingrad
69. Voroponovo
70. Pitomnik
71. Gumrak Station
72. Red October
73. Spartakovka
74. Rynok
75. Erzovka
76. Dubovka
77. Dikova Balka
78. Sadki
79. Orlovka
80. Kuzmichi
81. Bolshaia Rossoshka
82. Samofalovka
83. Baburkin
84. Zapadnovka
85. Dmitrievka
86. Illarionovskii
87. Marinovka
88. Siding Prudboi
89. Sovetskii
90. Sokarevka
91. Peskovatka
92. Malonabatovskii
93. Vertiachii
94. Kotluban
95. Shirokov
96. Panshino
97. Kachalino Station
98. Alaev
99. Ilovlia Station
100. Trekhostrovskaia
101. Nizhne-Akatov
102. Evlampievskii
103. Bolshenabatoyvskii
104. Golubinskii
105. Mostovskii
106. Lozhki
107. Berezovskii
108. Kalach
109. Kumovka Station

110. Liapichev Station
111. Siding Lozhki
112. Verkhne-Chirskii
113. Rychkovskii
114. Nizhne-Chirskaia
115. Bolshaia Osinovka
116. Tuzov
117. Zrianinskii
118. Lysov
119. Ostrov
120. Savinskii
121. Surovikino
122. Plesistovskii
123. Verkhne Osinovka
124. Sekretev Station
125. Oblivskaia
126. Tsymla Station
127. Morozovskii
128. Valkovo Station
129. Gusynka
130. Klinovyi
131. Krasnoe Selo
132. Iasinovskii
133. Novovasilevskii
134. Osinovskii
135. Arzhanovskii
136. Ozery
137. Petrovka
138. Kalach-Kurtlan
139. Lipovskii
140. Zotovskii
141. Maniolin
142. State Farm No. 1
143. Malaia Donshinka
144. Perelazovskii
145. Bolshaia Osinovka
146. Bolshaia Donshinka
147. Pronin
148. Pichugin
149. Chernyshevskaia
150. Chistiakovskaia
151. Evlantevskii
152. Bokovskaia
153. Konkov
154. Karasev
155. Tusynka
156. Astakhov
157. Peschanyi
158. Independent State Farm No. 86
159. Blinovskii
160. Korotkovskii
161. Klinovoi
162. Bolshoi
163. Zhirkovskii
164. Verkhne-Cherenskii
165. Evstratovskii
166. Vlasov
167. Svechnikovskii

168. Verkhne Buzinovka
169. Golubaia
170. Oskinskii
171. Platonov
172. Srednii
173. Krainii
174. Blizhnaia Perekopka
175. Shokin
176. Sirotinskaia
177. Logovskii
178. Melo-Kletskii
179. Kletskaia
180. Verkhne-Solomakovskii
181. Ozerki
182. Raspopinskaia
183. Verkhne-Fomikinskii
184. Serafimovich
185. Izbushenskii
186. Elanskii
187. Iagodnyi
188. Singin
189. Kalmykovskii
190. Nizhne-Kalininskii
191. Verkhne-Krivskoi
192. Nizhne-Krivskoi
193. Rynbyi
194. Veshenskaia
195. Gorbatovskii
196. Ushakov
197. Bokovskaia

Key
A   Position of Soviet and fascist troops at the end of November 18, 1942
B   Direction of the blows of Soviet forces on November 19–23, 1942. Position of the Soviet and fascist troops at the end of November 23, 1942.
C   The advance of Soviet units after the completion of the encirclement of the fascist troops.
D   Position of Soviet and fascist troops at the end of November 30, 1942.

Units
German
198. Units of the 8th Rumanian Cavalry Division
199. 7th Rumanian Army Corps
200. 5th Rumanian Cavalry Division
201. 4th Rumanian Infantry Division
202. 6th Rumanian Army Corps
203. 1st Rumanian Infantry Division
204. 18th Rumanian Infantry Division
205. 2nd Rumanian Infantry Division
206. 4th Panzer Army area of operation
207. 29th Motorized Division
208. 4th Panzer Army Headquarters

209. 297th Infantry Division
210. 4th Army Corps
211. 371st Infantry Division
212. 6th Army area of operations
213. 71st Infantry Division
214. 295th Infantry Division
215. 100th Jaeger Infantry Division
216. 79th Infantry Division
217. 24th Panzer Division
218. Units of the 14th Panzer Division
219. 305th Infantry Division
220. 389th Infantry Division
221. 94th Infantry Division
222. 16th Panzer Division
223. 3rd Motorized Division
224. 60th Motorized Division
225. 14th Panzer Corps
226. 51st Army Corps
227. 113th Infantry Division
228. 76th Infantry Division
229. 8th Army Corps
230. 384th Infantry Division
231. 6th Army Headquarters
232. 11th Army Corps
233. 44th Infantry Division
234. 1st Rumanian Cavalry Division
235. 376th Infantry Division
236. 376th Infantry Division
237. 1st Rumanian Cavalry Division
238. 15th Rumanian Infantry Division
239. 4th Rumanian Army Corps
240. 13th Rumanian Infantry Division
241. 3rd Rumanian Army area of operations
242. 6th Rumanian Infantry Division
243. 5th Rumanian Army Corps
244. 5th Rumanian Infantry Division
245. 14th Rumanian Infantry Division
246. 1st Rumanian Panzer Division
247. 7th Rumanian Cavalry Division
248. 48th Panzer Corps
249. 22nd Panzer Corps
250. 22nd Panzer Corps
251. 1st Rumanian Panzer Division
252. 2nd Rumanian Army Corps
253. 9th Rumanian Infantry Division
254. 11th Rumanian Infantry Division
255. 1st Rumanian Army Corps
256. 7th Rumanian Infantry Division
257. Italian "January" Blackshirt Brigade
258. 2nd Italian Infantry Division
259. 9th Italian Infantry Division
260. 62nd Infantry Division
261. 8th Italian Army area of operations
262. 7th Rumanian Cavalry Division
263. 3rd Rumanian Army Headquarters
264. 4th Rumanian Army Headquarters

Soviet
265. 28th Army totals: 2 – Rifle Divisions,
3 – Rifle Brigades, 1 – Tank
Division
266. 91st Rifle Division
267. 51st Army area of operations
268. 76th Fortified Region
269. 51st Army Headquarters
270. 51st Army totals: 4 – Rifle Divisions;
1 – Mechanized Corps, 1 – Cavalry
Corps, 1 – Tank Brigade, 1 –
Motorized Rifle Brigade
271. 302nd Rifle Division
272. 126th Rifle Division
273. 4th Cavalry Corps
274. 4th Mechanized Corps
275. Stalingrad Front totals: 24 – Rifle
Divisions, 15 – Rifle Brigades, 1 –
Mechanized Corps, 1 – Cavalry Corps,
1 – Tank Corps, 7 – Tank Brigades,
2 – Motorized Rifle Brigades
276. 15th Guards Rifle Division
277. 57th Army totals 2 – Rifle Divisions,
1 – Rifle Brigade, 1 – Tank Corps, 2
– Tank Brigades, 1 – Motorized Rifle
Brigades
278. 4th Mechanized Corps
279. 13th Tank Corps
280. 177th and 45th Independent Machine
Gun Artillery Battalions
281. 143rd Rifle Brigade
282. 422nd Rifle Division
283. 13th Tank Corps
284. 57th Army Headquarters
285. 36th Guards Rifle Division
286. 169th Rifle Division
287. 38th Rifle Division
288. 157th Rifle Division
289. 154th Naval Infantry Brigade
290. 204th Rifle Division
291. 29th Rifle Division
292. 66th Naval Infantry Brigade
293. 7th Rifle Corps
294. 64th Army Headquarters
295. 64th Army totals: 5 – Rifle Divisions,
5 – Rifle Brigades, 2 – Naval
Infantry Brigades
296. Stalingrad Front Headquarters
297. 62nd Army: 13th, 37th, 39th Guards
Rifle Divisions, 45th, 95th, 112th,
138th, 193rd, 284th, 308th Rifle
Divisions, 92nd, 115th, 124th, 149th,
160th, 42nd Rifle Brigades
298. 62nd Army Headquarters
299. 99th Rifle Division
300. 64th Rifle Division
301. 116th Rifle Division
302. 226th Rifle Division
303. 299th Rifle Division
304. 66th Army Headquarters

305. 343rd Rifle Division
306. 233rd Rifle Division
307. 260th Rifle Division
308. 66th Army totals: 6 – Rifle Divisions, 1 – Tank Brigade
309. Don Front totals: 24 – Rifle Divisions, 1 – Tank Corps, 6 – Tank Brigades
310. 24th Army totals: 9 – Rifle Divisions, 1 – Tank Corps, 1 – Tank Brigade
311. 24th Army Headquarters
312. 16th Tank Corps
313. 84th Rifle Division
314. 273rd Rifle Division
315. 173rd Rifle Division
316. 298th Rifle Division
317. 49th Rifle Division
318. 214th Rifle Division
319. 120th Rifle Division
320. 24th Rifle Division
321. 4th Guards Rifle Division
322. 65th Army Headquarters
323. 65th Army totals: 9 – Rifle Divisions, 2 – Tank Brigades
324. 40th Guards Rifle Division
325. 23rd Rifle Division
326. 321st Rifle Division
327. 258th Rifle Division
328. 252th Rifle Division
329. 304th Rifle Division
330. 27th Guards Rifle Division
331. 76th Rifle Division
332. 4th Tank Corps
333. 93rd Rifle Division
334. 3rd Guards Cavalry Corps
335. 277th Rifle Division
336. 333rd Rifle Division
337. 63rd Rifle Division
338. 21st Army totals: 6 – Rifle Divisions, 1 – Tank Corps, 1 – Cavalry Corps
339. 96th Rifle Division
340. 333rd Rifle Division

341. 277th Rifle Division
342. 346th Rifle Division
343. 346th Rifle Division
344. 26th Tank Corps
345. 124th Rifle Division
346. 119th Rifle Division
347. 47th Guards Rifle Division
348. 14th Guards Rifle Division
349. 1st Tank Corps
350. 5th Tank Army Headquarters
351. 8th Cavalry Corps
352. 5th Tank Army totals: 6 – Rifle Divisions, 1 – Motorized Rifle Brigade, 2 – Tank Corps, 1 – Cavalry Corps, 1 – Tank Brigade
353. 278th Rifle Division
354. 203rd Rifle Division
355. 197th Rifle Division
356. 1st Guards Army totals: 6 – Rifle Divisions, 1 – Motorized Rifle Brigade
357. Southwestern Front headquarters
357A. 21st Army Headquarters off-map north and right of 93A
357B. Southwestern Front totals 18 – Rifle Divisions, 3 – Tank Corps, 2 – Cavalry Corps, 1 – Tank Brigade, 1 – Motorized Rifle Brigade
357C. 8th Cavalry Corps
358. omitted
359. 321st Rifle Division
360. 119th Rifle Division
361. 1st Tank Corps
362. 26th Tank Corps
363. 4th Tank Corps
364. 3rd Guards Cavalry Corps
365. 252nd Rifle Division
366. 76th Rifle Division
367. 27th Guards Rifle Division
368. 304th Rifle Division
369. 333rd Rifle Division
370. 258th Rifle Division

Source: Basic data from K.K. Rokossovskii *Velikiye podedn na Volge* (Moskva: Voenizdat, 1965) map 21.

the 1st and 26th Tank Corps and the 8th Cavalry Corps—was thrown into the breach.

Toward 3:00 P.M., the 21st Army, after smashing units of the 15th and 13th Rumanian Infantry Divisions, broke through the defenses of the enemy in the direction of Zakharov and committed into the breach the mobile group of the Army consisting of the 4th Tank Corps and the 3rd Guards Cavalry Corps.

The rifle units, after overcoming strong enemy resistance, advanced by the close of the day a distance of 10 kilometers in the direction of the main attack. About 8:00 P.M. on November 19, the mobile group of the Army had reached the Zakharov-Tsymlovskii line, a distance of 25 kilometers.

In the course of November 20, the attacking units of the Front repelled the attacks of the immediate strategic reserves of the enemy (1st Rumanian, 14th German and 22nd Panzer Divisions). By the close of November 20, in two days of offensive operations, the shock group of the Front—after smashing the 13th, 14th and 9th Rumanian Infantry Divisions and inflicting heavy losses upon the units of the 15th, 5th, and 6th Rumanian Infantry Divisions and the leading units of the 14th and 22nd German Panzer Divisions—had advanced a distance of 35 to 40 kilometers and was continuing to develop the success toward Verkhne–Buzinovka.

The units covering the group (left flank of the 63rd Army and a part of the 5th Tank Army) successfully attacked in a southwestern direction and by the close of the third day of the offensive (November 21) reached the line of Gorbatovskii, Star Pronin, Medvezhii, and Kalach-Kurtalakskaia, moving a distance of 60 to 70 kilometers.

About the same time, a part of the forces of the 5th Tank and the 21st Armies surrounded the remnants of the 5th, 6th, 13th, and 15th Rumanian Infantry Divisions in the areas Verkhne-Fomikhinskii, Bolshaia Osinovka, and Raspopinskaia and fought a battle for the destruction of this group.[14] The tank corps, by pounding the rear of the enemy, developed the attack in the direction of Kalach.

From November 22–23, the troops of the Front were assigned the mission of moving to the Bokovskaia-Chernishovskaia line and establishing a rigid defense on the Chir River. The tank corps of the 5th Tank Army were given the mission of capturing Surovikino and cutting the railroad to Stalingrad-Likhaia (1st Tank Corps) and Kalach (26th Tank Corps).

By pursuing the uncoordinated and disorganized groups of the enemy in a south and southeasterly direction, the troops of the Front carried out the main part of their mission. The 26th Tank Corps, after forcing the Don River, captured the town of Kalach on November 22. On November 23, all of the 5th, 6th, 13th, and 15th Rumanian Infantry Division were captured.

On November 24, units of the 4th and 26th Tank Corps reached the region of Sovetskii, where they joined with units of the 4th Mechanized Corps of the Stalingrad Front, completely closing the ring of encirclement.

As a result of the four days of operations (from November 19–23), a 120-kilometer wide breach was made in the enemy's front along the Chir River. The rate of movement in the operation was rather rapid. The depth of the main blow—amounting to 140 kilometers—was covered in the course of four days, making an average of 35 kilometers per day.

Upon reaching the Don River on November 27, the 21st Army became operationally subordinate to the Don Front.

The troops of the Southwestern Front started preparations for a new operation aimed at smashing the enemy group on the Chir River and the middle course of the Don River.

In the course of the operations, the troops of the Southwestern Front captured about 55,000 prisoners and destroyed up to about 34,000 soldiers and officers of the enemy. We captured more than 1,000 guns; 235 tanks; 3,200 machine guns and a great quantity of other forms of armaments; ammunition; and military stores. The 3rd Rumanian Army ceased to exist.

The Don Front

At 8:50 A.M. on November 19, after an artillery preparation, units of the 65th Army assumed the offensive from the line of Kletskaia and Malshaia Iarkova in the direction of Mukovninskii.

In cooperation with the 24th Army, the units of the 65th Army had the mission of encircling and destroying the units of the 376th, 44th, and 384th German Infantry Division on the defensive on the line of Osinki, Sirotinskaia, and Trekhostrovskaia.

After meeting stubborn resistance and repelling counterattacks of the enemy reserves, the formations of the 65th Army advanced during the first day a distance of 6 to 7 kilometers on the right flank, while advances on the rest of the front were slight. For increasing the power of the blow, a division of the second echelon was committed to action on November 20 on the right flank of the Army. The attacking Army fought not only the German units but also units of the 1st Rumanian Cavalry Division and units of the 14th and 24th German Panzer Divisions, and 3rd German Motorized Division brought from the area of Stalingrad.

Beginning on November 20, units of the left flank of the 65th Army, by active operations of the separate detachments, tied down the enemy on the Sirotinskaia-Trekostrovskaia line; and created a threat to the rear of the enemy group on the right side of the Don. From November 20–22, the battles west of the Don River were of a particularly stubborn character. The advancing units of the 65th Army, after repelling repeated counterattacks of infantry and tanks of the enemy, advanced in the direction of the main blow at the rate of 5 to 6 kilometers per day. Toward the close of November 22, the units of the Army seized Verkhne-Buzinovka. About this time, the mobile units of the Southwestern Front captured the town of Kalach and reached the Don River north of Kalach, creating a direct threat to the crossings on the Don River in the area of Peskovatka and Vertiachii. Because of this, the enemy, while conducting rearguard actions, began a hasty withdrawal to the east side of the Don

River for effecting a junction with the main Stalingrad group, abandoning equipment, arms, and great quantities of various kinds of supplies.

On the morning of November 22, after a powerful artillery preparation, units of the right flank of the 24th Army started an offensive in the direction of Vertiachii and Peskovatka for the purpose of cutting off the enemy group on the other side of the Don from the river's crossings and preventing them from effecting a junction with the main forces of the German 6th Army.

Having encountered heavy fire resistance and an organized system of enemy fortifications and entanglements, the attacking units of the 24th Army were unable to advance. In long and hard battles, both sides suffered heavy losses. The Germans tried at any price to hold the crossings on the Don River in order to protect the withdrawal of the group on the west to the east bank of the river and their junction with the main forces. At the same time, the Germans concentrated up to 150 tanks in the region of Malonabatovskii to protect the crossings from capture from the west. On the morning of November 24 on the left wing of the Front, an offensive was started by units of the 66th Army, which moved to the left flank a distance of 8 kilometers and joined units of the Stalingrad Front in the area of Rynok.

By November 25, units of the 65th Army had cleared the west bank of the Don River of the enemy, the remnants of which fled to the east bank. On or about November 27, units of the 65th Army reached the area of Vertiachii and continued to pursue the enemy in a southeasterly direction.

The troops of the Don Front did not fully succeed in encircling the German group on the west side of the Don, but they inflicted serious losses upon the group. The Germans abandoned almost all of their artillery (about 400 guns), 300 tanks, and a great deal of other armaments. The enemy suffered heavy personnel losses—killed, wounded, and taken prisoner.

The Stalingrad Front

On November 20, 1942, after an hour's artillery preparation, units of the 64th, 57th, and 51st armies moved to the attack in the planned directions.

The 64th Army, by striking a blow with the left flank in the direction of Gavilovka, provided a covering from the north for the action of the main forces of the Front. Meeting stubborn resistance and repelling counterattacks of the immediate reserves of the enemy, the attacking units advanced slowly covering 2 to 5 kilometers by the close of the day.

The 57th Army, by striking its main blow with two rifle divisions and one rifle brigade on a front of 8 kilometers, broke through the defenses of the enemy in the first half of the day, and advancing a distance of 6 to 8 kilometers, brought the 13th Mechanized Corps into the breakthrough at 4:00 P.M. in the direction of Blinnikov, Vypasnoi, and Rokotino.

The 51st Army, striking its main blow with two divisions from the area around Tsatsa and Barmantsak in the direction of Plodovitoie and covering on this sector the commitment into the breakthrough of the 4th Mechanized and the 4th Cavalry Corps, attacked with one rifle division from the area between Lakes Sarpa and Tsatsa in the direction of the Privolzhskii State Farm cover the operation of the main group of the Army from the north. About 1:00 P.M., after breaking the enemy resistance, some units of the Army advanced 7 to 8 kilometers. The 4th Mechanized Corps, at 2:00 P.M., moved through the combat formation of the division in the direction of Plodovitoie, Verhkne-Tsaritsynskii, and Sovetskii.

In two days of the offensive (November 20–21), the armies smashed the 1st, 2nd, and 18th Rumanian Infantry Divisions and inflicted serious defeat upon the 20th Rumanian Infantry Division and the 29th German Motorized Division, with counterattacks made by units of the 57th Army. During this time, the units advanced from 4 to 16 kilometers (57th Army) up to 30 kilometers (51st Army).

By the close of the second day of the offensive, the mobile units debouched as follows: the *13th Mechanized Corps* on the Nariman and the "8th of March" Collective Farm line, after having engaged in uncoordinated battle in this area and having repelled the counterattacks of motorized infantry and tanks of the enemy; the *4th Mechanized Corps*, not encountering any serious resistance, in the area Verkhne-Tsaritsinskii and Zeti, advancing a distance of 50 to 60 kilometers; and the *4th Cavalry Corps*, moving into the breach behind the 4th Mechanized Corps, pursued the remnants of the defeated Rumanian divisions, and encountering weak resistance, advanced a distance of 50 kilometers and debouched on the morning of November 22 in the area of Abganerovo.

Continuing to develop a successful offensive, the units of the front, by the close of November 22, had enveloped the Stalingrad group of the enemy from the southwest on the Nariman-Varvarovka-Rokotino line along the west bank of the Chervlenaia River. By noon on November 22, the 4th Mechanized Corps reached the Karpovka-Sovetskii line, having completed jointly with the mobile units of the Southwestern Front the encirclement of the Stalingrad group of the enemy.

Further attempts to advance were unsuccessful. The enemy succeeded in rushing reserves to the threatened direction and, utilizing the position of the Stalingrad fortified area, organized a fairly stable defense.

In the operations carried out, the troops of the front smashed units of the 6th Army Corps and the 4th Rumanian Cavalry Corps, inflicted heavy losses on the units of the 29th German Motorized and 24th Panzer Divisions. We captured 15,000 soldiers and officers.

The enemy lost more than 70,000 in killed and wounded. We captured the following: 457 tanks; 38 airplanes; 870 guns; more than 1,000 machine guns; 1,100 mortars; 1,266 antitank guns; more than 2,500 submachine guns; 35,000 rifles, 1 million shells; 5 million cartridges; more than 200 motor vehicles; and a great deal of other kinds of military equipment.

In tightening the ring of encirclement, the 21st and 65th armies of the Southwestern Front, as a result of intense battles, reached the line of (all exclusive) Marinovka, Dmitrievka and Borodin by the end of November 30.

The 66th Army of the Don Front advanced with its left flank to the area of Rynok and joined with units of the 62nd Army of the Stalingrad Front. Hence, by the end of November 30, we had converted the operational encirclement of the enemy group at Stalingrad into a tactical encirclement. After completing the encirclement, the troops had before them the task of carrying out an organized and systematic offensive to split the encircled group into isolated groups and destroying them separately. This task was carried out by the troops of the Don Front in the subsequent stages of the operation.

Conclusions

1. The operations carried out between November 19–22, 1942 for the encirclement of the German offensive army of 330,000 men equipped with powerful modern military equipment showed the high level of military training of the commanders and men of the Red Army and marked the beginning of a new chapter in Soviet military art at its highest stage—the tactics of maneuvering large formations on the field of battle for the purpose of encircling and destroying the personnel and military equipment of the enemy.

2. The encirclement and subsequent smashing of the elite group of the enemy marked the beginning of a new stage of the Great Patriotic War—"the mass expulsion of the enemy from the land of the Soviets" (Stalin)—as a result of which the enemy suffered irreplaceable losses in the Northern Caucasus, the Kuban, in the Donbas, and on the other fronts of the Great Patriotic War.

3. The success of the operation for the encirclement of the Stalingrad group of the enemy was made possible first of all by the correct selection of the time for passing to a general counteroffensive. The stubborn and long drawnout battles on the approaches to Stalingrad, the heroic defense of the 62nd Army's troops, and the many months of battle on the immediate flanks of the Stalingrad group wore the enemy out, decimated his forces, and, in this way, destroyed his faith in the ultimate success of his operations.

BFS—D

4. The selection of the direction for the main blow was a decisive requirement for success in battle and is indicative of the level of operational-strategic military leadership. The striking of the main blow against the weakest link in the operational formation of the enemy (the Rumanians) sped up the operation but was not the primary cause of the German's defeat at Stalingrad.

5. The most important condition ensuring the successful execution of the operations for the encirclement of the Stalingrad group of the enemy was the sudden counterattack of the Red Army. Tied down by the continuous flank battles in the area between the Don and the Volga rivers and with relative quiet in the other sectors, the enemy never thought of the possibility of a serious counterattack against the more distant flanks of his offensive group.

Having underestimated the strength of the Red Army and overestimated his own forces, the enemy was shaken by the sudden blow and was demoralized by the great scope of the operations of the Red Army and the deep penetration of its mobile units into the operational rear of the Stalingrad group.

Hence, the new methods of conducting operations employed by the Red Army and the mass employment of large mobile units constituted one of the more important reasons for the victories.

6. The secrecy maintained as to the aims of the operation and the concealed documentation of troops were the reasons for the surprise. The experience of the Stalingrad operation teaches us that even in operations involving the equipment of large forces and on several fronts with intelligent leadership, that we must maintain secrecy and surprise, despite the long period needed to prepare such operations. The most important requirements for maintaining secrecy of such operations will be

● revealing the aims of operations to a limited number of personnel only in that period when it is necessary for making the preparations;
● giving oral assignment of missions to the executors during the preparation period to the extent necessary for them to carry out their missions, greatly broadening the orientation in proportion to the moment of approaching action;
● concealing concentrations of troops and means of reinforcement in the designated areas, forbidding movement in the daytime, and carefully camouflaging troops in the areas of concentration;
● carefully organizing the commandant's headquarters support in the areas of the troops' concentration and preventing the penetration into the aforementioned areas of persons not connected with the given large formations (or smaller units); and
● forbidding the concentrated troops to conduct reconnaissance with their own forces, leaving at their disposal for this purpose sufficiently

strong reconnaissance units and organs of combat security from the troops previously operating in the area.

7. The speed and impetuosity of the troops affecting the breakthrough and encirclement of the enemy depends upon the completeness and the care with which the operation is prepared. The successful operations of the units of all branches of the service in the battle of Stalingrad were prepared over a long period by intense work of the command personnel and staffs of all ranks in the study of the enemy and the locality, and also in the organized cooperation between the branches of the service in the locality.

The timely carrying out of war games by the senior and higher command personnel and their staffs were, without a doubt, very profitable.

8. Carefully planned and continuous conduct of reconnaissance made possible the timely discovery of the enemy's defense system, the grouping of his forces and means, his system of engineering installations, entanglements, and the character of the locality. In the study of the enemy, a great part was played by the local military operations of the front and the verification by reconnaissance in force of the groups of the enemy for several days before the attack.

9. Strategic cooperation of the branches of the service was organized in a rather precise manner. The rifle troops made passageways for the tanks through the defensive zone of the enemy and covered the action of the mobile groups from the flanks, drawing the counterattacks of the tactical and strategic reserves of the enemy and making possible complete freedom of action for the mobile groups.

Operating in the zone of the interior, the mobile groups disorganized the system of troop control and the work in the rear of the enemy, destroyed unit by unit the enemy reserves hastening to the front line, and cooperated with the rifle troops in distracting the enemy in the tactical depth of his defensive dispositions and in moving the infantry behind the mobile groups in the operational depths.

In addition to the great achievements of the fronts operating in the encirclement of the Stalingrad units of the enemy, we should also mention the most essential *weaknesses* in the planning of combat and direction of troops.

1. The unsuccessful actions aimed at cutting off the enemy groups on the other side of the Don River from the main forces of the 6th German Army resulted from underestimating the power of resistance of the encircled enemy groups and the measures that they could take for saving themselves.

For carrying out the mission of cutting off the enemy group on the other side of the Don (i.e., on the right side) from the crossings on the Don, it would have been necessary to have large formations possessing great strategic mobility and power of penetration. This mission could have been carried out more easily by the 4th Tank Corps but not by the 3rd Guards Cavalry Corps. The latter could have more successfully carried out the mission of providing liaisons between the two tank shock groups operating toward Kalach and Nizhne-Gerasimov. In addition, the blow of the 24th Army toward Vertiachii was too late and was not carried out in sufficient strength.

2. The direction of troops on the south wing of the Stalingrad Front was not planned thoroughly. The dual mission assigned to the 51st Army (breakthrough to Kalach and to cover the operations of the southwest) could not fail to affect adversely the command of troops operating in the direction of Kotelnikovo (the army staff was 90 kilometers from this group of troops). It would have been more appropriate to subordinate the 4th Mechanized Corps to the 57th Army or to bring the Mechanized Corps into one group subordinate to the front.

3. We did not make proper use of the 13th Mechanized Corps. It was given the narrow tactical mission of seizing the region of Nariman and Gavrilovka, and as a result, the Corps lost all of two days in aimless battle in this area, enabling the enemy to organize a defense on the Karpovka-Tsybenko line.

4. The command of the Stalingrad Front underestimated the possibility of an enemy countertattack from the southwest direction and failed to take immediate steps for strengthening ourselves on the line of the Aksai River and to seize and hold firmly, first of all, the most important centers and roads in the region of Krugliakov and Aksai.[15] The front had at its disposal the necessary personnel and equipment (machine gun/artillery battalions on the east bank of the Volga, approaching reserves, and so on).

For a number of reasons, first of all the careful preparation of the operations as a whole by the *Stavka* and its representatives on the spot (Marshals of the Soviet Union, Comrades Zhukov, Vasilevskii, and Voronov), the aforementioned mistakes and a number of less essential weaknesses did not have any serious consequences.[16] However, it goes without saying that these mistakes in concurrence with some other circumstances could have led to serious complications in carrying out the will of the *Stavka*.

Under the difficult winter conditions of very limited communications in an area with few inhabited localities, the High Command of the Red Army made the plans for military operations unparalleled in the military art, and the troops carried them out in a skillful manner in three or four days—operations that represented the beginning of the utter defeat of the 330,000 enemy shock troops at Stalingrad.

In conclusion, it will be interesting to note how the enemy reacted to the successful results of our offensive operations in the period of

November 19–24, 1942. Several days after the completion of the first stage of the operation (November 28), the staff of the 7th German Army Corps reported in a secret document "Conclusions from the Experience of the Great Offensive of the Russians at Stalingrad." The essence of this document in evaluating operations of the troops of the Red Army is the following:

1. *Preparation*. Excellent camouflaging of all units of the strategic concentration, especially the concentration of tank formations.
   - Successful radio silence of the attacking units, especially of tanks, carried out on a large scale.
   - Movements only at night.
   - An extremely careful feeling out of all the fronts by the method of ordinary actions of shock detachments (strength up to a regiment) separated by long intervals of time for the purpose of determining precisely the weak places on the front. This reconnaissance in force was particularly intense two days before the beginning of the offensive.
   - Renunciation of artillery fire for adjustment.
   - The intensification of air attacks against the bases of supply and against the staffs for many days before the beginning of the attack.

2. *Execution*. The rapid concentration of forces in the main direction; brief, concentrated artillery preparations, with commitment of the normal number of heavy guns and a large number of rocket guns.
   - The offensive of the infantry was supported by only a small number of tanks.
   - The first thing after the breakthrough was the commitment of tank brigades (corps), with deep operational objectives; in this case, the tank brigades cooperated with the cavalry.
   - Maneuvered and firm direction of troops in a situation whose rapid development was surprising even for the enemy.

3. *Tactical observations*. When a breach was made in the main defense zone, the accompanying infantry, for the first time, was mounted on moving tanks and was carried at a fast pace to the forward edge of the defense or forward to the points of penetration so that, by exploiting the gains of the tanks, they had an opportunity to advance without delay.

   The tank units committed to battle and having operational objectives are followed closely by the infantry units—for example, one infantry battalion to one tank battalion.

4. *Tactical conclusions*. Tanks breaking through into the main defense zone should be subjected to the concentrated fire of all the weapons of the infantry and artillery—independently of the

attacks made by antitank guns—in order to inflict as heavy losses as possible upon the tank-borne troops.

● The enemy infantry breaking through on tanks should be immediately subjected to a counterattack by the local reserves. Besides, our infantry should always bear in mind that the field of vision of the tanks of the enemy is very limited and that it is not necessary to overestimate the tank danger.

● The effectiveness of the reinforced tank groups breaking through into the depths of the area of battle is decreased considerably if we can separate and hold up the sensitive infantry which follows on trucks behind the tanks. By this means, it is possible for each rear unit on the defensive to delay a great deal the breakthroughs of the enemy or even to stop him. In these cases, we should always bear in mind that as soon as infantry separated from the tanks is attacked even by weaker German forces, it can be routed and destroyed.

It is proposed that we send these conclusions to all subordinate units.

Editor's Notes

1. The Rumanian formations occupying both flanks of the 6th German Army were a mixed bag with regard to military value. While the troops were up to strength and undoubtedly personally brave, the officer corps was ill prepared to lead a modern combat force; the formations were underequipped; and the national motivation for involvement in the struggle was lacking. Particularly absent was the lack of a modern antitank gun.

   It was only on November 30 that Hitler finally sought to remedy that problem. See *Kriegstagebuch des OKW (War Diary of the OKW)*, Band 1942, p. 1054. A Rumanian infantry division supposedly contained 13,100 men and up to 60 AT guns. The average of the latter was much lower. A Rumanian cavalry division contained 7,600 men and was somewhat better equipped with antitank guns. The problem, however, was not in numbers of antitank guns, but rather in the quality of the weapons. Many units were equipped with 37 mm antitank guns, which were hopelessly outmoded against Soviet armor. See Kehrig, p. 667, Appendix 9, for a breakdown of Rumanian forces.

2. German forces had nothing like 1,666 tanks even if one supposed the previously abandoned wrecks counted for some advantage in positional warfare. See Kehrig, *Stalingrad*, p. 665, Anlage 5.

3. This was the 48th Panzer Corps with the 1st Rumanian and 22nd German Panzer Divisions. A great deal of faith was placed in this formation, but as previously indicated, it was severely understrength.

4. An order of battle for the three Fronts may be found in the Appendix.

5. The Don Front was commanded by Lieutenant General K. K. Rokossovskii. The Southwestern Front was commanded by Colonel General N. F. Vatutin.

6. The 5th Tank Army was commanded by Lieutenant General P. L. Romanenko.

7. The 21st Army was commanded by Lieutenant General I. M. Chistiakov.

8. The 65th Army was commanded by Lieutenant General P. I. Batov.

9. The 24th Army was commanded by Major General I. V. Galinin.

10. The 57th Army was commanded by Major General F. I. Tolbulkhin, and the 51st Army was commanded by Major General N. I. Trufanov.

11. The 62nd Army was commanded by Lieutenant General V. I. Chuikov.

12. The 64th Army was commanded by Major General M. S. Shumilov.

13. The 28th Army was commanded by Lieutenant General V. F. Gerasimenko.

14. Antonescu directed a personal appeal to Hitler that perhaps prompted the order to the 48th

Panzer Corps to try and save the encircled Rumanian formations. *IVOVSS* vol. 3, p. 36, lists 27,000 prisoners.

15. Eremenko later stated that it was he and not *Stavka* that believed the German thrust would come from the area around Kotelnikovo. *Stavka* and Vasilevskii indicated Tormosin and the bridgehead on the Chir River as the most likely jump-off points for the relief effort. However, Stalin did order reinforcements to the area in the form of three tank regiments (60 tanks). See A. Eremenko, *Stalingrad* (Moscow: *Voenizdat*, 1961), pp. 393–95.

16. None of these officers were marshals at the time of the battle, but they were subsequently promoted. Thus, the author is speaking in the current sense.

Stalingrad represents a striking achievement for Soviet armored forces. Through the massed use of tank formations, the Red Army achieved a depth of penetration not seen in previous battles with Germany and its allies. The utilization of a special combined arms formation, the 5th Tank Army, ensured the power and speed necessary to cover the distances to Kalach. Past efforts by the 1st and 4th Tank armies during the defensive fighting had failed to find either a doctrine or an organizational structure that matched the successes of the German Panzer divisions. For the 5th Tank Army, plans were laid and war games conducted prior to final concentration. Sufficient strength was allocated by Stavka, and as a result, Stalingrad became an important first step in the maturity of Soviet tank troops. The lessons mentioned in this section were learned the hard way, but learned they were—and increasingly effective tactical operations became the rule, not the surprise—Ed.

5

Action of the Mobile Group of the 5th Tank Army in a Breakthrough

Conditions under which the Mobile Troops Are Committed into a Breach

The commitment of a mobile group into a breach is a complicated stage of the operation and requires careful preparation and a great deal of work in the organization of cooperation of the large mobile formations with the attached supporting units of reinforcement and the large rifle formations effecting the breakthrough.[1] Hence, for carrying out the preparatory work for commitment of the mobile group into the breach, it is necessary to allow sufficient time (3 to 5 days and sometimes more).

The preparatory work for commitment in a breakthrough starts immediately after the arrival of the first echelon of the staff of the mobile group in the area of concentration. By this time, the commander of the mobile group usually receives from the higher command the general decision and the mission of the mobile group. Without waiting for the completion of the concentration, the commander of the mobile group, with the commanders of the large formations and some of the commanders of the staff, goes to the area where commitment into the breach will take place, carries out a reconnaissance of the intermediate position area and the march routes to it, and also gets a general idea of the situation from the commanders of the units of combined arms on the sector where the commitment into the breach is to take place.

The main work is the planning of cooperation by the combined arms formations on the sector where commitment into the breach is to take place. The main work in the planning of cooperation with the units of combined arms and artillery in the period when one moves into the breach, and with aviation in the period of operation in the depths of enemy defenses, is carried out while the mobile units are in the intermediate position area. At this time, one prepares the material, plans for supplying the operation with material and equipment, and assembles and studies all the data pertaining to the situation.

In the period of preparation, one should determine the intermediate position area and the jump-off line for deployment and beginning of the movement into the breach and the route of movement of the large formations to the jump-off line, indicating the time by which the march route should be free of troops and the rear of the units of combined arms executing the breakthrough.

The cooperation of the mobile group with the unit of combined arms is planned by the commanders of the Army (or Front if the mobile group carries out the mission on the scale of a Front).

One of the most responsible moments is the selection of the time of the beginning of the movement of the mobile group into the breach. If the mobile group begins the movement into the breach before the enemy defenses have been completely broken through, it may be drawn out into a combat of combined arms, or it may be obliged to wait for the execution of the breakthrough, and during this time it could be under the action of the fire of aviation and long-range artillery. When the mobile group goes into battle, it can, of course, ensure a great tactical victory and hasten the breakthrough. However, what actually results in nearly all cases is that the mobile group suffers such heavy losses that it is weakened for the execution of its basic mission.

If movement into the breach starts too late, the enemy may have time to bring up his immediate reserves or carry out a regrouping of its forces and equipment in order to close the breach that has been made or organize a solid defense on one of the rear lines which the mobile group has to break through independently. In this case, the mobile group must deploy for battle before going in to the strategic depths of the enemy defenses.

The command of the mobile group should take special care to ensure maximum rapidity and decisive penetration into the breach and freedom of action in the depths of the enemy defenses. Hence, during the time of planning for cooperation, one fixes a line in the depths of the defenses of the enemy, after the seizure of which the mobile group begins movement into the breach. We prepare beforehand the roads and the cross-country routes of march, organize traffic regulation over these routes, and determine the method of passing through our own troops.

The beginning of movement of the mobile group into the breach should be coordinated with the actions of the units of combined arms effecting the breakthrough so that the mobile group will be on the line of the advancing infantry at the moment when it completes the crossing of the main defense zone of the enemy and the seizure of the area of artillery positions. In case of a well-organized and firmly held defense, it will be advantageous to commit the mobile units into the breach after the seizure of the second defense zone by the units of combined arms.

The time for *commitment* of the mobile group into the breach is usually determined by the commander of the armies (front). However, as experience has shown, this time will usually be the moment rather of *preparation* for the movement, because the precise time of the movement can be determined only during the breakthrough itself. Hence, in addition to the time for commitment into the breach, it is also good to agree on the signal upon which the movement of the groups begins. At the beginning of the movement into the breach, the commander of the mobile group and the commanders of its formations direct their small units, moving in the combat formations themselves.

The zone for commitment of the mobile group into the breach should assure freedom of maneuverability with an opportunity to deploy for battle with at least a part of the forces, if the situation requires it. In order to meet this requirement it will be desirable for the tank (mechanized) corps to have a zone of 6 to 10 kilometers on the front and not less than 2 to 4 routes of march; they should also have on each flank a zone of 3 to 5 kilometers for protecting the flanks from mortar fire and observed effective artillery fire. In cases when the commitment into the breach is effected in broken terrain, making it difficult to observe and to conduct aimed artillery fire, the width of the front of the breakthrough may be less. But in this case, the mobile group must go into the breach in deeply echeloned formations, something that naturally renders maneuvering more difficult and increases the time required in deploying for battle and for the passage of the mobile group through the zone of tactical defenses of the enemy.

Experience shows that the enemy usually tries to close up a breach made on his front, to gain time for the shifting of strategic reserves into the area of the breach. Hence, in order to ensure successful commitment of the mobile groups into the breach, the commander of the army (front) must, in the period of the preparation for the operation and the planning of cooperation, consider measures for widening the frontage of the breakthrough and neutralizing the fire weapons of the enemy on his flanks. He must also take measures for delaying the approach of reserves from the rear.

In order to secure as much freedom of action as possible for the mobile units, the units of combined arms should strive not only to effect an overall breakthrough into the tactical depths of the enemy defenses but also to widen at once the frontage by operating toward the flanks of the enemy, thus protecting the echelon for exploiting the breakthrough from enemy flank counterattacks. To have the mobile groups move at a normal rate of speed when committed to the breach, it is necessary to plan for restoration and repair of torn-up roads and bridges, for laying out cross-country march routes, and for the method of separating the march route of the mobile group from the artillery units and rear forces. The security of the route of movement of the echelon for exploiting the breach should be assigned to specially detailed engineer units subordinate to the commander of the mobile group.

For the neutralization of the artillery and mortars of the enemy on the flank, for the planning of a box barrage for the zone of movement, and for the accompanying of the mobile group into the depths of enemy defenses, it is advisable to assign a special artillery group. The forward observation posts of this artillery should be in tanks equipped with radio sets accompanying the leading units of the mobile groups.

The cooperation of the mobile group with the supporting aviation is usually planned on a front or army scale on the basis of the stages of the operation. In the period of preparation for commitment into the breach, in addition to covering the concentration and the jump-off area of the mobile group and upon the request of the commander of the mobile group, aviation will conduct reconnaissance and take aerial photographs of the zone of commitment of the mobile group over the whole depth of the enemy defenses and will secure information concerning the areas of concentration of enemy reserves.

In the period of action of the mobile group in the depths of enemy defenses, aviation should conduct special reconnaissance for the mobile group and, jointly with the group, strike the approaching reserves of the enemy, at the same time covering it from enemy aviation.

The most effective cooperation with aviation, as combat experience has proved, may be realized if in the period of action of the mobile group in the depths of enemy defenses one assigns to it a part of the aviation, and in particular, combat–support aviation. A part of the fighter aviation should be able to land on airfields in the area of the action of the mobile group in the rear of the enemy, organizing from there the covering of the mobile group. In all cases, a representative (preferably a commander of the aviation attached to or supporting the mobile group) with the necessary means of signal communications should be with the staff of the mobile group. By this means, in the period of action in the depths, the commander of this group can, through him, assign to aviation additional missions at any moment. The basic missions of aviation, however, should be assigned in the period when cooperation is planned.

The mobile group will strive to penetrate as quickly as possible into the depths of the enemy defenses, and hence, as a rule, its formations should not engage in combat with separate centers of defense and centers of resistance located on the routes of movement but should block them. Upon encountering large tank units of the enemy, the mobile group sends against them some antitank artillery and units of tanks for action from ambush and some antitank infantry weapons. Having covered itself with these means, the mobile group outflanks the enemy tanks with its main forces and strikes a blow first of all at his infantry to isolate it from the enemy tanks, paralyze its action, and deprive it of routes of approach. After the tanks of the enemy have used up their supplies, lost their ability to maneuver, and have been partially destroyed by our antitank weapons, artillery, and aviation, they may be definitively crushed by the combined efforts of our tanks, rifle troops, antitank weapons, and aviation.

These theoretical statements pertaining to the employment of mobile groups verified by the experience of the Great Patriotic War are known to the commanding personnel of the Red Army. It would not be necessary to disseminate them if in combat practice there had not been cases when large tank or mechanized units, intended for the exploitation of successes, were used for effecting a breakthrough jointly with the infantry and even independently of it, as a result of which they were exhausted prematurely and could not exploit the successes. All this shows that the preparation, organization, and technique of committing mobile units into breaches and the exploiting of successes have not been studied sufficiently either by units of combined arms or by the tank commanders.

The flank blows of the mobile units in the initial period of the offensive operations of the Southwestern and Stalingrad Fronts for the encircle-ment and crushing of the German–Fascist group to the west of Stalingrad gave convincing examples of the planning of a breakthrough and its exploitation by large mobile groups. One of the characteristic and instructive examples in this respect is the operation of the mobile group of the 5th Tank Army, and from it we can seek the practical solution of the theoretical problems mentioned above.

Missions of the 5th Tank Army and the Planning of the Operation

The Situation at the Beginning of the Operation

The Southwestern Front, having operated on the enveloping flank of our forces, consisted of the 63rd (later the 1st Guards), the 21st Combined Arms, and the 5th Tank Armies. The latter was shifted from the Briansk Front and, toward November 6, completed concentration on the north bank of the Don River. The Army had the following in its makeup: six rifle divisions, the 1st and 26th Tank Corps, the 8th Guards Tank Brigade, two separate tank battalions, the 8th Cavalry Corps, and the 8th Separate Motorcycle Regiment.[2]

For the reinforcement of the Army the following were assigned: nine artillery regiments from the reserves of the *Stavka*; eight destroyer–antitank artillery regiments; five *PVO* artillery regiments of antiaircraft defense; an antiaircraft artillery division; four mortar regiments; four Guards Mortar regiments; seven Guards Mortar battalions (M–30); and other means of reinforcement. In addition to this, we attached to the Army three combat air support regiments.

The Mission of the 5th Tank Army

The 5th Tank Army, operating on the left wing of the Southwestern Front, had as its mission the effecting of a breakthrough of the enemy defenses in the direction of State Farm No. 2 and Independent State Farm No. 86 and, operating subsequently toward Perelazovskii and Kalach together with units of the 21st Army, to crush the 3rd Rumanian Army and the approaching operational reserves of the enemy. On the third day of the operations, the 5th Tank Army, by debouchment into the Kalach-Richkovskii area, was to complete the encirclement of the Stalingrad group of the enemy in cooperation with the troops of the Stalingrad Front. For proportionally covering the operations from the west as we advanced in the direction of Kalach and Richkovskii, the 5th Tank Army was to hold with a part of its forces, a front along the Chir River on the Bokovskaia-Nizhne–Chirskaia sector.

In accordance with reconnaissance data the Army had before its front the 9th, 14th, and 5th Rumanian Infantry Divisions. These divisions occupied positions with good engineer installations and a system of company and battalion centers of resistance; their forward edge of defense being on the line of Bolshoi, the south slope of Elevations 220.0 and 210.1, and Bazkovskii.

At a distance of 2 to 4 kilometers behind the forward edge, the enemy had previously prepared a second defense zone, equipped in the same manner as the first, but weaker in engineer installations. On the line of Pronin, Peschanii (Ust–Medveditskii), and Perelazovskii, in accordance with reconnaissance data, we assumed the presence of up to two infantry divisions. Actually, however, in the course of the operations on this sector, the Army fought the Rumanian 7th Cavalry Division (in dismounted formation), units of the 1st Rumanian Panzer Division, and the 22nd German Panzer Division. The total depth of the operational defenses of the enemy was 50 kilometers. The main defense zone had, on an average three to four light earth-and-timber pillboxes to each kilometer of front, covered by mine fields, and on certain sectors barbed-wire entanglements.

On the sector of operation of the 26th Tank Corps, the enemy had up to 30 artillery antitank batteries, about 450 machine guns, and up to 150 tanks and armored cars, giving on an average up to eight guns and 20 machine guns to a kilometer of front.

The terrain in the area of the breakthrough was an open steppe, broken by a large number of ravines. The lack of roads and the presence of a large number of steep upgrades and downgrades hindered the movement of tanks and especially of motor vehicle transport; then, too, the absence of natural cover required strong protection by antiaircraft guns and aviation.

On the right, the area of operations was covered by the line of the Chir River, on which the enemy was able to organize a defense. On the other hand, with the capture of this line, the attacking units could cover themselves on the right flank in carrying out the forcing of the Don River and the capture of Kalach.

When our troops debouched at Station Chir they cut one of the main railway lines feeding the Stalingrad group of the enemy. When our tank group moved into the area of Kalach and Rychkovskii jointly with the troops operating northwest and southwest of Stalingrad, it had an opportunity to surround the enemy group in the bend of the Don River.

Preparation of the Operation

In accordance with the decision of the Army command, on November 12 the troops took up their jump-off position for an offensive, having in the first echelon four divisions, three of which were used in the direction of the main blow. In the second echelon, there were two rifle divisions.

The echelon for exploitation of the breakthrough consisted of the 1st and 26th Tank Corps (without the 216th Tank Brigade), the 8th Cavalry Corps, and the 8th Motorcycle Regiment.[3] The main shock force of the echelon was the tank corps, whose mission it was to move into the breach made by the rifle divisions, to crush the operational reserves, and on the third day of the operations after having captured the town of Kalach, to move to the Don River on the Kalach-Nizhne–Chirskaia Front and establish a connection with the troops of the Stalingrad Front.

Following the 1st Tank Corps, the 8th Cavalry Corps jointly with the rifle divisions, was to create a solid front of defense along the Chir River from Bokovskaia up to Niizhne–Chirskaia, covering in this way the action of the tank corps from the southwest and the west.

From the means of reinforcement the tank corps received the following: two destroyer antitank regiments, two *PVO* artillery regiments, and two Guards Mortar regiments.

On the front of the breakthrough of the 5th Tank Army, the density of guns was 35 to 50 guns to one kilometer of front. Four gun artillery regiments constituted the Army artillery group. The Guards Mortar battalion of M-30s and the Guards Mortar regiments made up the Army mortar group, which was used on the front of the 47th Guards and 119th Rifle Divisions.

As groups of direct support for the rifle troops we used the following: the 216th Tank Brigade (from the 26th Tank Corps) and the 510th and 511th Flamethrower Tank Battalions.

For purposes of concealment, the concentration areas of the 5th Tank Army were 30 to 60 kilometers from the front line. The movements of the troops were carried out exclusively at night. The masking of the areas of concentration was obligatory. All radio traffic was forbidden. In spite of the fact that in taking up the jump-off position for the offensive the troops had to cross to the south bank of the Don River, the deployment of the primary forces of the Army was, in the main, a surprise for the enemy, even though enemy air reconnaissance noticed the intense movement along the roads and over the crossings, and the presence of new units (especially cavalry units) on the south bank of the Don. From November 10 enemy aviation subjected the inhabited localities, the areas of concentration of the units and the crossings, to regular aerial bombardment; however, the scale of concentration was not revealed to the enemy.

For the purpose of masking the regrouping of the forces, we carried out the following measures: Before the front of the Army, we deployed the 47th Guards and 119th Rifle Divisions and left in place the combat security forces of the 14th Guards Division, previously on the defensive in this sector. In carrying out all the preparations and planning of the operation, we observed the strictest secrecy. The command personnel were informed of the plan of operations only within the limits of their missions and functions. Thus, the preliminary decision of the Commander of the 26th Tank Corps was known only to the commanders of the brigades, their assistants for the political units, and the chiefs of staffs. In the staff of the Corps, the only ones knowing about the decision were the Deputy Commander of the Corps, the Chief of Staff, his deputy for the political unit, and the chief of the operations and training section. The mission of the tank corps was not made known to all of the personnel until the eve of the attack on November 18.

The engineer preparations of the base of operations for the offensive by the troops of the first echelon were also carried out exclusively at night. As a result of all of these measures, we succeeded in effecting complete strategic surprise. From the statements of prisoners, we found out the amount of information the enemy had concerning preparations for the offensive; but the grouping of our forces, the direction of the main blow, and the time of the attack were not known to the enemy. In addition to this, the enemy apparently was too late in obtaining information pertaining to the preparation of the offensive, and hence, he did not have the time for regrouping his forces and taking countermeasures.

From November 12–16, the main task of the Army was replenishing supplies. Simultaneously, the tank corps, from their jump-off position, which was 15 to 20 kilometers from the front line, carried on reconnaissance of the routes of movement to the forward edge of the defenses of the enemy. The reconnaissance of the locality up to the forward edge was conducted by all the personnel of the echelon for the exploitation of the breakthrough, down to tank commanders. In addition to this, special column leaders were trained.

The data of all kinds gathered by reconnaissance gave information not only concerning the system of defense of the forward edge of the enemy but also his reserves farther back. We ascertained that the divisions of the first echelon had before them only enemy combat security. Hence, for the purpose of finding out the real forward edge of the defense and misleading the enemy as to the scale of the offensive being prepared, we undertook reconnaissance in force on November 17, with reinforced battalions from each rifle division of the first echelon. During the morning, we started a methodical processing of the artillery targets assigned for the support of each of the battalions. In the second half of the day, the battalions assumed the offensive, drove away the combat security during the night of the November 18, and advanced to the forward edge of the defenses of the enemy. On the following morning, the battalions renewed their offensive, but upon encountering strong resistance and enemy counterattacks, they began to dig in on the lines reached.

Hence, we reached the goal set for reconnaissance. By reconnaissance in force, we ascertained the real forward edge of the defenses of the enemy, and we learned from the statements of prisoners that the enemy had the impression that our offensive had failed.

The Course of Operations and Actions of the Tank Corps in the Breakthrough

At 8:50 A.M., on November 19, after 18 minutes of artillery preparation, units of the 5th Tank Army assumed the offensive along the whole front. The divisions of the first echelon, advancing in the main direction, encountered weak resistance on the forward edge of the defenses. As we advanced into the depths, the resistance of the enemy increased, and the movement of the rifle troops was slowed up. On the whole, the attack of the right flank of the 14th Guards Rifle Division was unsuccessful.

Upon the signal of the beginning of the attack by the rifle troops, the tank corps started from their jump-off positions in the following formation: the *1st Tank Corps*—in two columns, having in the right column the 117th Tank Brigade, the 33rd Destroyer Antitank Artillery Regiment, the 89th Tank Brigade and in the left column, the 159th Tank Brigade, the Corps Command, and the 44th Motorized Rifle Brigade (the *PVO* regiment of antiaircraft defense assigned to the Corps was distributed by batteries and by brigades); and the *26th Tank Corps* along four march routes in two echelons.

The 1st Tank Corps was assigned for its action a sector of about 8 to 9 kilometers on the front, and the 26th Tank Corps, one of 12 to 14 kilometers. Hence, the total width of the sectors of action of the tank corps was about 20 to 22 kilometers. Each of them went into the breach itself on sectors of 5 to 6 kilometers, having their inner flanks adjacent to each other and having on their outer flanks a free zone of 5 to 6 kilometers.

The tank formations moved ahead. The motorized riflemen of the 1st Tank Corps moved along the left march route under cover of tank brigades moving along the right march route. In the 26th Tank Corps, the motorized rifle brigades moved in the second echelon along all the march routes. The antitank artillery in the 1st Tank Corps moved directly behind the tank brigade along the right flank march route, and in the 26th Corps, it moved along the left march route. By this method, we had cover from the flank tank attacks of the enemy not only for each tank corps separately but for all the tank group of the echelon used for exploiting the breakthrough.

At 1:00 P.M., the tank corps reached the line of the attacking rifle troops.[4] By this time the defenses of the enemy had still not been breached completely. The tank corps, after breaking through the defenses on the march, began a rapid advance toward the south, although the 26th Tank Corps had to change its combat formation, rearranging it to harmonize with the breakthrough of the defenses of the enemy.

The attack of the 26th Tank Corps was more powerful and impetuous; after crushing in its sector of movement units of the 5th and 14th Rumanian Infantry Divisions of the enemy by dawn on November 20th, it had captured Novotsaritsinskii and Perelazovskii where it crushed the staff of the 5th Rumanian Army Corps and captured a large amount of booty. The tanks, upon approaching Perelazovskii, opened fire while on the move, and the motorized riflemen, by riding on the machines, quickly got within range of rifle and machine-gun fire and captured

Perelazovskii from the flanks and rear. The attack of the Corps was so heavy and impetuous that the dumbfounded enemy, offering very little resistance, threw away his weapons and began to surrender in groups. The 19th Tank Brigade, moving on the left flank of the Corps, was held by the enemy in the area of Korotkovskii and Zhirki and was not able to join the Corps in Perelazovskii until the morning of November 21. The 1st Tank Corps operated in a less impetuous manner and could not overcome through movement the strong resistance which it encountered at Peschanyi (Ust-Medveditskii).

The enemy was demoralized by the operations of the tank corps, lost control, and began a disorderly withdrawal toward the south. A considerable part of his group surrendered. The enemy, in trying to stop the advance of the forces of the Army, threw into the area of Peschanyi a part of the 22nd German Panzer Division and some small units of the 15th Rumanian Infantry Division. Into the area of Pronin, the enemy shifted the 7th Cavalry Division in dismounted formation. The enemy's 1st Rumanian Panzer Division began to move toward Verkhne-Fomikhinskii to execute a counterattack toward the west to cut off our rifle troops from the tanks.

Hence, on the first day of the operation, we broke through the enemy defenses; and units of the 5th Tank Army crushed the 14th and 5th Rumanian Infantry Divisions, but the mission laid down in the plan of operations of the Army were carried out only by the 47th Guards Rifle Division and the 26th Tank Corps. The reason for this was that the 1st Tank Corps and the 8th Cavalry Corps, instead of going around the enemy in Peschani and exploiting the success in depth, engaged the enemy in battle and slowed up the rate of exploitation of the breakthrough. The reason for the holding up of the right flank of the mobile group was also the poor cooperation between the 1st Tank and the 8th Cavalry Corps. Reconnaissance was unable to discover in due time the presence of the 22nd German Panzer Division; hence, clashing with its units in the area of Peschanii was to a certain extent unexpected.

At dawn on November 20, units of the 5th Tank Army renewed the offensive for the purpose of exploiting the gains of the first day and jointly with units of the 21st Army, destroying the 3rd Rumanian Army.

The 1st Tank and the 8th Cavalry Corps and the 8th Motorcycle Regiment fought all day for Peschanyi and toward evening captured it. The enemy began to fall back slowly toward the south. On the evening of November 20, the 1st Tank Corps, having encountered stubborn enemy resistance, changed its direction toward Bolshaia Donshchinka. Due to the absence of roads, the Corps moved along a single march route.

The 26th Tank Corps spent the whole day clearing the enemy out of the region of Perelazovskii and carried on combat with units of the 1st Rumanian Panzer Division, despite the fact that, by utilizing the delay in the movement of our forces, the Rumanian divisions could have escaped from the blows of the 21st Army by moving south.

Throughout the day the advance of the Army was held up by hard fighting in the area of Peschanii. On the left flank of the Army, the counterattacks of the 1st Rumanian Panzer Division did not give the 124th Rifle Division an opportunity to join up with units of the 21st Army and surround the Rumanian units.

On November 21, the troops of the Army were ordered to accelerate the execution of the mission laid down in the plan of operation, and the 124th and 119th Rifle Divisions were ordered to make an attack toward the southeast and join up with units of the 21st Army.

On the night of November 20–21, the 1st Tank Corps executed a march, and by the morning the leading elements reached Bolshaia Donshchinka, where the Corps encountered the strong resistance of the 22nd German Panzer Division and the remains of the shattered Rumanian divisions. Without engaging in battle, the Corps turned toward Perelazovskii and Lipovski, destroying on its way the trains and the withdrawing units of the enemy. Toward the close of the day, a part of the Corps was concentrated in the region of Lipovski, where it refueled.

At 1:00 P.M. the 26th Tank Corps, after joining with the 19th Tank Brigade, which had moved forward, began a swift advance toward Kalach and destroyed the approaching enemy reserves and those units withdrawing under the blows of the 21st Army. The right flank divisions with cavalry and tanks reached Gorbatovskii and by about midnight finished clearing out the enemy and then dug in, thus making it possible for the left flank of the 1st Guards Army to accelerate its advance toward the south.

Throughout the day, the 47th Guards Rifle Division pursued the enemy, who was withdrawing in panic. After capturing Varlamov, the Division began a rapid advance toward Chernyshevskaia. The 8th Cavalry Corps engaged in some hard fighting with the 22nd German Panzer Division, while slowly pressing forward from Peschanyi to the south.

The divisions of the left wing of the Army, after successfully repelling the counterattacks of the enemy, did some hard fighting toward the close of the day for the capture of Korotkovskii and Zhirki.

Hence, the mission laid down in the plan of operations for the three days was not carried out, because the enemy group in the center of the 5th Tank Army on the region of Bolshaia Donshchinka held up the debouchment of the 8th Cavalry Corps on the Chir River, and through local attacks, the enemy held up the advance of the left flank of the Army. Consequently, on November 21, the action of the Army consisted chiefly of widening the breach.

The tank corps advanced slowly, even though they did not encounter

Battle for Stalingrad

any organized resistance in the direction of their movement. The 1st Tank Corps continued to lag behind, whereas the 26th Tank Corps, toward the close of the day, was fighting on the Plesistovskii-Ostrov line and by a night attack, captured Ostrov. The 1st Tank Corps concentrated in Lipovski and refueled. Toward the close of the November 21, there was a gap of 30 to 40 kilometers between the two tank corps and close cooperation between them was not successful.

The tasks of the Army on November 22, were to advance rapidly to the line of the Chir River in order to prevent the enemy from bringing up reserves and, at the same time, to cover further action of the tank corps in the direction of Stalingrad from the southwest. In carrying out this mission on the night and the day of November 22, the tank corps moved quickly. By the end of the day, the 1st Tank Corps had concentrated in the Tuzov and Zrianinskii areas and had dispatched reconnaissance parties in the direction of Surovikino and Rychkovskii. The 26th Tank Corps reached the Don in the area of Kalach and crossed the 19th Tank Brigade onto the east bank of the river. By the close of November 22, the Tank Corps were even with each other, and the gap between them was closed.

A significant episode occurred in the 26th Tank Corps in the capture of a crossing over the Don River. After seizing the area of Ostrov after 12:00 A.M. November 22, the Commander of the Corps decided by taking advantage of the darkness of night to capture by surprise a crossing on the Don. For this purpose, he detailed Lieutenant Colonel Filippov, the commander of the 14th Motorized Rifle Brigade, to lead a forward detachment made up of two companies of the Motorized Rifle Brigade, 5 tanks of the 157th Tank Brigade, and some armored cars from the 15th Reconnaissance Battalion.[5]

The forward elements, moving into the rear dispositions of the enemy on machines with the headlights switched on, approached the crossing. The ruse was successful; the Germans took the column for their own and allowed it to reach the crossing without opposition. After crushing the guards at the crossing, the detachment captured it and organized for defense. Meanwhile the main forces of the Corps were engaged in combat on the line of the Collective Farm Pobeda Oktiabr, where the enemy, based on a previously prepared antitank area, offered stubborn resistance.

The leading detachment tried to capture the town of Kalach on the march, but, upon encountering stubborn resistance, it assumed the offensive at the crossing and conducted battle under encirclement until the arrival of the main forces. Hence, due to the successful ruse and the impetuosity of the action, a crossing on the Don River was captured and held, an operation that considerably facilitated the subsequent action for the capture of Kalach.

On November 22, the 159th Rifle Division on the right flank captured Kamenka and approached Bokovskaia. The 21st Cavalry Division (of the 8th Cavalry Corps), while pursuing the withdrawing enemy, approached Verkhne-Maksai but upon orders of the commander, turned toward the south and began to push into the area of Chernyshevskaia to a junction with the main forces of the Corps. Toward 3:00 P.M., the 47th Guards Rifle Division debouched on the Chir River, captured Demin and Chernyshevshaia, and proceeded to fortify the new line.

In the morning, the 8th Motorcycle Regiment and a company of tanks carried out an impetuous attack against Oblivskaia. Although the Regiment could not capture the place, it succeeded in destroying 25 airplanes parked on the airfield. By the close of the day, the Regiment began to concentrate in Perelazovskii, destroying on its way the withdrawing Rumanian units and reserves of the enemy.

The 119th Rifle Division captured Korotkovskii, and in the predawn of November 23, it captured Zhirki, continuing the offensive with the mission of joining up with the units of the 21st Army in the area Verkhne-Cherenskii.

During the night, the 124th Rifle Division captured Karagichev, and toward the end of the day, stormed and captured Verkhne-Fomikhinskii. There, after uniting with units of the 21st Army, it completed the encirclement of the remains of the 3rd Rumanian Army.

The enemy east of Verkhne-Fomikhinskii, feeling that the ring of encirclement would soon be closed, broke out at 12:00 P.M. with a group of 30 tanks, 68 machines, and infantry from the area of Zhirki. They joined up with units of the 22nd German Panzer Division in the area of Bolshaia Donshchinka, where this group of the enemy obstructed, as it did before, the debouchment of our units on the Chir River. For its liquidation, the commander of the Army ordered the 346th Rifle Division and the 8th Guards Tank Brigade to make a night march.

On November 23, the main forces of the 1st Tank Corps put itself in order in the area of concentration. With a part of its forces, the corps made an attack toward Surovikino and Richkovskii. By 4:00 P.M., the 26th Tank Corps had completely mopped up Kalach.

The 8th Motorcycle Regiment, operating in separate detachments, destroyed the rear and the withdrawing units of the enemy groups at Bolshaia Donshchinka.

The 159th Rifle and the 47th Guards Rifle Division dug in on the lines reached. The attempts of the 159th Rifle Division to capture Bokovskaia were not crowned with success, because the enemy brought up 20 to 30 tanks and a regiment of German infantry.

The 8th Cavalry Corps, giving up the unsuccessful frontal attacks of the enemy in the area of Bolshaia Donshchinka, undertook to bypass this group. By the close of the day the corps reached Naumov, Petroka, and

Arzhanovskii, throwing the enemy back toward the south.

The 346 Rifle Division, by a night march, reached Bolshaia Donshchinka and jointly with the 8th Guards Tank Brigade engaged in combat for the capture of this inhabited locality. After capturing Zhirki, at 2:00 P.M. the 119th Rifle Division reached Verkhne-Cherenskii, where it crushed the withdrawing column of the 1st Rumanian Panzer Division and joined up with units of the 21st Army to complete the definitive encirclement of the units of the 3rd Rumanian Army. The 124th Rifle Division also joined up with units of the 21st Army. The encircled Rumanian units laid down their arms.

Hence, the three-day mission by the 5th Tank Army for the defeat of the 3rd Rumanian Army and the encirclement of the Stalingrad group was carried out in a period of five days. The rifle divisions (with the exception of the 47th Guards and 159th) and the 8th Cavalry Corps could not reach the Chir River line because of the enemy's stubborn defenses in the area of Bolshaia Donshchinka. On the morning of November 24, the Army started the liquidation of this group. As a result, the 22nd German Panzer Division was finally destroyed, and only remnants of it were able to break through on the morning of November 25 to Chernyshevskaia.

On November 25, the rifle divisions began to debouch on the Chir River for organizing a defense on this line. On November 24, the 1st Tank Corps advanced in the direction of Surovikino, and the 26th Tank Corps was reassigned to the Commander of the 21st Army. Later on, after the capture of Sokarevka, the 26th Tank Corps operated jointly with units of this Army for the encirclement of the Stalingrad group. In these battles, the units of the Corps were employed in the majority of cases as groups for direction support of the rifle troops.

General Conclusions

Taking the operations of the 5th Tank Army as an example, we may draw certain general conclusions concerning the character of the actions of the mobile group in the operational depths of the enemy.

We must suppose that on the first day of the commitment of the mobile group into the breach, the combat actions will generally consist of clashes with the local reserves of the enemy approaching the area of the breach. The mobile group should destroy these reserves as it moves along and complete its action by concentrating in some area in the rear of the enemy to put itself in order.

The mobile group operating in the depths of the enemy defenses should take full advantage of its maneuverability without allowing itself to be drawn into a prolonged battle with small strongpoints and enemy groups trying to hold up its advance. The centers of resistance should either be bypassed by the formations of the mobile group or destroyed from the march. Then, too, it is necessary, of course, while in movement to change the march formation for executing detours or for deploying parts of the forces for attack.

If the commander of a mobile group or the commanders of large formations get timely information from their reconnaissance concerning such centers of resistance, the loss of time in executing detour maneuvers may be reduced to a minimum. The decision to bypass the center of resistance should be made in due time. If this is not done, an unexpected clash with the enemy will necessarily lead to a reduction in the rate of advance. In the operation considered, the 1st Tank and 8th Cavalry Corps had an unexpected encounter with units of the 22nd German Panzer Division in the area of Peschanii, engaging it in battle instead of remaining under cover and bypassing the enemy. In doing this we lost more than a day, allowing the enemy to put his disorganized units in order and bring up reserves from the rear; later on, this delay showed its effect by slowing up the operations as a whole. As a result of the loss of time by the 26th Tank Corps in Perelazovskii and in refueling and bringing up the 19th Tank Brigade, several units of the enemy succeeded in escaping the blows of the 21st Army.

It may happen that the enemy will succeed in concentrating his mobile reserves in the area of the breakthrough and that by means of these he will try to close the breach and even stop the offensive of the units of combined arms. In this case the mobile group should at first concentrate its attacks against the approaching reserves and not try to reach its basic goal until after the execution of this mission. The actions of the mobile group in crushing the approaching enemy reserves should be rapid, in order that there be no delay in carrying out the basic mission. Sometimes, it will be more advantageous to detail a part of the forces of the mobile group as a cover against the approaching reserves to hold up the reserves until the units of the combined arms approach and to continue with the main forces to carry out the encirclement of the main group.

The precise objectives that the mobile group will attack in the depths of the enemy defenses and the sequence in which it will attack them will depend each time on the specific situation. Sometimes it should act at once both against the reserves and against the units withdrawn by the enemy from the front for occupying a new defensive zone and in this way cooperate with our troops operating on the Front.

While operating in the depths of the enemy defenses, the mobile group will conduct various forms of battle. The most characteristic of these are march approach, for getting closer to the enemy reserves or for reaching the routes of withdrawal of the main group's units; encounter battle with the strategic reserves; or offensive combat against the enemy, quickly assuming the offensive in the intervals, switch lines, and rear lines.

A peculiarity of these combat actions is their short duration and the speed of maneuver for a blow against the flanks and rear of the enemy. The basic purpose of the action is to break up the forces of the enemy, surround them in small groups, and destroy them unit by unit. The actions should be bold. Even small units of a mobile group should not hesitate to wedge in deeply into the enemy dispositions, to infiltrate through his combat formations and demoralize his rear and command, to spread panic among his forces, and in this way to contribute to the success of the main forces of the mobile group. The pursuit of the retreating enemy should lead to his complete destruction.

At the beginning of the movement into the breach, each unit entering into the makeup of the mobile group should work in close operation with the air. Hence, for signal communication with the main forces and aviation, reconnaissance must have adequate signal communications equipment. In the period of battle in the depths, the commander of the mobile group must have reserve forces and means for reconnaissance.

Immediately after reconnaissance, we should send out the detachments for making movement possible. Among their missions will be the removal of the separate obstacles along the routes of movement, the marking of detours and the regulation of movement. A part of their work, however, should be the reconnaissance of the locality. In actions in the depths of the defenses, guides selected from the local inhabitants can play an important part, as experience showed in the operations in question. Thus, when we captured the crossing on the Don River, at Kalach, the detailed forward detachment quickly reached the crossing with the aid of a guide.

From November 19–25, the rifle divisions, by battle, reached the line of the Chir River after moving a distance of 35 to 60 kilometers, an average of 6 to 10 kilometers a day. During this period the tank corps, while fighting, moved a distance of 130 to 150 kilometers, an average of 20 to 25 kilometers a day. Such rates of movement must be regarded as satisfactory, but they are far from being the maximum for a mobile group. Under other circumstances, with the best cooperation, direction of battle, and security of the tank units, the rates of movement could be greater. Thus, the 25th Tank Corps, operating on the right wing of the Southwestern Front, had an average daily rate of movement of 48 to 50 kilometers.[6]

The tank corps, jointly with the cavalry and other mobile troops and reinforced by artillery and aviation, showed themselves in the given operation to be an effective means of the Front command for exploiting successes and for crushing the approaching enemy reserves by separate units.

The example of the given operation confirms the correctness of the general rules accumulated in the course of the Great Patriotic War for the employment of tank units as echelons for exploiting successes.

At the same time, the experience of the operations showed the necessity of centralized direction of the mobile groups, actions in the hands of a single command subordinate to the Military Council of the Front. Such centralization makes possible greater mobility in the direction of the actions of the tank corps in the enemy's operational depths than could be achieved by the commander of the 5th Tank and 21st Armies of the Southwestern Front.

Editor's Notes

1. An excellent study of tank operations is A. Radzievskii, *Tankovii udar* (Moscow: *Voenizdat*, 1977).
2. A technical study of the Army's operations may be found in Iu.V. Plotnikov, *Osobennosti boevogo primeneniaia soedinenii 5-i Tankovoi Armii v kontrnastuplenii pod Stalingradom* (Moscow: *Voenizdat* 1969). The Military Soviet of the Army consisted of Lieutenant General P. L. Romanenko as Commander, Major General of Tank Troops G. L. Tumanian as political member, and Major General A. I. Danilov as Chief of Staff. The six rifle divisions were 14th Guards, 47th Guards, 119th, 124th, 159th, and 346th.
3. The commander of the 26th Tank Corps was Major General of Tank Troops A. G. Rodin; the 1st Tank Corps was commanded by Major General of Tank Troops V. V. Butkov.
4. In fact, by midday the rifle troops and their supporting armor had only advanced 4 to 5 kilometers. This was less than the initial objectives which were set at 6 kilometers for 47th Guards and 119th Rifle Divisions. See R. Mazurkevich "Taktika obshchevoiskovovo boia," *Voenno istoricheskii zhurnal* No. 11 1982, p. 19. The attack appeared to be bogging down and a decision was made to commit the tank reserves. Although this resulted in heavier than anticipated casualties, it did allow for a breakthrough.
5. This was Lieutenant Colonel G. N. Filippov, who subsequently became a Hero of the Soviet Union.
6. The 25th Tank Corps was commanded by Major General of Tank Troops P. P. Pavlov.

The crushing Soviet offensive of late November 1942 presented the German High Command with a terrible dilemma: Should the 6th Army remain in Stalingrad, encircled by superior forces and unsupplied in the midst of winter; or should von Paulus break out toward the new German lines west of Kotelnikovo? Hitler's decision to remain on the Volga necessitated a massive relief effort. While the Luftwaffe struggled to supply the 6th Army, von Manstein endeavored to break through to von Paulus by relief operation Wintergewitter (Winter Storm). The Soviet responses, detailed herein, reveal both the collapse of German strategic options and the evolving skill of the Soviet General Staff. The timing and execution of the Soviet countermoves spelled the end of any hope for outside relief for the 6th Army—Ed.

6

The Kotelnikovo Operation

The Kotelnikovo operation, which is one of the most important stages in the crushing of the Germans at Stalingrad, was carried out from December 12 to 30, 1942. This operation included two stages: the first, from December 12–23, was a defensive battle for the purpose of wearing out the enemy troops by mobile defense; the second, from December 24–30, was a determined offensive of our troops and the defeat of the Kotelnikovo group of the enemy.

General Situation at the Beginning of the Operation

After the encirclement of the Stalingrad group of the enemy, the units of the left wing of the Southwestern Front developed a successful offensive, clearing out the enemy from the area of the middle course of the Don. The left flank group of the Stalingrad Front advanced in the general direction of Kotelnikovo (51st Army and 4th Cavalry Corps) and toward Elista (28th Army).

While operating in the Kotelnikovo direction the 51st Army reached

114

the following line toward November 26: Gromoslavka, Kapkinskii, Zhutov No. 1, Aksai, Peregruznyi, Umantsevo, and Obilnoe. The 61st Cavalry Division was shifted into the area of Sharnutovskii. For the further development of the offensive, it was necessary to capture Kotelnikovo, since it was the most important road center in the given operational direction.

The commander of the 51st Army decided first to capture Kotelnikovo on November 27 with the forces of the 4th Cavalry Corps, for which purpose the 81st Cavalry Division was to strike from the north from the area of Verkhne-Iablochnyi and the 61st Cavalry Division from the east from the region of Sharnutovskii. The 81st Cavalry Division succeeded in penetrating to the north edge of Kotelnikovo, but upon encountering here some strong enemy counterattacks, it was forced to withdraw into the area of Nizhne-Iablochnyi and Verkhni–Iablochnyi. The offensive of the 61st Cavalry Division was also unsuccessful, because it was met by the counterattacks of an infantry regiment, reinforced by 40 tanks, and was forced to withdraw to the region of Vershin-Sal.

The second attempt to capture the area of Kotelnikovo by concentric blows was also unsuccessful. The offensive of the 51st Army units, starting on December 3 met heavy counterattacks of enemy infantry and tanks from the areas of Kotelnikovo and Pimen-Cherni. The 61st Cavalry Division was engaged in battle in the jump-off position for the attack and did not set out.

In the second half of the day of December 4, the enemy, again committing to battle the 6th German Panzer Division that had arrived, assumed the offensive in two directions: one group consisting of 100 tanks against the 81st Cavalry Division units from the area of Maiorskii; the second, having in its makeup as much as a regiment of infantry with 30 tanks, struck a blow at the left flank of the 302nd Rifle Division.[1] As a result of the battle, the 81st Cavalry Division, after suffering heavy losses, withdrew to the line of Verkhne-Kurmoiarskaia, Verkhne-Iablochnyi, and the 832nd Infantry Regiment of the 302nd Rifle Division was thrown back in the direction of Chilekov.

On December 5, the 51st Army, after repelling the attacks of the enemy, assumed the defensive on the line of Gremiachaia, Darganov, Sharnutovskii, Vershin-Sal, and Peredniaia Elista. The 4th Cavalry Corps, covering the right flank of the army, dug in on the line of Verkhne-Kurmoiarskaia and Verkhne-Iablochnyi. By this time, after the battles for completing the encirclement of the Germans, the 13th Mechanized Corps from the area of Sovetskii was concentrated in the region of Aksai.

By December 6, the German command succeeded in stopping the disorderly withdrawal of the Rumanian divisions, in putting into their composition some detachments of German troops, in assigning them to tanks, and in organizing a defense on the line Zakharov, Kurmoiarskii, Pimen-Cherni, Verskin-Sal, Kenkria, and Peredniaia Elista.[2]

The enemy forces in the Kotelnikovo direction consisted by this time of three Rumanian infantry divisions (the 18th, 1st, and 4th, shattered in the preceding battles); gendarme detachments of Rumanians and Germans; some small, mixed tank units; the 6th German Panzer Division, shifted from France into the area of Kotelnikovo; and remains of the 5th and 8th Rumanian Cavalry Divisions, which had also suffered considerable losses in the preceding battle.

From December 6–12, the enemy made repeated attacks against the positions of our units, chiefly for the purpose of reconnaissance. Simultaneously, the German command intensified preparations for an operation aimed at breaking through the defenses of our troops in order to join up with the 6th German Army encircled at Stalingrad. For this purpose he concentrated shock groups in the area of Tormosin and Kotelnikovo under the overall command of General Field Marshal von Manstein. Large forces were quickly moved into the area of Kotelnikovo. On December 12 the 23rd German Panzer Division arrived here from the North Caucasus, and the relative strength of the sides in the Kotelnikovo direction had changed by December 12 in favor of the enemy. His forces here amounted to about 30,000 bayonets and sabers, 266 field guns, 280 tanks, and 1,253 machine guns.

Hence, by December 12, the enemy had succeeded in creating a considerable superiority in personnel and equipment in the Kotelnikovo direction, and his tank units were concentrated on a narrow front to the northeast of Kotelnikovo in the area of Pimen-Cherni.[3]

The Character of the Area of Combat Operations

The area of combat operations was a hilly steppe-plain, cut up by the beds of rivers and brooks, gullies and ravines. The majority of the ravines run in an east–west direction, but there are some which run in a north--south direction.

The Myshkova, Aksai, and Aksai–Kurmoiarskii rivers are narrow and shallow and can be forded over almost their entire course, but due to the steepness of their banks, they are not always easy to cross and require careful preliminary reconnaissance and work on the banks.

By the time of the combat operations all the rivers had frozen and had lost their importance as natural antitank barriers. However, they were good as defense lines and were used both by our own troops and those of the enemy for the organization of defense. The ravines were filled with deep snow and interfered a good deal with the movement of tanks.

The absence of forest and other cover created unfavorable conditions for the masking of troops and the execution of maneuvers. There were only a few roads properly prepared for traffic, but the firm ground and the shallow snow cover made possible the movement of all kinds of transport means even outside the roads. The ravines, however, which were filled with snow, interfered with the movement of transports and frequently made it entirely impossible.

The Offensive of the Kotelnikovo Group of the Enemy

The Breakthrough and the Advance of the Germans to the Aksai River

By a thrust from the areas of Tormosin and Kotelnikovo, the German command intended to break through the outer front of our troops and establish a strategic liaison with the encircled 6th Army. The Kotelnikovo group was to strike along the railway from Kotelnikovo to Chilekov and further on through Gromoslavka toward Marinovka.

The attempt of the enemy Tormosin grouping to break through the front of our troops in the area of Nizhne-Chirskaia was not successful. But the combat actions in the Kotelnikovo direction were carried out in the following manner. Beginning on December 12, after concentrating up to an infantry division and 100 tanks in the area of Pimen-Cherni and carrying out a strong air, artillery, and mortar preparation, the enemy struck at the left flank of the 302nd Rifle Division, defending the line Elevation 129.0 and Krutoi pond [see map 5—Ed.].

In spite of the considerable numerical superiority of the Germans, the units of the Division met the attack with strongly organized fire. However, as a result of the weak antitank defense, due chiefly to its lack of depth, they were forced by heavy fighting to withdraw in the direction of Chilekov and Nebikov. Because of the subsequent repeated attacks of the tank units of the Germans, some of the units of the Division withdrew to the Zaria Railway siding, where they organized a defense by December 14.

After pushing into the region of Nebikov, the Germans began to widen the breach in the direction of Verkhne-Iablochnyi. With the approach of the enemy group to Verkhne-Iablochnyi from the northeast, this point was also attacked from the south. However, the units of the 81st Cavalry Division, which were on the defensive here, successfully repelled in the course of the day all the attacks and by the close of the day drove back the tanks and the infantry of the enemy.

During this time the main forces of the enemy advanced to Chilekov and Nebikov, without encountering any resistance, because here, in the depth of the 51st Army, there were no units. After capturing Nebikov, the German command sent groups of tanks toward the southeast, and toward the close of the day, the enemy succeeded in capturing Koshara No. 2 and Elevation 158.0.

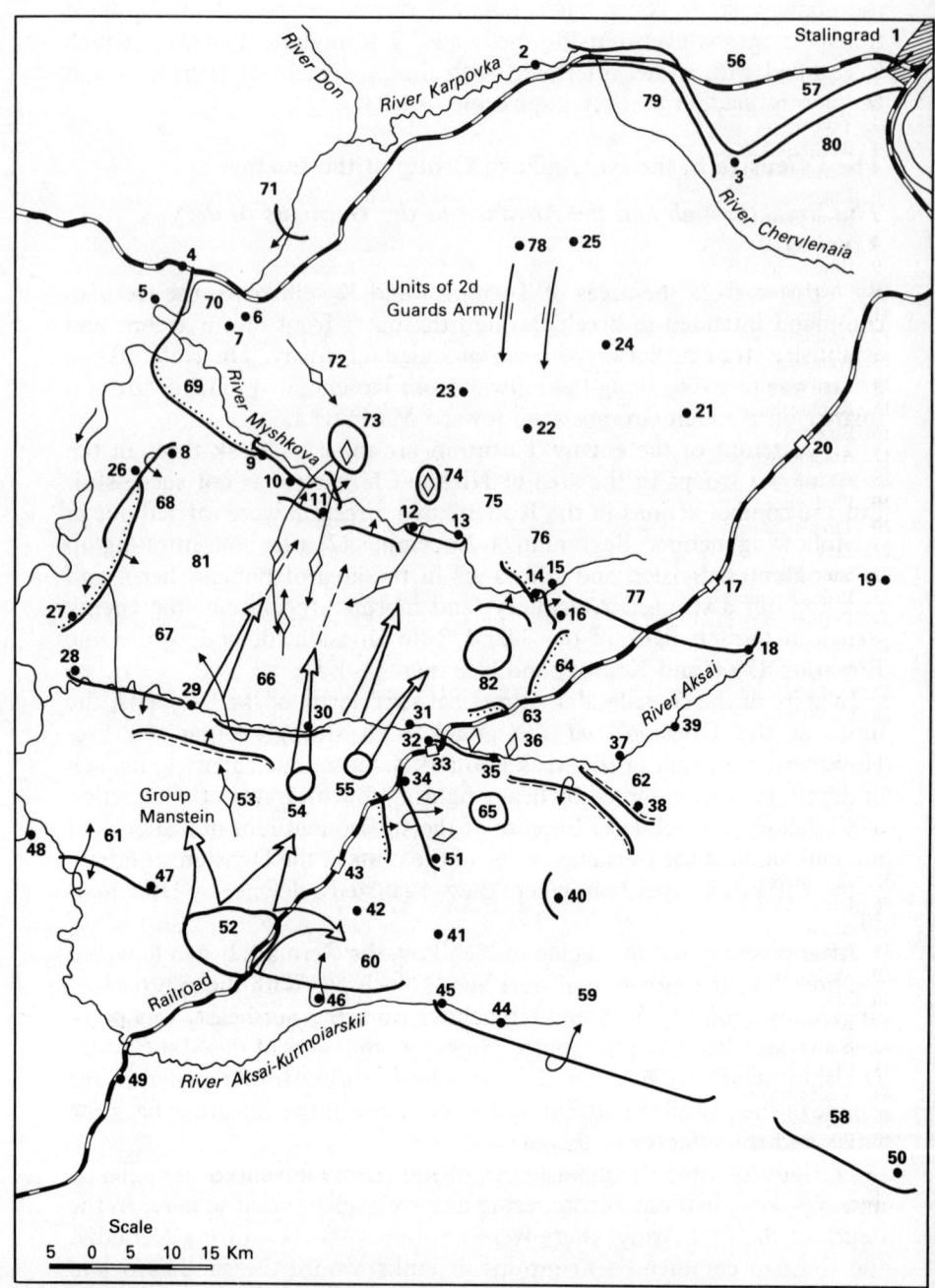

Source: A.I. Eremenko, *Stalingrad,* map supplement (Moskva: Voenizdat, 1961), map 19.

Map Five
"The German Relief Effort of December 12 to 23 1942"

Cities
1. Stalingrad
2. Marinovka
3. Tsybenko
4. Rychkovskii
5. Verkhne-Chirskaia
6. Logovsk
7. Ermokhinskii
8. Shabalinskii
9. Ilmen-Chirskii
10. Chernomorov
11. Nizhne-Kumskii
12. Gromoslavka
13. Ivanovka
14. Vasil'evka
15. Kapkinskii
16. Birzovoi
17. Abganerovo Station
18. Abganerovo
19. Plodovitoe
20. Tinguta Station
21. Zety
22. State Farm Krep
23. Eriko-Krepinskii
24. Verkhne-Tsaritsynskii
25. Buzinovka
26. Verkhne Rubezhnyi
27. Podstepinskii
28. Gorodskoi
29. Novoaksaiskii
30. Zalivskii
31. Antonov
32. Krugliakov
33. Zhutovo Station
34. Birukovskii
35. Zhutov No. 1
36. Lenin State Farm
37. Aksai
38. Peregruznoe
39. Shelestovo
40. Zhutov No. 2
41. Koshara No. 2
42. Nebykov
43. Chilckovo Station
44. Sharnutovskii
45. Darganov
46. Pimen-Cherni

47. Verkhne-Iablochnyi
48. Verkhne-Kurmoiarskaia
49. Kotelnikovo
50. Obilnoe
51. Ternobyi State Farm

German Units
52. Group Manstein consisting of 6th, 23rd, & 17th, Panzer Divisions and 2nd, 18th, 1st, 4th Rumanian Infantry Divisions and 5th, 8th, Cavalry Divisions
53. 17th Panzer Division
54. 6th Panzer Division
55. 23rd Panzer Division
56. 6th Army
57. 4th Panzer Army

Units
Soviet
58. 91st Rifle Division   Frontline on December 12, 1942
59. 126th Rifle Division
60. 302nd Rifle Division
61. 81st Cavalry Division
62. 126th Rifle Division   December 15–19
63. 13th Mechanized Corps
64. 302nd Rifle Division
65. 13nd Mechanized Corps and units of the 302nd Rifle Divison December 13-15
66. 61st Cavalry Division
67. 81st Cavalry Division
68. 300th Rifle Division on December 12
69. 300th Rifle Division on December 14
70. 315th Rifle Division on December 12
71. 7th Tank Corps on December 12
72. 7th Tank Corps on December 19
73. 4th Mechanized Corps
74. 235th Tank Brigade counterattack of December 14-15
75. 20th Independent Tank Brigade counterattack of December 14-15
76. 1378th Rifle Regiment of the 87 Rifle Division
77. 38th Rifle Division
78. Units of the 2nd Guards Army
79. 57th Army
80. 64th Army

Source: A.I Eremenko, Stalingrad, map supplement: (Moskva: Voenizdat, 1961), map 19.

On the rest of the sectors of the 51st Army our troops successfully repelled on this day numerous attacks of German infantry and tanks; these attacks were especially violent on the left wing of the Army, on the sector of the 91st Rifle Division in the area of Vershin-Sal and further toward the east.

In order to prevent the advance of enemy tanks in the north and northeast direction, the 13th Mechanized Corps (17th and 62nd Mechanized Brigades, 41st Tank Regiment) was shifted into the areas of Zhutovo, Biriukovskii, and Collective Farm Ternovyi.[4] By the close of December 12, the 41st Tank Regiment had occuped Zhutovo; the 17th Mechanized Brigade had reached the line Elevations 73.3 and 103.3; and the 62nd Mechanized Brigade had reached the line Elevation 135.7 and Collective Farm Ternovyi. At the same time, the 13th Tank Brigade had concentrated at Peregruznyi.

In the course of the night, the Germans brought up to the place of the breakthrough about 200 tanks and a division of motorized infantry. On the morning of December 13, they continued to exploit the breakthrough, directing their main efforts along the railroad toward Biriukovskii and toward Zalivskii and Verkhne-Kumskii, where they succeeded by the close of the day in capturing Shestakovo, Zalivskii, and Verkhne-Kumskii.[5]

On the right flank of the 51st Army, the enemy's motorized infantry, reinforced by tanks, tried by an attack from the north with a simultaneous attack from the east and south to drive the 81st Cavalry Division from Verkhne-Kurmoiarskaia, Nizhne-Iablochnyi, and Verkhne-Iablochnyi to make possible freedom of maneuver for the units advancing toward the north. On this sector of the front, there was heavy fighting all day. The enemy did not succeed in capturing Verkhne-Iablochnyi until evening, and his attacks against Nizhne-Iablochnyi and Verkhne-Kurmoiarskaia were successfully repulsed by our units. It was not until December 15th that the 81st Cavalry Division and the 85th Tank Brigade were withdrawn behind the Aksai River. By this time the 61st Cavalry Division, after battles in the area of Sharnutovskii, had moved into the area of Dorofeevskii and had become a part of the 4th Cavalry Corps.

The attacks of the enemy against the left flank of the Army, on the sector Darganov and Vershin-Sal on December 12–13, were successfully repulsed by the units of the 126th and 91st Rifle Divisions. Hence, toward the end of the second day of the offensive, the enemy with separate groups of tanks and infantry had wedged into the center of the dispositions of the 51st Army to a depth of 40 kilometers. The Army then extended over a front of as much as 160 kilometers and unable to create a sufficient depth of defense.

In view of the approach of the enemy to the Aksai River, the 4th

Mechanized Corps from the area of Pervomaisk was directed into the areas of Shebalinskii and Nizhne-Kumskii.[6]

On December 14 there was very heavy fighting for Collective Farm Ternovyi, Samokhin, and Darganov. By stubborn resistance and vigorous counterattacks, our troops repelled the thrusts of the enemy and inflicted heavy losses upon him. By the close of December 14, after violent attacks, the enemy succeeded in taking possession of the center of Collective Farm Ternovyi and, on the left flank of the 23rd German Panzer Division, captured Darganov.

On December 15, the 4th Mechanized Corps, by an impetuous advance from the northwest, north, and northeast attacked Verkhne-Kumskii from the march, destroying here up to 50 tanks and up to a battalion of infantry. Toward the close of the day, the Corps had captured this point.

On December 14, the Commander of the Stalingrad Front decided to withdraw the troops of the right wing and the center of the 51st Army behind the Aksai River. During the night of December 14–15, the units of the 51st Army were moved up to the Aksai River. By the close of December 15, the 4th Cavalry Corps reached the line of Gorodskoi and Dorofeevskii; the 13th Mechanized Corps organized a defense on the Krugliakov-Kovylevka line; the 302nd Rifle Division concentrated in the areas of Zaria Railroad Siding and Kamenka; and the 126th Rifle Division occupied a line for defense of Aksai and Peregruznyi. The rest of the units of the Army—91st Rifle Division and units of Fortified Region No. 76—defended the previous line.[7] In order to create a defense in depth, the 87th and 300th Rifle divisions, arriving from the reserves of the *Stavka*, were moved to the line of the Myskhova River. The 300th Rifle Division occupied the Kovylevka-Nizhne-Kumskii line; the 87th Rifle Division, Ivanovka and Kapkinskii.

Concentration of Troops for a Counterattack

On the Aksai line, the enemy was held until December 19. In violent and continuous battles along the whole front and especially to the west of the railroad, the enemy suffered heavy losses; the forces of the Germans and their Rumanian allies were harassed and their equipment used up; and all efforts to break through to the north were unsuccessful. At the price of heavy losses on the Aksai River, the enemy succeeded in occupying Generalovskii, Vodianskii, Zalivskii, Shestokov, and Krugliakov.

The *Stavka* assigned to the troops of the Stalingrad Front the mission of crushing the Kotelnikovo group of the enemy, and for this purpose, on December 15, the 2nd Guards Army was subordinated to the command of the Stalingrad Front.[8] It had the following in its makeup: the 1st and 13th Guards Rifle Corps and the 2nd Guards Mechanized Corps, stationed in the region of Cherkasov, Kolpachkii, and Buzinovka. This Army was given the mission to concentrate as follows by the morning of December 17: the *1st Guards Rifle Corps* in the area of Liapichev, Bratskii, Verbovskii; the *13th Guards Rifle Corps* in the area of State Farm No. 3, Eriko-Krepinskii, and Collective Farm Krep; and the *2nd Guards Mechanized Corps* in the areas of Station Tinguta and the forest to the southwest of this place.

On December 18, in order to create a powerful shock group, the following were made subordinate to the commander of the 2nd Guards Army: the 7th Tank, the 4th Mechanized, the 4th Cavalry Corps, and the 300th Rifle Division.[9] Simultaneously, steps were taken to reinforce the defenses on the line of Myshkova River. The *300th Rifle Division* assumed the defensive on the Zimovskoi-Shebalinskii sector; the *98th Rifle Division* deployed around Nizhne-Kumskii and Gromoslavka; the *3rd Guards Rifle Division* was moved into the Ivanovka-Kapkinskii area; the *87th Rifle Division* was sent to the 51st Army and assumed the defensive with two regiments on the Birzovoi-Gniloaksaiskaia line (one regiment was on Elevation 147.7, south of Verkhne-Kumskii).

The 38th Guards Rifle Division was taken from the makeup of the 64th Army for reinforcing the 51st Army and was assigned the mission of firmly holding the junction area between the 2nd Guards and 51st Armies on the Kapkinskii-Elevation 124-Station Abganerovo line. In the area Verkhne-Tsaritsynskii and on State Farm Krep, we concentrated anti-tank reserves (20th Tank Destroyer Brigade, 565th Destroyer Antitank Regiment, 90th and 91st Guards Mortar Regiments) with the mission of acting in case of necessity in a north and south direction.

By the morning of December 18, the 2nd Guards Army was to be ready to debouch on the Kovylevka-Shebalinskii-Gromoslavka line for attacking the Kotelnikovo group of the enemy in the general direction from Gromoslavka toward Kotelnikovo. The 2nd Guards Mechanized Corps was to be used for independent action south of the Aksai River. The 5th Shock Army was to cooperate with the offensive of the 2nd Guards Army on the west bank of the Don, and the 51st Army was to strike along the railroad toward Kotelnikovo.[10]

Battle on the Line of the Myshkova River
(December 19–23)

After suffering considerable losses in equipment and personnel in the battles for the capture of the Aksai River line, the enemy was forced to stop his advance temporarily and to bring fresh forces into the region of Generalovskii and Zalivskii. By December 19, units of his 17th Panzer Division came up, the forward elements of which were noticed by our reconnaissance in the area of Kotelnikovo as early as December 10.[11]

At noon on December 19, up to two motorized infantry regiments of the enemy with 60 tanks supported by strong aviation (on this day, the enemy made a total of 1,400 airplane flights) attacked the units of the 3rd Guards Mechanized Corps[12] and the 378th Rifle Regiment of the 87th Rifle Division, which were on the defensive on the ridge of the elevation south of Verkhne-Kumskii. After a violent attack, the enemy captured Verkhne-Kumskii, Nizhne-Kumskii, and Chernomorov but was not able to cross to the north bank of the Mishkova River.

No less fierce in character was the battle in the area of Vasil'evka, where the enemy, after regrouping units of the 6th German Panzer Division, sent tanks with motorized infantry against our right flank and captured Vasil'evka and Kapkinskii.

At the time of the attack against Vasil'evka there was also an attack by units of the 23rd German Panzer Division against the sector of Zaria Railroad Siding and Birzovoi, but even here all the attacks of the enemy failed.

Having lost hope of breaking through our front in a north direction, the enemy on December 20–23, limited himself to insignificant fighting for the purpose of reconnaissance. Only the area of Vasil'evka was there any fighting of a rather active character.

The command of the Stalingrad Front continued to reinforce its shock group. The 4th Cavalry Corps was brought into the Logovskii-Ermokhinskii area; the 7th Tank Corps was concentrated in the Demkin area; and the 2nd Guards Mechanized Corps was concentrated in the area around Eriko-Krepinskii and State Farm Krep. On December 22, the 3rd Guards Mechanized Corps was brought into the area of Tinguta Station for reorganization. Hence, in the period December 20–22, we completed the planned regrouping.

The Withdrawal of the Enemy from the Myshkova River

As a result of the 13 days of heavy fighting on the line of the Aksai and Myshkova rivers, the enemy suffered heavy losses, his troops were tired out, and his equipment depleted. During this period, his losses in killed and wounded alone amounted to 8,000 men, and he lost 160 tanks, 92 guns, 85 mortars, 189 machine guns, and 82 airplanes. The attempt to join up with the encircled 6th German Army across the line of the Myshkova River was not successful.

The successful offensive of the troops of the Southwestern Front in the area of the middle Don and the concentration of the 2nd Guards Army north of the Myshkova River not only excluded the possibility of a breakthrough of the von Manstein grouping into Stalingrad but created a real threat for all the Kotelnikovo group of the enemy. The German command decided upon an immediate withdrawal of the Kotelnikovo group from the Myshkova River toward the southwest.

On December 21–22, units of the enemy were taken from the south bank of the Myshkova River and concentrated to the south of Gromoslavka and Vasil'evka. In accordance with reconnaissance data, up to 300 tanks and five motorized regiments were concentrated in this area as early as December 22. On December 23 the enemy undertook to move into the area of contact between the 2nd Guards Army and the 51st Army in the general direction of Vasil'evka and Birzovoi and captured the latter.

The attempt to exploit this success toward Tebektenerovka was not successful. In the night of December 23–24, the enemy began to withdraw toward the south. The circumstances required immediate pursuit of the withdrawing enemy.

Offensive of the 2nd Guards Army and the 51st Army

Grouping and Missions

On December 23, the command of the Stalingrad Front decided to assume a determined offensive beginning on the morning of December 24, striking its main blow with the forces of the 2nd Guards Army and with the right flank of the 51st Army in the general direction of Kotelnikovo.

The Front Commander, in the presence of the Corps commanders, verbally gave the order to the Commander of the 2nd Guards Army. This Army was assigned the mission of destroying the enemy moving toward the north from the Aksai River and subsequently of capturing Kotelnikovo. Hence the 2nd Guards Army and the 51st Army were, in reality, to make a frontal assault to gain time for the command.

Action on December 24–25

On the morning of December 24, the troops on the left wing of the 5th Shock Army, the 2nd Guards Army, and the 51st Army started an offensive. The 1st Guards Rifle Corps struck the main blow toward Verkhne-Kumskii; the 24th Guards Rifle Division, toward the close of the day, captured Verkhne-Kumskii. As early as December 25, they approached the Aksai River, after capturing Novaksaiak. The 98th Rifle Division, after breaking the resistance of the enemy, captured Zagotskot, and by the close of December 25, reached the northern edge of Zalivskii, where it engaged in a hard-fought battle [see map 6—Ed.].

The units of the 13th Guards Rifle Corps, with the cooperation of the units of the 7th Tank and 2nd Guards Mechanized Corps, reached the north bank of the Aksai River toward the end of December 25. The 3rd Guards Rifle Division, after capturing Moiseev, was drawn into a hard battle for Shestakov and Anotonov. The 49th Guards Rifle Division, with one regiment, engaged in battle together with units of the 3rd Guards Rifle Division for Antonov on the Aksai River and had two regiments 7 kilometers northeast.

The 6th Mechanized Corps was drawn into the region of Aksai and Peregruani.[13] The 387th Rifle Division remained in the area of Farm No. 1 and Tebektenerovka. The 7th Tank and the 2nd Guards Mechanized Corps operated along the Gromoslavka-Shestakov highway because movement outside the road was hindered by ravines filled with snow.

By the close of December 25, the forward elements of the 300th Rifle Division, covering the right flank of the 2nd Guards Army, reached the area of Rychkovo. At this same time the 4th Cavalry Corps reached the areas of Ilmen-Chirskii, Kovylevskii and Shebalinskii.

The offensive on the right flank of the 51st Army also developed successfully. The 87th Rifle Division, supported by the 13th Tank Brigade, captured Birzovoi by the close of December 24 and made contact with units of the 49th Guards Rifle Division south of Kapkinskii.

In the period December 24–25, there was stubborn fighting on the sector of the 87th and 302nd Rifle Divisions. As a result of this, the enemy was pushed toward the northwest, where he came under the blows of units of the 49th Guards Rifle Division and started to withdraw in a southwestern direction.

THE 13TH MECHANIZED CORPS ON THE NORTH BANK OF THE AKSAI RIVER

After the units of the 302nd and 87th Rifle Divisions reached the line of the Aksai River, this Corps, jointly with the 13th Tank Brigade, moved into the area of Baga-Malan for pursuit of the withdrawing groups of Germans.

On the morning of December 24, the left wing of the 51st Army, the enemy began an attack on the sector of Fortified Region 76. Strong points Obilnoe, Nurga, and Shebeneryi were surrounded. The troops of the Fortified Region conducted a hard battle. Peredniaia Elista was subjected to attack at the same time.

Hence, in the first two days of the offensive our troops advanced, while fighting, a distance of 8 to 20 kilometers and pushed the rear guards of the enemy beyond the Aksai River. The main forces of the German 6th, 17th and 23rd Panzer Divisions, after rather heavy losses even in the period of the fighting for Aksai and the Myshkovo, continued to withdraw hastily toward Kotelnikovo.

The Pursuit of the Enemy December 26–29

The concluding phase of the Kotelnikovo operation started on December 26. The 2nd Guards Army, after overcoming the resistance of the enemy

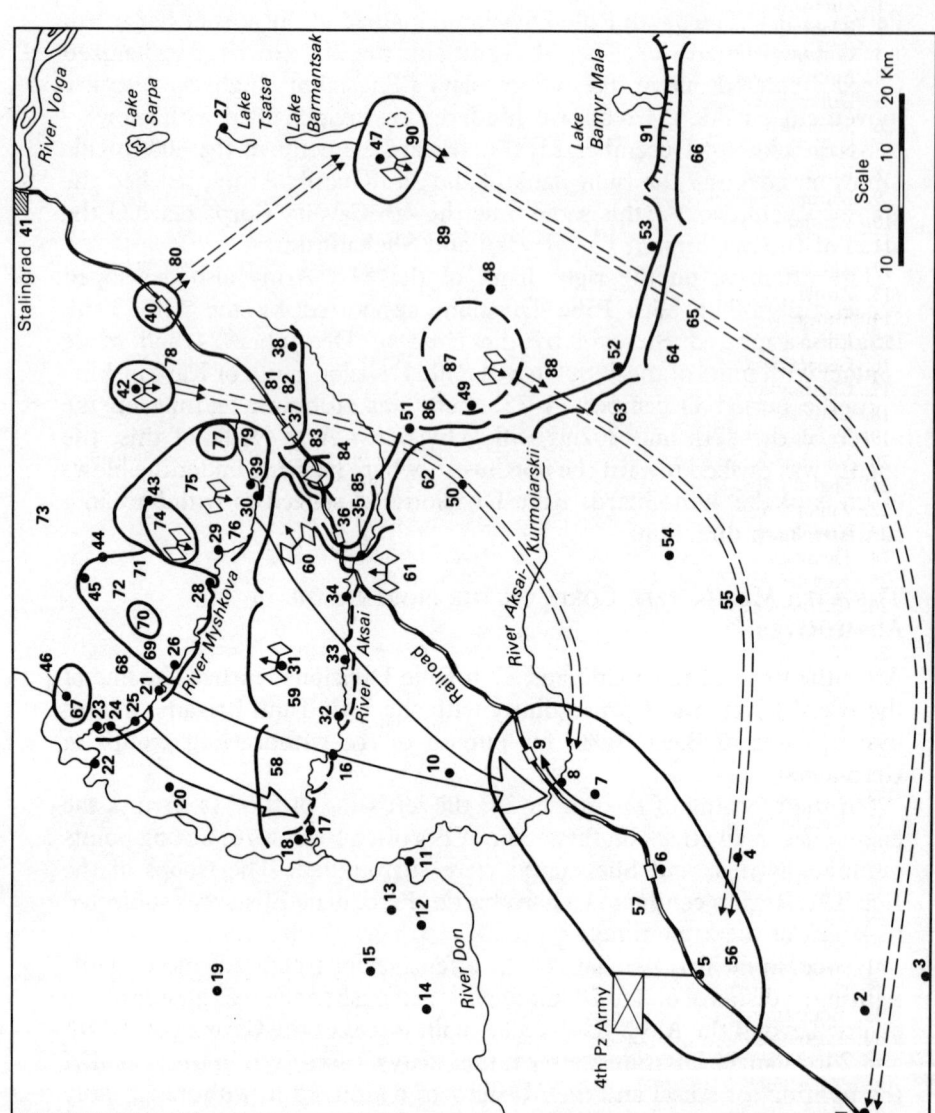

Source: Basic data from A.I. Eremenko, *Stalingrad,* map suppliment (Moskva: Voenizdat, 1961), map 21.

Map Six
"The Plan by the Stalingrad Front for the Defeat of the German Kotelnikovo Grouping"

Cities
1. Zimovniki
2. Il'ichev-Ternovskii
3. Glubokii
4. Andreevskaia
5. Dubovskoe
6. Semichnaia
7. Nagol'nyi
8. Kotelnikovo
9. Kurmoiarskii
10. Verkhne-Iablochnyi
11. Verkhne-Kurmioaskaia
12. Aginov
13. Zirnyi
14. Mineav
15. Elifanov
16. Generalovskii
17. Chausovskii
18. Gorodskoi
19. Tormosin
20. Verkhne-Rubezhnyi
21. Shabalinskii
22. Zimovskii
23. Ermokhinskii
24. Demkin
25. Kovylevskii
26. Chernomorov
27. Tsatsa
28. Gromoslavka
29. Ivanovka
30. Vasil'evka
31. Verkhne Kumskii
32. Birykov
33. Zalivskii
34. Shestakov
35. Krugliakov
36. Zaria Station
37. Kapkinskii
38. Tinguta Station
39. Stalingrad
40. Zety
41. State Farm Krep
42. State Farm No. 3
43. Bratskii
44. Logovskii
45. Tunditovo
46. Tolochkin
47. Baga-Malan
48. Zhutov No. 2

49. Peregruznyi
50. Kenkria
51. Obilnoe
52. Verkhne Salsk
53. Shebalin
54. Zavetnoe
55. Kichkino

Units
German
56. 4th Panzer Army
57. SS Motorized Division "Viking"
58. 6th Army Corps
59. 17th Panzer Division
60. 6th Panzer Division
61. 23rd Panzer Division
62. 8th Rumanian Cavalry Division
63. 4th Rumanian Infantry Division
64. 1st Rumanian Infantry Division
65. 57th Sapper Battalion/6th Rumanian
    Infantry Division
66. 5th Rumanian Cavalry Division
Soviet
67. 4th Cavalry Corps
68. 300th Rifle Division
69. 24th Rifle Division
70. 33rd Guards Rifle Division
71. 7th Tank Corps
72. 1st Guards Rifle Corps
73. 2nd Guards Army
74. 2nd Mechanized Corps
75. 13th Guards Rifle Corps
76. 3rd Guards Rifle Division
77. 387th Rifle Division
78. 6th Mechanized Corps
79. 49th Guards Rifle Division
80. 3rd Guards Mechanized Corps
81. 38th Rifle Division
82. 254th Tank Brigade
83. 87th Rifle Division
84. 13th Mechanized Corps
85. 302nd Rifle Division
86. 126th Rifle Division
87. 13th Mechanized Corps
88. 91st Rifle Division
89. 51st Army
90. 3rd Guards Mechanized Corps
91. 76th Fortified Region

Source: Basic data from A. I. Eremenco, *Stalingrad*, map supplement (Moskva: Voenizdat, 1961), map 21.

on the Aksai River, continued to move toward the south. For pursuing the withdrawing German units in the Kotelnikovo direction, we sent out the 7th Tank Corps, the main forces of which reached Kotelnikovo on December 27, and engaged in a hard battle with the infantry and tanks of the enemy. The 2nd Guards Mechanized Corps moved behind the 7th Tank Corps in the second echelon, and by the close of December 27, was still in the area of Generalovskii and Dorofeevskii.

For bypassing Kotelnikovo on the southeast toward Nagolnyi (5 kilometers southeast of Kotelnikovo), we threw forward the 6th Mechanized Corps. A mobile group of forces consisting of the 3rd Guards Mechanized Corps and the 13th mechanized Corps were sent in pursuit of the German and Rumanian divisions in the general direction of Zavetnoe (80 kilometers southeast of Kotelnikovo).

The advance of strong mobile groups in three directions split the withdrawing troops of the enemy into separate groups isolated from each other. Hence, favorable conditions were created for destroying them unit by unit. The 1st Guards Rifle Corps, by a forced march, moved behind the 7th Tank Corps. By the close of December 28, forward elements of the 24th Guards Division and of the 98th Rifle Division reached the area 3 to 4 kilometers north of Kotelnikovo. By the close of December 28, parts of the 7th Tank Corps—jointly with the approaching forward elements of the 24th Guards Rifle Division and 98th Rifle Division— penetrated the town and engaged in street fighting with the enemy. On December 29 Kotelnikovo was captured by our troops.

On December 26, the 6th Mechanized Corps crushed the 1st and 4th Rumanian Infantry Divisions in the area of Darganov and Sharnutovskii, turned with a part of its forces toward Pimen-Cherni, and with its main forces continued the pursuit of the enemy in the direction of Nagolnyi. On December 28, parts of the Corps occupied Karaichev and on December 29 seized Nagolnyi. The isolated units of the 17th and 23rd German Panzer Divisions withdrew behind the Sal River.

The offensive of the 13th Guards Rifle Corps also developed successfully. On December 28, its units joined battle with the isolated groups of the enemy on the Gremiachii–Pimen–Cherni Front, and moving behind the 6th Mechanized Corps, reached the Lenin Estate-Karaichev Front by the close of December 29.

A mobile group of forces consisting of the 3rd Guards and 13th Mechanized Corps carried out its mission in a brilliant manner. On December 27 the 13th Mechanized Corps occupied Iki-Zorgakin and Dogzmankin, capturing 1,500 Rumanian soldiers. On this day units of the 3rd Guards Mechanized Corps reached Kiselevka and Ketcheneri. On December 28, while pursuing the Rumanian units, the 13th Mechanized Corps, together with the 13th Tank Brigade, reached the Sal River on the sector Novo-Ilovlinskii and Nikolskii, encircling and destroying up to two regiments of the enemy in the area around Shabalin. The 3rd Guards Mechanized Corps, while pursuing and destroying the isolated units of Rumanians, occupied Zavetnoe. Subsequently, the 3rd Guards Mechanized Corps was assigned the mission of capturing Zimovnikii.

Units of the 51st Army moved behind the units of the 6th Mechanized Corps, which had been pushed forward behind the mobile group of the 3rd Guards and 13th Mechanized Corps. On December 26, the 87th Rifle Division, jointly with units of the 6th Mechanized Corps, captured State Farm Ternovyi and Samokhin and by December 28 moved out into the area of Karaichev and Budarka.

On December 28, the 126th Rifle Division reached the areas of Verkhne-Kuzhny, Krylov, and Shabalin, where it encountered resistance from the remains of the 4th Rumanian Infantry Division. Having forced the Rumanian units back in a southerly direction, on December 29 the Division concentrated in the Atamanovka-Novo–Ilovlinskii area. On December 28, the 91st Rifle Division reached the area of Zavetnoe.

During all the later phase of the operations, the units of the Fortified Region 76 remained at the strong points and conducted battles from the encirclement until the approach of the 3rd Guards Mechanized Corps units.

By the close of December 30, after inflicting a crushing defeat upon the withdrawing enemy group, the forces reached the following lines: *2nd Guards Army*, the line Verkhne–Kurmoiarskaia, Semichnyi, Nagolnyi, and Karaichev, having moved a part of its forces to the right bank of the Don; the *51st Army* on the line of Station Semichnyi, Andreevskoe, Sirotskii, and Valuevka, with the *3rd Guards* and *13th Mechanized Corps* on the approaches to Zimovnkii. From this line, the troops of the 2nd Guards and the 51st Army were given a new mission for further pursuit of the enemy.

Hence, by December 30, the Kotelnikovo operation was successfully completed. The efforts of the German command to join up with the 6th Army encircled at Stalingrad was a complete failure. From this time, the 22 divisions compressed in the ring of our forces were doomed.

In the course of the battles from December 12–30, the Kotelnikovo group of Germans suffered a great defeat. The German–Rumanian units lost the following: 16,300 dead, wounded, and prisoners out of a total of 34,500 men, 303 tanks out of 400, and 306 guns out of 481.

General Conclusions

From the course of the Kotelnikovo operations we must draw the following conclusions.

1. The experience of the Great Patriotic War showed repeatedly that when a group of enemy forces was encircled the German command always

tried by counterattacks from the outside to break out of the ring of encirclement. Hence, operations for the encirclement of large groups of the enemy require reliable operational security, which may be obtained either by defense on suitable lines of the outer ring of encirclement or by active offensive actions.

In the first period of the Kotelnikovo operation, December 12–23, the strategic security of the troops of the Don Front, operating for the destruction of the 6th Army of von Paulus, were carried out by the methods of maneuvering defense of the 51st Army. After the concentration of the 2nd Guards Army on the line of the Myshkova River, the operations of the Don Front were secured by the offensive of the 2nd Guards Army and the 51st Army. In planning an operation for encirclement, it is necessary to have strong maneuverable reserves for the strategic security of our own actions.

2. The success of maneuvering offense depends upon the preparation of a number of successive lines of defense and the organization of brief but strong counterattacks. The troops of the 51st Army did not have previously prepared defense lines, and even such a good line as that of the Aksai River was not organized for defense. This circumstance complicated to a considerable degree the conditions under which our troops fought right up to the Mishkova River line.

The maneuvering defense of the units of the 51st Army was active, that is, accompanied by a large number of counterattacks. Thus, on December 13, in the area of Verkhne-Kurmoiarskaia and Verkhne-Iablochnyi, units of the 4th Cavalry Corps repelled by a brief counterthrust a heavy attack by a German regiment of motorized infantry supported by 150 tanks. On December 14, in the area of elevation 135.7, the 62nd Mechanized Brigade, having 11 tanks in all, repelled by a counterattack an offensive of enemy's motorized infantry reinforced with 50 tanks. The enemy suffered considerable losses and withdrew to the jump-off position.

Experience showed that local, energetic, and skillfully planned counterattacks tire out enemy personnel, wear out his equipment, and weaken his offensive power.

3. The units on the defensive in the direction of the main blow of the enemy should always be ready for stubborn defense, even though cut off from adjacent units; for defense with exposed flanks; and for defense under conditions of encirclement. Centers of defense, left in the rear or on the flanks of an enemy effecting a breakthrough, oblige the enemy to use up a considerable number of his forces and equipment for blocking the defense and for covering his own flanks. This situation necessarily leads to a breaking up of his shock group and, on the whole, to the weakening of the force of his blow.

With our troops providing a firm defense on the flanks, the breakthrough in the center of the 51st Army and the wedging of the enemy into the depths of our dispositions did not lead to a breaking up of strategic defense. Because the flank units of the 51st Army—on the right, units of the 4th Cavalry Corps; on the left, units of the 126th Rifle Division—held their ground and successfully repelled the attacks of the enemy, the latter was forced to divert a considerable part of his forces from the direction of the main blow when protecting his flanks, thus weakening the force of his blow at the place of the breakthrough.

4. The selection of the moment for starting a counteroffensive is always one of the most complicated problems in the command of troops. Starting a counteroffensive prematurely may lead to a weakening of the offensive possibilities and in this way may prevent one from reaching the established goal. A counteroffensive after some delay will necessarily lead to one of two things: either the enemy will have time to occupy a suitable line and prepare for defense, or—and this is the most frequent case of all—will slip away, and the thrust will be to no avail.

The 2nd Guards Army and the 51st Army assumed the offensive on the morning of December 24. The enemy, however, after unsuccessful attempts on December 20–22 to break through our front, began on the evening of December 23 to withdraw his units behind the Aksai River under cover of strong rear guards. Hence, the offensive of the armies was delayed, and the attacking units, during the first days of the offensive, had to conduct battle only with the rearguards of the enemy. His main forces escaped the blow. This shows that the moment for passing to the counteroffensive was misssed.

In selecting the moment for transition to the counteroffensive, reconnaissance of all kinds—the data of which should be prepared and carefully studied and checked by a special commander of air and ground reconnaissance—plays a very important part. In the Kotelnikovo operation, beginning on December 21, the reconnaissance furnished information concerning the initial movements of the enemy. The situation revealed by this information indicated that the command the staffs should intensify all kinds of reconnaissance and secure verification of the reports coming in. But this was not done, thus a big mistake was made—one which could not be corrected in the course of the offensive that had already started.

5. The offensive and energetic pursuit should be completed by the destruction of the withdrawing enemy. Tank, mechanized, and cavalry formations should try to reach the routes of withdrawal of the enemy.

For the pursuit of the withdrawing units of the enemy we sent out mobile groups of forces over a broad front: the *7th Tank Corps* west of the line of the railroad, in the general direction of Kotelnikovo; the *6th Mechanized Corps*, east of the line of the railroad, through Pimen-Cherni toward Nagolnyi, and a mobile group consisting of the *3rd Guards* and

13th Mechanized Corps in the general direction of Zavetnoe. This method of pursuit enabled us to break up the enemy into separate groups isolated from each other and to strike them in detail, but the mobile groups did not move out upon the route of withdrawal of the main group of the enemy. The rifle divisions, moving behind the mobile groups, mopped up the enemy in the inhabited localities and passed through or bypassed the tanks and motorized riflemen.

The decisive condition for a successful and uninterrupted pursuit is adequate supplies for the forces engaged, especially ammunition and fuel for the tank, motorized, and cavalry units. In the meantime, in the Kotelnikovo operation, during the pursuit, a number of tank and mechanized corps were poorly supplied with fuel. Thus, in the 7th Tank Corps, the machines had only a one-third to half-full tank, and 50 per cent of the T-70 tanks did not participate in the battle because they had no fuel.

Editor's Notes

1. The 6th German Panzer Division and two infantry divisions were ordered by Hitler from France on November 4 to serve specifically as reserves for the 3rd Rumanian and 8th Italian Armies. See *Kriegstagebuch des Ober–Kommandos der Wehrmacht*, Teilband II, p. 902. The 6th Panzer Division contained 141 tanks on December 11, 1942. See M. Kehrig, *Stalingrad* (Stuttgart: Deutsche Verlags-Anstalt), p. 328, footnote 73.
2. Army Group Don, as the reformed units were designated, was originally to consist of German–Rumanian formations under the command of Marshal Antonescu, the dictator of Rumania. The Soviet breakthrough disrupted this plan.
3. The distribution of Soviet forces of the Stalingrad Front was a follows: (*total*) 38.5 divisions, 274,000 men, 578 tanks, 1,663 guns (76 mm and above), 1,179 antitank guns, and 2,175 mortars (82 mm and above). Of those forces, facing the 6th German Army were 18.5 divisions, 100,000 men, 62 tanks, 793 guns, 525 antitank guns, and 1,074 mortars. The forces facing the Army Group Don comprised the remainder. See Rokossovskii, *Velikaia pobeda na Volge*, p. 369. The initial German offensive was not mounted with a Fascist superiority but rather with a concentration of assets.
4. The 13th Tank Corps was organized as a mechanized corps during the Stalingrad battle and was renamed as a mechanized corp on January 9, 1943. The commander of the 13th Tank Corps was Major General T. I. Tanaschishin. In this book the 13th Tank Corps will be uniformly designated as the 13th Mechanized Corps to better reflect its actual combat formation and so as not to confuse the reader. The Corps also contained the 61st Mechanized Brigade.
5. In fact, there was no German motorized division assigned to 57th Panzer Corps. At the commencement of the relief effort, the 57th Panzer Corps had the battle strength of one Panzer Division. See Kehrig, *Stalingrad*, p. 328.
6. The commander of the 4th Mechanized Corps was Major General V. T. Volskii. Its history is chronicled in A. Samsanov, *Ot Volgi do Baltiki* (Moscow: *Nauka*, 1963, 1973).
7. A *fortified region* was a special formation of the Red Army. It usually consisted of several machine gun and artillery battalions assigned to defend a particular area of frontage. It did not have to be a static unit.
8. For a history of the 2nd Guards Army, see *V nastuplenii gvardiia* (Moscow: *Voenizdat*, 1971). The Army was organized on the base of the 1st Reserve Army (2nd Formation) in October 1942. In December the veteran units attached to the Army were ordered by *Stavka* to concentrate in the region of Kalach and to drive on Rostov. The Army was commanded by Lieutenant General R. Ia. Malinovskii.
9. The 7th Tank Corps was commanded by Major General of Tank Troops P. A. Rotmistrov.

10. The commander of the 5th Shock Army was Lieutenant General M. M. Popov. On December 26th he was replaced by Lieutenant General V. D. Tsvetaev. In December the Army contained 71,000 men, 252 tanks, and 814 guns and mortars. See Rokossovskii, *Velikiia pobeda na Volge*, p. 370. The 57th Panzer Corps had 101 tanks on the evening of December 18. See Kehrig, *Stalingrad*, p. 366, footnote 42.

11. The 17th Panzer Division was not a major reinforcement, having already suffered losses in previous combats. It totaled only 44 tanks. Total strength remaining in the three Panzer Divisions was only 101 tanks. See Kehrig, p. 366, footnote 42.

12. The name of the 4th Mechanized Corps was changed to the 3rd Guards Mechanized Corps upon orders of the People's Commissar of Defense.

13. The commander of the 6th Mechanized Corps was Major General of Tank Troops S. I. Bogdanov.

The Soviet plan for the final destruction of the encircled German forces at Stalingrad was entitled "Koltso" (Ring). The operational significance of Koltso was in the experiences derived by the General Staff in the first major Soviet encirclement/destruction inflicted on the Wehrmacht during the war. For the first time, Soviet forces faced the problems of sealing off a pocket and reducing its area. On land and in the air, Stavka *handled new complex strategic and operational issues. The error in computing the strength of the von Paulus grouping, as will be discussed, necessitated significant alterations of the initial Soviet plan. That* Stavka *mastered all the difficulties and conducted additional simultaneous diversions to allow an unhampered reduction of the pocket, demonstrates an excellent evolving awareness of the strategic possibilities of its forces: a point often overlooked in the search for German might-have-beens—Ed.*

7

Liquidation of the Encircled Stalingrad Group of the Enemy

The brief outline given below, drawn up on the basis of the materials of the Operations Section of the General Staff, is devoted exclusively to the final stage of the Stalingrad operation. It includes a survey of the offensive operation of the Don Front in the period from January 10 to February 2, 1943. During which the German–Fascist troops, encircled in the region of Stalingrad and consisting of the 4th Panzer and 6th Armies, were finally crushed and captured.

The Stalingrad Group of the Enemy (Its Composition and its Intentions About January 10, 1943)

Toward the end of November 1942, as a result of the powerful concentric attacks of the Southwestern Front, the Don Front, and the Stalingrad

134

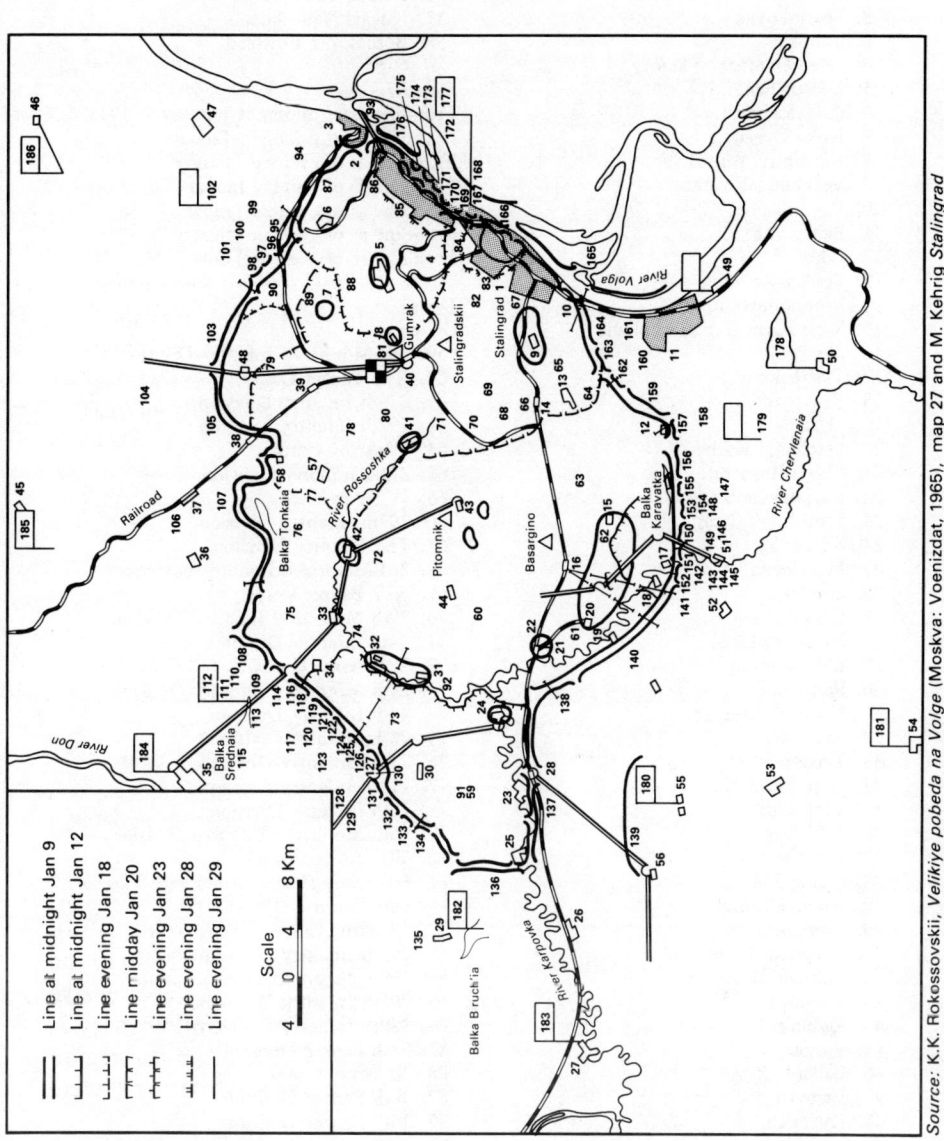

Line at midnight Jan 9
Line at midnight Jan 12
Line evening Jan 18
Line midday Jan 20
Line evening Jan 23
Line evening Jan 28
Line evening Jan 29

Scale
4   0   4   8 Km

Source: K.K. Rokossovskii, *Velikiye pobeda na Volge* (Moskva: Voenizdat, 1965), map 27 and M. Kehrig *Stalingrad* (Stuttgart:: Deutsche Verlags-Anstalt, 1974), p. 667, Appendix 9.

Map Seven
"The Destruction of the Stalingrad Pocket"

Cities
1. Stalingrad
2. Spartakovka
3. Rynok
4. "Red October" Factory
5. Gorodishche
6. Orlovka
7. Balka Desiataia
8. Kamennyi Buerak
9. Verkhne Elshanka
10. Kuporosnoe
11. Beketovka
12. Elkhi
13. Peschanka
14. Voroponovo Station
15. State Farm Gornaia Poliana
16. Basargino
17. Tysbenko
18. Kravtsov
19. Skliarov
20. Peschanyi Karber
21. Novyi Rogachik
22. Karpovkaia Station
23. Voroshilov Camp
24. Karpovka
25. Marinovka
26. Sovetskii
27. Ilevka
28. Siding Prudboi
29. Illarionovskii
30. Poltavskii
31. Novo-Alekseevskii
32. Baburkin
33. Zapadnovka
34. State Farm No. 1
35. Vertiachii
36. Kotluban
37. Samofalovka
38. Siding 564
39. Konnyi Siding
40. Gumrak
41. Gonchara Farmstead
42. Bolshaia Rossoshka
43. Pitomnik
44. Dubinin
45. Fastov
46. Balka Dikova
47. Erzovka
48. Kuzmichi
49. Lesobaza
50. Ivanovka
51. Varvarovka
52. Vypasnoi
53. Buzinovka
54. Verkhne-Tsaritsynskii

55. Novyi Put
56. Sredne-Tsaritsynskii
57. Novaia Nadezhda
58. Borodkin Farmstead

Map Key
Frontline as of midnight January 9, 1943
Frontline as of midnight January 12
Frontline as of evening January 18
Frontline as of midday January 20
Frontline as of evening January 23
Frontline as of evening January 28
Frontline as of evening January 29

Units
German
59. 3rd Motorized Infantry Division
60. XIV Panzer Corps
61. 376th Infantry Division
62. 297th Infantry Division
63. IV Army Corps
64. 371st Infantry Division
65. IV Army Corps
66. 297th Infantry Division
67. 71st Infantry Division
68. 3rd Motorized Infantry Division
69. XIV Panzer Corps
70. 29th Motorized Infantry Division
71. 44th Infantry Division
72. VIII Army Corps
73. 29th Motorized Infantry Division
74. 44th Infantry Division
75. 76th Infantry Division
76. 113th Infantry Division
77. 113th Infantry Division
78. 76th Infantry Division
79. 60th Motorized Infantry Division
80. VIII Army Corps
81. 6th Army Headquarters with Flag and date "until 1- 15 -43"
82. LI Army Corps
83. 295th Infantry Division
84. 100th Jaegar Infantry Division
85. 305th Infantry Division
86. 389th Infantry Division
87. 24th Panzer Division
88. XI Army Corps
89. 16th Panzer Division
90. 16th Panzer Division
91. Units of the 1st Rumanian Cavalry Division
92. Units of the 14th and 25th Panzer Division
93. 149th Rifle Brigade
94. 159th Fortified Region

95. 116th Rifle Division
96. 7th Guards Tank Regiment
97. 99th Rifle Division
98. 226th Rifle Division
99. 299th Rifle Division
100. 64th Rifle Division
101. 124th Rifle Brigade
102. 66th Army Advanced Headquarters
103. 343rd Rifle Division
104. 1030th Regiment/ 260th Rifle Division
105. 1026 Regiment/ 260th Rifle Division
106. 1028th Regiment/ 260th Rifle Division
107. 54th Fortified Region
108. 49th Rifle Division
109. 84th Rifle Division
110. 273rd Rifle Division
111. 8th Guards Tank Regiment
112. 24th Army Advanced Headquarters
113. 233rd Rifle Division
114. 971st Regiment / 273rd Rifle Division
115. 252nd Rifle Division
116. 214th Rifle Division
117. 91st Tank Brigade
118. 9th Guards Tank Regiment
119. 27th Guards Rifle Division
120. Observation Post No. 2
121. 10th Guards Tank Regiment
122. 24th Rifle Division
123. Observation Post No. 1
124. 14th Guards Tank Regiment
125. 304th Rifle Division
126. 5th Guards Tank Regiment
127. 173rd Rifle Division
128. 23rd Rifle Division
129. 47th Guards Tank Regiment
130. 15th Guards Tank Regiment
131. 51st Guards Rifle Division
132. 293rd Rifle Division
133. 277th Rifle Division
134. 298th Rifle Division
135. 1st Guards Tank Regiment
136. 96th Rifle Division
137. 52nd Guards Rifle Division
138. 15th Guards Rifle Division

139. 120th Rifle Division
140. 115th Fortified Region
141. 156th Motorized Rifle Brigade
142. 254th Tank Brigade
143. 235th Tank Brigade
144. 234th Guards Tank Regiment
145. 189th Guards Tank Regiment
146. 29th Rifle Division
147. 154th Naval Infantry Brigade
148. 35th Tank Regiment
149. 166th Tank Regiment
150. 36th Guards Rifle Division
151. 38th Rifle Division
152. 422nd Rifle Division
153. 204th Rifle Division
154. 90th Tank Brigade
155. 143rd Rifle Brigade
156. 157th Rifle Division
157. 66th Naval Infantry Brigades
158. 38th Motorized Rifle Brigade
159. 169th Rifle Division
160. 113th Fortified Region
161. 7th Rifle Corps
162. 93rd Rifle Brigade
163. 97th Rifle Brigade
164. 96th Rifle Brigade
165. 77 Fortified Region
166. 13th Guards Rifle Division
167. 348th Regimental Artillery Battalion
168. 416th Independent Artillery Battalion
169. 284th Rifle Division
170. 92nd Rifle Brigade
171. 39th Guards Rifle Division
172. 156th Fortified Region
173. 45th Rifle Division
174. 95th Rifle Division
175. 138th Rifle Division
176. 400th Independent Artillery Battalion
177. 62nd Army Headquarters
178. Don Front Headquarters
179. 64th Army Advanced Headquarters
180. 57th Army Advanced Headquarters
181. 57th Army Headquarters
182. 21st Army Advanced Headquarters
183. 21st Army Headquarters
184. 65th Army Headquarters
185. 24th Army Headquarters
186. 66th Army Headquarters

Source: K. K. Rokossovskii, *Velikiye pobeda na Volge* (Moskva: Voenizdat, 1965), map 27 and M. Kehrig *Stalingrad* (Stuttgart: *Deutsche Verlags-Anstalt, 1974*), *p. 667, Appendix 9.*

Front—organized and carried out in accordance with the plan of the *Stavka* of the Red Army—the large group of German–Fascist troops surrounded west of Stalingrad, between the Volga and the Don rivers, was completely encircled.

The encircled group of German–Fascist troops was comprised of the following:

● *4th Army Corps*—before October 1942, the Schwedler group of the 4th Panzer Army, which became a part of the 6th Army; the 297th, 371st German and 20th Rumanian Infantry Divisions, and the remnants of the 1st Rumanian Cavalry Division;

● *the 8th Army Corps*—76th, 113th, and 44th Infantry Divisions, and, before it was broken up, the 384th Infantry Division;

● *the 11th Army Corps*—60th Motorized Division, 16th Panzer Division, 24th Panzer Division, and, before it was broken up, the 94th Infantry Division;

● *the 51st Army Corps*—305th, 389th, and 295th Infantry Divisions, 100th Jaegar Division, 71st Infantry Division, and the 79th Division, before it was broken up; and

● *the 14th Panzer Corps*—29th and 3rd Motorized Divisions, 14th Panzer Division, and 376th Infantry Division.

A total of 22 divisions including 15 infantry, three motorized, three tank, and one Rumanian cavalry. The divisions of the enemy were well supplied with all kinds of the latest military equipment, a fact which is proved by the large amount of booty captured.

We should note that the reconnaissance organs of the front, using the statements of prisoners concerning the losses of their units, made a mistake in their calculations and estimates of the numerical strength of the encircled enemy group. The numerical strength of this group, in accordance with the data of the reconnaissance section of the staff of the Don Front, was as follows: 75,500 men; 1,977 guns of various calibers; 366 mortars; 6,881 machine guns; 34,730 submachine guns; and 245 tanks.

The final composition of the encircled group was precisely determined by a comparison of the losses, booty, and prisoners of the enemy with statements by Colonel Von Kulovski, the general staff officer (*Ib*) in charge of supply and administration (*Generalquartiermeister*) at the field forces headquarters.[1] By the end of November 1942, the encircled group of the enemy numbered up to 330,000 men, including the rear, units of reinforcement, and service personnel. By the time of the all-out offensive of the troops of the Don Front, on January 10, 1943, the encircled troops had suffered losses of up to 140,000 from hunger, cold, and disease and up to 190,000 soldiers and officers.

At the time in question, we still did not know precisely the plans of the German High Command with respect to the group encircled at Stalingrad; but separate statements of captured generals and the whole course of subsequent events confirmed that the German High Command still had the intention of joining up with the encircled group from the direction of Kotelnikovo and Verkhne-Chirskaia, to restore and reorganize the front, and to hold after this the area of Stalingrad [Colonel Von Kulovsky, a prisoner of war, said, for example, that the bend of the Don River and Stalingrad was to serve in the spring of 1943 as a base for an attack from Stalingrad toward the north and the departure for Moscow]. This was also necessary in order to remove the threat hanging over the Caucasus and, at the same time, to conserve the prestige of Hitler and his military policy in the eyes of Germany and its vassals.

The German High Command, as we can see, did not permit the encircled group to carry out an independent action to escape from encirclement; it made no serious efforts to do so. The attempt to come to its rescue by attacks from the west and northwest with a specially prepared army group under the command of General Field Marshal Manstein was unsuccessful. This time the German High Command was unsuccessful in carrying out the customary operation for coming to the rescue of the encircled troops—oftentimes successful in the past—namely, a halfway attack, formation of a corridor, and after this, the restoration of the front or the bringing out of the encircled troops. The plans of the German High Command were foiled by the timely counterattack of troops (5th Shock and 2nd Guards Armies) that we brought up and committed against the Tormosin and Kotelnikovo group of Germans.

The situation could have been made otherwise complicated if the German High Command had decided upon an independent withdrawal of the von Paulus group from encirclement by moving toward the west and southwest. It is possible that, in this case, they could have succeeded in withdrawing from the ring of encirclement a part of the personnel of the group, after losing the equipment and weapons. But the plan in mind prevailed over what was called for by the situation. The help expected from the west did not arrive, and the encircled troops were definitively isolated. The only means that they had for communicating with the rear areas was transport planes, and their only means of signal communications was their radio.

In this situation, which had developed on the Don Front toward the end of November 1942, it was very important for the staff of the Front to have a correct idea of the composition of the enemy group and its possibilities. Any miscalculation made by the reconnaissance organizations of the Don Front staff in the appraisal of the enemy could have led to serious complications in the situation in the area of the middle course of the Don, if the encircled group had acted in a different manner. That is, if, by decisive actions, it had made an effort to escape from encirclement at the very beginning without waiting for help from the outside.

After the failure at Kotelnikovo, the German High Command evidently decided toward the end of December to continue to hold the area of Stalingrad, even at the cost of losing 22 of its best divisions. Because of the situation that was developing (about this time) in the Millerovo direction, it was necessary for the Germans to tie down as many of our forces as possible in the area of Stalingrad to gain time and take measures for the restoration of their front, in which some large breaches had already been made; and to protect the continuing withdrawal of their Caucasus group, which about this time was also under threat of strategic encirclement, into the Rostov area.

Preparation of the Operation on the Don Front

The Combat Operations of the Don Front, November 24, 1942–December 12, 1942[2]

On November 24, 1942, the units of the left flank of the 66th Army, after discovering the withdrawal of the enemy from the area of Rynok, passed to the offensive and advanced a distance of 2 to 8 kilometers by the close of the day. In this sector, the enemy withdrew to a line more favorable for defense, consisting of some dominating elevations—135.4, 144.4, 147.6, and 145.1—to shorten his front and to meet the 3rd Motorized Division shifting to the southwest sector of the ring of encirclement. After fortifying himself on the line mentioned above and forming armored fire positions with his own tanks and ours, left from the period of the summer and fall tank battles, the enemy offered stubborn resistance and did not give the units of the 66th Army an opportunity to develop their offensive any further.

The units of the 66th Army were not able, by heavy pressure, to utilize the enemy's withdrawal to break through his defenses on the new line without a well-organized pursuit and breakthrough Gumrak and Gorodishche for a union with formations of the 62nd Army in Stalingrad. The failure of the 66th Army in this case is also explained by the passivity of the units of the 62nd Army, which were not sent out for action in a northwest direction; we did not take advantage of the situation for improving our position. The total result of the advance of the left flank of the 66th Army was its union with a part of the forces of the 62nd Army isolated in the area of Rynok and Spartakovka.

After the capture of Vertiachii and Peskovatka by the troops of the Don Front with the 21st, 65th, and 24th Armies, the attempt made on December 2–3 to break through the defenses of the enemy on the west and northwest sector of the ring of encirclement was unsuccessful. The troops of the armies mentioned were extended in the preceding offensive battles of encirclement lasting for many days. The command, cooperation, and the rear were not properly organized. The artillery could not give the rifle troops the necessary support in the offensive against the enemy. Able to consolidate his position quickly and successfully on the line of Elevations 122.9, 121.3, 124.5, 126.7, 129.0, and 135.1, the enemy covered the main directions leading into the center of the ring of encirclement.

The enemy was able to organize strong defenses by withdrawing to this favorable line for defense, by occupying the outpost area on the heights and by placing his main forces in the fortified positions of the middle ring of Stalingrad fortified area along the Rossoshka and Chervlenaia Rivers. To these positions, he shifted units that had not been mauled too badly from the other sectors of the rings of encirclement, and these units held up our advance by strongly organized fire and counterattacks using infantry and tanks. The line of elevations on which the enemy fortified himself dominated the dispositions to the west of his locality up to the Don River. It enabled the enemy to observe the advance of our troops, to conceal the depths of his defenses and rear from our ground observation, and to cover at the same time his landing strips and airdromes set up east of the Rossoshka River from observation and artillery fire. This also explains the subsequent efforts of the enemy to hold this line at all costs.

Up to December 12, when the enemy made a counterattack from the direction of Kotelnikovo, our troops carried out a partial regrouping; brought up reserves, artillery, and rear organizations; conducted reconnaissance and combat to improve our positions; and fought with varying success to capture and hold the elevations in the west and south sectors of the ring of encirclement.

The terrain in the area of encirclement, where events of the concluding phase of the operation took place, exerted a substantial influence upon the actions of the troops of both sides. The battlefield had an area of about 1,450 square kilometers located between the Volga and Don rivers along the ring of Orlovka, Kuzmichi, Borodin, Collective Farm No. 1, Dmitrievka, Marinovka, Karpovka, Novyi Rogachik, Rokotino, Tsybenko, and Elkhi. For the most part it was bare, without vegetation; rolling, with a gradual and gentle transition from one undulation to the next steppe; cut up by deep ravines, running from the west toward the east. The open terrain makes orientation and masking difficult for the troops. In the winter time, orientation in this locality is still more complicated by the presence of snow cover. The terrain gradually rises from the west toward the east and has many elevations; the crests and ridges are, for the greater part, plateaus with a barely perceptible convexity.

The elevations and their crests enabled the defense to use the flat trajectory of the infantry fire and small-caliber artillery in a very effective manner and they also gave the defense a great advantage in observing both the battlefield and the depths of the dispositions of the attacker. Observation was possible to an average distance of 5 to 6 kilometers. The possession of the dominating heights and of the inhabited localities by the enemy made it easier for him to organize defenses, to conduct fire, and to take antitank measures. The frequent occurrence of elevations alternating with ravines in the possible directions for the action of our tanks and infantry made it possible for the enemy to organize deep defenses and centers of resistance, coordinated with a system of flanking fire by machine guns, submachine guns, and antitank guns.

The character of the terrain made it possible for the enemy to make extensive use of oblique fire and flank fire at close and average ranges and from reverse slopes. Placing fire positions on the reverse slopes subjected the attacking rifle troops wedging into the defenses to the whole firepower of the defense. Thus the rifle troops could not, due to the absence of reference points, correctly designate the targets for the artillery and mortars supporting it. Here, the maneuverability and actions of the tanks could be carried out only against the crests of the elevations, in comparatively narrow corridors between the ravines, easily covered by fire or antitank artillery, engineer entanglements, and mine fields.

The enemy's possession of fortified lines along the east bank of the Rossoshska and Chervlenaia rivers, a number of fortified, inhabited localities (Gorodishche, Gumrak, Karpovka, Alekseevka, etc.), and of the Stalingrad fortified area helped the enemy to a certain extent in organizing its defense in the ring of encirclement. During the fall battles, even before encirclement, the enemy was able to fortify himself strongly in the northern, eastern, and southeastern sectors of the ring. In the subsequent battles, he was able to hold the sectors and from them offer strong, organized resistance.

In addition to this, after the great fall–summer tank battles, on the battlefield in the north in the area of Orlovka, Collective Farm Opytnoe Pole, and Kuzmichi both our own knocked-out tanks and those of the Germans were left on the battlefield, and the enemy used them as armored fire positions.

The inhabited localities in this area are few in number and located chiefly along the ring of encirclement and within it, close to the banks of the rivers and streams. Hence, the majority of the inhabited localities were in the hands of the encircled enemy. Our units had at their disposal only a few inhabited localities, the majority of which were burned or destroyed in the preceding battles.

The area of the city of Stalingrad, stretched out along the right bank of the Volga, facilitated the conduct of defensive battle and hindered offensive operations, which consisted of long, drawn-out street fighting.

This hindered the freedom of maneuver of the units of the 62nd and 64th Armies operating in the southwestern sector.

The enemy's possession of the Stalingrad railway center made supply and evacuation difficult for the troops of the Don Front, especially for the units of its south sector, with their communications greatly extended and cut by the Volga.

The numerous deep ravines with steep banks and many spurs in this steppe area where the battle of Stalingrad was fought played an important part in the fighting.[3] They served as places for concentration and cover for the reserves, staffs, and rear organizations and were also utilized as cross-country march routes for the covered approach of reserves, artillery, and tanks. In the ravines, the troops were also protected from the cold winter winds that blew continually. Usually these same ravines served as targets for bombing from the air and fire concentrations from artillery and mortars.

Supplying the troops in this area with fuel—especially for the units of the Red Army, which were operating for the most part outside of inhabited localities at temperatures of 25 to 30 degrees below zero—developed into a special problem. Fuel for heating the troops and preparing warm food for them could not be secured close by due to the conditions prevailing in the locality, and it was necessary to bring it up from the rear. For this, it was necessary to have additional transport means and service personnel. For the enemy, having in his hands all the inhabited localities with their wooden structures, the problem of securing fuel was solved much more easily.

The snow cover did not have any great influence upon the operations of the troops, because it was not deep and, as a result of thaws, was converted into an ice crust that even facilitated the movement of motor vehicle transport off the roads. Only the snowdrifts in the ravines were troublesome; they rendered difficult the utilization of the ravines for the quartering of troops and required a great deal of work in clearing the roads at the places where drifts intercepted the ravines.

The Preparation of the Troops for the General Offensive (December 12, 1942–January 9, 1943)

For the command of the Red Army, it was extremely undesirable to have in the rear of its advancing troops the encircled group of the enemy, still capable of active operations and having in its possession the Stalingrad junction of railways leading to Salsk-Tikhoretskaya-Rostov and Likhava-Shakhty-Rostov. The operational situation required that the command settle accounts as quickly as possible with this enemy group in order to release our troops and protect railway transport for reinforcement and further development of the offensive toward Rostov or some other no less important direction.

The successful development of events in the area of the middle course of the Don and the necessity of crushing and destroying as quickly as possible the group of German–Fascist troops, surrounded and completely isolated between the Don and Volga rivers in the area west of Stalingrad, required (and at the same time made possible) a division of fronts. The 5th Shock, 2nd Guards, 51st, and 28th Armies of the Stalingrad Front, moving toward the west, received about January 1, 1943, an independent mission and formed a part of the South Front to continue operations in the Rostov direction. A part of the forces of the Stalingrad Front (62nd, 64th, and 57th Armies), holding the ring of encirclement on the east and south, were placed in the makeup of the Don Front, which was also assigned the mission of capturing or destroying the encircled troops of the enemy.

After the elimination of the threat of an enemy breakthrough from Kotelnikovo, the troops of the Don Front started systematic preparations for the final smashing and destruction of the encircled troops of the enemy in accordance with the plan received and known as *Koltso* (Ring). The plan was drawn up by the staff of the Front about December 26, 1942. The basis of the plan was set forth in the directives of the Chief of the General Staff of the Red Army, Marshal Comrade A.M. Vasilevskii, (No. 01/op November 30, 1942).[4] In accordance with the plan, we were to break up the encircled enemy into separate parts and then destroy them. This plan was approved by the *Stavka* of the Red Army.

For carrying out the mission of smashing and destroying the encircled 6th German Army, we used the 21st, 65th, 24th, 66th, 62nd, 64th, and 57th Armies, which had the following effectives on January 9, 1943:[5]

	Armies							
Military Units in Formation	*65th*	*21st*	*24th*	*66th*	*62nd*	*64th*	*57th*	**Total**
Rifle Divisions	8	7	4	6	6	5	3	39
Rifle Brigades	—	—	—	2	1	7	—	10
Tank Brigades	1	—	—	—	—	1	2	4
Independent Tank Regiments	6	1	1	1	Sig. Co.	2	2	13
Artillery reinforcement:								
(a) Artillery regiments of the reserves of *Stavka*	27	2	1	2	4	10	9	55
(b) Artillery mortar regiments	—	3	—	2	2	—	1	8
(c) *PVO* Artillery regiments	5	4	1	—	1	1	1	13
Guards Mortar Brigades	4	—	—	—	—	1	—	5
Guards Mortar Regiments	9	1	1	2	2	1	1	17
Fortified Regions	—	—	—	—	—	2	—	2
Independent machine gun artillery battalions	—	—	5	5	4	—	5	19

In the reserves of the Front, there were 1 tank brigade, 3 independent tank regiments, 1 independent tank battalions, and 2 *PVO* antiaircraft artillery regiments. At the beginning of operations, we had about 280,000 men in these formations; about 4,000 weapons, not counting the Guards' Mortars; about 6,300 mortars of various calibers; and 232 tanks in formations, including 121 heavy, 58 medium, and 45 light. We should state that almost all the rifle units, tank units, and units of combined arms were weak in numerical strength at the beginning of the offensive as a result of combat losses. In the majority of the divisions, there were not more than 4,000 to 5,000 men, and the equipment of the tank units was not up to standard strength.[6]

In the period of preparation for the all-out offensive, the Army Air Forces of the Front continued the fight against the transport aviation of the enemy, and the troops captured Elevations 126.7 (Kazachii, Kurgan), 121.3, 122.9, and 137.2, thus securing for themselves a more favorable jump-off position. In this same period, the 65th Army, operating in the direction of the main attack, received reinforcements, bringing the strength of its divisions up to 7,000 men.

THE PLANNING OF THE OPERATIONS

The plan of the offensive operations of the troops of the Don Front to defeat and destroy the German–Fascist group encircled in the area of Stalingrad provided for attacks against the intersecting directions to break through the defenses of the enemy, breaking up his forces into separate parts and capturing or destroying those garrisons that continued to resist.

The chief blow was to be struck from the northwestern sector of the ring of encirclement from the west toward the east, from the front Elevations 131.7 and 122.9 (front of breakthrough, 20 kilometers) in the general direction of Baburkin, Gonchar Farmstead, Stalingradii State Farm, and the village of Krasnyi Oktyabr. The purpose of this attack was to split the encircled group from the west to the east and then to destroy the parts separately.

For striking the main blow, we used the troops of the 21st, 65th, and 24th Armies. In this attack, the 65th Army was assigned the leading role; it was to attack over the entire front (12 kilometers), having five rifle divisions in the first echelon and three divisions in the second. These reinforcements (see table on page 144) made it possible to create a density of artillery on its sector of 130 guns to a kilometer of front. To the right of the 65th Army, the 21st Army was to attack with its left flank on a front of 4 kilometers with the forces of two rifle divisions, reinforced by one tank regiment, two artillery regiments, and three mortar regiments of the *Stavka* reserves. On the left, the 24th Army—with three rifle divisions reinforced by one tank regiment, two artillery regiments, and two battalions of high-powered artillery from the *Stavka* reserves—was to attack with its right flank on a 4-kilometer front.

Secondary attacks were to be made from the northeastern and southern sectors of the ring of encirclement. The first engaged units of the 66th Army—five rifle divisions, one tank, one artillery, and two mortar regiments of the *Stavka* reserves, and two Guards Mortar regiments— with a center on a 7-kilometer front in the direction of the Drevni Val Siding and Novaia Nadezhda Farmstead. The second attack involved units of the 64th and 57th Armies from the Popov-Rokotino Front (12 kilometers) with the forces of four divisions, three naval brigades, and two tank brigades reinforced with 12 *Stavka* artillery regiments, four Guards Mortar regiments (M-13s), and one heavy Guards Mortar brigade (M-30s) in the general direction toward Kravtsov and Station Voroponovo.

In the selection of the direction of the main and secondary attacks, the command of the Don Front proceeded from the following considerations.

1. On the front of the main attack, the troops of the enemy on the defensive were chiefly those that had been badly mauled in the fighting of November and December 1942, and their combat ability had been reduced by the retreat, losses suffered, and other causes connected with the encirclement.

2. The main attack had to be made against the basic enemy forces under encirclement. Its purpose was to break them up and, at the same time, enable our troops to gain their rear, aerodromes, and control points, that is, to strike their most sensitive objects of defense.

3. It bears remembering that the enemy had occupied and reinforced the line of the western sector over a short period after the withdrawal of his units from behind the Don and, hence, the defense was weaker than, for example, on the north sector, where the enemy had successfully defended himself over a period of four months and had had sufficient time for reinforcing his defense with engineer works. In addition to this, on the defense lines of the north sector, the enemy had divisions that were more stable and less shaken up and that had repelled the attacks of our troops in the fall battles of 1942.

4. The striking of blows in the directions mentioned above did not require any complicated regrouping of forces.

5. The conditions of the locality made possible a better utilization of the shock power and capacity for maneuvering of tanks in the directions selected. The numerous ravines, running in the directions of the attacks, gave to the tank units a certain freedom of maneuverability and made it easier for them to move into the depths of the ring of encirclement.

The beginning of the general offensive was set tentatively for the morning of January 6 and depended upon the time of arrival of replacements and ammunition. It was expected to take seven days to carry out this operation. The operation was divided into three phases:

● *1st phase* (two days): destruction of the western part of the encircled group and arrival on the line of Novaia Nadezhda Farmstead, Gonchar Farmstead, Elevation 115.6, and Peschanka.
● *2nd phase* (two days): destruction of the enemy in the area of Peschanka, Stalingrad, and Gumrak.
● *3rd phase* (three days): the final mopping up (with a part of the forces) of all the area of the separate groups of enemy still resisting.

The relative strength of forces by January 10, 1943, on the Don Front was the following:

Name	Troops of the Don Front	Troops of the Encircled Enemy	Ratio
Men	281,000	190,000[1]	1.5:1
Guns	3,770	6,200	1.0:2.0
Mortars (without Guards Mortars)	6,300	1,500	4.2:1.0
Machine guns	7,300	13,700	1.0:1.9
Submachine guns	30,000	10.700	3.0:1.0
Rifles	164,000	157,000	1.0:1.0
Tanks	250	1,800[2]	1.0:7.2
Motor vehicles	9,400	81,000	1.0:8.6

Remarks: 1. The data concerning the numerical strength of the enemy are given on the basis of summarized information concerning losses sustained by the enemy during the period of the operations (from January 10 to February 2, 1943).
2. Included in the 1,800 tanks of the enemy are, of course, also the tanks knocked out in previous battles, left on the field of battle, and suitable for use by the enemy as armored firing positions.

In the relative strength, it is necessary to bear in mind that the data pertaining to the numerical strength of the enemy requires correction, especially with regard to the number of guns and mortars, a part of which were captured by our units or damaged and, possibly, were not used by the enemy in battle. In addition to this, in the study of the relative strength, it is also necessary to take into account the following:

1. The number of bayonets among the troops of the Don Front was certainly less than those of the enemy, nearly all of which, with his rear units—to say nothing of the security units—could be used on the fighting line.

2. The progressive decrease, in the course of battle, of the quantity of ammunition, food, and fuel at the disposal of the enemy.

3. The lowering of the morale of the encircled troops of the enemy, as a result of heavy losses, worsening of the supply situation, losses in territory, losing battles, and so on.

4. Improvement in the fighting spirit of the soldiers of the Red Army as a result of victories in the destruction and crushing of the encircled German–Fascist group.

5. Shortening of the width of the front and the increase in the density of the combat formations of the troops of the Don Front in the course of successful combat operations.

From the table given, we can see that the troops of the Don Front had only a slight numerical advantage over the enemy, who was on the defensive. The most favorable advantage was the relative strength in mortars and submachine guns. In other respects, the relative strength was in favor of the enemy. Hence, in the evaluation of the successes on the Don Front and in the actions against the encircled troops of the enemy, it is necessary to take into account the remarks made above. In addition to this, we should not forget the influence of the leaflets dropped in enormous numbers by our air forces over the territory occupied by the enemy before the beginning of the general offensive. The leaflets made known to the soldiers and officers the text of the ultimatum that had been rejected by the command of the encircled German troops.

UTTER DEFEAT AND DESTRUCTION OF THE ENCIRCLED ENEMY TROOPS
(January 10–February 2, 1943)

The *Stavka*, in the person of the representative of the Headquarters of the Supreme Command of the Red Army, Colonel General of Artillery N.N. Voronov, and the Commander of the Don Front Lieutenant-General K.K. Rokossovskii, in order to avoid useless loss of life, gave on January 8, 1943, the following ultimatum to the command and to all the officers and troops of the German forces encircled at Stalingrad.

To the commander of the German 6th Army Colonel General von Paulus or his deputy and to all the officers and troops of the encircled German troops at Stalingrad.

The German 6th Army, units of the 4th Panzer Army, and

the units of reinforcement assigned to them have been completely surrounded since 23 November 1942.

The units of the Red Army have encircled this group of German forces with a solid ring. There is no foundation for any hope of saving our troops by an offensive of the German forces from the south and southwest. The German troops hastening to help you have been smashed by the units of the Red Army and the rest of these forces are withdrawing to Rostov.

German transport aviation, bringing you a famine ration of food, ammunition, and fuel, has been forced oftentimes, as a result of the successful and determined advance of the Red Army, to change airdromes and to fly from a long distance to the encircled troops. This same German transport aviation has suffered heavy losses in airplanes and crews as a result of the action of Russian aviation. Its assistance to the encircled troops has become ineffective. The situation of your encircled troops is serious; they are suffering from hunger, disease, and cold. The severe Russian winter has only started. The severe frost, cold winds, and snowstorms are still ahead, and your soldiers are not provided with winter uniforms, and are living under unsanitary conditions. You, as commander, and all the officers of the encircled troops understand very well that you have no real chance of breaking through the ring of encirclement. Your position is desperate and further resistance is useless. Under the conditions which have developed, your situation is hopeless; and in order to avoid useless loss of life, we propose that you accept the following conditions of capitulation: (1) All the encircled German troops, including you and your staff, are to cease resistance; (2) You are to surrender to us all the personnel, armament, military equipment and military property in good condition. We guarantee life and safety to all officers and soldiers who cease resistance and, after the termination of the war, return to Germany or some other country, depending upon the desire expressed by the individual.

All the personnel surrendering may keep their military uniform, various insignia and orders, personal effects, valuables, and the higher officers may keep their silent weapons (i.e., swords, daggers—Ed.). All officers, non-coms., and soldiers surrendering will be given normal rations immediately. All the wounded, sick, and frostbitten will be given medical attention. Your answer is expected by 1000 hours Moscow time 9 January 1943 in written form through your personal representative, who must come in a light vehicle, with a white flag, along the road toward Konnii Siding-Kotluban Station. Your representative will be met by Russian officers acting as agents in the area "B" 0.5 kilometers southeast of Siding 564 at 10:00 A.M. on 9 January 1943. If you reject our proposal for capitulation, we warn you that the troops of the Red Army and the Red Air Force will be obliged to carry out the work of destroying the encircled German troops and for this you will bear the responsibility.

The command of the encircled German–Fascist troops refused to accept the aforementioned ultimatum, offered through parlementaires on two occasions (January 8 and 9). After the refusal of the encircled troops to lay down their arms, the troops of the Don Front, on the morning of January 10, 1943, started a determined offensive for the purpose of crushing, capturing, or destroying the resisting enemy.

The offensive started with a powerful artillery preparation against the main of resistance of the encircled enemy. At 9:00 A.M., the troops along the ring of encirclement moved to the attack of the fortified positions.

By the close of January 13, the resistance of the enemy had been broken in the western and southern sectors of the ring of encirclement. Units of the 65th and 21st Armies, advancing from the west, reached the west bank of the Rossoshka River and entirely cleared Dmitrievka, Marinovka, and Karpovka of the enemy. The right flank units of the 57th Army and units of the left flank of the 64th Army, having overcome stubborn resistance, reached at this same time the line Gornaia Poliana State Farm to Rokotino. There they occupied a favorable position, making it possible by a turning of the flanks and action along the front of the enemy to roll up his combat formations. On January 14, the Commander of the 57th Army made good use of this position, and as early as the close of the day, the shock group of the Army had cleared the east bank of the Chervlenaia River of the enemy, seizing the areas of Staryi Novyi Rogachik, and Karpovskaia Station. By these successful operations of the 57th Army, the success of the subsequent advance of troops of the front operating from the west and southwest was assured.

As a result of the gaining of the flanks of the units of the enemy, on the defensive on the east bank of the Rossoshka River, by the shock group of the 57th Army and the further operations of this group, on the morning of January 15, the enemy started a disorderly retreat toward Stalingrad, showing very little resistance and throwing away equipment and armament. Between January 15–17, the enemy was definitely defeated. On these days, the units of the 24th Army also won victories. During the three days of offensive operations, the troops of the Front advanced 15 to

20 kilometers and reached the edge of Gonchar Farmstead, Alekseevka, and Peschanka, having cleared the enemy from more than half of the area he previously occupied in the ring of encirclement. Besides, the enemy suffered heavy losses in killed, wounded, and prisoners (more than 30,000). In addition, we captured a great deal of equipment and weapons: in motor vehicles alone more than 15,000; about 1,000 guns; 370 airplanes, and so on.

Only in the sectors of (exclusive) Gumrak, Voroponovo Station, Peschanka, and Staro-Dubovka did the enemy succeed—and then only for a short time—in stopping the advance of the right flank of the 21st Army, units of the 57th Army, and the left flank of the 64th Army. Here the enemy held up the advances of our forces by making use, for defensive purposes, of dominating heights and fortified towns and villages; by bringing up fresh forces taken from other sectors of his front; and by strongly organized fire and counterattacks. The Military Soviet of the Front assigned to these armies the following task: to use the time before January 21 for preparation, putting the units in order, replenishing supplies, and careful reconnaissance of the enemy. They were again ready to assume the offensive on the morning of January 22.

By this time, the units of the 24th, 65th, and 21st Armies were continuing the advance and reached the line of Novaia Nadezhda Farmstead and Gumrak.

Again assuming the offensive along the whole front on the morning of January 22 and having broken the enemy resistance in the Voroponovo-Peschanka area, the troops of the Front began a gradual advance, breaking the resistance of the garrisons and pressing eastward toward Stalingrad the remnants of the broken enemy units. By January 26, the units of the 64th Army captured the southern edge of the central part of Stalingrad. And the troops of the 21st Army joined up with parts of the 62nd Army in the area of the village of Krasnii Oktiabr and Mamaev Kurgan, separating the enemy withdrawing into the area of Stalingrad into two isolated groups, a northern group and a southern group.

On January 26, the fate of the encircled enemy was already sealed. The Stalingrad railroad junction was practically cleared of the enemy and was quickly restored by the timely bringing up of railroad units. Beginning on January 26, the situation that had developed in the area of Stalingrad made it possible for the *Stavka* to begin placing in reserve certain parts of the forces of the Don Front and to send them to other active sectors of the fronts of the Red Army.

From January 27 to February 2, the troops of the Front continued to attack, capturing in succession first the southern group and then the northern group of the enemy, with the remnants of these units surrendering in mass with their officers and generals. We also captured the staff of the German 6th Army, headed by von Paulus, commander of the 6th Army, who had received the day before the Knight's Cross and the title of Field Marshal.*

On February 2, 1943, the troops of the Don Front completed the liquidation of the encircled German–Fascist group, having cleared Stalingrad of the enemy. Beginning on February 2, the troops of the Front, having carried out their mission, ceased military action, and started regrouping and bringing units into the area for loading and transporting by railroad into new areas. From this day on, Stalingrad was in the deep rear. The great Volga waterway was also free and began preparation for spring navigation.

Summary, Conclusions, and Deductions

The Battle of Stalingrad and Its Concluding Phase

The offensive operation for smashing and destroying the large encircled group of Germans, well equipped with all kinds of modern weapons, will pass into the history books of the Great Patriotic War of the Soviet Union against the Fascist invaders as one of the most brilliant pages. As yet, the history of warfare records no case when a large encircled group of the enemy was completely crushed and not a single one of its soldiers escaped from the ring of encirclement, and all equipment and armament in enormous quantities fell entirely into the hands of the victors as war booty.

The encirclement and subsequent complete defeat at Stalingrad of 20 elite divisions of the German Army, famous for their victories in Europe, exerted a great influence upon the whole course of the winter campaign of 1942–43; inspired still greater confidence in the strength and power of the Red Army; strengthened faith in the great ability and skill of its field commanders among our troops and officers and among our people and our friends; and sowed panic and feelings of uncertainty and fear among the troops and leaders of the enemy. This was the greatest defeat ever suffered in the history of warfare by an enemy overconfident and ready to risk too much.

Losing a large territory (480,000 square kilometers), masses of weapons and equipment prepared for the spring and summer campaign of 1943, bases and dumps; witnessing the smashing of large units and armies of the Germans, Rumanians, Hungarians, and Italians; and suffering great losses in personnel (about 1,200,000) seriously undermined the prestige of the German High Command and the German General Staff who had prided themselves upon their infallibility and precise methods of

*For data as to the number of prisoners and war booty, refer to "The Stalingrad Group of the Enemy."

planning and operational leadership. The utter defeat at Stalingrad also showed its effect on the morale and combat ability of the soldiers of the German Army and its vassals. After the encirclement at Stalingrad, the Hitlerite forces, at the least threat to their flanks, began to fear encirclement and quickly abandoned solid lines of defense previously occupied. The German soldier was highly reluctant to go to the Eastern Front. Such is the general summary of the Stalingrad operation.

The basic idea used in the planning of the operation for crushing the encircled enemy—namely, that of breaking up his group into separate, smaller groups by powerful blows from the west—was conceived a long time before the beginning of the general offensive and soon after the troops of the Don Front captured the areas of Vertyachii and Peskovatka on the left bank of the Don. This idea was laid down in operational Directive No. 01 of November 30, 1942, by the representative of the *Stavka*, Comrade Marshal A.M. Vasilevskii to provide for immediate action (beginning December 2) of the troops of the Don and Stalingrad Fronts against the encircled units of the enemy withdrawing from the west and northwest from behind the Don and not yet having time to fortify themselves and to organize their defenses. However, by reason of the complicated situation—extended line of troops, lagging of the artillery and the rear organizations, numerical weaknesses of the units, and later on, the complications on the Kotelnikovo sector due to the approach of large tank forces of the enemy on this sector—it was impossible for our troops to carry out this mission at that time.

The aforementioned Directive also laid the battle of preparations for warding off possible counterattacks of the enemy from the outside for the purpose of rescuing the encircled forces. For such an eventuality, the Directive provided for the creation of reserves: up to three divisions and four tank–destroyer artillery regiments in the area of Kalach and further south and three divisions (from the *Stavka* reserves) in the areas of Verkhne-Buzinovka and Verhkne-Tsaritsynskii. In subsequent planning of the operations by the staff of the Don Front, its general idea and direction of the attacks remained practically the same.

A great weakness in the planning of the operation was the miscalculation by the staff of the Front in estimating the strength of the encircled enemy. As a result, errors were made in the determination of the stages of the operation and the fixing of periods for their realization. In reality, the enemy was much stronger and more numerous than the reconnaissance organizations estimated by the Front. This explains the drawing-out of the operations, which, instead of lasting 7 days as planned, lasted 23 days. In the end, this delayed the release and withdrawal of the strategic reserves for other sectors where they were needed.

The failure of the encircled enemy to make any determined effort to break out of encirclement saved our troops from a situation that might have been serious. At the same time, the passive attitude of the German–Fascist troops encircled in the area of Stalingrad was the result of a great strategic error on the part of the German command, an underestimation of the strength and capacity for action of the Red Army.

Preparing an attack from the side of Kotelnikovo, the German command did not have enough aerial reconnaissance at that time and therefore did not have any knowledge of the resources the Red Army possessed. The German command did not have any possibility of concealing their mobile group, which had advanced toward Kotelnikovo and further to the northwest for a breakthrough and linkup with the surrounded troops of von Paulus' Sixth Army. The presence of only a weak screen from the cavalry in this direction (the 81st Cavalry Division) undoubtedly would have led the German command into error and would confirm all future activity. The activities of the German Kotelnikovo grouping, because of their lack of reconnaissance, appreciation of the Red Army, and of action by the surrounded troops to be met, thus doomed to failure the plans of the German command to rescue the surrounded troops, to reestablish the front, and to retain for itself the region of Stalingrad.

Among the negative phases resulting from an underestimation of the condition of the enemy and the planning of the operation itself, we should also mention the absence of a short-range attack by the units of the 57th Army in the direction east of Prudboi and Karpovka to meet the enveloping left flank of the 21st Army, operating with the mission of liquidating the salient Dmitrievka, Marinovka, and Karpovka. The absence of such an attack enabled the enemy on January 10–11 to escape the blows of our units without any special difficulties or losses to withdraw to the east and also rendered difficult from the very beginning the action for breaking up the enemy group.

Among the defects in the planning, we should also mention the unfortunate choice of direction for delivering the second attack (on the basis of strength of the group and missions) on the sector of and with the forces of the 66th Army, which had before it units of the enemy stubbornly defending themselves, mauled very little during the past battles, and having well-equipped defenses. The repeated offensive operations of the 66th Army, in previous battles on this sector, were unsuccessful, and the troops did not have the confidence, enthusiasm, and persistence necessary for an offensive. In comparison with the other shock sectors of the front, the 66th Army had received only a small amount of artillery reinforcement. For striking the strong and well-organized defense of the enemy on this sector, the artillery assigned to the Army from the *Stavka* reserves consisted of one artillery regiment and two mortar regiments, was clearly insufficient, and of course, it could not assure a breakthrough on a front of 7 kilometers. The tank reinforcement of the Army consisted of only one tank regiment, used already in the preceding battles and having in its formation only a few tanks. Hence, in the zone of this Army, success did not appear until the end of the operation, when the resistance of the enemy was broken everywhere and when the units of the 24th and 65th Armies gained the rear of the enemy units defending themselves against the 66th Army.

The positive planning of the plan of operations of the Don Front, the combat intentions, and the directions of the main and secondary attacks were the following:

- the effort to break up the encircled group into separate parts by powerful blows from the west toward the east and then to destroy the separate isolated garrisons.
- the pinning down of the forces of the enemy by secondary blows along all of the main directions.
- the direction of the attacks along the shortest routes leading into the areas of the basic vital centers (airdromes and landing fields, points of control, areas of the centers of signal communications and staffs, communications, and fortified centers) and objects of the defenses of the encircled enemy.
- the making of the attacks in such a way that, after the breakthrough, we could direct the action of our troops along the combat formations of the defenses of the enemy for gradually rolling them up, in order to deny the enemy an opportunity to hold a fortified line.

Among the most instructive actions of the troops in this operation and the ones deserving attention were the skillful and energetic operations of a comparatively small group of the 57th Army. This group made good use of its flank position for rolling up the combat formations of the enemy defenses and subsequently developing its offensive by a turn of 90 degrees in the direction of Basargino Siding and Voroponovo against the enemy who had been disorganized by these actions.

The actions of our artillery, which played an exceptional part in this operation, are of special interest. The Front command—taking into account the lack of personnel in the combat formations, resulting from the numerical weaknesses of the rifle units and formations—was obliged to assign to the artillery the basic task of carrying out the operation. The artillery, by accompanying the rifle troops with powerful fire and utilizing wheeled vehicles, neutralized the resistance of the enemy and destroyed his fire positions and personnel. The mass of the artillery and mortar fire, directed against the encircled troops, helped to increase the lack of confidence, feelings of despair, and panicky attitude among the ranks of the enemy and, to a considerable degree, facilitated the actions of our rifle troops.

The breaking up of the encircled enemy into separate groups was not achieved in the course of the operations. It was not until the end of operations in the area of Stalingrad that the troops of the Don Front were able to separate the enemy into two isolated groups, a northern group and a southern group. The failure of the troops of the Front in this respect is explained by the efforts of the enemy to escape each blow every time there was a threat on his flanks. The enemy's possession of a large territory enabled him to carry out this maneuver with comparative impunity right up to the time that he moved into the area of Stalingrad.

The concluding phase of encirclement was the decisive stage in the operation for encirclement and destruction of the large enemy group made up of troops of combined arms. In carrying out the missions of this stage of the operations, the command had to do the following:

● direct the maximum effort, chiefly of the mobile equipment, for smashing unit by unit the fresh forces of the enemy—generally highly mobile forces saturated with tanks—approaching from the outside to help or rescue the encircled group.

● locate reserves in the basic directions and paths for warding off possible enemy attacks, having as their aim the breaking of the ring of encirclement from the inside and escaping from it.

● to close the ring of encirclement tightly without leaving a single sector unswept by the fire of artillery, mortars, and machine guns.

● assure the rapid forward movement of the units and formations (large units of combined arms), creating a new outer front, and in this way force removal to a greater distance of the airdromes and bases feeding the encircled group. The command also had to render difficult the giving of assistance by counterattacks from the outside, and, at the same time, to facilitate the creation and development, among the encircled troops of the enemy, a feeling of being in a hopeless situation.

● have all the forces of aviation, antiaircraft artillery, and machine guns engage in actions for the purpose of destroying the transport aviation of the enemy supplying the encircled group and keeping out of the area of encirclement.

● detail special artillery and mortar units for conducting fire against landing fields and airports of the encircled enemy at the moment of landings by combat and transport planes.

● to use the captured artillery and ammunition for conducting uninterrupted harassing fire against the places of concentration of enemy troops within the ring of encirclement.

● interfere with radio communications of the encirled enemy with the outside front, with the forces approaching to render assistance, and with aviation, by utilizing radio equipment especially designed for putting interference into the atmosphere.

● utilize the less mobile mortar, artillery, and machine gun units of the Fortified Regions for reinforcing the units outflanking the ring of the encircled enemy.

In the planning and directly carrying out of the missions for smashing and destroying the large encircled operational group of the enemy, it was necessary for the command to do the following:

1. To direct the main forces and equipment and to take advantage of the weakest places in the defenses of the encircled enemy, within a short time and in the most effective manner, to strike a stunning blow and break up his defensive group into separate parts.
2. In the course of the offensive, to seek out in the general system of the enemy defenses those objectives, which when attacked, would weaken the resistance of the enemy and lower his combat power. These objectives include reserves, airdromes and landing fields, control points, ammunition dumps, stores of food and fuel, basic communications, and routes for the maneuver of reserves.
3. To select directions to these objectives for the main and secondary attacks leading over the shortest routes into the rear of the fortified lines and to the centers of resistance of enemy defenses and, at the same time, to take possible action against the combat formations of the defense for the purpose of rolling them up.
4. To tie down the defense by active operations along the whole front of the ring of encirclement to deprive the enemy of all opportunities to maneuver his reserves or to take out units from the less active sectors.
5. To prevent or render difficult, by the action of aviation and long-range artillery, the maneuvers of the reserves of the enemy within the ring of encirclement.
6. By all measures, to deprive the enemy of an opportunity to recover lost positions by counterattacks or to fortify himself on a line seized and to facilitate in this way, the lessening of the area of encirclement, the decrease in the distance for the conduct of fire, and making possible an increase in the density of fire by all forms of infantry weapons.

Editor's Notes

1. The (*Ib*) for the 6th Army was Major General von Kunowski. He is misidentified in the original.
2. The Military Council members for the Don Front were Commander—Lieutenant General (after January 15, 1943, Colonel General) K. K. Rokossovskii; Political Member (appointed December 24, 1942) Major General K. F. Telegin; and Chief of Staff Lieutenant General M. S. Malinin.
3. The ravines identified in the study are the "*balkas* listed on Soviet maps. A good discussion of the terrain and difficulties presented by these topographical features may be found in F. W. von Mellenthin, *Panzer Battles* (Norman, Okla.: University of Oklahoma Press, 1956), pp. 161–62.

4. At the time of the battle, Vasilevskii was a colonel general. He is misidentified in the text.
5. A complete Order of Battle for the Don Front may be found in the Appendix.
6. Reinforcements were obtained by draft replacements from *Stavka* (20,000) and stripping men from the rear areas and the hospitals (10,000) See K. K. Rokossovskii, *A Soldier's Story* (Moscow: Progress, 1985), pp. 158–59.

Cavalry played an integral role in the combat operation of the Red Army during the early years of the Great Patriotic War. During 1941, Stavka greatly expanded the number of its cavalry units, although the new divisions were only one-half the strength of the prewar units. By December, the operational lessons of the previous campaigns encouraged the formation of a new, larger organization. In the winter battles of 1941–42, cavalry corps became the desired operational organization. During the summer–fall 1942 campaign this configuration was regularly employed, although additional support units often were attached to enhance the striking power of the cavalry units. This chapter, one of the largest on arms of service, clearly reveals the continuing debate over the proper role and utility of these formations.[1]—Ed.

8

Cavalry in the Offensive Operations Around Stalingrad

Large cavalry formations participated in the offensive operations for the encirclement and destruction of the Stalingrad group of the enemy. From November to December 1942, the following participated in the operations of the Southwestern, Don, and Stalingrad Fronts.

Northwest of Stalingrad—the 8th Cavalry Corps (21st, 55th, and 112th Cavalry Divisions) and the 3rd Guards Cavalry Corps (the 5th and 6th Guards and 32nd Cavalry Divisions).

South of Stalingrad—4th Cavalry Corps (61st and 81st Cavalry Divisions).

The general mission of the cavalry corps in the first period of the operation was to go into the breakthrough made by the units of the Southwestern, Don, and Stalingrad Fronts; to penetrate into the operational depths of the enemy, smash his reserves and staffs, break up signal communications, cut routes of communication; and, in cooperation with the large formations attacking from the Front, to close the ring of

159

encirclement, isolating the Stalingrad group of the enemy from his other units operating west and southwest of Stalingrad.

At the beginning of the operation the effectives of the corps were the following:

	3rd Guards Cavalry Corps	8th Cavalry Corps	4th Cavalry Corps
Men	22,512	16,134	10,284
	+24[1]	--1,874[2]	--1.172
Horses	18,057	14,908	9,284
	—3,752	—2,379	—988
Rifles and carbines	14,102	10,974	7,354
	—1,388	—1,014	—1,777
Submachine guns (PPSh)	2,153	1,369	566
	+193	—607	--757
Light machine guns	374	366	264
	--94	--32	--64
Machine guns (DShK)	40	33	0
	+5	+4	--61
Antitank rifles	388	188	140
	+10	--146	--11
76 mm guns	70	66	32
	0	+4	--26
45 mm guns	55	35	24
	+9	--3	0
37 mm antiaircraft guns	21	6	8
	--29	--12	--4
120 mm mortars	44	37	16
	. 0	--7	0
82 mm mortars	108	66	46
	+22	--8	+10
50 mm mortars	294	123	118
	+96	--43	+10

Remarks:
1. + = over strength
2. - - = under strength.

From this table, one can see that the 3rd Guards Cavalry Corps was most nearly up to required strength. The considerable shortage of horses in all the corps is noticeable. This made it necessary to have dismounted troops in the regiments. The weakness in antiaircraft weapons was also seriously felt in the organization of the antiaircraft defense of the cavalry in the period of its action in the breakthrough.

In the survey given below of the military actions of the cavalry, we deal principally with questions of strategic employment of the cavalry corps; the tactics of the actions of cavalry are discussed only in a general way.

Operations of the 8th Cavalry Corps

The General Situation and Missions of the Corps

The 8th Cavalry Corps, after a march from the area of Eltsa (544 kilometers; had concentrated by November 8, 1942, in the areas of Tiukovnoskii, Krutovskii, and in the ravines south of these points on the right bank of the Don River, 12 to 15 kilometers from the front line, and became operationally subordinate to the Commander of the 5th Tank Army. The Corps was assigned the mission of following the 1st Tank Corps into the breakthrough on the front (reference point 223.0, Bolshoi) and of exploiting the gains in the general direction toward Pronin to reach the Pronin-Karaseev region by the close of the 1st day of the offensive and to seize with strong forward elements crossings at Chistyakovskoi and Chernushevskaia. On the second day of the offensive, the 8th Cavalry Corps was to reach the region Ust-Griaznovskii, Leonov, and Siniapkin.

On the right, the 14th Guards Rifle Division was to reach the line of reference point 211.5, State Farm No. 2, and Frunze State Farm by the end of the first day. On the left the 47th Guards Rifle Division debouched on the line of Station Seniutkin and reference point 207.0.

Before the front of the shock group of the 5th Tank Army, units of the 7th, 11th, 9th, 14th, and 5th Rumanian Infantry Divisions occupied defense positions on the line Ribnii, Verkhne-Krivskoi, Yiagodnyi, Bolshoi, and reference points 219.5 and 223.0. In the depths of the defensive dispositions, the enemy executed trench works in the area Blinovskii, Station Seniutkin, and Ust-Medveditskii. The reserves of the enemy were noticed in Perelazovskii, up to 120 tanks; in Fomikhinskii and Chernushevskaia, up to two infantry divisions.

In the period of the operation, the 8th Cavalry Corps was reinforced with the 174th and the 179th Tank Destroyer Artillery Regiments, the 35th Guards Mortar Regiment, the 586th *PVO* Antiaircraft Artillery Regiment, and the 511th Tank Flamethrower Battalion. In the beginning of the operation, a part of these forces was not supplied with fuel, ammunition, and motor transport (174th Tank Destroyer Artillery Regiment).

The commander of the 8th Cavalry Corps decided to move into the breakthrough with the main group on his right flank. The 112th Cavalry Division, with a battalion of the 35th Guards Mortar Regiment and a battalion of the 148th Mortar Regiment, moved in the first echelon of the right column of the Corps. The second echelon was made up of the 21st Cavalry Division, with a battalion of the 35th Guards Mortar Regiment and a battalion of the 148th Mortar Regiment. The march route of the right column was Tuikovnovskii, Chebotarevskii, Bolshoi, and Blinovskii.

The left column was formed by the 55th Cavalry Division with the

263rd Independent Horse Artillery Battalion. Behind it moved the staff of the 8th Cavalry Corps with a training battalion and the 8th Independent Destroyer Antitank Battalion. The march route of the left column was Krutovskii, Chebotarevskii, Kalmykovskii, Klinovoi, and Independent State Farm No. 86. The 174th Tank Destroyer Artillery Regiment, the 586th *PVO* Antiaircraft Artillery Regiment, and the 511th Tank Flamethrower Battalion were to constitute the reserve of the commander of the 8th Cavalry Corps, moving along the march route of the left column.

In the period of the preparation of the operation by the commander and staff of the 8th Cavalry Corps and the Commanders of the 21st, 55th, and 112th Cavalry Divisions, cooperation was planned in the locality with the commanders of the rifle divisions of the 5th Tank Army effecting the breakthrough.[2] The commanders of the cavalry divisions were at the command posts of the rifle troop commanders. The staff of the 8th Cavalry Corps worked out a schedule for commitment into the breakthrough and gave it to the staffs of the divisions ahead of time. There was also timely coordination of cooperation with the 1st Tank Corps, which, in accordance with the orders of the commander of the 5th Tank Army, was to move ahead of the 8th Cavalry Corps.

Going into the Breakthrough and the Battles of November 19–20, 1942

At 7:30 A.M. on November 19th the artillery offensive started on the front of the 5th Tank Army. The artillery preparation for the attack continued for an hour and 20 minutes, after which the rifle divisions of the shock group moved to the attack and by 12:00 noon had captured the first line of the fortified positions of the Rumanians.

At 9:00 A.M., the units of the 8th Cavalry Corps started from the jump-off area and concentrated immediately behind the combat formations of the rifle troops. At 1:00 P.M., after the columns of the 1st Tank Corps and of the 8th Motorcycle Regiment passed the former main line of resistance of the enemy, the columns of the 112th and 55th Cavalry Division moved into the breach.

Due to the weather conditions, enemy aviation did not appear in the air on this day. Radio communications with the staffs of the division and the staff of the 5th Tank Army functioned continuously.

After the battle of November 19–20 at Blinovskii and Ust-Medveditskii and the repulse of the counterattack of the enemy from Station Seniutkin, the units of the Corps arrived in the area of Blinovskii and Ust-Medveditskii. By the close of November 20, the units had fortified themselves and conducted reconnaissance in the zone of their operations.

At 7:00 P.M. on November 20, an order arrived from the commander of the 5th Tank Army to place the 21st Cavalry Division at the disposal of the commander of the 1st Guards Army for a joint attack against Gorbatovskii and the destruction of the remainder of the 7th, 9th and 14th Rumanian Infantry Divisions defeated the day before. Simultaneously, the commander of the 5th Tank Army assigned to the 8th Cavalry Corps—55th and 112th Cavalry Divisions, the 35th Guards Mortar Regiment, the 586th *PVO* Antiaircraft Artillery Regiment, the 179th Tank Destroyer Artillery Regiment, and the 511th Tank Flamethrower Battalion—the mission of seizing through Bolshaia Donshchinka the Russkaia Sloboda-Petrovka area in joint operation with the 1st Tank Corps.

Actions on November 21–24

Parts of the Corps, by a night march, moved in the direction Malaia Donshchinka and Bolshaia Donshchinka. By the morning of November 21, they engaged in stubborn fighting with the reserve units of the 5th Rumanian Army Corps, reinforced by tanks of the 1st Rumanian Royal Panzer Division.

In the area northwest of Bolshaia Donshchinka after some prolonged and fierce fighting, the 112th Cavalry Division, by an attack in mounted and dismounted formations, drove back up to a regiment of Rumanian infantry with 25 tanks in the direction of Medvezhii.

The 55th Cavalry Division, after capturing Malaia Donshchinka from the march, engaged in hard fighting during the day with the 44th Rumanian Infantry defending Bolshaia Donshchinka. By a night attack of dismounted troops with the support of tanks and with simultaneous envelopment from the west and southwest, the village was cleared of the enemy by 2:00 A.M., and during the operation, we captured a large amount of booty, including 18 guns. During the day, two JU-87 airplanes were shot down.

In the meantime, with the mission of advancing ahead of the 8th Cavalry Corps, the 1st Tank Corps moved in the general direction Bolshaia Donshchinka—Russkaia Sloboda. Upon approaching Bolshaia Donshchinka, they ran into the fire of antitank guns and did not attack the village but moved in a southeastern direction, losing contact with the cavalry.

At 10:30 A.M. on November 22, we discovered a motorized column of the enemy moving from the direction of Zhirkii toward Independent State Farm no. 861. Consisting of up to 200 motor vehicles with 20 tanks, at 11:30 A.M., the column turned and moved into the rear of the combat formations of the 55th and 112th Cavalry Divisions. The commander of the 8th Cavalry Corps ordered the Independent Antitank Battalion, the training battalion, and the artillery of the 55th Cavalry Division to prepare for all-around defense and repel the attack of the enemy. He ordered the main forces of the Corps to continue with the execution of their mission. Simultaneously, the commander of the 55th Cavalry Division reported the approach from the east and southeast of the enemy tanks and motorized infantry.

By the artillery fire of the 55th Cavalry Division and the 35th Guards Mortar Regiment, the attack by enemy tanks was repulsed. The column of the 22nd German Panzer Division—after losing 27 tanks and 60 trucks and leaving more than 600 soldiers and officers dead, 16 machine guns, 40 motorcycles, and 150 prisoners on the battlefield—withdrew in a southern direction, infiltrating between the combat formations of the 112th and 55th Cavalry Divisions. Enemy aviation cooperating with the tanks was driven off by the antiaircraft artillery of the 55th Cavalry Division, with one JU-87 being shot down.

At 10:00 A.M. on November 22, the 112th Cavalry Division with the staff of the 8th Cavalry Corps, started toward Krasnoiarovka and Arzhanovski with the intention of cutting off the escape routes of the 5th Army Corps, the 1st Royal Rumanian Panzer Division, and the 22nd German Panzer Division.

By 7:00 P.M. the 112th Cavalry Division reached the area of Krasnoiarovka and assumed the defensive on a front running northeast and east along the banks of the Chir River. At midnight the cut-off units of the enemy made an attempt to break through the division's position but was repulsed and had to withdraw to Russkaia Sloboda and Petrovka. Then, however, in accordance with orders of the commander of the 5th Tank Army, the 35th Guards Mortar Regiment, the 179th Antitank Artillery Regiment, and the 511th Tank Flamethrower Battalion were detached from the 8th Cavalry Corps. Up to this time, the 174th Antitank Artillery Regiment had been left in the rear for lack of fuel.

The commander of the 8th Cavalry Corps, which was with the 112th Cavalry Division, ordered by radio the commander of the 55th Cavalry Division to attack from the rear the withdrawing enemy motorized–mechanized columns, and to destroy them in cooperation with the 112th Cavalry Division. The 55th Cavalry Division, after repelling a tank attack of the enemy and having no liaison with the staff of the Corps and the 112th Cavalry Division, left Bolshaia Donshchinka at 2:00 A.M. on November 23 to carry out the radio order received from the Commander of the Corps. In Medvezhii the leading detachment of the Division overtook the tail of the enemy motor column, attacked it, and captured 22 motor vehicles, fuel servicing trucks, and 12 prisoners. At 5:00 A.M. tanks and 250 motorcyclists of the 22nd German Panzer Division broke into the tail of the column of the 55th Cavalry Division on the march, conducting automatic fire from their machines. The attack was repulsed.

From November 23–24, units of the Corps conducted battle for the encirclement and destruction of the enemy in the areas of Petrovka, Russkaia Sloboda, and Ozery. The 112th Cavalry Division, operating from the region of Krasnoiarovka through Arzhanovskii, and the 55th Cavalry Division, after capturing Petrovka and Russkaia Sloboda, advanced through Zakharchenskii toward Ozery.

Beginning November 21, enemy aviation began to display great activity with as many as 180 airplane sorties. On the 23rd, the 112th Cavalry Division at Arzhanovskii, for a period of six hours, was subjected to air attacks by groups of 10 to 30 airplanes. On this day the enemy carried out a total of over 300 airplane sorties.

The Action in the Area of Oblivskaia (November 24–December 3, 1942)

On November 24th, the commander of the 5th Tank Army assigned to the 8th Cavalry Corps the task of capturing Oblivskaia and the crossing of the Stalingrad–Likhaia railroad for the Chir River. For carrying out this mission, units of the Corps, starting from the Ozery-Arzhanovskii region on the evening of November 24, made a march of 50 to 60 kilometers and by the morning of the 25th reached the approaches of Oblivskaia from the north.

At 6:00 A.M. on November 25, the 112th Cavalry Division deployed for an attack against Oblivskaia toward the south from Frolov; however, the attack of the Division was broken up by continuous attacks of enemy aviation made throughout the day. The enemy, taking advantage of the weakness of the antiaircraft weapons of the Corps and the complete absence of our fighter aviation, made continuous attacks against the combat formations of the Division with groups of up to 50 airplanes.[3]

The 55th Cavalry Division, upon approaching Chugunka, at about 7:00 A.M. on November 25, was also subjected to attack by about 20 enemy airplanes, the attack being continued until the approach of darkness, with the result that the Division was pinned down to the spot. It was not until 2:00 A.M. on November 26 that the Division placed its units in order and started an advance toward Oblivskaia.

On November 25, the units of this division lost in killed and wounded by enemy aviation 559 men (including four regimental commanders, one chief of staff, and 12 commanders of cavalry squadrons) and 915 horses. Also a great deal of equipment was disabled.

At 5:00 A.M. on November 26, the units of the Corps deployed for an attack against Oblivskaia; the 55th Cavalry Division attacked in the direction of Riabovskii and Ptitsesovkhoz; and the 112th Cavalry Division made an attack against the railroad station of Oblivskaia and the hospital. At dawn on November 26, enemy aviation started powerful and continuous raids. Everything was pinned to the ground. The airplanes dive bombed, machine gunned, and even chased individual horsemen. When a gun or machine gun opened fire, two or three airplanes immediately dived upon it. The antiaircraft artillery, having fired all its shells, remained silent; and fighter aviation, in spite of timely calls for support made through the liaison officer of the staff of the Mixed Air Corps, did not appear.

The units of the 55th Cavalry Division lost in killed and wounded up to 1,000 men and 1,500 horses; and the 112th Cavalry Division lost 322 men and 473 horses. The attack of the Corps against Oblivskaia was broken up by the action of enemy aviation exclusively.[4]

On the following days, up to December 4, the units of the Corps put themselves in order, repelled the counterattacks of the enemy infantry and tanks of the enemy, and made an unsuccessful attack against Oblivskaia lasting three days (December 1–3).

Despite the fact that the joint actions of the Corps and of the 40th Guards Rifle Division (which had arrived) for the capture of Oblivskaia were directed by the Deputy Commander of the 5th Tank Army, the attacks were not successful because of the weakness in cooperation. On December 4, the 112th Cavalry Division turned over its sector to the infantry and was transferred to the Chir River, assuming the defensive on the Deev–Glukhmanovskii line and seized by units of the 55th Cavalry Division as early as December 1.

The Actions of the 21st Cavalry Division from November 21–December 1, 1942

The 21st Cavalry Division, detached from the composition of the 8th Cavalry Corps on November 20, received the following mission from the commander of the 1st Guards Army: to cooperate in the smashing of the rest of the 7th, 9th, and 14th Rumanian Infantry Divisions in the areas of Rubaskin, Singin, and Gorbatovskii.

On November 21, the units of the Division deployed from Karaseev and conducted an offensive against the Frunze State Collective Farm Number 2. After repelling three counterattacks of the units of the 9th Rumanian Infantry Division and after two days of stubborn fighting, the 21st Cavalry Division captured the Frunze State Collective Farm Number 2 by dawn on November 23. It destroyed in the action over 800 soldiers and officers of the enemy; smashed the staff of the 9th Infantry Division; and captured operational documents, two flags, 12 guns, 40 machine guns, 28 trucks, more than 100 vehicles with ammunition, and also other booty. Having broken the defense of the enemy, the Division started in pursuit in cavalry formation, and after stubborn fighting, captured Gorbatovskii and Ushakovo by the close of November 23.

On November 24, a new order was received from the commander of the 5th Tank Army, namely, to move to the line of Starikov, Novosergievka, Paramonov, and Varlamov to cover from the west the attack of the main group of the Army against Morozovskii and Oblivskaia. During the night, the Division executed a 60-kilometer march, and by the morning of November 23 reached with the 17th Cavalry Regiment the Starikov-Novosergievka line, having before it the demoralized remnants of the 14th Rumanian Infantry Division. The 112th Cavalry Regiment in Krasnaia Zaraia attacked a company of the infantry, cut to pieces 60 soldiers and officers, captured a large amount of booty, and reached the area of Paramonov, having before it the small isolated units of the 7th Rumanian Infantry Division.

At 4:00 A.M. on November 25, the remains of the 22nd German Panzer Division, trying to break out of encirclement in the area of Russkaia Sloboda, broke through the positions of the 47th Guards Rifle Division and penetrated into Chernyshevskaia. After stubborn street fighting however, they were driven out by units of the 21st Cavalry Division and 47th Guards Rifle Division. At 2:00 P.M., from the direction of Russkaia Sloboda, the enemy threw into the attack 27 tanks and 300 trucks with motorized infantry and the 67th Cavalry Regiment was cut off from the main forces of the Division.

On November 27–28, the units of the Division repelled the violent attempts of the units of the 22nd Panzer Division of the enemy to break out of encirclement and of the Rumanian infantry and German tanks, which were outside of the ring of encirclement, to assist this effort to escape. The 17th Cavalry Regiment, south of Novosergievka, attacked and cut to pieces the 4th Engineer Battalion of the 14th Rumanian Infantry Division. The 112th Cavalry Division and the reconnaissance battalion of the 21st Cavalry Division repelled, over a period of three days, several attacks of infantry and tanks of the enemy; and the 112th Cavalry Regiment counterattacked five times in mounted formation, cutting to pieces more than 500 Rumanian soldiers and officers.

The 67th Cavalry Regiment conducted battle for three days from encirclement. At 4:00 P.M. on November 28, up to a regiment of the 7th Rumanian Infantry Division with four tanks carried out an offensive from Ust-Griasnovskii toward Varlamov, but the regiment repelled the attack, knocking out two tanks, and then drove the enemy from Ust-Griaznovskii and escaped from encirclement.

The Losses and Booty of the 8th Cavalry Corps

Despite the fact that the 8th Cavalry Corps operated in a secondary direction, it suffered considerable losses in killed, wounded, and missing during the 12 days of the operation from November 19 to December 2.

With the units of the 8th Cavalry Corps, we destroyed during this same

	Staff & Units	21st Cavalry Division	55th Cavalry Division	112th Cavalry Division	Total
Commanding personnel	25	129	135	129	418
Non-commissioned commanding personnel	50	253	380	424	1,107
Soldiers	324	642	1,844	1,647	4,457
Total	399	1,024	2,359	2,200	5,982
Horses	502	952	2,919	2,657	7,030

period 6,730 enemy soldiers and officers, 35 tanks, and 10 airplanes. We captured three flags; 1,064 prisoners; 130 tanks; 67 guns; 163 machine guns; 707 motor vehicles; 7,300 rifles, 19 supply dumps; and a great deal of other booty.

For the display of daring in battles with the German invaders, for persistance, courage, discipline and good organization, and for heroism of the personnel, the People's Commissariat of Defense of the USSR, by Order no. 78 of February 14, 1943, changed the designation of the 8th Cavalry Corps to that of 7th Guards Cavalry Corps.[5]

Operations of the 3rd Guards Cavalry Corps

The Concentration of the 3rd Guards Cavalry Corps

Up until October 27, 1942, the 3rd Guards Cavalry Corps was in the reserves of the commander of the 63rd Army. Then, in accordance with a directive of the *Stavka*, the Corps after four night marches moved a distance of 142 kilometers by the morning of November 1 and concentrated in the area of Bezymianka, Archedinskaia, and Abramov (75 kilometers north of Kletskaia). In the area where it was previously stationed there was left an operating radio network, from corps to division to regiment, but in the new region of concentration the use of radio communications was forbidden.

The Corps was brought up to full strength. There was a shortage of horses in the 32nd Cavalry Divison and in four cavalry squadrons, which were dismounted. Deliveries of food and forage, especially the latter, to the units in the new region of concentration were greatly delayed, and there were no local supplies at all. In addition to this, neither the Corps nor the Army depots had any horseshoeing materials, and 75 percent of the cavalry horses still had on the poor summer shoes at a time when freezing had already started and when there was icing. It was not possible to carry out the reshoeing before the start of the operations.

On November 5, the Corps was made operationally subordinate to the commander of the 21st Army and was assigned the following mission: by night marches, to concentrate in the areas of Lastushinskii, Podpe-shinskii, and Orlovskii to go into the breakthrough on the front of the 76th Rifle Division.

By the morning of November 8, the Corps had concentrated in the jump-off area, which was crowded with artillery and the rear establish-ments of the rifle divisions of the 21st Army (which were in the departure base of operations for the offensive in the area of Kletskaia). The enemy aviation discovered the concentration of the cavalry, and on November 8–9, the Corps was subjected to continuous attacks, losing 190 men and 461 horses killed and wounded. In view of the fact that the beginning of the offensive was delayed because of a shortage of equipment—upon the solicitation of the Commander of the Corps—on November 10, the Corps was again moved into the area of Ugolskii, Otrozhkii, and Budylga (32nd Cavalry Division); Enlovskii and Kletsko-Pochtovskii, (5th Guards Cavalry Division); and Vershinin, Maloulanovskii (6th Guards Cavalry Division).[6] The staff of the Corps was at Vershinin. From 10–18, we continued to bring up ammunition, food, and forage and to issue winter uniforms. In this period, we also carried out a reconnaissance of the crossings over the Don River and the jump-off areas, in preparation for commitment in the breakthrough, and the solving of problems of cooperation with the rifle divisions of the 21st and 65th Armies.

For the crossing of the echelon over the Don River, the exploitation of successes and the supplying of the shock group of the 21st Army, we prepared 12 bridges and ferry crossings. The area of the crossings was continuously bombarded by the heavy artillery of the enemy. From November 8–17, enemy aviation bombarded the crossing continuously, making it unfit for use. The ferry crossings, due to the heavy cold that set in on November 16, were frozen and also unfit for use.

The Situation and Mission of the 3rd Guards Cavalry Corps

On November 16, an order was received from the Commander of the 21st Army, assigning to the Corps the following mission:

> The 3rd Guards Cavalry Corps with the 1250th Tank Destroyer Regiment of the 5th Tank Destroyer Brigade, the 21st Guards Mortar Regiment, with one artillery regiment of the 3rd Anti-Aircraft Division, and the assistance of one combat-support aviation wing—following the 4th Tank Corps—is to pass through the combat formations of the 293rd and 76th Rifle Divisions, striking a blow in the direction Selivanov, Verkhne-Buzinovka, and in coop-eration with the 4th Tank Corps to smash and destroy the reserves, staffs, and rear establishments of the enemy, preventing the

approach of his strategic reserves from the rear. By the close of the day, it is to reach the area (exclusive) Erik, Verkhne-Buzinovka, Svechnikovskii, where it is to dig in.

The task of the second day of the offensive required the following of the Corps:

With the previous units of reinforcement, to strike a blow in the direction Osinovka, Bolshenabatovskii, and, in cooperation with the 4th Tank Corps, continue the smashing of the reserves and staffs of the enemy, reaching by the close of the day the Don River on the line: Golubinskii, Bolshenabatovskii, Kalachkin, Evlampievskii, sending out strong reconnaissance parties to the northeast. The forward units are to capture crossings over the Don River.

At the beginning of the operation, the rifle divisions of the 21st Army occupied jump-off positions for a breakthrough of the defensive zone of the enemy.

Before the front of the shock group of the 21st Army and the right flank of the 65th Army the following were on the defensive: units of the 13th and 15th Rumanian infantry divisions, the 7th Assault Battalion, and the 2nd Regiment of the 1st Rumanian Cavalry Division. The second defense line on Gromki, reference point 196.7, and reference point 218.8 was defended by units of the 15th Rumanian Infantry Division and separate small units of the 7th Rumanian Infantry Division. Trench work was being carried out in the rear of the dispositions of the enemy, on the Vlasov-Tsymlovskii-Platonov line. Units from the 3rd Motorized and 14th Panzer Divisions of the 6th German Army in the region of Stalingrad were moved into the area of Verkhne-Buzinovka and Tsymlovskii.

The Commander of the 3rd Guards Cavalry Corps decided to commit the Corps in the breakthrough on the front (exclusive) Gromki, reference point 218.8, having the main group on the left flank. The missions were assigned to the divisions in the following manner. The 5th Guards Cavalry Division with the 1st Battalion of the 21st Guards Mortar Regiment and the 1st Battalion of the 152nd Mortar Regiment, in exploiting the successes of the rifle troops, seized the area of Vlaskov and Selivanov and by the end of the first day reached the area Nizhne-Buzinovka and (exclusive) Erik, sending out forward detachments to Sukhanovskii. The subsequent mission was developing the actions toward Sukhanovskii and Krasnyi Skotovod State Farm, reaching the line of Golubinskii and Malo-Golubinskii by the end of the second day, and seizing crossings on the Don River.

The 6th Guards Cavalry Division with the 2nd Battalion of the 21st Guards Mortar Regiment, 4th Guards Tank Regiment, 1250th Tank

Destroyer Artillery Regiment, and the 8th Independent Horse Artillery Battalion, operating in the direction of reference point 218.8, reference point 227.3 were to capture Tsymlovskii and Platonov. By the close of the first day they were to reach the area Verkhne-Buzinovka, sending out a forward detachment to Osinovka. The subsequent mission was to exploit the successes toward Osinovka and Evlampievskii and to reach the area of Luchenskii and Kalachkin by the close of the second day, after having seized crossings on the Don River.

The 32nd Cavalry Division, with two battalions of the 152nd Mortar Regiment, moving along the march route of the 6th Guards Cavalry Division, was to assist its advance and by the close of the second day to reach the area of Malonabatovskii, Evlampievskii, and Bolshenabatovskii.

The 5th Tank Destroyer Brigade, an artillery regiment of the 3rd *PVO* Antiaircraft Division, a training battalion, and the 3rd Guards Separate Tank Destroyer Battalion were to constitute a reserve of the commander of the corps.

At 10:30 P.M. on November 18, a radio signal was received from the staff of the 21st Army ordering the immediate departure of the Corps and its concentration in the jump-off area, before commitment in the breakthrough, on the south bank of the Don River northwest and north of Kletskaia. At 5:00 A.M. on November 19, after a march of 35 to 40 kilometers in sleet, the units of the Corps reached the crossings on the Don River, but of these only one had survived the long-range artillery bombardment of the enemy, namely, a bridge on the western edge of Nizhne-Zatonskii that had been half-destroyed. Because of low clouds and a heavy, overcast sky, enemy aviation did not appear. The cavalry crossed over the ice. The gun and *tachankas* (light animal-drawn vehicles for transportation and mounting of machine guns) were moved by hand over the half-destroyed bridge.

By 3:30 P.M., the units of the Corps had concentrated in the area assigned to them. The Corps Commander and the Commanders of the divisions, with the commanders of the staff, were already at the command posts of the commanders of the rifle divisions. Liaison for cooperation was also established with the 4th Tank Corps, which was to make an attack against Evstratovskii and Manoilin and seize by the close of the first day the area of State Farm Pervomaiskii and Evseev.

Action of the 3rd Guards Cavalry Corps on November 19–20, 1942

At 7:00 A.M. on November 19, the units of the first echelon of the 21st Army began an artillery offensive. The artillery preparation for the attack continued for fifty minutes, after which the rifle divisions moved to the attack. By 3:00 P.M., after breaking the stubborn resistance of the enemy, they had broken through the enemy defenses and were beginning to move forward. The 76th Rifle Division broke through the defenses of the enemy and reached, with its forward units, a line 1 kilometer north of Platonov, Tsymlovskii, Selivanov, and Vlasov, where enemy fire forced it to dig in.

The units of reinforcement of the 3rd Guards Cavalry Corps, supporting in the period of the attack the echelon of the 21st Army, could not be shifted in time to support the Corps. The 4th Guards Tank Regiment went to Kletskaia for replenishing its fuel and ammunition; the artillery and the 21st Guards Mortar Regiment also replenished their ammunition. The advancing rifle troops not only did not clear the enemy mine fields but in going through them did not mark the passageways in the zone where the cavalry was committed in the breakthrough. Hence, for clearing the passageways it was necessary to put forward the engineer cavalry troops of the 5th and 6th Guards Cavalry Divisions, and this held up the movement of the Corps into the breakthrough for an hour or two.

The 4th Tank Corps, upon reaching the area of Vlasov and encountering strong enemy resistance at Pervomaiskii State Farm, was not able to advance and halted for the night.

At 4:00 P.M., after crossing the mine fields, the divisions of the 3rd Guards Cavalry Corps passed through the combat formations of the 293rd and the 76th Rifle Divisions and moved into the breakthrough. In developing the attack from the march, the units of the 5th Guards Cavalry Division seized by the end of the day the areas of Vlasov, Selivanov, and Tsymlovskii, capturing war booty and prisoners. The 6th Guards Cavalry Division engaged in the some hard fighting beyond Platonov, repelling counterattacks of enemy infantry and tanks from the north and northeast.

At 5:00 A.M. on November 20, the units of the 5th Guards Cavalry Division departed in two columns for carrying out the subsequent task. At 2:30 P.M., after having occupied Maiorovskii, the units of the Division on the march to the east of this point were counterattacked by two regiments of the 1st Rumanian Cavalry Division, and toward the southeast they were attacked by 16 enemy tanks. The 20th Guards Cavalry Regiment, in mounted formation, attacked the Rumanian hussars, cutting to pieces more than 150 cavalrymen and capturing 300 prisoners, more than 800 saddle horses, their saddles, and other war booty. The remnants of the Rumanian cavalry scattered along the ravines. The tank attack was repelled by artillery fire. At 11:00 P.M., the units of the Division started for Nizhne-Buzinovka along the march route of the forward detachment.

The 6th Guards Cavalry Division and two regiments of the 32nd Cavalry Division continued the hard fighting in Platonov, driving the enemy from the northeastern and northern parts of the State Farm. The

Commander of the 21st Army, after arriving at the command post of the Corps commander, ordered the units of the 76th Rifle Division to attack and capture Platonov; he ordered the 6th Guards and the 32nd Cavalry Divisions to leave a screening force at the State Farm, then to go around the flank of the enemy through Selivanov, and continue the execution of its mission.

As soon as the enveloping movement of the cavalry was noticed, the enemy left Platonov and, throwing away its equipment, began a hasty withdrawal in a southeastern direction. Seeing the withdrawal of the enemy, the 65th and the 85th Regiments of the 32nd Cavalry Division— left as a screening force—broke through into the State Farm and captured 13 guns, three machine guns, 20 motor vehicles, and other booty. The enemy left on the State Farm more than 150 dead soldiers and officers and three disabled tanks. At 11:00 P.M., the 6th Guards Cavalry Division occupied Svechnikovskii without a fight.

The Action of the Corps on November 21–22, 1942

Throughout the night the units of the 3rd Guards Cavalry Corps continued to move in a southeastern direction. At about 7:00 A.M. on November 21, as the 5th Guards Cavalry Division was approaching Nizhne-Buzinovka, enemy aviation made several attacks, but the cavalry units scattered quickly and suffered small losses. At 8:00 A.M., the 20th Guards Cavalry Regiment attacked two companies of the 3rd German Motorized Division that had occupied Nizhne-Buzinovka and, after a brief battle, drove them from the State Farm. At 11:30 A.M., the enemy counterattacked the units of the Division with 15 tanks and a company of submachine gunners from Sukhanovskii. The attack was repulsed and, while pursuing the enemy, the Division captured Sukhanovskii by 6:00 P.M., driving from the State Farm a regiment of the 1st Rumanian Cavalry Division and repelling at 10:00 P.M. a counterattack of a German company with six tanks.

At 6:00 A.M. on November 21, after a 40 kilometer night march, the 6th Guards Cavalry Division, together with the 18th Guards Cavalry Regiment, attacked Verkhne-Buzinovka, which was occupied by two battalions and 27 tanks of the 14th German Panzer Division. The enemy offered stubborn resistance and made some unsuccessful counterattacks.

At 10:00 A.M., the Commander of the Corps ordered the Commander of the 6th Guards Cavalry Division to leave a screening force and to encircle the State Farm from the south, following behind the 32nd Cavalry Division directed toward Osinovka. The 197th and the 65th Cavalry Regiments were assigned the task of attacking Verkhne-Buzinovka from the north. With the departure of the columns of the 32nd Cavalry Division toward the south, the enemy made a counterattack from

Verkhne-Buzinovka, but was thrown back to the State Farm and immediately began a hasty withdrawal to Osinovka. Having penetrated into Verkne-Buzinovka, the 197th Cavalry Regiment captured six guns, 32 motor vehicles, 30 motorcycles, and some dumps with ammunition and food. The enemy left about 100 dead soldiers and officers and 19 prisoners.

At 4:00 P.M., the units of the Division, after some hard fighting, captured Osinovika, where the 6th Guards and 32nd Cavalry Divisions halted for four hours. Beginning on the morning of November 22, the 5th Guards Cavalry Division moved into the area of Krasnyi Skotovod State Farm where, in the course of the day, the Division did some hard fighting with an enemy infantry battalion. By 5:00 P.M., the Division captured the State Farm, together with some war booty.

ACTIONS OF THE CORPS ON NOVEMBER 22–26, 1942

By dawn on November 22, the 6th Guards and 32nd Cavalry Divisions reached the area of Eyvlampievskii and Bolshenabatovskii. The forward detachment of the 6th Guards Cavalry Division, upon discovering that Evlampievskii and Bolshenabatovskii were occupied by large enemy forces (up to three battalions of the German 3rd Motorized Division and the 16th Panzer Division with 70 tanks), turned toward the south and up to the northern edge of Malo-Golubinskii.

The main forces of the Division, having overtaken on the march the column of the 32nd Cavalry Division, deployed at 8:00 A.M.—having in the first echelon the 23rd and 28th Guards Cavalry Regiments and in the second echelon the 25th Guards Cavalry Regiment—and attacked Evlampievski in mounted formation. When met by heavy artillery mortar and machine-gun fire, the cavalry troops dismounted and continued the attack in dismounted formation. At 10:00 A.M. the dismounted cavalry troops penetrated the State Farm and quickly captured it, and a cavalry squadron of the 23rd Regiment, having taken a position in the mounted formation on the east edge, captured a German airdrome with 19 FW-53 [sic—Ed.] airplanes in good condition and ready for flying. In addition to this, it captured in the village up to 300 trucks and other war booty. In battle it destroyed up to 200 enemy soldiers and officers.

The 32nd Cavalry Division, after deploying to the right of the 6th Division, started an attack at 12:00 P.M. against Bolshenabatovskii, encircling it from the northeast. The 6th Guards Cavalry Division, after putting its units in order, made an attack in the direction of Luchenskii and Kalachkin. The 5th Guards Cavalry Division, continuing its night march, repelled and destroyed some small groups of the enemy and by dawn on November 23, captured Golubinskii and Malo-Golubinskii. In this area, the division captured 55 tanks, two armored cars, 25 guns, over

300 trucks and 100 light motor vehicles, 42 motorcycles, 1,500 rifles, 630 wagon teams with military supplies, more than 600 horses, and other war booty. At the airport at Malo-Golubinskii, the enemy left 36 damaged partially burned airplanes.

The 32nd Cavalry Division, while advancing against Bolshenaba-tovskii, encountered strong resistance from the enemy, who realized that the arrival of cavalry in the areas of Golubinskii, Malonabatoskii, and Bolshenabatovskii was the completion of the operational encirclement of the Stalingrad group and rushed tanks and infantry from Stalingrad to meet the 3rd Guards Cavalry Corps. During the day the enemy made four counterattacks with tanks and infantry against the units of the 32nd Cavalry Division. By the end of November 23, the 86th and 65th Cavalry Regiments captured the northern edge of Bolshenabatovskii and began street fighting, while the 197th Cavalry Regiment moved to the eastern edge of the State Farm and cut the road to the east.

On the road from Malonabatovskii to Trekhostroskaia, the enemy concentrated over 100 tanks of the 14th and 16th Panzer Divisions and executed continuous counterattacks against the units of the 6th Guards Cavalry Division. At dawn on November 23, the units of this Division fought their way to the Malonabatovskii-Trekhostrovskaia road and brought it under effective fire. The enemy attacked continuously, but all the attacks of his tanks and infantry were repulsed.

At 8:30 A.M. on November 24, the 18th, 25th, and 23rd Guards Cavalry Regiments of the 6th Guards Division captured Malonabatovskii by a general attack, destroying in two days of continuous battle over 200 enemy soldiers and officers and 50 tanks and capturing more than 300 motor vehicles. The units of the Division lost up to 800 men in killed and wounded.

At 10:00 A.M. on November 24, the units of the 32nd Cavalry Division from the north and the 17th Guards Cavalry Regiment from the south, by joint attack, captured Bolshenabatovskii, throwing the enemy back in a northeastern direction and capturing a large amount of war booty.

By the close of the day, the forward units of the 76th Rifle Division reached the area of Evlampievskii and took up defense positions in this area. The seizure by the units of the 3rd Guard Cavalry Corps of the area of Golubinskii, Bolshenabatovskii, Malonabatovskii, and Evlampievskii and the seizure by the units of the 4th Tank Corps of the town of Kalach cut off the Stalingrad group of the enemy from his troops operating west of Stalingrad. This was, in reality, the completion of the operational encirclement of the von Paulus group.

The units of the Corps, while remaining in the seized area, quickly put their units in order. At 6:00 P.M. on November 24, an order was received from the commander of the 21st Army assigning to the units of the Corps and to the 76th Rifle Division the mission of smashing the enemy group northeast of Bolshenabatovskii and then moving into the area of Trekhostrovskaia. The Corps, having regrouped during the night, started an attack at dawn on November 25, with the 32nd Cavalry Division toward Kartuli, the 5th Guards Cavalry Division, and the 76th Rifle Division to the north of this point.

At 2:00 P.M. on November 25, an order was received from the commander of the 21st Army for the dispatching of one cavalry division into the area of Pobeda Oktiabr State Farm for protecting the right flank of the army from the direction of Nizhne-Chirskaia. At 5:00 A.M., the 6th Guards Cavalry Division, leaving the 25th Regiment to protect the left flank of the Corps, departed from the area of Pobeda Oktiabr State Farm.

During the day of November 25, the units of the 5th Guards and 32nd Cavalry Divisions and the 76th Rifle Division did some hard fighting with the infantry and tanks of the enemy in the area of Kartuli and to the north of this place. At 2:10 P.M. the following order was received from the Commander of the 21st Army:

> The 3rd Guards Cavalry Corps (without one cavalry division) jointly with the 76th Rifle Division, 1st, 2nd and 4th Tank Regiments are to attack at 10:00 A.M. on November 25th, in the direction of Peskovatka, Vertiachii, crush the enemy and by the close of the day reach the lines: 76th Rifle Division—Kulturnyi Stantsiia (5 kilometers east of Kislov), reference 73.3; the 3rd Guards Cavalry Corps with two cavalry divisions and three tank regiments, the line (exclusive) Bolshaia Rossoshka, Bolshaia Krutenka (15–25 kilometers northeast and east of Peskovatka).

Beginning at 4:00 P.M., the Division, having left a screening force, began to break off combat and start the concentration for crossing the Don River south of Bolshenabatovskii, the crossing to the south bank of the Don to be started with the approach of darkness. The enemy bombarded the crossings with artillery from the area of Kartuli. In the daytime, enemy aviation bombarded the crossings, and the antiaircraft artillery of the corps shot down two JU-88 airplanes. By dawn on November 26, the 5th Guards and 32nd Cavalry Divisions had completed the crossing and had concentrated in the forest 2 kilometers south of Malonabatovskii.

At 5:00 A.M., the 86th Cavalry Regiment of the 32nd Cavalry Division approached Peskovatka and began to move into the village but ran into an ambush of two enemy battalions. The Regiment suffered heavy losses, but still it was able to escape from encirclement and reach the main forces of the Division. The 121st Cavalry Regiment, moving at the head of the column of the main forces, was also subjected to a fire attack, had to dig in, and could not render timely assistance to the 86th Cavalry Regiment.

At 9:30 A.M. on November 26, a new order was received from the commander of the 21st Army to send the 6th Guards Cavalry Division into the area of Richkovskii and make it subordinate to the Commander of the 1st Tank Corps. At 11:30 A.M. a third order came in directing that the sector be turned over to the unit of the 277th Rifle Division and that the Corps move rapidly into the area of Chir Station. At 1:30 P.M. on November 26, the units of the 5th Guards and 32nd Cavalry Divisions began to cross back to the west bank of the Don.

War Booty and Losses of the Corps

The Corps, which operated in the direction of the main attack and jointly with the 4th Tank Corps, closed the ring around the German groups in Stalingrad in the period November 19–26, destroyed and captured 5,798 enemy officers and soldiers, disabled and burned 167 tanks and six airplanes. The units of the Corps captured the following: 35 tanks and 19 airplanes in good condition, 108 guns of various calibers, 182 machine guns, 930 trucks and 152 light motor vehicles, 960 troop horses and more than 1,000 draft horses, 11 army dumps with ammunition, food, forage and quartermaster supplies, and a large quantity of other war booty.

The units of the Corps sustained the following losses in killed, wounded, and missing:

	Staff & Units	5th Guards Cavalry Division	6th Guards Cavalry Division	32nd Cavalry Division	Total
Commanding personnel	14	246	234	261	755
Non-commissioned commanding personnel	71	376	609	713	1,769
Privates	196	1,676	2,286	2,626	6,784
Total	281	2,298	3,129	3,600	9,308
Horses	230	1,699	2,412	2,100	6,441

Operations of the 4th Cavalry Corps

Concentration and missions of the 4th Cavalry Corps

By November 8, the 4th Cavalry Corps, which was subordinate to the Commander of the Stalingrad Front, concentrated in the region of Svetlyi Iar, Raigorod, and Solodniki. The reconnaissance battalions of the divisions, merged into a cavalry group, were subordinate to the commander of the 51st Army and operated on the left flank of the army in the sector of the 91st Rifle Division.

In going to the area of concentration, the units of the Corps executed a long march (350 to 550 kilometers). Because of the delays in receiving feed, the horses were weak. The Corps was far from being up to strength in men, horses, motor vehicle transport, and armament.

From November 8–19, the units of the Corps, while in the region of concentration, made preparations for the operation. The commanders and staffs studied the locality, the main line of resistance of the enemy, his defensive installations, flanks, side roads and so on and got acquainted with the plans of attack of the rifle divisions effecting the breakthrough.[7] They worked out the problems of cooperation in the course of the offensive, especially with the 4th Mechanized Corps, which was to precede the offensive of the 4th Cavalry Corps; they reconnoitered the areas of the jump-off positions, marked out the roads, selected observation posts, and established signal communications with the units of the 51st and 57th Armies.

For the reinforcement of the Corps, we assigned the 149th Tank Destroyer Artillery Regiment consisting of five 76 mm batteries with "ZIS-3" (3-ton trucks), in which, instead of 76 machines, there were only three. At the beginning of the operation, the Corps had 1.5 units of fire, five days rations of food and forage, and one fuel fill.

On the sector of the breakthrough of the 51st Army, units of the 93rd Infantry and 5th Jaegar Regiments of the 1st Rumanian Infantry Division were on the defensive. The reserves—about one battalion with tanks— were in the Sredniaia Lasta and Zakharov; up to a regiment with tanks were in Plodovitoie; and the staff of the 6th Rumanian Army Corps was known to be in Abganerovo.

On November 19, the commander of the Stalingrad Front assigned to the Corps the following missions: in the night preceding November 20, it was to occupy jump-off positions in preparation for going into the breakthrough in the area of Siangerdyk, Algoi, Kharbulia, and Gashun; on November 20, it was to move into the breakthrough between Lakes Tsatsa and Barmantsak, and, following behind the 4th Mechanized Corps, it was to capture Abgenerovo and Abganerovo Station by the close of November 21, destroying the withdrawing units of the enemy.

After completing, during the night preceding November 20, a 45-kilometer march, the units of the Corps concentrated by dawn in the area of Siangerdik, Algoi, Kharbulia, and Gashun. From the beginning of the artillery offensive, the commanders and staffs of the corps and divisions were at the observation posts, following the development of the defensive radio communications with the staffs of the 51st Army and with the divisions that were functioning continually.

Commitment into the Breakthrough and the Capture of Abganerovo

At 11:30 P.M. on November 20, the commander of the 4th Cavalry Corps gave orders for the commitment of the Corps into the breakthrough and the capture of the area of Abganerovo. The divisions were committed into the breach in a single echelon along two roads, having the reserves of the Commander of the Corps (training battalion, four independent tank destroyer battalions, and the 149th Tank Destroyer Artillery Regiment) behind the 61st Cavalry Division. The movement of the cavalry was held up by the columns of the 4th Mechanized Corps, which delayed its departure for the jump-off position and blocked all the roads with machines loaded with motorized rifle troops, ammunition, and fuel.

At 8:00 P.M., the 61st and 81st Cavalry Divisions began to move into the breach. By this time, reports had been received of the capture of Plodovitoie by the units of the 4th Mechanized Corps and the forward battalion of the 126th Rifle Division. After the breakthough of the front by units of the 51st Army, the enemy withdrew in the general direction of Abganerovo, offering weak resistance in places.

The commander of the Corps decided to destroy the enemy group in the region of Abganerovo and Abganerovo Station, by enveloping them simultaneously from the north and from the south.

At dawn on November 21, the leading detachments of the Division drove off the covering units of the Rumanian 1st and 4th Infantry and 5th Cavalry Divisions between Plodovitoie and Abganerovo, inflicting upon them losses and capturing prisoners and booty. At 10:30 A.M., the units of the Corps reached Abganerovo, and after a brief battle by attacks in mounted cavalry formation they captured the town. The enemy hastily withdrew toward the west and south. In view of the fact that the horses were tired out, the pursuit was conducted for only a short distance. The 227th Regiment of the 81st Cavalry Division captured Abganerovo Station by 2:00 P.M., straining the cavalry to the very limit.

The fighting of the 61st Cavalry Division at Umantsevo and Sharnutovskii on November 22–26

In the night preceding November 22, the Deputy Commander of the Stalingrad Front arrived in Abganerovo and assigned an independent mission to the 61st Cavalry Division (reinforced by a battery of the 149th Tank Destroyer Regiment, a Guards Mortar battalion, and three armored cars). Namely, it was to move along the march route Abganerovo-Kurgan Solianoi into the region of Umantsevo and operate in the rear of the units of the 4th Rumanian Infantry Division, which was defending itself in the region of Tundutovo, Sadovoe, and Obilnoe against our 91st Rifle Division. In the battle for Abganerovo and Abganerovo Station, the units of the 4th Cavalry Corps captured more than 100 guns, 18 machine guns, 300 horses, 3,000 artillery shells, 1,500 mortar shells, dumps with ammunition, food, and fuel. The 81st Cavalry Division lost 10 men killed and 13 wounded; the 61st Cavalry Division lost 17 men killed and 21 wounded. The losses of the enemy amounted to about 300 men killed and over 600 prisoners.

Leaving Abganerovo at 10:00 A.M. on November 22, the 61st Cavalry Division during November 22–24 did some effective fighting against units of the 8th Rumanian Cavalry Division in the area of Kurgan Solianoi and Umantsevo. Making extensive use of wide and close encirclement and of attack in mounted formation, in combination with the battle of small dismounted units, the Division occupied Umantsevo on November 24. The 8th Rumanian Cavalry Division suffered a severe defeat, losing all of its artillery; and the remnants of its 2nd, 3rd, and 4th Cavalry Regiments were scattered in disorder.

At 2:00 A.M. on November 25, the Commander of the 61st Cavalry Division received from the Commander of the 51st Army an order by radio to concentrate at Darganov by the close of the day. By this time the 126th Rifle Division of 51st Army was conducting a battle with the counterattacking units of the enemy southwest of Aksai. The 91st Rifle Division moved into the area of Umantsevo. Neither the Commander of the Division nor the staff of the 51st Army had any information concerning the enemy in the direction of the action of the 61st Cavalry Division. At 6:00 P.M. on November 25, the Division moved from Umantsevo, having in its forward detachment the 213th Regiment with a battery of the 13th Independent Horse Artillery Battalion and a battery of the 149th Tank Destroyer Artillery Regiment.

During the approach to Yergin at 12:00 P.M., we observed six medium tanks of the enemy coming from the State Farm. Fairly soon eight more tanks came with a company of submachine gunners who opened fire. A battery of the 149th Tank Destroyer Artillery Regiment deployed and opened fire. After a brief exchange of shots, the tanks withdrew toward Sharnutovskii. The 213th Cavalry Regiment, in pursuing the enemy, captured Yergin at 9:30 P.M. Continuing to advance, the regiment encountered on the eastern outskirts of Sharnutovskii fire from an enemy company with four heavy tanks, after which it engaged the enemy.

The Commander of the Division decided to attack with the 222nd Regiment from the north, with the 213th Regiment from the south, and to capture the village by the morning of November 26. At midnight, the units started the attack, encountering stubborn resistance from the German infantry, which defended the place house by house. The actions of the enemy infantry defending itself in the village was supported by more than 15 tanks. At the same time, 29 tanks attacked the battle formation of the 222nd Cavalry Regiment and, after neutralizing three batteries, moved back into the village. Being faced by up to three battalions with 45 tanks and having suffered considerable losses, the Commander of the Division decided to break off the engagement and withdraw the units to Umantsevo. At 10:00 P.M., the Division began to withdraw, and by 5:00 P.M. on November 27, had concentrated in Umantsevo, assuming the defensive here and putting its units in order. In this battle, the Division suffered heavy losses in personnel, horses, and equipment. The enemy lost six burned-out and crippled tanks.

The Capture of the Town of Aksai by the 81st Cavalry Division

After capturing Abganerovo, the units of the 81st Cavalry Division stationed themselves in the north part of the town. They were then assigned the mission of organizing for antitank defense and conducting reconnaissance to the northwest and west. The enemy fortified himself on the line west and northwest of Abganerovo, while conducting vigorous tank reconnaissance along the Aksai-Abganerovo highway.

The commander of the 4th Cavalry Corps, seeing an increase in the activity of the enemy, decided on November 23, to capture Aksai, advance to the main route of the withdrawal of the enemy, block his actions on the north, and throw him back from the railroad.

By the close of November 22, the 126th Rifle Division had concentrated in the area of Abganerovo. The Corps Commander ordered the Commander of the 81st Cavalry Division to move at dawn on November 23, with one regiment through the Ilich Collective Farm to the route of withdrawal of the enemy and with the rest of the units to capture Aksai, striking a blow through Vodinskii. The training battalion, with a battery of the 149th Tank Destroyer Artillery Regiment, operated on the Shelestov sector, with the mission of capturing Peregruzny. The 4th Tank Destroyer Battalion and a battery of the 149th Tank Destroyer Artillery Regiment were in the reserves of the Corps Commander.

At 6:00 P.M. on November 22, the units of the 81st Cavalry Division departed from Abganerovo, having in the forward detachment the 216th Cavalry Regiment, which, 6 kilometers southwest of Abganerovo, engaged in battle with a Rumanian battalion with artillery and 16 tanks on the defensive on the line of Krutenkaia ravine, cutting the highway at Aksai. The first attack of the 216th Regiment was repelled by the enemy, but after having brought up some artillery, the Regiment repeated the attack. The enemy, leaving three crippled tanks, began a withdrawal toward Shelestov, clinging at the same time to each line. After a volley fired by the Guards Mortar battalion, the Rumanian infantry began to fall back rapidly toward Aksai, covering itself with tanks deployed on a wide front. With their fire, supported by gun and mortar fire from farther back, they held up the advance of the Regiment. After a brief but stubborn battle, the Regiment captured Shelestov and at 12:00 P.M. penetrated the eastern edge of Aksai.

The 227th Cavalry Regiment, advancing from Abganerovo Station toward Gniloaksaiskaia and Aksai, met the resistance of a Rumanian battalion with two artillery and mortar batteries and 14 tanks. After a hard battle, the enemy withdrew toward Aksai, leaving nine crippled tanks in Gniloaksaiskaia. After sending a cavalry squadron along the railroad, the main forces of the Regiment turned toward Ilich Collective Farm and reached the southwest edge of Aksai.

The 232nd Cavalry Regiment, after driving the enemy from Vodinskii, attacked the north edge of Aksai, which was finally captured by the units of the Division at 12:00 P.M.. After a short battle, Peregruzny was captured at 5:00 P.M. by the training battalion. The enemy lost 17 burned-out and crippled tanks and more than 300 men. The 93rd Infantry Regiment of the 1st Rumanian Division was definitively smashed. In the town, we captured 12 guns, depots of food, uniforms, ammunition, and other war booty.

The Battle of the 81st Cavalry Division at Kotelnikovo

On November 24, at Aksai, the Commander of the 4th Cavalry Corps received orders to concentrate by the morning of November 25 in the area of Gromoslavka and Nizhne-Kumskii and to reach the right flank of the 51st Army covering the action of its units at Zhutovo Station and Krugiakov. We brought up from Abganerovo to Aksai the 126th Rifle Division, which had the mission of advancing toward Kevalevka where we had observed a strong group of German–Rumanian infantry with tanks. On November 24–25, the 302nd Rifle Division executed a march from Plodovitoie and Kapkinskii; the 91st Rifle Division engaged in hard fighting south and northeast of Sadovoe.

After a brief battle with German motorized units, the 81st Cavalry Division captured Gromoslavka and Nizhne-Kumskii by 12:00 P.M. on November 25. At 10:00 P.M., an order was received for making the 4th Cavalry Corps operationally subordinate to the Commander of the 51st Army. The mission—the 81st Cavalry Division with Corps units—starting out in the night before November 26 along the march route of Gromoslavka, Verkhne-Kumski, Generalovskii, Verkhne-Iablochnyi, and Kotelnikovo—was to reach the area of Kotelnikovo by the close of November 26 with the forward units. On the morning of November 27, it was to capture Kotelnikovo in cooperation with the 302nd and 126th Rifle Divisions, advancing from the east along the railroad and from Pimen-Cherni. By the close of November 26, the 61st Cavalry Division was to reach Kotelnikovo from the southeast.

The 81st Cavalry Division had to march more than 95 kilometers during the day. Reports had come in of the concentration at Kotelnikovo of the remains of the 17th, 85th, 93rd Rumanian Infantry, and the 38th Rumanian Artillery Regiments and of the approach of the German infantry and tanks from the direction of Salsk. The staff of the Corps did not have any communications with the 126th Rifle Division moving along the railroad, because the staff of the 51st Army did not give any general call signs.

After setting out from the occupied area, the 81st Cavalry Division and the Corps units concentrated by 3:00 P.M. on November 26 for a long halt in the area of Generalovskii. Small groups of enemy motorized infantry and tanks were withdrawing toward the south without accepting battle. Upon arriving by airplane, the liaison officer of the staff of the Front reported that, during the attack against Kotelnikovo, the 4th Cavalry Corps would be reinforced by a tank battalion and by a Guards Mortar battalion, which would arrive by the close of November 26. At 3:10 P.M., a radio message was received from the commander of the 61st Cavalry Division announcing that the Division in the area of Sharnutovskii was engaged in hard fighting with enemy tanks.

At 7:00 P.M., the Commander of the 4th Corps ordered the 81st Cavalry Division and three batteries of the 149th Tank Destroyer Artillery Regiment to attack Kotelnikovo, striking along the highway and cutting the route of withdrawal of the enemy toward the west. The 61st Cavalry Division was ordered by radio to break off the engagement with the enemy and, during the night before November 27, to advance to Kotelnikovo and attack from the east in cooperation with the 81st Cavalry Division. After this, radio communication with the 61st Cavalry Division was interrupted. As we learned later, after the battle at Sharnutovskii, it withdrew toward Umantsevo; the 126th Rifle Division, in the course of November 26–27, did some stubborn fighting in the area of Krugliakov, Zhutovo, and Kovalevka. The 81st Cavalry Division had to operate at a distance of 60 kilometers from the 126th Rifle Division and at a distance of 95 kilometers from the 61st Cavalry Division. There was very little information concerning the enemy. It was not until after the battle of November 28 that we obtained from the staff of the 51st Army an intelligence report containing air reconnaissance data about a group of 40 tanks, 100 armored cars, and 50 motor buses 5 kilometers north of Lotelnikovo, the movement of up to 30 motor vehicles along the Zakharov–Kotelnikovo road, and the concentration in the latter of up to a regiment of infantry.

At 10:00 P.M. on November 26, the 81st Cavalry Division started out from the long halt, and by the morning of November 27, its leading detachments (the 232nd Cavalry Regiment) approached the northwest edge of Kotelnikovo. During the day, the enemy offered stubborn resistance, repeatedly counterattacking with tanks and submachine guns the combat formations of the regiments of the 81st Cavalry Division. At 1:00 P.M., the enemy transferred on trucks from Zhutovo Station two echelons with infantry and artillery, which after unloading on the roads near Kurmoiarskaia, struck the flanks and rear of the units of the Division advancing toward Kotelnikovo from the north.

During the night preceding November 28, the Division, having suffered considerable losses in battle, withdrew and concentrated in the areas of Zakharov and Pokhlebin.

In the course of the battle, it was learned that the enemy had in Kotelnikovo up to three battalions of Rumanian infantry, the 114th Motorized Regiment of the 6th German Panzer Division, up to 50 tanks with 8 to 10 artillery batteries, and numerous mortars and large-caliber machine guns. The enemy organized a double line of defense with trenches of full profile, prepared earth- and-timber pillboxes in the stone houses, strung barbed-wire entanglements, and laid mine fields on the approaches to the town from the northwest, north, and west.

The 81st Cavalry Division in its attack against a large well-fortified town—defended by a strong garrison and having no assistance from the 126th and the 302nd Rifle Divisions and the 61st Cavalry Division (held up by the enemy) and not having received the tank battalion or Guards mortar battalion assigned for reinforcement—failed in the battle of November 27 and suffered heavy losses.

The Battle at Poklebin on December 4, 1942

On November 29, the 302nd Rifle Division, while pursuing the withdrawing enemy, reached with its mainforces the Chilekov- (exclusive) Nebikov front. The 126th Rifle Division captured Nebikov and with its left flank approached Pimen-Cherni. Both divisions moved forward slowly, being held back by the enemy. The 4th Cavalry Corps (without the 61st Cavalry Division) passed to the defensive on the line of Verkhne-Kurmoiaskaia, Nizhne-Iablochnyi, and Verkhne-Iablochnyi. Its 61st Cavalry Division, reaching the Poperechnyi-Budarka line, engaged in heavy fighting.

The activity of the enemy increased. The tank reconnaissance of the enemy was persistent and deep. Enemy aviation had control of the air. our reconnaissance constantly encountered tanks, armored cars, and motorized infantry of the enemy. On the Zakharov-Kotelnikovo sector, we observed up to 30 motor vehicles, and on the Zhutov-Kotelnikovo sector, 10 railway echelons moving south. The enemy forces in the area of Kotelnikovo continued to increase. The cavalry reconnaissance of the Division could not penetrate into the depths of the enemy dispositions to determine the grouping of his forces and the approach of his fresh reserves, because it was thrown back by the motorized infantry and tanks. The 85th Tank Brigade, being without fuel, had concentrated in Generalovskii; it arrived on November 28, to reinforce the 4th Cavalry Corps. The situation of the units of the Corps was also extremely serious. There was only enough food for two days, and the only forage was hay. There was no fuel, and the batteries of the 149th Tank Destroyer Artillery Regiment were obliged to remain where they were.[8]

At 5:00 P.M. on November 29, the commander of the 4th Cavalry Corps received a field order from the 51st Army, in which the following mission was assigned:

By the close of November 29, fight your way into the defenses of Kotelnikovo, fortify yourself, and wait for the general attack on November 30, 1942, using the forward detachments for this purpose.

The Corps (without the 61st Cavalry Division) was to attack Kotelnikovo from the west; the 302nd Rifle Division from the northeast and the east, and the 126th Rifle Division from the east and southeast. The 61st Cavalry Division with its forward detachments captured Meliorativnyi Siding and Semichnaia Station and was to prevent the enemy withdrawal toward the south.

At 9:15 P.M. on November 29, the Commander of the Corps received from the staff of the 51st Army a second coded telegram.

You are to continue the battle for Kotelnikovo. Before 1200 hours on 30–11 you are to bring up artillery and carry out a reconnaissance. Attack against the enemy in Kotelnikovo is to start at 1200 hours on 30 November 1942.

There was no signal communications with the 61st Cavalry, 302nd, and 126th Rifle Divisions.

At midnight on November 29, the 81st Cavalry Division started to carry out its mission. On November 30, the Commander of the 51st Army suspended the execution of the operations, ordering the units of the 4th Cavalry Corps to fortify themselves and hold the Veselyi, Safronov, and Verkhne-Iablochnyi line; to conduct reconnaissance to the west and to the south; to bring up fuel; and to prepare for the capture of Kotelnikovo.

Before December 2, the units of the Corps fortified themselves on the occupied lines and brought up fuel. The enemy brought up reserves and fortified Kotelnikovo, Semichnaia, Maiorskii, and Pokhlebin.

The 249th Guards Mortar Battalion, having two "salvos," arrived on December 2, for the reinforcement of the 4th Cavalry Corps. At 3:00 A.M.

on December 2, an order was received from the commander of the 51st Army.

4th Cavalry Corps (without 61st Cavalry Division), with the 85th Tank Brigade, covering itself from the Don River, is to reach the line Maiorski–Zakharov by 1100 hours on December 2 and by the close of December 2, capture the west part of Kotelnikovo. With one reinforced regiment you are to capture Meliorativny Siding. After capturing Kotelnikovo you are to develop the attack along the railroad toward Dubovskoe. The 302nd Rifle Division will advance on the left and by the close of December 2, this Division is to capture the east part of Kotelnikovo.

The Commander of the Corps gave preliminary orders for readiness by the morning of December 2 for action aimed at the capture of Kotelnikovo while at the same time reporting to the Commander of the 51st Army the absence of fuel in the 85th Tank Brigade.

On December 2, the Army Commander gave the following order: Execution of order for the capture of Kotelnikovo to stop until special instructions.

On December 2–3, the units of the Corps and of the 85th Tank Brigade replenished their fuel up to one "fill." The staff of the 51st Army gave the following order: "On the morning of December 3, you are to start carrying out the order of December 1 of the Commander of the Army for the capture of Kotelnikovo."

By this time, all the Kotelnikovo base of operations had passed into the hands of the enemy. Kotelnikovo, Maiorskii, Zakharov, Pokhlebin, and Semichnaia were converted into strong points. The forces of the enemy, especially the tanks, had concentrated in the area of Kotelnikovo. The great movement of motor vehicles from the crossing on the Don toward Kotelnikovo indicated the approach of reserves.[9]

The 302nd Rifle Division was drawn into some hard fighting in the area of Gremyschi station and was unable to advance. The 126th Rifle Division passed to the defensive in the area of Pimen-Cherni.

In carrying out the order of the commander of the 51st Army, the 4th Cavalry Corps (without the 61st Cavalry Division), reinforced by the 85th Tank Brigade and the Guards Mortar Battalion, started on the morning of December 3 from the occupied area. At 7:00 A.M., the forward units of the 81st Cavalry Division encountered strong resistance in the area of Pokhlebin but hurled back the enemy and captured the village. Further attempts to advance toward Maiorskii were repulsed by the enemy. The latter, while intensifying artillery and mortar fire from Maiorskii,

Zakharov, and Kotelnikovo, carried out several tank attacks that were repulsed by the destroyer artillery of the regiment, the artillery of the division, and of the 85th Tank Brigade.

The prisoners of war and the reconnaissance data indicated concentration in the area of Maiorskii, Zakharov, and Kotelnikovo of the 6th German Panzer Division arriving from France. Having appraised the situation and fearing the encirclement of the 81st Cavalry Division in the area of Pokhlebin, the Commander of the 4th Cavalry Corps asked the Commander of the 51st Army about the withdrawal of the Corps to the line of Verkhne-Kurmoiarskaia, Safranov, and Verkhne-Iablochnyi. The Commander of the 51st Army gave the following order: "Carry out the previously assigned mission, capturing before dawn Maiorskii, Zakharov, Semichnaia. The beginning of the offensive is at 7:00 A.M. on 4-12-1942."

On the morning of December 4, the Commander of the Corps could not make a second report to the Commander of the 51st Army concerning the necessity of the withdrawal, because neither the Commander nor the Chief of Staff were with the Staff of the Army. As late as 7:00 P.M. on December 3, the units of the Corps received an order to continue the offensive.

At 10:00 A.M. on December 4, the enemy opened artillery fire of great density and, from 11:00 A.M. to 1:00 P.M., attacked the dispositions of the 81st Cavalry Division in the area of Pokhlebin with 150 tanks and motorized infantry. In repelling the tank attack, all artillery participated, including the 113th Antiaircraft Artillery Regiment arriving during the night and the antitank rifles. After capturing Pokhlebin, small groups of enemy tanks moved north toward Veselyi and Verkhne-Kurmoiarskaia.

At 2:00 P.M., the 81st Cavalry Division was completely encircled; the tanks and motorized infantry of the enemy began to tighten the ring of encirclement. The Division conducted stubborn battle during the day, and it was not until darkness came on that it began to withdraw, by groups, toward Nizhne-Iablochnyi.

The commander of the Corps reported all the circumstances to the Commander of the 51st Army and received orders to withdraw the units of the 81st Cavalry Division to the line of Verkhne-Kurmoiarskaia, Nizhne-Iablochnyi, and Verkhne-Iablochnyi.

The losses of the 81st Cavalry Division in killed, wounded, and missing amounted to 1,897 men and 1,860 horses. The units lost fourteen 76 mm guns, four 45 mm guns, four 107 mm mortars, and eight 37 mm antiaircraft guns. Among those killed were the Commander of the Division Colonel Baumstein; Chief of Staff Lieutenant Colonel Terekin, and Chief of the Political Section Regimental Commissar Turbin.[10]

The enemy left on the field of battle 69 burning and disabled tanks.

The Defensive Battle of the 4th Cavalry Corps
(December 6, 1942–January 1, 1943)

After the battle at Pokhlebin, the main group of the enemy concentrated in Kotelnikovo from where it subsequently carried out an attack against Zhutov, Abganerovo, Gromoslavka, Kapkinskii, and Nizhne-Kumskii. Enemy aviation had control of the air and constantly bombarded the units of the 4th Cavalry Corps and inflicted upon it considerable losses. The 302nd and 126th Rifle Divisions engaged in heavy defensive fighting on the previous lines.

The Corps placed itself in order and fortified the lines it occupied, securing the right flank of the 51st Army and the concentration of the shock armies. On December 9, the 61st Cavalry Division joined the Corps, after occupying the Biriukov-Vodianskii-Zalivskii line.

In accordance with the orders of the commander of the 51st Army, four strong points were to be organized on the sector of the corps: Verkhne-Kurmoiarskaia, Nizhne-Iablochnyi, Safronov, and Verkhne-Iablochnyi. In addition to this, upon the arrival of the 61st Cavalry Division, the latter was to pass to the defensive on the occupied line.

On December 12, the enemy's main forces of the Kotelnikovo group passed to the counteroffensive for the purpose of breaking through from the southwest the ring of encirclement tightening around the German 6th Army at Stalingrad. From December 12–17, the 4th Cavalry Corps protected by hard fighting the concentration of the 2nd Guards Army, tying down considerable forces of the enemy.

In this period, the 61st Cavalry Division, operating on the left flank of the Corps, carried on some hard fighting and held up on the front the approaching reserves of the enemy in front of the rifle divisions fighting at Verkhne-Kumskii and Gromoslavka. In this battle the Division suffered heavy losses in men and horses from enemy tanks and aviation, especially from the latter.

The Corps, having lost up to 60 percent of its strength during 45 days of continuous fighting, was becoming weaker still each day. Its combat equipment for opposing the pursuing tank groups had become clearly insufficient. On December 18, the Corps became subordinate to the Commander of the 2nd Guards Army and withdrew to the line of the Myshkovo River, where it relieved the units of the 300th Rifle Division and assumed the defensive. With the advance of the units of the Red Army, the 4th Cavalry Corps was placed in the reserves of the Front to be brought up to strength by replacements.

Results of the Operations of the 4th Cavalry Corps

From November 19 to December 18, 1942, the units of the Corps inflicted heavy losses upon the enemy. The 2nd, 3rd, and 4th Cavalry and the 3rd Artillery Regiments of the 8th Rumanian Cavalry Division, the 6th Regiment of the 5th Cavalry Division, and the remnants of the 5th Jaeger, 85th, and 93rd Infantry Regiments of the 1st Rumanian Infantry Division were all completely shattered. Heavy losses were inflicted upon the 11th Panzer and 114th Motorized Regiments of the 6th German Panzer Division, which, after the battles at Kotelnikovo and Pokhlebin, were reorganized into a brigade.

In all, the units of the 4th Cavalry Corps destroyed more than 3,000 soldiers and officers of the enemy and captured 148 guns, more than 50,000 artillery shells, 3,000 mortar shells, many rifles, machine guns, mortars, motor vehicles, and 15 dumps with ammunition, fuel, and Class I supplies. In battle it destroyed and captured 102 tanks, three armored cars, and more than 300 motor vehicles with troops and loads of supplies.

The units of the Corps, in unequal battle with large tank and infantry forces of the enemy, lost up to 65 percent of their equipment.[11]

Conclusions Pertaining to the Strategic Employment of Cavalry

1. The operations of the Great Patriotic War, in which large masses of cavalry took part, proved that only by operating as Front-level assets in cooperation with the shock group of the army can cavalry corps produce the maximum strategic effect.

Nevertheless, while having three cavalry corps, the command of the Fronts carrying out the Stalingrad operation subordinated all of the cavalry to the commanders of the armies. Again the cavalry units were placed in an unfavorable situation when used by certain army commanders for carrying out secondary missions. They were deprived of means of reinforcement, broken up into units, and in the end unable to produce the strategic effect that they could have had if they had been employed correctly.

The employment of the 3rd Guards Cavalry Corps, which should have cooperated with the 4th Tank Corps by attacking at the junction area between the 21st and 65th Armies, was particularly characteristic. In this case, it would have been entirely obvious to ask permission to combine the action of these corps into one cavalry–mechanized group immediately subordinate to the front command for striking a powerful blow in the general direction of Kalach. Such a concentrated attack by a tank and a cavalry corps against the Rumanian troops and the separate German garrisons in the depths of the breakthrough could have saved the cavalry from useless losses and could have speeded up the encirclement of the German group east of Kalach by several days. The Front command preferred to employ both the tank and the cavalry corps independently, subordinating the one and the other to Army command, and the latter was not able to organize cooperation between the cavalry and tanks in the course of the operations. As a result, they acted separately.

We can see the same but more unfavorable results in the operation of the 5th Tank Army. Here the command of the Army was completely unable to organize cooperation between the 1st Tank and 8th Cavalry Corps. The cavalry, which should have moved with the second echelon, behind the tanks for exploitation of the success was, in reality obliged— because of the absence of the proper cooperation between them in the course of the operation—to make its way with its own forces. Nor did the command of the Stalingrad Front organize a powerful cavalry–mechanised group for exploiting gains. Instead, it directed its mobile units separately: the 4th Mechanized Corps toward Tinguta and the 4th Cavalry Corps toward Abganerovo.

2. The Field Service Regulations of the Red Army, on the basis of the experience of the Great Patriotic War, state that in offensive operations the large cavalry units should be reinforced assigned tanks, rifle, artillery, and Guards Mortars divisions and special units from the reserves of the *Stavka*.

Following the letter of the Regulations, the commands of all the armies, upon receiving cavalry corps as subordinate forces, did assign to them means of reinforcement; but in the majority of cases, this reinforcement was in name only. For example, the means of reinforcement assigned to the 8th Corps—the 152nd Howitzer Artillery Regiment and the 510th Flamethrower Tank Battalion—did not arrive at all. The 174th and 179th Tank Destroyer Artillery Regiments arrived in such condition that they were not fit for fighting. Those in the composition of the Corps did not fire a single shot and were soon left in the rear for lack of fuel. The 35th Guards Mortar Regiment and the 511th Flamethrower Tank Battalion were taken from the Corps on the third day of the operation, and at the time of the mass action of enemy aviation at Oblivskaia, the 586th *PVO* Artillery Regiment almost ran out of shells. For this reason the Corps, weakened by the command of the 5th Tank Army by one division (the 21st Cavalry Division) and deprived of all means of reinforcement, was left to its own resources in the critical moment of the operation.

After the battle at Kotelnikovo on November 27, the command of the 51st Army assigned the 85th Tank Brigade to the 4th Cavalry Corps, but it had almost no fuel, and it could not cooperate effectively with cavalry.

The command of the 21st Army gave considerable reinforcements to the 3rd Guards Cavalry Corps in the form of army artillery and mortars, and the Corps operated under better conditions than the 8th and 4th. But the absence of tanks in the 3rd Corps—in operations against large tank groups of the enemy in the area of Evlampievskii, Bolshenabatovskii and Malonebatovskii on November 22–24—obliged the cavalry divisions to carry on a long and stubborn battle without the help of tanks. The results were that it suffered excessive losses and could not carry out its mission in time.

We did not practice the assignment of rifle units to the cavalry corps at all, while the experiences of the Great Patriotic War showed such reinforcement to be advantageous.

3. Northwest of Stalingrad, the cavalry was made operationally subordinate to the commanders of the 5th Tank Army and the 21st Army, which undoubtedly employed it first of all in the interest of their armies. On the second day of the operation, the Commander of the 5th Tank Army began to break up the 8th Cavalry Corps, which was subordinate to him, into separate parts. When the Corps went into the breach and carried out its mission for the first day, we took from its composition the strongest division—namely, the 21st—and sent it out to execute a secondary mission—one of cooperation with the 1st Guards Army in striking the demoralized remnants of the 7th, 9th, and 14th Rumanian Infantry Divisions. This mission could have been successfully assigned to the 14th Guards Rifle Division operating on the right of the 8th Cavalry Corps, and the Corps could have been sent in full strength to fight the infantry and the units of the 22nd German and the 1st Rumanian Panzer Divisions.

If we remember that at the same time the Commander of the Army also took from the 8th Cavalry Corps almost all its means of reinforcement (except the 586th *PVO* Regiment, which had almost no ammunition), the ineffective manner in which the command of the 21st Army employed the cavalry becomes still more evident. The command of the 21st Army did not disperse the cavalry, but even here there was some fractioning of it. At the moment of the hardest fighting against German tanks and infantry in the area east of Bolshenabatovskii and Malonabatovskii, the Commander of the 21st Army took from the 3rd Guards Cavalry Corps, makeup the 6th Guards Cavalry Division, which was sent at first to carry out a passive mission in the preparation of a defensive line in the area of Pobeda Oktiabr State Farm. This was a mission for which a less mobile unit would have been more appropriate. The 6th Guards Cavalry Division was then reassigned to the commander of the 1st Tank Corps for an attack against Chir Station and Rychkovskii.

On the second day of the operation, the command of the Stalingrad Front actually eliminated his two-division 4th Cavalry Corps, sending the 61st Division for the execution of an independent mission and subordinating the 81st Division two days later to the commander of the 51st Army. As a result of this, the 61st and 81st Cavalry Divisions, operating separately in a secondary direction won a number of tactical victories in the beginning. Subsequently, however, in battles with superior forces of German tanks and infantry of the von Manstein group, the divisions suffered heavy losses. Hence, as an operational unit, the 4th Cavalry Corps was not effectively employed; because of the fact that it was broken up.

Something that was highly characteristic of the command of troops of combined arms was the taking of reconnaissance battalions from the composition of the 61st and 81st Cavalry Divisions and employing these special units as organic cavalry on the sector of the 91st Rifle Division.

4. In the treeless area around Stalingrad, the concealment of the concentration of large masses of cavalry from enemy airplanes was possible only on conditions that we had mastery of the air and a powerful system of antiaircraft defense for the cavalry itself. In the given operation, such conditions did not prevail. Hence, the bringing of cavalry into the jump-off area before committing it in the breakthrough had to be carried out at the very last moment, secretly and under cover of darkness. However, only the command of the Stalingrad Front organized in a correct manner the bringing up of the 4th Cavalry Corps into the jump-off area before committing it in the breakthrough. By a 45-kilometer night march, the Corps was concentrated in the areas of Siangerdyk, Amoi, Kharbulia, and Gashun, and after an 8-hour rest, moved into the breakthrough on November 20.

The Commander of the 5th Tank Army concentrated the 8th Cavalry Corps in the jump-off area before sending it into the breakthrough on November 8, that is, 11 days before the beginning of the operation. It is quite natural that enemy aviation noticed ahead of time the concentration of cavalry on the south bank of the Don River and inflicted upon it serious losses even before it was sent into the breakthrough.

The Commander of the 21st Army also concentrated the 3rd Guards Cavalry Corps in the jump-off area 11 days before commitment in the breakthrough. The presence of the Corps in the initial area was discovered by enemy aviation, which in two days disabled 190 men and 461 horses of the Corps. It was only upon the request of the Commander of the Corps on November 10 that the Corps was again led back into the area of concentration. In adition to the heavy losses that were entirely unnecessary, another result of the enemy's discovery of the direction of attack was that the Corps marched 70 kilometers to no purpose and lost 10 days of precious time needed for reshoeing the horses.

5. The security provided by the Army command for the forcing of the Don River at Nizhne-Zatonskii by the 3rd Cavalry Corps was highly characteristic. In the direction of the main attack, 12 ferries and bridge crossings were prepared with Army equipment. The bridge work was carried out without taking any masking precautions; the work was carried out leisurely, without any cover by antiaircraft guns and within the range of enemy artillery. The result was that at the time of the approach of the Corps instead of 12 crossings, there was only one bridge and it was half-

destroyed; the rest had been knocked out by enemy aviation and artillery. The Corps began the crossing during the daytime, without sufficient air cover. Artillery and vehicles were crossed by hand over a single half-destroyed bridge, and it was only by exceptionally favorable circumstance—namely, the presence of heavy clouds and fog, during which enemy aviation did not appear in the air—that it was possible to send the cavalry into the breakthrough successfully.

6. The missions assigned to the cavalry corps were characterized by their great depth. For example, on the first day of the operation, the 8th Cavalry Corps were assigned the task of going into the Pronin-Karasev area (up to 55 to 60 kilometers, after having thrown out forward detachments to the crossings at Chistiakovshaia and Chernushevskaia (an additional distance of 22 to 25 kilometers). On the second day of the operation, it was to seize the area of Ust-Griaznovakl, Leonov, and Siniapkin (a total depth of more than 120 kilometers).

On the first day of the operation, the 3rd Guards Cavalry Corps was assigned the mission of seizing the areas of (exclusive) Erik, Verkhne-Buzinovka, and Svechnikovskii (depth up to 60 kilometers), and on the second day, to reach the Don River in the areas of Golubinskii, Bolshenabatovskii, and Evlampievakii (more than 120 kilometers).

The immediate mission of the 4th Cavalry Corps was defined as the capture of Abganerovo at a distance of 65 kilometers from the front line.

It is necessary to emphasize that the commitment of the cavalry in the breakthrough actually took place between 12:00 noon and 8:00 P.M.—that is, toward the end of the short November day—hence, the missions of the first day were too deep for the cavalry to carry out. In the attack against Kotelnikovo on November 27, the Commander of the 51st Army ordered the 81st Cavalry Division to march a distance of 95 kilometers in a day.

7. In the course of the operation the Army command did not carry out any cooperation. The 8th Cavalry Corps was committed in the breakthrough behind the 1st Tank Corps, which was to make an attack ahead of the cavalry up to the line Ust-Medveditskii, and from there to turn toward Lipovskii, while the 8th Corps attacked toward Star Pronin to protect the right flank of the shock group of the 5th Tank Army.

In reality, after commitment in the breakthrough, the 8th Corps, on the line of Blinovskii and Ust-Medveditskii, moved up on a level with the point of the column of the 1st Tank Corps. When the 55th Cavalry Division engaged the enemy beyond Ust-Medveditskii, the units of the 1st Tank Corps were no longer in front of the combat formations of the cavalry but behind them. In precisely the same way the 112th Cavalry Division, after engaging the enemy at Blinovskii, moved not behind the rifle troops but in front of them.

The 8th Corps engaged the enemy at Bolshaia Donshchinka and to the west. The Corps was then attacked from the rear by the 22nd German and the 1st Rumanian Panzer Divisions, which had broken through, and it fought these units until they were defeated in the night of November 23 without any support from the units of the 1st Tank Corps.

The 3rd Guards Cavalry Corps was also to go into the breakthrough behind the 4th Tank Corps and crush the operational reserves of the enemy in cooperation with the 4th Tank Corps. In reality, the 4th Tank Corps, on the first day of the operation, advanced only up to the area of Vlasov and, upon encountering stubborn enemy resistance at this place, stopped for the night, without continuing its southward movement toward Pervomaisk State Farm, Evseev.

On November 20, the units of the 4th Tank Corps cooperated with the 5th Guards Cavalry Division in the battle for Vlasov and Salivanov, but after this the 4th Tank Corps moved in the direction of Manoilin and on toward Kalach. The 4th Tank Corps did not render any assistance to the units of the 3rd Corps in the hard fighting against the units of the 14th and 16th Panzer and 376th Infantry Divisions in the area of Bolshenabatovskii, and Malonabatovskii on November 22–24.

The artillery and Guards mortars of the 5th Tank and 21st Armies, assigned to the 3rd Guards and 8th Cavalry Corps, participated in the general attack of the armies and were switched to support the cavalry only after a great delay.

The rifle troops of the 21st Army, in whose zone of advance the 3rd Guards Cavalry Corps was committed in the breakthrough, not only failed to make passageways in the mine fields and entanglements of the enemy for the cavalry, but did not even mark the passageways that it made for itself.

The Commander of the 51st Army, having sent the 4th Cavalry Corps (actually, only the 81st Cavalry Division) for an attack against Kotelnikovo—occupied by large forces of infantry and tanks of the enemy—did not plan cooperation between the cavalry and the 302nd Rifle Division advancing along the railroad line. Here, in reality, the cavalry fought an isolated battle with numerically superior enemy forces defending fortified towns, at a distance of 60 to 95 kilometers from the adjacent unit. This made it possible for the enemy to bring up reserves and drive off the 81st Cavalry Division, inflicting upon it heavy losses.

The offensive of the 81st Cavalry Division against Kotelnikovo from December 1–4 was carried out by sudden efforts of short duration, with very little organization, and the staff of the 51st Army was obliged to change his attack orders three times because the offensive was not provided with the proper security.

8. The lack of organized cooperation between cavalry on the one hand and tank and mechanized units, rifle divisions, and aviation on the other could have been remedied to a considerable degree by the control of these

units in the course of the operation itself. However, in the control of the cavalry there were many great weaknesses.

The Commander of the 5th Tank Army, after changing the direction of the attack of the 8th Cavalry and 1st Tank Corps toward Bolshaia Donshchinka, did not provide for cooperation between these two mobile units in battle at Bolshaia Donshchinka. Tied down by battle with the tanks and motorized infantry breaking out of encirclement, the cavalry could not, because of the delay of the 47th Guards Rifle Division, turn over the destruction of this group to the infantry and continue its movement toward Oblivshaia.

Bled white during the time of the air attacks and not covered from the air, the units of the 55th and 112th Cavalry Divisions did not have the strength to break the resistance of the enemy garrisons in Oblivskaia. More so as by the order of the commander of the 5th Tank Army on December 1, the 55th Cavalry Division had been sent toward the west for assuming the defensive on the Deev-Glukhmanovskii sector. In the period of December 1-3, the attack against Oblivskaia was carried out by only the 112th Cavalry Division. The units of the 40th Guards Rifle Division, approaching Oblivskaia—which, on November 29, under the direction of the second in command of the 5th Tank Army, were to attack the station jointly with the 112th Cavalry Division—put off the attack seven times, without informing the cavalry in due time, as a result of which the latter suffered losses in isolated attacks.

In the course of the operation, especially in its first period, the command of the 21st Army directed the actions of the 3rd Guards Cavalry Corps in a more effective manner. However, even between the units of the 3rd Cavalry and the 4th Tank Corps, there was not sufficient cooperation in the course of the operation, and the cavalry with its own forces and without the support of tanks was obliged to overcome the resistance of the enemy in fortified towns in the face of rather strong tank forces.

In the second period of the operation, the control of the 3rd Guards Cavalry Corps by the Army command became more tentative. The missions were changed quickly, and the cavalry divisions were shifted around a great deal by frequent changes in the direction of the actions.

The command of the 51st Army not only failed to direct the actions of the 4th Cavalry Corps in the course of the operations, but its Commander could not even find the Commander of the Army or the chief of staff at the proper moment in the night of December 4, when it was completely evident to him that the 81st Cavalry Division was in danger of being crushed by superior forces of enemy tanks and infantry.

9. The Army command, after the cavalry corps was placed at its disposal, oftentimes continued to regard it as a temporarily assigned unit and did not make the necessary effort to provide the cavalry with

adequate supplies. Even in the areas of concentration, the cavalry divisions experienced great difficulty in bringing up Class I supplies and especially forage. Upon arrival in the jump-off areas—where a large number of units were crowded together and the supply route from the supply station had a length of about 200 kilometers (for the divisions of the 3rd Guards Cavalry Corps upon approaching the south banks of the Don River)—the bringing up of supplies became a still more difficult problem; the area itself was stripped of everything by the German troops. The units were saved only by the large number of captured motor vehicles and fuel, and an exceptionally great burden was placed upon the divisional transports.

10. The Army command and the army replenishment units did not show the least concern in planning for shoeing the horses on time for the winter. It would soon be necessary to operate in a roadless area in the presence of ice. The command of the cavalry units did not have sufficient time for reshoeing the horses, because the cavalry had carried out a useless march from the area of concentration to the jump-off area and return. As result of this, the loss of horses in this operation was exceptionally high, and the losses were caused not only by enemy aviation and guns but also from exhaustion, loss of shoes, and being disabled from other causes.

The experience of the Stalingrad operation enables us to draw some very valuable conclusions pertaining to the combat operations of cavalry. Among these are the following:

1. There was extensive employment of cavalry regiments and even "divisions of maneuver" and numerous successful attacks in mounted formation against badly shattered infantry, especially against the Rumanian cavalry.
2. In a number of cases, there was successful alternation of the operations' combination of dismounted and mounted units.
3. The cavalry units obtained experience in the capturing of fortified towns and villages by enveloping them from the flanks, from the rear, cutting the routes of withdrawal of the enemy.
4. The cavalry units learned to conduct successful battle against enemy tanks with their own equipment.

General Conclusions

The battle of Stalingrad proved once again that large cavalry units, in offensive operations, are a powerful strategic means of the command for the exploitation of successes. In order to have the most effective employment of cavalry units, the following are necessary:

1. Mass employment of cavalry in the direction of the main attack, in cooperation with tanks and mechanized units, both as strategic means of

the front and, in certain cases, even as reserves of *Stavka*. The breaking up of cavalry units by reassigning them to the army command, and more so to the commanders of the units of combined arms, should not be permitted.

2. The sending of large cavalry units against the main group of enemy forces in directions making possible wide freedom in strategic maneuver by these cavalry units, in order that the cavalry itself will not have to break through fortified enemy positions and conduct long, drawn-out battle with garrisons in fortified towns and villages.

3. Assignment to the large cavalry formations of motorized riflemen (in the winter, sleds), tank units, artillery, and motor reserves of *Stavka* antitank and antiaircraft equipment, combat engineers, and special units.

4. Assignment of fighter aviation, as a rule making it operationally subordinate to the commander of the cavalry unit, to cover from the air the concentration, maneuver, and combat operations of the cavalry.

5. Independent supplying of the large cavalry formations with open railheads for cavalry divisions and the placing of motor vehicles and transport aviation at the disposal of the commander of the cavalry unit.

6. Giving to the cavalry units, after the completion of the front and army operations, time for rest, for bringing up the rear establishments, for distributing replacements that arrive, and for putting units in readiness for the next mission.

Editor's Notes

1. For an excellent overview of Soviet cavalry see A. Ia. Soshnikov, *Sovetskaia kavaleriia* (Moscow: *Voenizdat*, 1984).

2. The 8th Cavalry Corps was commanded by Major General M. D. Borisov. The other comanders were: 112th Cavalry Division, Major General M. M. Shaimuratov; the 21st Cavalry Division, Major General N. P. Iaknun; and the 55th Cavalry Division, Colonel I. T. Chalenko.

3. Compare these and comments found in Chapter 10 to those found in more modern Soviet air histories such as R. Wagner, ed. *The Soviet Air Force in World War II* tran. (New York: Doubleday & Co., 1973), or to I. Timokhovich, *Operativnoe iskusstvo Sovetskikh VVS v Velikoi Otechestvennoi Voiny* (Moscow: *Voenizdat*, 1976).

4. This destruction clearly reflects the continuing concern over the utility of cavalry. The losses of the 55th Cavalry Division mirror the defeats suffered in 1941, but the debate continues to highlight the inability of the Soviet General Staff to unambiguously draw final conclusions. In fact, this ambiguity had existed in all armies since 1914 and has been thoroughly reviewed in Edward Katzenbach, "The Horse Cavalry in the Twentieth Century: A Study in Policy Response" in Morton Halperin and Arnold Kanter, eds., *Readings in American Foreign Policy* (Boston: Little, Brown and Company, 1973), pp. 172–90.

5. For a complete history of the 7th Guards Cavalry Corps, see M. Dokuchev, *V boi shli eskadrony* (Moscow: *Voenizdat*, 1984).

6. The 3rd Guards Cavalry Corps was commanded by Major General I. A. Pliev. The other units were commanded by: the 5th Guards Cavalry Division, Colonel N. S. Chepurkin; the 6th Guards Cavalry Division, Colonel A. I. Belogorskii; and the commander of the 32nd Cavalry Division, unknown to the editor, is possibly Colonel G. F. Maliukov.

7. The 4th Cavalry Corps was commanded by Lieutenant General T. T. Shapkin. The other

commanders were: the 81st Cavalry Division, Colonel V. G. Baumstein; the 61st Cavalry Division; Major General Ia. K. Kuliev.

8. In World War I, fodder was a serious concern for all cavalry, even in stationary positions. For Great Britain, the largest item of export to the continent during the war had been horse fodder. The problems of logistics was one of the primary unsolved difficulties for the Soviet Union during the battle.

9. This grouping was von Manstein's relief effort. The large number of vehicles came from assembling the 6th, 17th, and the 23rd Panzer Divisions.

10. These are staggering losses for a single division. Average divisional strength was supposedly 3,000 to 3,500 men.

11. Once again, this reflects the fragility of these formations and the continuing search for the proper role. Certainly 65 percent losses mean the formation was unfit for combat.

Artillery enjoyed an exceptional reputation in the Red Army and had amply demonstrated its power on several occasions in the past, notably in Yelnia in August 1941. Stalingrad represented a new high point in the power of Soviet artillery to influence combat operations. Soviet guns and mortars virtually tripled over the time of the defensive fighting, going from 4,282 to 12,078. Density increased from 10 to 13 guns per kilometer of front to 40 to 60 guns and mortars by November. New tactics, including a single rolling barrage, and air–artillery cooperation provided increased effectiveness. As a result, Soviet artillery greatly enhanced its offensive power and readily assisted Red Army troops both in the breakthrough and in the subsequent reduction of the Stalingrad pocket—Ed.

9

Artillery in the Offensive Operations at Stalingrad

The survey of the combat employment of artillery below is devoted to the breakthrough of the defensive zone on the flanks of the Stalingrad group of the enemy before the completion of its strategic and tactical encirclement.[1]

The breakthrough of enemy defenses in the Don Bend and in the areas to the northwest, north, and south of Stalingrad was carried out with strategic cooperation between three fronts. In conformity with this, we shall consider in succession the action of artillery of the Southwestern, Don, and Stalingrad Fronts.

Operations of the Artillery of the Southwestern Front

The Preparatory Period of the Operation

The Southwestern Front, created by a decision of the *Stavka* at the end of October, 1942, had in its makeup the 1st Guards, 5th Tank, and 21st

Armies. The positions of the armies from November 19–30, 1942, are shown (*see map 4—Ed.*).

In the plan of encirclement of the Stalingrad group of the enemy, the mission of the Southwestern Front in general outline was the following: to break through the front of the enemy defenses on the sector Rybnyi, Bolshoi, and Kletskaia; and then by a swift offensive of the mobile group in the general direction of Kalach—in cooperation with the mobile units of the left wing of the Stalingrad Front—to encircle the 6th German Army west of Stalingrad.

A part of the forces of the Front (1st Guards Army and cavalry) provided security from the west for the action of the 5th Tank Army and its mobile group on the line of the Chir River.

In keeping with the mission assigned and the decision of the Commander of the Front, the artillery commander, at the beginning of November 1942, determined the measures to be carried out and received approval of them.[2] The work carried out by the artillery commander of the Front and his staff in the preparatory period of the operations included the following basic problems:

● instruction, distribution, and control in the reception and concentration of the reinforcing artillery units;
● the drawing up of a plan of air cover for the points of unloading in the areas of concentrations of the troops;
● instructions concerning the method for deployment of the artillery arriving at the fire positions, providing a network of observation, with engineer works and masking;
● instructions pertaining to organization for reconnaissance of the enemy;
● instructions pertaining to the preparation of personnel of the units for offensive battle;
● orders pertaining to the method of planning the artillery offensive; and
● organization of control of artillery in the offensive operation.

In order to provide an adequate supply of ammunition, instructions were given to place in the hands of the troops at the divisional distribution points the following: mortar shells of all calibers and gun shells for 45 mm and 76 mm guns at the rate of two units of fire each; the shells for 76 mm divisional artillery to the amount of 2.5 units of fire; and, for the rest of them, three units of fire each. In addition to this, we created Front reserves to the amount of 0.5 units of fire of all kinds of rounds.

The breakthrough was planned on the sector of the 5th Tank Army and the 21st Army; hence, the basic grouping of artillery was created in the zone of action of these Armies. The concentration of the artillery units was planned between October 28 and November 3. However, delays in railway transports and the considerable elongation of the columns of artillery regiments on the roads—regiments that were transferred from the Don and Voronezh Fronts—disrupted the plan of concentration, and its execution was drawn out almost up to the beginning of the operation. For example, the 518th Gun Artillery Regiment arrived at the 5th Tank Army the day before the operation, November 18.

The Task of the Armies and the Grouping of Artillery

In conformity with the directive of the Front, the grouping of the artillery at the beginning of the operation was arranged in the following manner. The 1st Guards Army had the mission of providing security for the right wing of the Front. Thus it was only its left flank, in cooperation with the 5th Tank Army, that struck a secondary blow in the direction of Bokovskaia. Hence, the basic grouping of artillery was created on the left flank of the Army. As artillery reinforcements, the Army had three tank destroyer artillery regiments and one gun artillery regiment from reserves of *Stavka*.[3] The greater part of the tank destroyer regiments were in the antitank mobile reserves of the commanders of the rifle divisions and in the period of the artillery preparations were drawn into the rifle troop support groups. Three batteries of the 1249th Tank Destroyer Artillery Regiment were in the reserves of the artillery commander of the Army. The maximum density of artillery was created in the zone of the 203rd Rifle Division, where, on a front 5 kilometers wide and having 204 guns and mortars, there were 41 pieces to the kilometers of front. The ratio to the enemy was 5:1.

The 5th Tank Army operated in the direction of the main attack in the general direction of Perelazovskii and Surovikino, breaking through the defenses of the enemy with three rifle divisions in a zone of 10 kilometers. In the second echelon, there were two rifle divisions, two tank corps, and one cavalry corps that were committed in the break-through for the exploitation of the success. One rifle division operated in a secondary direction.

As artillery reinforcement, the Army had the following: four gun artillery regiments, five howitzer artillery regiments, eight tank destroyer regiments, four Guards Mortar regiments, one Guards Mortar battalion, four mortar regiments, and a *PVO* antiaircraft defense battalion.

In the direction of the main attack of the army, there operated with the divisions of the first echelon 10 artillery regiments of *Stavka* and the artillery of the rifle divisions and the tank corps of the second echelon. In the secondary direction, we employed a part of the tank destroyer artillery regiments of the reserves of *Stavka* and artillery of the cavalry corps.

For the Army grouping, general support included the 396th, 213th, 312th, and 1092nd Gun Artillery Regiments and a grouping of Guards

Mortar units including the 35th, 62nd, 75th, and 85th Guards Mortar Regiments. The artillery ratio in the direction of the main attack of the Army was 5:1.[4]

The 21st Army struck the main blow in the general direction of Verkhne-Buzinovka and Peskovatka. It had the mission of completing the encirclement of the enemy's Stalingrad group with its right flank in cooperation with the units of the Stalingrad Front on the line of the Stalingrad–Kalach railway.

In the direction of the main attack, there operated three rifle divisions, reinforced by 11 *Stavka* reserve artillery regiments and the artillery of two rifle divisions of the second echelon. The general support for the Army grouping included the 1166th, 1107th, and 648th Gun Artillery Regiments, while the mortar units consisted of the 86th, 88th, and 21st Guards Mortar Regiments. In the secondary direction, there existed one rifle division, reinforced by two tank destroyer regiments. In the second echelon, two rifle divisions, one tank, and one cavalry corps were commited into the breakthrough for exploiting the success. For reinforcing the Army, there were two gun artillery regiments, six tank destroyer artillery regiments, three Guards Mortar regiments, and one Guards Mortar battalion. Together, these forces gave a ratio of 6:1 in our favor on the direction of the main attack.

On the whole, the ratio of rifle troop forces in the direction of the main attack was favorable, while in the case of artillery it was 2.5:1.0, with a total density over the entire offensive front of 12 guns per kilometer.

THE PLANNING OF COOPERATION

In the preparatory period, the troops had at their disposal sufficient time for the organization of cooperation. The missions during the period of the offensive, the target layout, and the fire plan with indications such as who would neutralize which targets and when were presented to the commanders, including the battery commanders, in plenty of time. The artillery commanders carried out joint reconnaissance with the commanders of the companies, battalions, and regiments. During these local reconnaissance missions to get acquainted with the targets, they arrived at mutual agreements as to the missions of the artillery. In the majority of cases, the targets were fired upon for adjustment during the preparatory period.

PROVIDING AN ADEQUATE SUPPLY OF AMMUNITION

In accordance with the plan of operations, it was necessary to accumulate the following amounts of ammunition (in units of fire):

At the beginning of the operations, the following had actually been brought up to the units and accumulated at the forward bases.

Armies	76 mm Div.Arty	122 mm	152 mm	82 mm Mortar	120 mm Mortar
1st Guards	1.95	1.95	2.20	1.70	1.95
5th Tank	3.95	3.95	4.20	2.70	2.95
21st	3.95	3.95	4.20	2.70	2.95

Armies	76 mm Div.Arty		122 mm		152 mm		82 mm Mortar		120 mm Mortar	
	I[1]	II[2]	I	II	I	II	I	II	I	II
1st Guards	1.8	1.2	1.0	—	2.0	0.6	0.7	0.4	1.2	1.0
5th Tank	2.1	0.9	1.1	0.2	0.6	2.4	1.0	1.2	1.2	1.0
21st	1.9	0.5	1.4	0.4	1.4	2.4	1.4	0.5	1.5	0.5

1. I = with the troops.
2. II = with the army artillery depots.

The expenditure of ammunition was planned on the basis of the following calculation (in units of fire):

Caliber	Issued for the operation	Expenditure by Units by day					Battle in depth	Total
		1	2	3	4	5		
50 mm	2	3/4	1/2	1/8	1/8	1/8	3/8	2
82 mm	2	3/4	1/2	1/8	1/8	1/8	3/8	2
120 mm	2	3/4	1/2	1/8	1/8	1/8	3/8	2
45 mm	2	3/4	1/2	1/8	1/8	1/8	3/8	2
76 mm Field	3	3/4	3/4	1/8	1/8	1/8	1 1/8	3
76 mm Division	3	1	1/2	1/8	1/8	1/8	1 1/8	3
122 mm	3	1 1/2	1/2	1/8	1/8	1/8	5/8	3
152 mm	3	1 1/2	1/2	1/8	1/8	1/8	5/8	3
37 mm AA	3	1 1/4	1/2	1/8	1/8	1/8	3/8	3[1]
85 mm	3	1 1/4	1/2	1/8	1/8	1/8	3/8	3[1]

1. Totals did not add in the original—Ed.

Breakthrough of the enemy defenses

The attack of the rifle troops was preceded by a powerful 80-minute artillery preparation. This included a 5-minute fire concentration at the beginning of the bombardment, followed by a 65-minute shelling intended to assist in the destruction and neutralization of observed targets. Finally, a 10-minute fire onslaught was to immediately precede the attack of the tanks and rifle troops.

In accordance with the artillery plan for the offensive, the preparation for the attack was to include powerful surprise attacks, delivered simultaneously by artillery and aviation over the depths of the enemy defenses. As a result, artillery and aviation had a prior agreement as to the objects to be neutralized during this period. However, the dense fog and heavy snowfall during the preparatory period before the attack prevented the operation of airplanes. Thus, some of its missions had to be assigned to the artillery, mostly to the general support grouping. Only ground attack aviation made a limited number of sorties, and even these were made only after the completion of the artillery preparation.

Immediately after the 10-minute artillery fire concentration, the close support tanks, jointly with the rifle troops, were to attack the main line of resistance and the immediate depths of the defenses. Separate tank regiments of the breakthrough forces operated in the direction of the main attack of the 5th Tank and 21st Armies.

At 7:30 A.M. on November 19, upon a signal (a volley of Guards Mortars), the artillery offensive was started with a powerful 5-minute fire concentration against the enemy's main line, as well as the centers of resistance in the depths of the defenses. This fire featured the simultaneous participation of all fire weapons, including those of the rifle troops. This powerful fire attack was unexpected by the enemy and had a stunning effect upon his troops. The individual soldiers and all of the small units fled in panic from their huts, dugouts, and trenches. In this manner, they suffered still heavier losses.

After this fire, for the next 65 minutes, there followed a period of destruction and neutralization. The fog and the heavy snowfall made it impossible to execute fire against specific targets. It was due solely to the careful and timely preparation of data, and the rather fully exposed fire system of the enemy, that it was possible to conduct sufficiently effective fire during this period. For the best observation and conduct of fire, the observation posts were placed toward the main line of resistance of the enemy defenses. The guns of battalions and regimental artillery and a part of the guns of the tank destroyer regiments were assigned for fire by direct sighting and thus conducted fire from distances of 300 to 400 meters. When the attack began, these guns moved with the combat formations of the rifle troops and the tanks operating with them. In this manner, they neutralized the fire positions that had escaped the artillery or that had reopened fire and were now obstructing the advance of the attacking troops.

The tank destroyer regiments were employed by preference in the combat formations of the rifle troops for the purpose of direct fire support against targets in the immediate area of the riflemen. The mortar regiments of the reserves of *Stavka*—batteries of 120 mm mortars of the rifle regiments and the 82 mm mortar companies—inflicted heavy losses upon the enemy through concentrated attack against groups of targets behind cover, against the personnel in trenches, and also by fire from the separate mortars and batteries.

During the first 5-minute fire concentration, the volleys of the Guards

Mortars were directed against the main line of resistance and served as a signal for the general fire concentration. For 65 minutes, volleys were executed at irregular intervals of time, varying from 10 to 20 minutes, against the basic centers of resistance in the immediate depths. In the last 10-minute fire concentration, the Guards Mortar units fired volleys from "H" minus 5 minutes to "H" hour against the strongholds of the main line of resistance.

The last 10-minute fire concentration of all the artillery, mortars, and divisional guns finally paralyzed the enemy's defenses. The volleys of the artillery and the mortars produced great destruction in the defense installations of the enemy. All the fire liaison between the strongpoints and the centers of resistance were destroyed, and it was only on certain sectors, at the very beginning of our attack, that independent enemy batteries tried to conduct fire. However, here they were also neutralized by the fire of the general support artillery grouping. The road was open for the rifle units.

Artillery provided support for the troops executing the breakthrough of the defensive zone of the enemy. By 12:00 noon on November 19, the Front Command made the decision to commit the mobile groups into the breakthrough battle.[5]

The Operations of Artillery during the Commitment of the Mobile Groups

The 26th and 1st Tank Corps, the 8th Cavalry Corps, and the 8th Motorcycle Regiment were committed into the breakthrough on the sector of the 5th Tank Army. The support for these units committed into the breakthrough was entrusted to the general support artillery of the army. Further support was made available through the artillery detailed to the units themselves (as a rule, tank destroyer regiments and Guards Mortar units). At the beginning of the artillery offensive the general support artillery grouping carried out counterbattery missions and executed fire concentrations against enemy staffs and centers of communication, places of probable concentrations of enemy personnel, and other unobserved targets. The absence of aviation for the direction of artillery fire and the poor observation from ground observer posts made it necessary to conduct fire in almost all cases by neutralizing unobserved targets utilizing the zone method.

The subsequent mission of the general support artillery grouping of the Army was to provide security for the commitment of the mobile forces to a depth of 10 to 12 kilometers. This was effected by the controlled fire of the Commander of the artillery grouping as the rifle units reached specific lines. A matter of great interest was the adequate provision of artillery fire for the actions of tanks in the depths: fire that was furnished on request through the artillery observer–fire corrector placed with the radio-equipped tanks. For this purpose, at the very beginning of the movement of the tank corps, we placed in the tanks of the forward brigades several previously trained artillerymen/observers: deputy of the commander of the battalion, chief of staff, and commander of a battery selected from each battalion of the regiments of the general support artillery grouping. These individuals directed the fire of the battalion over all the depths of their range of fire from their main firing positions.

Beforehand, we worked out a method of target designation. This method of accompanying the tank troops requires careful organization and smooth functioning of radio communications between the tanks and the artillery. In the 5th Tank Army, when the distance of the radio tank from the combat formations of the artillery increased, the radio sets in the battalions did not receive the radio signals. The same thing happened in the 21st Army as a result of the weakness of the radio sets of the artillery regiments. For this purpose, we need radio sets of the type 5-AK and RSB.[6]

The further mission of the general support army group in the exploitation of the success in the direction of the main attack consisted of giving fire support to the flanks. In this case, the employment of box barrages with the participation for this purpose of the artillery groups or infantry support (especially of howitzer regiments of the reserves of *Stavka*) proved to be worthwhile.

The example of the general support grouping of the 21st Army confirmed the necessity of distant fire concentrations against towns and villages occupied by the enemy and his staffs. Distant fire attacks should be made not only in the direction of the main attack but also on the flanks of the breakthrough. By such attacks, we disorganized the morale of the enemy, broke up the control of troops, and disoriented the enemy to the direction of the main attack of our troops.

It was for this purpose that the artillery commander of the 21st Army, after the breakthrough of the defensive zone of the enemy, reassigned only a part of the general support grouping to the commanders of the rifle divisions. Two regiments of it were in the hands of the artillery commander of the Army, and by changing the combat formations forward by the battalions, they helped the support groups of the rifle troops and the mobile group by striking and destroying the centers of enemy resistance when these groups called for fire.

Actions of the Tank Destroyer Regiments in the Makeup of the Mobile Groups

The most widely employed means for supporting the mobile groups in operations into the strategic depths were the tank destroyer regiments with 76 mm guns. At the beginning of the commitment into the breakthrough, the 33rd Tank Destroyer Artillery Regiment was assigned to the 1st Tank Corps; the 1241st Tank Destroyer Regiment was assigned to the 26th Tank Corps; the 8th Motorcycle Regiment received the 481st Tank Destroyer Regiment; the 4th Tank Corps, the 1180th Tank Destroyer Regiment; and the 331st Howitzer Artillery Regiment, the 8th Cavalry Corps; the 174th and 179th Tank Destroyer Regiments, the 152nd Howitzer Artillery Regiment, and the 3rd Guards Cavalry Corps were assigned to the 5th Tank Destroyer Brigade.

The tank destroyer artillery regiment, while possessing mobility, constituted a powerful antitank weapon and helped in the execution of the missions of fire support during the elimination of centers of resistance in the depths. Hence, the assignment of them to mobile groups was well warranted. For example, the 1241st Tank Destroyer Artillery Regiment, in the makeup of the 26th Tank Corps, accompanied the brigade combat formations of the first echelon. While moving only one kilometer behind the line of our riflemen, it was forced to deploy for combat with enemy antitank means which appeared in the path of movement of the Corps.

Subsequently, over the depth of the tank raid (132 kilometers), the Regiment was moved ahead for combating the antitank means. On the way to Kalach, the Corps encountered a strong center of resistance in Perelazovskii, which had as many as 15 to 20 antitank guns and 15 tanks. The skillful employment of its capacity for maneuver and the adequate cross-country capacity for travel due to the means of traction (*Willys*) made it possible to break the resistance of the enemy quickly and, at the same time, to inflict heavy losses upon the enemy.[7] The batteries of the regiment were quickly deployed in cooperation with their tanks in a semicircle on the flanks and rear of the enemy and brought under fire all the strongpoints.

In a single battle, the 1241st Tank Destroyer Regiment destroyed by fire, eight enemy tanks and up to 15 antitank guns. The resistance of the enemy was broken, and it was possible for the Corps to continue the execution of its missions.

During its advance to Kalach, the Corps had to cross the Don River over the two crossings that the enemy held in this region. The leading brigades, unexpected by the enemy, seized these crossings under the cover of darkness. During the night, a part of the leading small tank units crossed to the other bank after seizing a small bridgehead for the deployment of the Corps. The 1241st Tank Destroyer Artillery Regiment received the following mission. With a part of its forces, it was to protect the captured bridgehead and the crossings, and with another part, it was to cover the flanks of the Corps during its approach to the crossings. The Regiment carried out this mission successfully.

A no less outstanding example was the operation of the 5th Tank

Destroyer Brigade, forming a part of the 3rd Guards Cavalry Corps. On November 24, while approaching the line of the Don River in the area of Bolshenabatovskii, the Corps was counterattacked by enemy tanks. In this battle with tanks, a decisive part was played by artillery, chiefly the small units of the 5th Tank Destroyer Brigade. Out of 100 tanks participating in these attacks, the Brigade knocked out and set fire to 22, and the enemy attack was broken up. The Brigade suffered slight losses (five 45 mm guns, six 76 mm guns and up to 300 soldiers), but the tanks of the enemy were prevented from moving into the area of operation of the Corps.

The operation of the 481st Tank Destroyer Artillery Regiment, supporting the 8th Motorcycle Regiment, may also serve as a useful example. Together with the Motorcycle Regiment, this Artillery Regiment gained the rear of the enemy up to the Morozovskii-Oblivskaia line. With its fire, it destroyed the personnel and equipment of the enemy, crushed his centers of communications and staffs, and disrupted the control of troops. During the clash with the enemy, the guns of the Regiment, by direct sighting, fired upon the personnel and the fire weapons of the enemy; in this way, they assured the successful execution of the mission of the 8th Motorcycle Regiment. During the fighting that took place while it was accompanying the 8th Motorcycle Regiment, the 481st Tank Destroyer Artillery Regiment destroyed 28 tanks, knocked out 16 antitank guns, and killed more than 800 Hitlerites. Experience showed that, in the unit of fire of tank-supported artillery, we should have armor-piercing and high-explosive fragmentation shells as well as shrapnel for combating enemy personnel.

As tank support artillery, we also detailed howitzer artillery regiments (331st Howitzer Artillery Regiment to the 4th Tank Corps). Experience showed that these regiments may also be used for accompanying tanks, operating chiefly during combat for the capture of large towns and villages and for eliminating centers of resistance. For example, the 331st Howitzer Artillery Regiment, during the time of operation with the 4th Tank Corps, moved all the time in its combat formations, suffering small losses. By joint operations with the 1180th Tank Destroyer Artillery Regiment, it assisted the Corps in the execution of its missions.

Effecting a Breakthrough

After crossing the Don River on November 23, the tank groups of the 5th Tank Army (26th Tank Corps) and the 21st Army (4th Tank Corps) captured Kalach.[8] On the line of the railroad east of Kalach, the 4th Tank Corps joined the right flank of the south group of the troops of the Stalingrad Front with its right flank. By this means, we completed the strategic encirclement of the Stalingrad group of the enemy.

During this time, the offensive of the main forces of the 5th Tank Army and the 21st Army successfully developed in the direction of the main attack. The enemy suffered heavy losses in personnel and equipment. The Rumanian units, unable to withstand the impetuous attacks and blocked at a number of points, surrendered by the thousands. In order to support the advance of the troops, the artillery units were constantly brought up to the combat formations of the infantry and, with their fire, supported its actions.

Upon the arrival of the units of the Army on the line of Rubashkin, Dubovskii, and Gorbatovskii, the units operating in the secondary direction (1st Guards Army) had much less success. The enemy brought up reserves and on November 25–28 with the support of several tanks and aviation understood, a number of counterattacks in the direction of Dubovskii and Gorbatovskii against units of the 14th Guards and 203rd Rifle Divisions. Artillery played the main part in repelling the counterattacks by directly laying the guns (45 mm and 76 mm) fired point-blank upon the advancing infantry of the enemy. Up to nine counterattacks against Dubovskii and Rubashkin were repelled, exclusively by artillery fire, with the killing of up to 3,000 soldiers and officers. Units of the 5th Tank Army, in a successful exploitation of the offensive, reached the Chir River on November 30 and occupied the Front—(exclusive) Bokovskaia and Chistiaovskaia—and engaged in fighting for Chernyshevskaia, Osinovskii, Sekretev, and (exclusive) Surovikino.

The 21st Army, cooperating with units of the Don and Stalingrad Fronts, forced the Don River and moved to the line of (exclusive) Marinovka and Peskovatka, where, in accordance with the decision of the *Stavka*, it was reassigned to the Don Front on November 27, 1942.

Summary of the Combat Activity of Artillery

In the fierce battle of November 19–30, the 5th, 6th, 13th, 14th, and 15th Rumanian Infantry Divisions were completely smashed. Heavy losses were inflicted upon the Rumanian 7th Cavalry and 1st Panzer Divisions as well as the German 14th and 22nd Panzer Divisions.

The impetuous action of the mobile units, their cutting of enemy communications, and the continuous action of the main forces of the attacking units, with heavy fire support by artillery, forced the enemy to leave all of his equipment and enormous quantities of ammunition and many motor vehicle transports.

By November 25, the enemy had brought up units of the 29th German Army Corps (62nd, 294th, and 298th Infantry Divisions), which, in point operations with the 7th and 11th Rumanian Infantry Divisions, started a counteroffensive on the right wing of the front and carried out continuous but unsuccessful counterattacks up until the end of November. All attempts by the enemy to break the resistance of our units were repelled by artillery fire and mortars.

In spite of the serious difficulties with transport means and the mobile character of the operations of the Southwestern Front, the artillery carried out, on the whole, its missions of supporting the advancing troops. The most successful were the tank destroyer artillery regiments.

The actual consumption of ammunition during November 19–30, 1942, is shown in the following table:

Type of Shell	Consumption by Army			Total for Front
	1st Guards	5th Tank	21st	
82 mm	39,504	92,720	53,166	185,390
120 mm	5,678	8,126	15,761	29,565
45 mm	7,626	44,572	16,586	68,784
76 mm Field	4,480	9,061	14,025	27,556
76 mm Division	16,546	59,023	43,651	119,220
122 mm Howitzer	1,954	14,456	7,062	23,472
152 Field Howitzer	507	3,871	4,579	8,957

The actual consumption (see tables on page 203) turned out to be much less than what was planned. For example, in 76 mm shells of the divisional artillery, it amounted to only 1.7 units of fire and for the 122 mm howitzers, it amounted to only 1.2 units of fire. The difference between planned consumption of ammunition and actual usage is explained by the rapid breakthrough of the enemy defenses and the skillful bypassing of the deeper enemy centers of resistance.

Operations of the Artillery of the Don Front

The Grouping and Missions of the Armies

In the period September–October 1942, the troops of the right wing of the Don Front seized a bridgehead on the right bank of the Don and, after widening it to include the area Ribnyi up to Kletskaia, protected the subsequent offensive operations from this sector with the 5th Tank and 21st Armies of the Southwestern Front.

After the regrouping and the taking of steps to organize its units and bring them up to full strength, the Don Front had the following in its composition on November 19, 1942.

Armies	Divisions	Artillery	Mortars		Total
			82 mm	120 mm	
65	9	598	603	142	1,343
24	8	710	602	138	1,450
66	6	497	499	143	1,139

The mission assigned to the Don Front was to deliver an attack on its right flank with the forces of one army, to assist the Southwestern Front in the encirclement from the west of the enemy Stalingrad grouping, and by a secondary thrust of the 24th Army toward Vertiachii, to separate the enemy forces west of the Don River from those in the area of Stalingrad.

The 65th Army struck the main blow with two divisions from the area of Kletskaia on a frontage of six kilometers and with two supporting divisions in the second echelon. The Army also struck a secondary blow with one division along the front of Melo-Melovskii and Malye Iarki. The divisions on the defensive passed to the offensive one after the other as the exploitation of the success progressed.

The 24th Army, having a shock group consisting of four divisions (two divisions of which were in the second echelon), broke through the enemy defenses on a frontage of four kilometers. By debouchment in the area of Vertiachii, it was to prevent the crossing of the Don by the enemy units withdrawing from the western bank of the river.

With its left flank, the 66th Army made an attack for the dual purpose of uniting with the right flank units of the 62nd Army to the north of Stalingrad and for tying down the enemy on the rest of this sector of the front.

For the development of the breakthrough on the front of the 24th Army, we planned to employ additionally the 16th Tank Corps for the purpose of assisting the 24th Army in gaining possession of the area of Vertiachii and with the further mission of preventing the enemy from organizing a defense on the line of the Rossoshka River.[9]

Characteristics of the Enemy Defenses

The main enemy line of resistance from the Volga River to the Don River passed along some commanding heights with partial utilization of the strongholds previously prepared by our troops for the defense of Stalingrad. The commanding heights concealed all the movements within the defensive area of the enemy.

On the right bank of the Don River, from Nizhne-Akatov up to Kletskaia, the main line of enemy resistance ran along elevations which were 100 to 150 meters higher than the locality occupied by our troops. As a result, the enemy had a view of the depths of our defenses to a distance of 40 kilometers. Taking advantage of his commanding heights, the enemy maneuvered freely, even by day, along the front close to the main line of resistance. The covers and blindages, prepared mainly along the slopes of the ravines, were only slightly vulnerable to artillery fire and bombing. In places where the enemy could not use the natural conditions for arranging living quarters, he dug deeply into the ground, while in the towns, the enemy used the cellars of the surviving structures.

As a rule, there were two lines of trenches on the main line of resistance. The trenches had emplacements for both heavy and light machine guns. In front of the trenches, there were barbed-wire entanglements and minefields. On the second line of trenches, the enemy prepared fire positions for mortars, and close to these, he prepared the same kind of positions for infantry weapons. Communications trenches, making possible concealed movements while standing erect, led from the trenches of the first and second lines back into the depths. In open places, the length of such communications amounted at times to 3 kilometers and more.

The Artillery Offensive

For supporting the offensive operations of the armies, the artillery was concentrated on the frontages of the enemy in the direction of the breakthrough. Density of concentration sometimes reached up to 35 guns per kilometer of front. For this purpose, a portion of the divisional artillery on passive sectors was reassigned for the time of the breakthrough to the divisions operating in the main direction.

On October 28, 1942, the artillery commanders of the Don Front were given instructions on how to prepare for the operation.[10] These instructions covered the following points:

- organizing additional reconnaissance of the main line of resistance and the depths of enemy defenses;
- planning the distribution of the reinforcing artillery units and the calculation of the density of artillery and mortar fire;
- regrouping the artillery units both on a front scale and also within the army;
- formulating a plan for attack by massed artillery fire and for the support of the commitment into the breakthrough of the 4th and 26th Tank Corps and the 3rd Guards Cavalry Corps;
- providing the artillery lanes for the 4th Tank and 3rd Guards Cavalry corps;
- planning fire control of the artillery groups;
- positioning the combat formations of the reinforcing artillery;
- planning for adequate provision of ammunition and the organization of transport of this ammunition to the troops;
- preparing emergency installations for field artillery depots and the reconnaissance of the routes of transportation;
- planning and organization antiaircraft defense;
- carrying out preliminary measures in the preparation of the commanding personnel of the artillery for the adjustment of fire from tanks;
- coding of the locality;

- issuing separate instructions pertaining to the firing of captured artillery;
- firing for destruction;
- instructions as providing to the method of march in the steppes and during the time of snowstorms.

Before the attack of November 19, the 65th Army executed an artillery preparation lasting for one hour and twenty minutes. The 24th Army began its attack after one hour of artillery preparation. And the 66th Army attacked without any preliminary artillery preparation, simultaneously executing with the attack a 5-minute fire concentration against the main line of enemy resistance. A characteristic feature was that the artillery preparation for the attack was not started with a period of destruction but with a powerful fire onslaught.

On the sector of the 65th and 66th armies, as a result of joint action, our units broke through the main line of enemy resistance on the very first day and moved into the depths of the defenses to a distance of 2 to 12 kilometers. In the rapid movement of our units, a major role was played by the artillery, both on the sector of the 65th Army and in the concurrent successful breakthrough of the units of the 21st Army operating on the right.

Fire Control

The support of the offensive operations by concentrated fire, through the employment of several artillery regiments, on the whole was provided in a timely manner. The fire control of the general support groups by their commanders and the direction of the fire by the artillery commanders of the divisional units were carried out directly from the respective observation posts. These commanders had telephone and, for some, radio communications with all the regiments forming a part of their group. Calls for scheduled fire were made by signals in accordance with the plan of fire. In the artillery groups for general support, target designation for unscheduled fire against the enemy artillery was usually carried out on the basis of coordinates, more rarely on the basis of the map and intersections by sound-ranging. In the divisions, it was done by reference points in the locality.

Against counterattacking enemy troops, both the general support artillery and the divisional regiments of artillery conducted fire by shifting from check targets and points into the areas of enemy movement. There was also target designation on the basis of the map. The insufficient provision of radio sets to the artillery regiments created great difficulties for fire direction. In actuality, artillery fire achieved good results from utilizing the tanks for correction and control, a method employed in the 5th Guards Artillery Regiment. In that unit, the response to calls for fire were made at the proper time, and the accuracy of fire was good.

There was almost no control of artillery during pursuit. In general, during changes in position over long distances, neither artillery commanders of divisions nor armies had an adequate number of radio sets, and their number of motor vehicles was extremely limited.

Cooperation of artillery with rifle troops, in both defensive and offensive operations, was assured by colocating the observation posts of the artillery commanders with those of the commanders of combined arms units. The commanders of artillery groups supporting the rifle troops as a rule, were, located with the commanders of the rifle regiments; and the commanders of batteries were with the commanders of rifle battalions and companies. In cases when joint observation posts did not give to the battery and battalion commanders a full view of the depths of the enemy defenses, the artillery commander selected his observation post to the side of, and sometimes behind, the combined arms units commanders. The artillery then dispatched a forward observation team to the combined arms commander's post and supplied his team with wire or radio communications.

Despite colocating headquarters, however, there were few calls from the combined arms commanders. In the majority of cases where calls were made, the requests were foolish in nature since they dealt with fire upon submachine gunners, individual motor vehicles, and other kinds of vehicles and not against the fire points of the enemy that were actually interfering with the advance of the rifle troops. Most of the battery and battalion commanders conducted fire against the enemy fire positions based upon their own initiative, making use of the reconnaissance data from the advanced observation posts and often entrusting to them the direct correction of fire.

In the offensive, the results of poor coordination of artillery fire with the fire of mortars, rifles, and machine guns revealed itself quite clearly. From the beginning moments of the attack against the main line of enemy resistance, the rifle troops did not coordinate their movements with rifle, machine-gun, or mortar fire. They took for granted that all the enemy fire positions were destroyed or, at the worst, would be neutralized by the artillery before the seizure of these positions. In view of this, at the moment of the attack, there was no general reinforcement of fire against the main line of resistance, because the artillery had lifted its fire into the depths. The machine guns and small-caliber mortars, which before the advance had conducted a weak fire against the enemy positions, had also begun to change their positions as the riflemen moved forward and thus completely stopped their fire. Movement by bounds of the fire weapons was not generally employed. Information concerning the jump-off lines of our rifle troops before the attack and the time necessary for them to move without stopping from the jump-off line to the main enemy line of resistance greatly facilitated cooperation. Despite a number of orders, the distance the rifle troops deployed before the attack from the main line of resistance varied a great deal. After the signal for the beginning of the attack, some time was necessary for initiating fire against the enemy fire positions, both on the main line of resistance and on positions within 200 to 300 meters from it.

During the advance of the rifle troops, the forward observation posts of the battery and battalion commanders, and sometimes even the commanders of batteries themselves, moved forward with these combat formations. On certain sectors, they even moved ahead of the rifle troops, depending upon the situation. Moving in this way made it possible to open fire in timely support of the rifle troops, but at the same time it caused a great loss of life in artillery commanding personnel, especially among the commanders of the headquarters sections and among the battery commanders.

At the same time, it is necessary to note that the rifle troops, while requiring that artillerymen move along with them, never thought of covering the artillery observation posts with their fire from the enemy machine gunners and even riflemen. It is quite obvious that artillery commanders cannot conduct observation, correct fire directions, and fight as riflemen all at the same time.

There have been cases when, because of the absence of rifle troops, the commanders and Red Army artillerymen were obliged with their own personal weapons to drive the enemy from a trench or elevation in order to procure a view of the enemy dispositions. For example, in the 1034th Rifle Regiment (24th Army), the commander of a regimental battery, following behind the tanks, penetrated an enemy trench in which he personally killed four soldiers and captured one; his senior scout killed four soldiers and one officer and captured a radio set in good condition. By capturing this trench, they secured a good observation post from which, by battery fire, they successfuly supported the combat of the rifle troops and the tanks. This was heroic action, but with a different kind of cooperation with the rifle troops, it would not have been necessary.

Cooperation with tanks was effected by the following measures: mutual coordination of artillery fire with the movement of tanks on the basis of specified lines, common signals by radio and rockets, and joint reconnaissance of the locality by the commanding personnel. For the correction of fire and for requesting artillery fire in combat support of the tanks, we placed in one tank brigade commander's radio tank a battery commander of the 5th Guards Artillery Regiment, who while moving in the combat formation of the tank brigade, requested and corrected the fire of the general support artillery against unobserved targets interfering with the advance of the tanks. As a result of the movement of this tank ahead of the combat formation of the tank brigade, the command tank was knocked out by the enemy with an armor-piercing shell. This experience teaches us that for any one combat tank brigade it is necessary to have two or three artillery fire correctors. In addition to this, the tank with the artillery commander should not move out ahead of the general combat formation of the tank unit.

The Movement of the Combat Formations of Artillery

Because of the poor condition of the horses and the concurrent lack of horses, the average speed of movement of the divisional artillery regiments was 3 kilometers per hour; for a day's march it was 25 to 30 kilometers. This level of performance was simply because the horses could not withstand long marches.

Due to the great shortage of tractors and motor vehicles, and also because of their poor mechanical condition, the average speed of movement of the artillery combat formations of the *Stavka* reserves was not more than 3 to 4 kilometers an hour with a daily march rate of 30 kilometers and a maximum daily rate of 40 kilometers. It was only the 122 mm howitzer regiments, utilizing the STZ-5 tractors, that executed daily marches of 60 to 80 kilometers. The tractor park was so over-utilized that, after marching 80 to 100 kilometers, it was necessary to undertake repairs lasting 1 to 2 days and sometimes even more for certain vehicles. For these reasons, during the offensive operations of November 19–30, certain artillery regiments of the reserves of *Stavka* left their equipment along the routes of march, and the units were greatly elongated.

One of the methods of increasing the maneuverability of artillery units is the selection of a single type of prime mover and the correct organization and timely repair of the automative equipment. But, without a radical change in the supply of equipment, this problem cannot be solved in a satisfactory manner.

OPERATIONS OF ANTITANK ARTILLERY

During offensive actions, the antitank artillery in the rifle divisions moved in the combat formations of the rifle troops, thus making possible the neutralization of the separate fire positions, the fortification of new positions, and the security of the flanks against enemy counterattacks. Such employment proved to be fully effective. In the 66th Army, the antitank artillery, in making possible the fortification work on the newly established positions, destroyed in a period of three days 20 tanks and additional personnel and machine guns.

Concrete results were obtained by the employment of tank destroyer brigades and regiments, both for the close support of the mobile groups committed into the breakthroughs and for action with them in raids. In these cases, the antitank artillery was generally used for protecting the flanks and for making possible the fortification of the new positions.

The fire positions of regimental artillery and the antitank guns were with the combat formations of the rifle troops in organized gun emplacements. During the offensive, the guns were moved by hand to new fire positions by the crews. During the offensive operation, there was a great shortage of horse traction, which is so much needed by the field artillery batteries and for antitank defense in steppe terrain. The open steppe and the absence of cover prevented us from keeping the limbers and horses close to the guns. During the shifting of the combat formations, the gun crews were unable to move the guns by hand in a timely fashion to keep up with the rifle troops due not only to the highly broken nature of the terrain but chiefly because the forward bounds were over long distances. In addition to this, the entirely open terrain with the great depth of visibility as a rule made the movement of the guns by horses impossible. This fact was due to the size of the target that enabled the enemy to very quickly knock out the gun as well as the horses and the personnel accompanying it.

The experiences gained in the final battles revealed that as traction means for the 45 mm and the 76 mm field artillery, we should have T-20 prime movers. These can be easily masked even in the steppe close to the fire positions. By reason of their great mobility and maneuverability, both on and off the roads, they assure the timely movement of the guns closely behind the combat formations of the rifle troops.

Operations of the Artillery of the Stalingrad Front

Missions of the Army and Front Artillery

In accordance with the decision of the Military Council of the Stalingrad Front, the breakthrough was effected by the forces of the 57th and 51st Armies.[11] The 64th Army, with its left flank, cooperated with the offensive of the 57th Army. In conformity with this, the 57th Army, advancing in the general direction of "balka" Blinnikova and Varvarovka broke through the enemy defenses on the frontage of Andreevka and Elevations 97.3 and 112.7 In cooperation with units of the 51st Army, the 5th Army destroyed the enemy Sarpinsk grouping. Upon arrival on the Chervlenaia River, the Army exploited the success toward the north and northeast into the rear of the enemy's positions around Beketovka.

The breakthrough sector selected for the 51st Army was between Lake Tsatsa and Lake Barmantsak. The secondary attack was designated for the front of Lake Sarpa and Lake Tsatsa.

As an echelon for exploiting the success, the Front command employed the 4th and 13th Mechanized Corps and the 4th Cavalry Corps. This mobile group was to complete the strategic encirclement of the enemy to the west of Stalingrad in cooperation with the mobile grouping attached to the Southwestern Front. Further, the former grouping was to secure the shock group of the Stalingrad Front from enemy action from the area of Kotelnikovo.

In accordance with the designated plan, the offensive of the armies was to be reinforced with the following units:

The 57th Army by the 762nd and 565th Tank Destroyer Artillery Regiments; the 1111th, 1104th, and the 1159th Gun Artillery Regiments of the reserves of *Stavka*; the 70th Guards Artillery Regiment of the reserves of *Stavka*; the 140th Guards Mortar Regiment of the reserves of *Stavka*; and by one battery of the 266th Gun Artillery Regiment of the reserves of *Stavka*.

The 51st Army by the 491st and 492nd Tank Destroyer Regiments; the 1105th Gun Artillery Regiment of the reserves of *Stavka*; the 85th Guards Howitzer Artillery Regiment; the 125th Guards Mortar Regiment; and the 1113th and 1170th *PVO* Antiaircraft Artillery Regiments.

In addition to the aforementioned units of reinforcement, we employed on the sector of the 57th Army during the artillery preparation for the attack artillery from a regiment of a division of the second echelon and the 4th Mechanized Corps. On the sector of the 51st Army, we also employed artillery from the 4th Cavalry Corps.

As a result of regrouping, we created for the period of the artillery offensive, the following density per 1 kilometer of frontage: for the 57th Army—the width of the breakthrough frontage was 14.5 kilometers with a total of 393 guns/mortars—the density was 27.1 per kilometer; and *the 51st Army*—the width of the breakthrough frontage was 14 kilometers and the number of guns/mortars was 331—the density was 23.9 per kilometer.

With the heavy artillery regiments, we created army artillery groups. In the 51st Army, special groups of mortar units were organized. In the 57th Army, the Guards Mortar units were assigned to the rifle divisions.

Preparation of the artillery offensive

In the preparatory period, the artillery units had from 10 to 13 days at their disposal for organization of reconnaissance and observation. In addition to having ground observation, the artillery of the 57th Army was strengthened by means of artillery instrument reconnaissance techniques and aerial spotter aviation. The subordination of these means to the Army, together with the reconnaissance of the regiments of the reserves of *Stavka* and the other divisions, made it possible by the beginning of the operation to have precise data about the enemy artillery. The precision of work of these forms of reconnaissance was subsequently confirmed by the large number of enemy guns knocked out and gun crews destroyed. Of the 30 batteries located by intersection, the accuracy of location was confirmed in 25 cases. The coordinates of the location of the artillery battalion of the 20th Rumanian Infantry Division, determined on the basis of a captured firing chart, coincided fully with the coordinates determined by our reconnaissance.

Special reconnaissance was not organized as well in the 51st Army. The Front did not have at its disposal artillery instrument reconnaissance equipment and aerial spotters to assign to the Army. As a result, the artillery of the Army depended on its own ground reconnaissance.

Three days before the beginning of the attack, the artillery staffs of the armies received aerial photographs of the separate sectors of the defense area of the enemy. The aerial photographs were prepared by orders of the artillery staff of the front.

By the beginning of the attack, reconnaissance of all kinds had ascertained the outline of the main line of resistance, areas where observation was being carried out, firing positions, the separate fire points, and the defensive installations of the enemy. However, we should note that it was not possible to determine the exact location of the fire system of the enemy in the depths of his defense in view of the fact that the enemy did not reveal his system of fire and deep reconnaissance was carried out to a very limited extent.

All the targets revealing themselves were combined in separate sectors. The staffs of the artillery of the armies gave instructions to the subordinate staffs, requesting them, in the planning of the artillery offensive, to conduct fire not against areas but against separate targets or groups of them.

In the period of preparations for the breakthrough, the questions of cooperation were worked out in special games applicable to the approaching tactical missions. However, we must note that while in the period of preparation cooperation was organized fairly well, it was often broken up in the course of the operation.

For the purpose of making the preparations for the offensive, fire for adjustments was carried out in the 57th Army the day before—and in the 51st Army, it was carried out two days before—the attack. The plans of the artillery offensive provided for the following.

THE 57TH ARMY

Beginning of the artillery attack was at "H" minus 1.15. The artillery preparation for the attack was started by a fire concentration against the fire points on the main line of resistance and in the immediate depths of the defenses of the enemy. The signal for the beginning of the preparation for the attack, apart from the signals indicated in the plan, consisted of volleys of Guards mortar units.

Subsequently, the fire concentrations were alternated with periods of neutralization and heavy lifting of fire. The volleys of the Guards Mortars at the end of the artillery preparation constituted the signal for the beginning of the attack. For the destruction of well-observed fire points of the enemy, we detailed guns for fire by direct laying for which we determined the targets beforehand and the time for their destruction. A part of the guns were prepared for destruction of targets revealing themselves in the course of the artillery preparation. For accompanying the attack of the tanks, we assigned tank support guns at the rate of one gun to the platoon of tanks.

For security of the junction area with the 64th Army, we prepared fire to be executed upon the request of the artillery commander of the 64th Army. Into the left flank divisions of the Army, we sent commanders with means of signal communications for observation and, in case of necessity, for opening and correcting fire.

THE 51ST ARMY

The beginning of the artillery offensive "H" minus 1.00. The artillery preparation for the attack was started by a fire concentration with subsequent transition to fire for destruction and neutralization.

The artillery preparation was completed by a fire concentration of all the fire means against the main line of resistance and against the areas where the batteries were disposed. This was followed by a period for accompanying the attack of the tanks and rifle troops up to the line of Elevation 87.0; fighting for the seizure of the line of Elevation 87.0 and Vasilev; the development of the rifle troops attack against Plodovitoe and the commitment in the breakthrough of the 4th Mechanized Corps; and fighting for the line of Plodovitoie and Elevation 107.0 and fortifications on this line. The details of the organization of the artillery fire are given in the plan of the artillery offensive of the 51st Army.

Providing an Adequate Supply of Ammunition

The quantity of ammunition planned for the first day of the artillery offensive and the actual consumption of ammunition in units of fire are given in the following table:

The considerable difference between the planned and actual ammunition consumption is explained by the weak resistance of the enemy after the breakthrough of his defenses and the economical expenditure of ammunition. By the end of the first day of operations, the artillery of the 57th Army had in the regiments/battalions one unit of fire of 76 mm shells and 0.6 units of fire of 122 mm shells.

Calibers	Planned		Consumed	
	57th Army	51st Army	57th Army	51st Army
76 mm divisional artillery	1.5	2.0	0.60	1.30
122 mm divisional artillery	1.5	1.5	0.55	0.15
122 mm regimental artillery	1.7	—	2.00	—
152 mm field howitzers	1.7	3.0	0.30	0.40

The breakthrough and the exploitation of the attack

At 7:30 A.M. on November 20, we started the artillery preparation for the attack, which was carried out strictly according to the plan of the artillery offensive. The enemy fire system in the main was neutralized, and the tanks and rifle troops, passing to the attack with minimum losses, occupied the enemy trenches on the main line of resistance. The enemy, showing weak resistance, began a withdrawal to the southeast, to the south, and to the west.

As a result of the breakthrough of the defensive area on the front of the 57th and 51st Armies on November 20, the enemy, closely pressed by our troops, continued the withdrawal, trying to pass to the counterattack on separate sectors for the purpose of joining up with the encircled Stalingrad group.

The combat operations, during November 21–30, developed in the following manner.

The 64th Army. On November 21, the enemy, in trying to regain the positions lost on November 20, made repeated attacks against the units on the offensive. From November 21 to November 30, the army undertook a number of offensive operations, but owing to the strong resistance of the enemy, it did not make any notable progress.

The 57th Army. As a result of our offensive, by November 25 the enemy had withdrawn to the line of "balka" Karavatka, Tsybenko, Kravtsov, Rokotino, and Station Rogachik, where he fortified his forces on a previously prepared defense position. At the same time, the right flank units of the Don Front had moved up to the line of Marinovka and Dmitrievka. Hence, the tactical encirclement of the enemy's Stalingrad grouping was completed.

Upon reaching the new line, the units of the 57th Army encountered obstinate resistance. To overcome this resistance, the units regrouped, replenished their ammunition, and positioned themselves for the purpose of destroying the encircled enemy grouping.

The 51st Army. The units of the Army, after breaking through the enemy defenses and smashing the opposing formations, reached the

Play of Attack by Massed Artillery Fire

Artillery Groups	Designation of Artillery units	Fire for Adjustment "H"—1 hour 48 min.	"H"—1 hour 18 min.	Artillery Preparation of attack from "H"—0100 to "H"				
				Fire Raid 15 minutes	Neutralization 15 minutes	Deliberate Fire against old targets & striking of new 10 minutes	15 minutes	Fire Raid 5 minutes
Army Group of General-Support Artillery	1105th Gun Artillery Regiment of *Stavka* Reserve	—	Sector No. 6 check pt. on "Tsentralnaia Elevation"	Sector No. 6 78th Batteries	77th, 80th, 81st, 82nd Batteries	Observation post on Sector No. 6 and batteries just revealing themselves	Neutralization of most harmful batteries and active observation posts	Sectors Nos. 1, 8
Army Group of General-Support Artillery	1168th Gun Artillery Regiment of *Stavka* Reserve	—	Sector No. 11 Srednaiaia Lasta Balka	102nd & 104th Batteries	Observation post on Sector No. 11—107th, 113th Batteries	105th, 11th Batteries	Neutralization of most harmful batteries and active observation posts	Sector No. 5
126th Rifle Division	Division Artillery 125th Mechanized Regiment. Two battalions of the 4th Mechanized Corps (only for Artillery preparation)	Sectors Nos. 1, 2, 8, 7, 11	—	Sectors Nos. 7, 8, 11	Trenches & *Dzots*[1] on Sectors Nos. 1, 2, 8	Neutralization of recently discovered targets on the main line of resistance of the enemy	Box barrage of targets of traditore[2] guns. Destruction of fire pts. and inf. on elevations "Gorbataya" and "Bugor"	Sectors Nos. 1, 8, 2
302nd Rifle Division	Division Artillery, 85th Regiments. One battalion of the 4th Cavalry Corps (only for artillery preparation)	Sectors Nos. 3, 4, 5, 9, 10	—	Sectors Nos. 4, 9 Batteries Nos. 107, 98	Trenches & *Dzots* on Sectors Nos. 3, 4, 5, 9, 10	—	Same on south slopes of Elevation "Gorbataya" and on Sectors Nos. 5, 10	Sectors Nos. 2, 3, 4

Notes 1. earth-and-timber pillboxes. 2. short-range surprise fire.

Accompanying the attack of the tanks and rifle troops up to the line of Elevation 87.0.	Battle for the capture of line Elevation 87.: 87.0, Vasil'ev,	Development of the rifle troops attack against Plodovitoie. Commitment of the 4th Mechanized Corps in to the breakthrough.	Battle for the line of Plodovitoie Elevation 107.0, fortification on this line.
—	—	—	—
Accompanies the tanks with fire and movement.	Organizes the antitank defense of the area occupied by the rifle troops. Destroys the fire points by direct laying.	Protect from counterattack the columns of the Mechanized Corps. Parallel with it they move toward the strong points of the enemy in the depth of the defenses and detroys them. The antitank reserves of the commander advance to the line of the old main line of resistance.	By wide maneuver on the sectors of the divisions, and by direct laying, they destroy the withdrawing and counterattacking groups of the enemy. The mission of antitank defense of the combat formations and the flanks of the rifle regiments is carried out with special care.
Accompanies the tanks with fire and movement.	Organizes the antitank defense of the area occupied by the infantry. Destroys the fire points by direct laying.		
They advance in the combat formations of the rifle troops.	They advance in the combat formations of the rifle troops.	—	—
They are to prepare volleys against areas: "Golova," "Chernaia," "Vulkan," Zakharov, Elevation "Troinaia."	They are to prepare volleys against elevations: "Golova," "Tsentralnaia," "Vulkan," Zakharov, Vasil'ev.	They are to prepare volleys against the areas: Farm 4, Grove "Sapog," Balka Tiagabuluk, Kordon Balka, Plodovitoie.	Prepares volleys against Plodovitoie, ravines west of Plodovitoie, Plodovitoie Road, Abganerovo, machine tractor factory, field telephone, junctions of roads on Elevation 107.0, Frolov.

Part II

Stages of the artillery attack — Designation of Artillery units	Fire for Adjustment "H"—1 hour 48 min.	Fire for Adjustment "H"—1 hour 18 min.	Fire Raid 15 minutes	Neutralization 15 minutes	Deliberate fire against old targets & striking of new 10 minutes	15 minutes	Fire Raid 5 minutes
Artillery Groups							
15th Guards Rifle Division — 43rd Artillery Regiment, 2 batteries of the 85th Guards Artillery Regiment	Sectors Nos. 14, 17, 13, Elevation 86	—	Sectors Nos. 14, 15, 16, 17	Trenches & *Dzots* on Sectors Nos. 16, 17, 13, and Battery 69	Deliberate fire against targets on Sectors Nos. 14, 15	Same on Sectors Nos. 13, 16, 17	Sectors Nos. 16, 17
Field Artillery and Antitank Defense — Group for Destruction and Blocking	—	—	—	—	—	Destruction of *Dzots* by direct laying	Continues destruction of *Dzots*
Group of Field Artillery	—	—	—	—	—	—	Pulls loaded guns to fire position and destroys AT guns
Battalion and Company Mortars (Guns of the Rifle-troops)	—	Advance *Dzots*	Against forward trenches with all the inf. weapons	—	Neutralize the recently appearing fire points in the trenches	Cover the *traditore* guns. Neutralize the fire positions in the trenches	Fire of all the infantry guns against forward trenches & *Dzots* until the tanks approach
Groups of Guards Mortar Units — 80th GM Regiment, 90th GM Regiment, 66th GM Regiment	—	—	Sectors Nos. 2, 3, 5, 10, 13; Signal beginning artillery offensive	—	Sectors Nos. 2, 7; Signal—fire by direct laying—2 battery salvos	2 battery salvos against Sectors Nos. 2, 7. Signal for following fire raid	Sectors Nos. 1, 3, 4, 5, 13. Sectors Nos. 2 Standing barrage

Accompanying the attack of the tanks and rifle troops up to the line of Elevation 87.0.	Battle for the capture of line Elevation 87; 87.0, Vasil'ev.	Development of the rifle troops attack against Plodovitoie. Commitment of the 4th Mechanized Corps into the breakthrough.	Battle for the line of Plodovitoie, Elevation 107.0, fortification on this line.
Successive concentration of fire on Sectors nos. 7, 11. Observation of batteries Nos. 80, 81, 77, 78, 82.	In agreement with the commander of the 15th Artillery Division neutralizes the firing point on Elevation "Golova" and Elevation "Tsentralnaia."	Accompanies the Mechanized Corps up to the line "Nos"; has a forward observation post Plodovitoie on Elevation "Tsentralnaia; it is subordinate to the commander of the 126th Rifle Division. It conducts successive concentrations of fire against Sectors 12 and "Vorota."	It is centralized through control by the Chief of Artillery of the Army. Fire missions depending upon the situation; observation posts on Elevation "Nos"; it is to prepare fire concentrations against Kulkova Balka.
Successive fire concentrations against Sectors Nos. 5, 9, 10; fire observation posts on Elevation "Vulkan"; fire observation of batteries Nos. 105, 113, 104, 102, 101, 98, 99, 100.	15 minutes of deliberate fire against fire point and observation posts on Elevation "Vulkan"; fire observation of batteries Nos. 111, 105, 104, 102.	Accompanying the Motorized Corps up to the line "Vorota." It has a forward observation post on Elevation "Vulkan"; it is subordinate to the commander of the 302nd Rifle Div.; successive concentrations of fire against Sectors Nos. 12 and "Vorota."	It is centralized by the control of the Artillery Chief of the Army. Fire missions depending upon the situation; observation posts on elevation "Podoshva." It is to prepare fire concentrations upon the exits from Plodovitoie toward the west and Elevation 124.8.
Successive concentrations of fire against the sectors designated by the commander of the 4th Mechanized Corps. The Divisional artillery changes fire positions after the 125th Mech. Reg. on line Kamishi, Elevation "Gorbataia"; the 125th Mech. Reg.—successive concentrations of fire against Sector No. 8. Changes fire position in the area of Elevation "Gorbataya".	Concentrations of fire against Sector No. 11.	Changes fire position on the line Elevation "Tsentralnaia," Sredniaia Lasta and prepares to repel the counterattacks from Grove "Sapog," Kordon Balka, and from Plodovitoie.	Neutralizes the fire points, observation posts and destroys the infantry in the following areas: Churche and east edge of Plodovitoie, Kazenina Balka. Prevents a counterattack from Grove "Sapog," "Paltsy."
Successive concentrations of fire against sectors indicated by the commander of 4th Mechanized Corps. Deliberate fire against Sector No. 10 and "Dalnaiaia Lasta."	Concentrates fire against Sectors Nos. 12, 11, Zakharov, "Troinaia." A battalion of the 4th Cavalry Corps joins the corps.	Relief of fire positions: 85th Guards Artillery Regiment in the area Sredniaia Lasta and "Vulkan," divisional artillery on the line, "Zakharov/"Troinaia." It repels the counterattacks from the southwest and from the direction of Plodovitoie.	Neutralizes the enemy in the area of "Topor," Krutaia Balka, Elevation 122.0, Elevation 107.0. Prevents counterattack from the south through Frolov.

following lines by November 30: *81st Cavalry Division,* Verkhne-Kurmoiarskaia; *302nd Rifle Division,* Elevation 129.0, Station Gremia-chaia, and Nebikov; *126th Rifle Division,* Pimen-Cherni, Darganov, and Sharnutovskii; *61st Cavalry Division,* Kanukovo; *91st Rifle Division,* Umantsevo; *76th Fortified Region,* Sadovoe. By this same time, the enemy, through the commitment of small groups of tanks (5 to 10 machines), had stopped the offensive of the Army. After bringing up fresh Panzer divisions, the enemy held the units of the Army on the line of Pokhlebin, Verkhne-Kurmoiarskaia, Pimen-Cherni, and Sharnutov-skii.

Brief Conclusions

1. The plan for the breakthrough on the flanks of the German Stalingrad group was carefully worked out and precisely organized. The break-through was carried out simultaneously on a broad front by the troops of three fronts; this action of our troops tied down by fire the maneuvering of the enemy. Furthermore, the blow was struck by surprise, with excellent troops, against the least stable enemy units.

2. The tactical zone of enemy defense was pierced on the very first day of operations to a depth making possible the commitment of the mobile reserves. The impetuous advance of these units, made without fear of becoming separated from the rifle units, rendered it possible to throw them into the rear of the main German grouping, thus practically closing the ring of encirclement by the fourth day of operations. With their main forces, the rifle units widened the operational breakthrough of the mobile groups and protected their line of communications. The enemy units left in the rear were blocked by specially assigned groups; the main forces, which affected the tactical encirclement of the main German group, did not allow themselves to be diverted by collateral missions.

The successful selection of the sectors of the breakthrough and the careful planning for reconnaissance of the enemy had great importance.

3. The artillery played a great part in the operations for effecting the breakthrough and the encirclement of the Germans at Stalingrad. The artillery, by effective and concentrated artillery fire, made it possible to break through the main zone of enemy defense. It constantly assisted the rifle troops and tanks in overcoming the main zone of defense. Artillery fire was effective in accompanying the mobile groups through the tactical zone of enemy defenses. By fire and movement, the artillery also supported the actions of the mobile groups in the strategic breakthrough. Thus, it helped to carry out the well-devised plan for the entire operation, and without its effective work, this plan could not have been realized.

4. The success of the work of the artillery was assured by the following:

● sufficient time for regrouping and for careful reconnaissance of the enemy (the artillery commanders and the staffs had the necessary time for organization of the artillery offensive and control of all the preparatory measures for the operation);

● the skillful control, by the commanders and artillery staffs, of the fire and movement of the artillery in the course of the operation;

● the excellent teamwork of the artillery units; and

● the carefully worked-out plan—followed in the main—of cooperation of artillery with rifle troops and tanks in the locality during the breakthrough.

5. Matters worthy of attention were the method of arranging the artillery preparation, a method whose value was confirmed by the results of battle, and the measures employed by artillery to eliminate the dangerous and harmful gap between the cavalry/artillery preparation and the beginning of the attack by the rifle troops and tanks.

6. In the course of the offensive, during action in the depth of the enemy defenses, the cooperation of rifle troops with artillery was often disrupted. However, the success of the breakthrough as a whole and the lack of stability on the part of the enemy, who was stunned by the attacks of the mobile groups into his operational rear, made it possible to avoid the consequences of the breakdown in cooperation between the rifle troops and the artillery.

The initiative of the artillery commanders in opening fire against targets interfering with the advance of the rifle troops was of great importance in the course of battle in the depths of the operational dispositions of the enemy.

Another matter worthy of attention and meriting detailed study is the work of the forward artillery observers, moving out ahead on tanks provided with radio, because the employment of such observers proved to be one of the most effective methods of promoting cooperation in mobile forms of battle.

7. The employment of tank destroyer artillery regiments and brigades in the operations for encirclement of the enemy Stalingrad group gave concrete results.

8. In the analysis of the action of the artillery, we observed team play and precision in its work not only within the army and Fronts but also between the Fronts. In the combat actions of the artillery, we took into account all the preceding experience of the Great Patriotic War and eliminated all the weaknesses encountered in the preceding operations. This was promoted to a considerable degree by the fact that not only the general but also the immediate control of artillery was carried out by the artillery commander of the Red Army Marshal Comrade Voronov. His fortunate selection of a command group made it possible for him to exercise control and have his orders carried out.[12]

Editor's Notes

1. The best reference on Soviet artillery is *Sovetskaia artilleriia v Velikoi Otechestvennoi Voine 1941–1945 gg.* (Moscow: *Voenizdat*, 1960). During the period of preparation, *Stavka* gave to the three fronts an additional 75 gun/mortar regiments. This number represented almost one-half of those currently in the reserves.

   An additional 115 Guards Mortar battalions were also provided to the fronts. This figure represented one-third of the total for the Red Army. See *IVOVSS* vol. 3, p. 20. On November 20, the three fronts had a total of one artillery and three antiaircraft divisions, 39 gun artillery regiments, 42 destroyer antitank regiments, 13 mortar regiments, 33 Guards Mortar regiments, and 35 antiaircraft regiments. The forces also possessed one heavy artillery battalion, 14 breakthrough artillery battalions, and five antiaircraft battalions. See "Kontr'nastuplenii pod Stalingradom v tsifrakh (Operatsiia'Uran')" *Voenno istoricheskii zhurnal* No. 3, 1968, p. 68, table 3. An artillery division comprised eight artillery regiments.

2. The commander was Lieutenant General of Artillery M. P. Dmitriev.

3. Tank destroyer artillery had been created by the People's Commissar of Defense's order of July 1, 1942. Previously designated simply as antitank artillery, the new title signified the enhancement of the arm of service. The designation provided new privileges, special insignia and rewards, and an upgrading of personnel.

4. As an example of fire concentration, the 5th Tank Army employed 2,166 guns/mortars-/Guards Mortars on the 35-kilometer front. On the 10-kilometer breakthrough sector, 1,067 artillery pieces were concentrated. The total of 13,500 guns/mortars concentrated in the three fronts was more than twice the number employed at Moscow in 1941–42. See also the Appendix.

5. Despite this praise for the artillery, it is well to keep in mind that the Soviet artillery, not being as mobile as necessary, had failed to achieve a complete breakthrough. As a result, on the Southwestern Front the attack gave the appearance of bogging down, and Soviet armor was inserted early so as to speed the attack as was discussed in chapter 5.

6. This rather mundane issue is often overlooked in more modern accounts of Soviet successes.

7. The faithful U.S.-built *Willys* was a powerful instrument for increasing the tempo of Soviet operations. Another tribute to Lend-Lease regardless of the limited numbers at this time.

8. The commander of 4th Tank Corps was Major General of Tank Troops A. G, Kravchenko.

9. The commander of the 16th Tank Corps was Major General of Technical Troops A. G. Maslov.

10. The artillery commander of Don Front was Lieutenant General of Artillery V. I. Kazakov.

11. The artillery commander of Stalingrad Front was Major General of Artillery V. N. Matveev.

12. At the time, N. N. Voronov was a Colonel General and not a Marshal.

Aside from the battles at Moscow, the Red Air Force had not faired well in engagements with the Luftwaffe. *The aerial combat near Stalingrad demonstrated the Soviet Forces' growing experience and their potential for future operations.*

Stavka *carefully planned the strategic aspects of the struggle for air supremacy at Stalingrad. The significant growth of Soviet air strength provided for* Stavka's *substantial concentration of fresh air units near Stalingrad such as seven independent air divisions and two Composite Air Corps for the counteroffensive. Numerical superiority, however, was achieved even before the opening of the offensive.*

Due to the disruptions of the German positions and the poor weather, Soviet aircraft flew five times the number of missions as German forces during the crucial five days following the opening of the attack. This important chapter details the results of those actions—Ed.

10

Action of the Army Air Forces in the Battle for Stalingrad

Throughout the period of the hard-fought Stalingrad battle ending in a brilliant victory for the Red Army, our aviation carried on intense combat activity and rendered great assistance to the ground forces in the defense of Stalingrad and in the rout and destruction of the Stalingrad group of the enemy.

In the fight for Stalingrad, we must consider two periods, with the first period of withdrawal of our forces toward Stalingrad and our defense of Stalingrad. This period started at the end of July, when the enemy, with his motorized–mechanized units and strong air support came into the Don Bend and created a direct threat to Stalingrad. The second was the attack of the Red Army with subsequent defeat and destruction of the Stalingrad group of the enemy (from November 19, 1942 to February 3, 1943). These periods differed from each other both in the character of the

229

missions and the conditions of their execution and in the characteristics of the methods of action employed by our aviation.

Operations of Aviation in the Period of the Withdrawal of Our Troops and in the Defense of Stalingrad

The three-month period of hard fighting on the approaches to Stalingrad and in the city itself had a great influence upon the subsequent course of events. The efforts of the enemy to capture the very important strategic point at all costs encountered the tenacious resistance of our troops. By destroying the personnel and military equipment of the enemy, we continued to hold not only a part of the city but also the bridgeheads north and south of Stalingrad that were necessary for a subsequent attack. In this hard fighting, the aviation of the 8th and 16th Air Armies, operating day and night in close cooperation with the ground forces played a very important role.[1]

The combat operations of our aviation during the defensive period were carried out under extremely difficult conditions. The enemy aviation, by constantly replacing its heavy losses on aircraft and personnel, always had a strength of 800 to 1,000 operating airplanes.[2] The presence of such a large number of aircraft gave the enemy a two-fold to three-fold advantage over our air units in the Stalingrad area.

Despite the unfavorable relative strength in the air, our air units were obliged to operate at all costs; the critical situation at Stalingrad made it necessary. The lack of planes necessitated an increase in the intensity of aerial operations, which for a long time averaged 3 to 3.5 sorties per day for each aircraft in flying condition. Our fighter planes in particular were obliged to engage in very intense activity, which, in addition to protecting the troops and the most important objectives from enemy air attacks, also had to cover the operations of our ground attack planes and our bombers since 60 to 70 percent of their combat missions involved encounters and air battles with enemy fighter planes.

As a result of the intense activity and operations in the face of strong enemy fighter and antiaircraft gun counteraction, our formations always had a large number of planes that were unable to fly. Usually, a considerable portion of the planes returning from combat had serious damage and thus had to undergo repairs lasting for extended periods. On certain days, the number of planes out of commission reached 60 to 70 percent. For example, on September 1, 1942, of the total strength of the 8th Air Army—193 fighters and 195 combat support planes and day bombers—there were 57 fighters and 69 combat support planes in need of repair.[3]

In the first days of September, we had a total of 270 planes in good condition (in the 8th and 16th Air Armies) in the Stalingrad area. Of these aircraft, 80 were fighters, 85 were combat support, 54 were day bombers, and 51 were night bombers. It is clearly evident that with such a number of airplanes to create an equilibrium of forces in the air was extremely difficult even on a narrow sector of the front and for a short period of time. The situation was complicated by the absence of the necessary number of fighter planes for accompanying the combat-support planes and the day bombers. As a result, the latter could not carry on combat operations with an all-out effort.

Enemy aviation, throughout the period of the defense of Stalingrad, dominated the air over the whole front.[4] This was evident from the data pertaining to the number of airplane sorties of our aviation (involving flying over the front line) and the number of enemy airplane flights over our territory:

	Soviet	German
August	10,590	20,600
September	14,080	18,200
October	14,747	26,000

We must bear in mind that of the total number of airplane sorties made by our air units a very large part were carried out at night (in September—6,692; in October—10,505), whereas the enemy aviation flew mostly in the daytime.[5]

The enemy aviation, utilized in mass against the main directions of operations of the German ground forces, carried out the following missions on the days of active operations on the ground: fighter planes, from daybreak to the onset of darkness, covered their troops on the battlefield and on the approaches to it; the bombers—in groups of 10 to 30 airplanes—constantly operated against our ground troops and attacked crossings on the Volga River, staffs, and the most important communications; at night single planes mined the channel of the Volga River. On certain days of intense combat activity our Aircraft Warning Service posts recorded 1,000 to 1,500 enemy air sorties. For example, on August 23, 1942, the day the enemy motorized–mechanized units broke through our defense on the sector of Verkhne-Gnilovskii and Peskovatka and then approached the western bank of the Volga in the Akatovka-Vinnovka area (12 kilometers north of Stalingrad), we counted 1,500 enemy airplane sorties—more than 50 percent of which operated against the city of Stalingrad.

To concentrate the efforts of our numerically small air force in the conduct of the most important missions was very difficult, because the enemy advanced simultaneously from several directions, and usually the situation developed everywhere in his favor.[6] For example, from July 23–August 1, 1942, the main efforts of our air forces were concentrated in the area of Verkhne-Buzinovka, Osinovka, Lipologovskii, and Eruslanovskii (25 to 40 kilometers northwest of Kalach) for the purpose of destroying the enemy group breaking through the sector of the 62nd Army and threatening to drive out our units on the east bank of the Don River. At the same time, a small part of our air units operated against the troops of the enemy in the area of Nizhne-Chirskaia, from where the enemy was advancing in northern and northeastern directions, striving to join up with the Verkhne-Buzinovka group and to surround our 62nd Army.

On August 2, the enemy started an attack from Kotelnikovo with two Panzer divisions and motorized infantry. On August 1, this attack broke through the defense of our troops in the area of Station Remontnoe and began to develop an energetic offensive along the Kotelnikovo–Stalingrad railroad. The enemy's great numerical superiority here made it possible for them to develop the attack very rapidly. By August 7, the enemy had occupied Siding 74 kilometers Tunguta, and Plodovitoie (35 kilometers south of Krasnoarmeisk). This constituted a direct threat to Stalingrad; hence, from August 2 all the efforts of our aviation had to be concentrated for action against the Kotelnikovo group of the enemy.

Diverting our aviation for use against the Kotelnikovo group of the enemy freed from its action the groups of forces around Verkhne-Buznikovka and Nizhne-Chirskaia. Toward the end of August 9, these groups reached the right bank of the Don River on the sector of Kamenskii, Kalach, and Rychkovskii, and a part of the forces of the 62nd Army were encircled in the area of Dobrinskii. This circumstance forced our aviation—without stopping its operations against the Kotelnikovo group breaking through to Stalingrad—to detail a part of its planes (chiefly from night aviation) to help the units of the 62nd Army to escape from encirclement and also to transport ammunition and food to them.

By the end of the first half of August, the situation was still more complicated. Having concentrated large forces in the area south of Kletskaia, the enemy began an attack on August 15 and, by the end of August 16, had occupied the eastern bend of the Don River and threatened to forge the Don River. In order to eliminate this threat, aviation had to operate in this direction. However, the operations of our aviation against the crossings and troop concentrations of the enemy in this period were still very much limited in scope because, after the hard fighting against the enemy groups in Verkhne-Buzinovka and Kotelnikovo, a great part of our airplanes were undergoing repair.

On August 23, we started active combat operations against the enemy group breaking through to the west bank of the Volga about 12 kilometers north of Stalingrad, the purpose of the fighting against this group was to prevent it from spreading out toward the south and in doing so to help defend the city itself.

The serious situation north of Stalingrad was complicated still further after the enemy assumed the offensive south of Stalingrad and subsequently broke through on August 31 into the inner ring of our defense on the approaches to the city, passing along the line of the Chervlenaia River. With only a small number of airplanes in good condition, our air force was obliged to fight the enemy in two directions—northwest and southwest of Stalingrad.

This brief list of the directions of active operations of the troops in the initial period of the fighting for Stalingrad is also characteristic of all the subsequent period of this heroic epic. It shows that our aviation was used in a purposeful manner: its efforts were always concentrated in the most important directions of action of our ground troops and contributed to the success of the execution of their combat missions.

Inasmuch as our troops were on the defensive, the importance of the direction of their operations was determined by the enemy troops' operations in these directions. Hence, the most important directions of operation of our troops were also highly important for the enemy, who usually employed the majority of their aviation at the same place. It is natural that a concentration of a large number of airplanes by both sides on a small sector of the front led to numerous air battles, the scale of which was sometimes rather large; in certain cases as many as 50 airplanes from both sides participated in these battles. The number of air battles was also large—on an average, 20 to 25 air battles took place every day. Inasmuch as each side tried to reach the target assigned to it at any cost, the battles were extremely tenacious and were accompanied by heavy losses of 20 or more airplanes a day.

In spite of the superiority of the enemy air force, our aviation inflicted serious damage upon the enemy both on the ground and in the air, especially in the latter. In only 20 days of combat operations (from July 20–August 10, 1942), 315 enemy airplanes—50 percent of which were fighters—were shot down in air battles and destroyed on airfields.

In trying to get control of the air at Stalingrad, the enemy did not limit themselves to numerical superiority in the air. In addition to this, they employed a number of other measures. In particular, they brought into action a large number of new modernized fighter planes, the Me-109G, possessing high speed, excellent armament, and more powerful armor in comparison with their predecessor, the Me-109F. They also made extensive use of their fighter planes for blocking our airports. Finally, in the Stalingrad direction, they used some specially prepared units and small units of "aces." In the middle part of August, the experienced 52nd Fighter Group appeared at Stalingrad. There was nothing new in the tactics of these German aces; they generally employed the old method of encountering a single small group of our combat–support planes and bombers on the approach to the objective for the purpose of engaging the escort fighters, with subsequent attack of the groups of combat–support planes or bombers by a second shock group of two to four planes. In addition to this, extensive use was made of the method of fighter "sweeps." In the final accounting, the whole of the measures of the enemy amounted essentially to the following: up to the middle of September the *Luftwaffe* had greatly hampered our aviation in the carrying out of its missions, and at the same time, it had carried out its own missions with relative impunity.

About this same time, the enemy also won several victories on the ground; their troops, suffering heavy losses in battles on the approaches to Stalingrad, broke through to the city on September 19. Heavy street fighting started. In trying to capture Stalingrad at all costs, the Germans at this same time brought into action new forces of tanks, motorized infantry, and aviation, and activity became still more intense.

The bombers of the enemy, flying in groups of 10 to 15 airplanes, constantly bombed our forces on the battlefield, the eastern part of this city, the crossings on the Volga, and also subjected to frequent air attacks the inhabited localities in the zone near the front and the Volga shipping on the Astrakhan-Kamyshin sector. By mass air attacks, the enemy expected to neutralize the fire system in our defense, paralyze control of troops, prevent the approach of the reserves, and disrupt supply in order to win a victory at Stalingrad in a few days and capture the city. Enemy fighter planes in groups of up to 18 planes constantly patrolled the battlefield in the direction of the active operations of their troops, blocked our airfields, and by making extensive use of sweeping flights by fighter–hunter aircraft, offered strong resistance to our aviation on the flight courses.

Our aviation, having suffered heavy losses during the time of the battles on the approaches to Stalingrad (especially in fighter planes) and having a high percentage of airplanes unfit for flying (up to 50 percent), was greatly inferior to the enemy in the air. The 8th and 16th Air Armies on October 1, 1942, had a total of 373 planes suitable for flying (71 fighter planes, 166 combat–support planes, 34 day bombers, and 102 night bombers) against not less than 850 enemy planes, including about 350 fighter planes.[7]

Such an unfavorable strength ratio for us gave enemy aviation almost complete control of the air. Under these conditions, the bombers of the enemy operated at average and low altitudes, in the majority of cases without the cover of fighter planes. Our combat–support planes and bombers, however, very often did not have an opportunity to carry out combat operations because of the absence of fighter planes for cover, even though our fighter planes carried on very active operations. On an average, they made not less then three sorties daily for each plane in flying condition. However, the necessity of carrying out such important missions as the covering of crossings over the Volga and railway transports absorbed almost all the activity of our fighter planes, and they could not provide reliable cover for the actions of the combat–support planes and bombers.

In this trying period lasting up until November, the most important air missions were cooperation with the ground forces in fighting the troops attacking on the battlefield, covering the most important objects, and reconnaissance. For combating enemy troop movements, attacks against enemy airdromes, and other similar missions, we rarely used our air forces, and when we did, we used a small number of planes. We must say that under these conditions, in view of the small number of planes we had and the constant and critical necessity of helping the ground troops hold the attacking troops of the enemy, we could not have employed our aviation in any other way.

The distribution of airplane sorties on the basis of missions was the following:

Execution of Missions	Number of Sorties	
	September	October
Attacking enemy troops	9,036	11,032
Attacking airdromes	280	483
Attacking railroad objects	91	217
Accompanying the combat-support planes & bombers	3,282	1,441
Covering objects	2,698	1,529
Intercepting of enemy airplanes	642	556
Reconnaissance of enemy troops	1,501	1,291
Transporting freight	47	282
Total	17,577	16,831

From this table we can see two-thirds of all the airplane sorties were carried out in making attacks against the troops of the enemy on the battlefield itself, and that only one-third were for the execution of all the other missions, including the accompanying of combat support planes and bombers. Such a distribution of our aviation efforts enabled us to keep the enemy under constant attack from the air (especially at night). This not only helped our hard-pressed troops at Stalingrad, but it also helped them to harass the forces of the enemy more effectively.

The small number of our fighter planes (especially in the latter period of our defense) and the presence of strong enemy counteraction in the air affected the combat operations of our aviation in a number of ways. For example, we made extensive use of night aviation for fighting enemy troops; we used day bombers at high altitudes without the cover of fighter planes. We attacked with combat–support planes from medium altitudes and organized a network of ground radio stations both for warning and for guiding the fighter planes to the enemy and also for directing air combat from the ground.

The employment of night aviation for combating enemy troops was not anything new. However, the scale on which this type of aviation was employed in the Battle for Stalingrad exceeded all previous employment in the Great Patriotic War. The blows of our night aviation against enemy troops were not only very important and a necessary supplement to the attacks of the planes operating in the daytime, but they also played a completely independent role—namely, these blows tired out and exhausted the troops of the enemy in a physical sense at the same time that they inflicted upon them certain losses in personnel, equipment, and transport means.

We can see from the data given in the table below the great importance of our night aviation:

Time of Action	Number of Airplane Sorties		Of these the following were for combat with enemy troops	
Month	Day	Night	Day	Night
			Total against the Troops	
August	8,508	4,087	—	6,267
September	10,885	6,692	2,622	6,414
October	6,326	10,505	1,582	9,450

Hence, from September to October, the main part of the airplane sorties against enemy troops was carried out by night aviation. A characteristic feature is that in proportion as the fight for Stalingrad became more and more intense, there was a decrease in the activity of our aviation during the daytime and an increase in activity at night.

As we have already stated, the basic purpose of the attacks of our night bombers (U-2, R-5, SB, DB-3, and units of IL-2s) was to tire out the personnel of the enemy, and this purpose was achieved. The continuous attacks throughout the night by small groups of bombers (one to three airplanes) at intervals of three to five minutes against the most important sectors, where the main part of the attacking enemy forces were concentrated, either forced the enemy to desist from attacking on these sectors or to attack at a slower pace because the troops of the enemy were physically and morally shattered and exhausted and as a rule were not able to overcome the persistence and stubbornness of the defense of our troops.

There were cases when the intensive actions of night bombers broke up the enemy preparations for attack. Thus, on September 7, 1942, our reconnaissance found that in the Gumrak-Kamenyi Buerak area the enemy had concentrated large forces. Hence on September 8, one could expect an attack in the direction of Aleksandrov. Our night aviation received the mission to make a concentrated attack on the night of September 7–8 and to break up the enemy attack, which was being prepared. The night bombers flew singly and in pairs throughout the night and continually struck the area of the enemy troop concentration. By morning, the target had been hit, and the attack of the enemy was broken up. A similar thing happened on the 22nd and 27th of September, when our night aviation also broke up enemy preparations for an attack along the valley of the Tsaritsa River and in the area of Elevation 102.0 (Mamaev Kurgan).

We must assume that in addition to harassing the enemy troops the night planes also inflicted upon them some appreciable losses in material and personnel. From September 13 to October 2, 1942—that is, in 20 nights—the night bombers of the 8th Air Army carried out 5,289 sorties and released 63,950 bombs, weighing from 2.5 kilograms to 500 kilograms (total weight: 1,600 tons) and expending 1,250 rocket shells, 6,417 incendiary projectiles with "YS," and 127,000 cartridges. According to the reports of the crews, they knocked out and destroyed during this time 200 motor vehicles, 20 gasoline tank trucks, 22 search lights, 45 guns, 50 mortars, 94 antiaircraft gun positions, three ammunition dumps, a fuel dump, 102 buildings serving as centers of enemy resistance, and in addition, caused up to 300 fires.

Of course the actual damage was greater, and this is attested to by the repeated cases when the enemy failed to attack on sectors subjected to intense attack by our bombers. This assumption is confirmed by the statements of German prisoners of war, who admitted the heavy losses and adverse psychological effects on their troops of the attacks of our night aviation; captured soldiers and even the officers generally called the U-2 airplane "Ivan the Terrible." The great effectiveness of the attacks of our airplanes at night is still further confirmed by the fact that beginning in September the enemy planned to defeat our night fighters. At first, enemy efforts consisted of operations against airdromes and the blocking of airdromes with their own night planes. at the end of September, the Germans began to employ special planes known as night "sweep" planes. These "sweep" planes (Me-110 aircraft) on light nights flew patrols on air alert missions against the probable directions of flight of our airplanes.[8]

The command of our ground troops had high praise for the night aviation operations. There were many cases when army commanders and commanders of troop formations thanked the units of night bombers operating on their sectors. The role of the U-2 airplanes in night operations was exceptionally important; thus, out of 10,505 night sorties carried out in October, 9,925 were made by the U-2. Even with the relatively small number (80 to 90) of airplanes of this type, we carried out in the course of the night up to 650 sorties and dropped 140 tons of bombs. Combat practice showed that on the basis of the number of sorties carried out the efficiency of the U-2 airplanes was considerably higher than in the case of any other types of night airplanes. On an average they carried out not less than five sorties during the night, whereas the R-5 and the SB aircraft flew only two to three sorties.

The large number of sorties flown by U-2 airplanes is explained by the fact that they operated from forward airdromes, located about 10 to 20 kilometers from the front line. At advanced airdromes, we used small areas on which slit trenches were dug or blinds constructed for protecting personnel in case of an enemy attack from the air. In such areas, as a rule we did not store any supplies; the battalions for servicing the airdromes brought us everything necessary for combat action at night.

The movement of the units to the advanced airdrome was done by single airplanes with the approach of darkness; the technical personnel came aboard the airplane to be served. The flights were carried out in the majority of cases without the night takeoff procedure. The takeoff/landing strip was marked by two lanterns, one of which served to mark the place where the plane touched the ground, and the other, the direction of the takeoff and of the landing. The lanterns were hidden by a cover that was lifted only when the airplane was about to land or takeoff.

We should mention that the high appraisal of the action of U-2 airplanes was due not only to the large number of sorties they made at night but also to the great precision and effectiveness of their attacks. In the course of all of the fighting for Stalingrad, our night aviation operated chiefly against the centers of resistance, motorized–mechanized units, and the fire positions of artillery—that is, the operations were principally against the battlefield, in the immediate neighborhood of the dispositions of our troops. Cases of bombs being released upon our own troops were very rare, even when our troops designated themselves poorly. We were able to avoid hitting our own troops only because the flight personnel generally knew the area of operation and unerringly found—even in the darkness of night—those objects that they wanted to bomb.

The night missions were usually assigned to the units on the basis of a (large-scale) sketch of the town, and besides that the aviation regiment was assigned an area (square) having 400 to 1,000 meters to the side (sometimes up to two kilometers. From this area each group was assigned a sector and oftentimes all of it. The missions were brought to the crews on the base airdromes before the takeoff for the advanced airdrome.

The operations were carried out by single airplanes, by pairs, and by flights. It was learned by experience that in the majority of cases actions by pairs and by flights were more effective than the action of single planes. In the flights with small groups, it was possible to achieve a more accurate approach to the target, and one could employ illumination for attacking the target and neutralize the antiaircraft weapons of the enemy if they opened fire.

The practice, instituted at first, of having aviation operate exclusively against a limited area throughout the night did not always justify itself. The enemy, having caught on to this method, moved their personnel back from the area of action to a distance of 800 to 1,000 meters just as soon as our airplanes started the attack, as a result of which our airplanes sometimes operated against an empty space. In order to avoid this, we subsequently began to employ a combination of different methods. If, however, it was necessary to operate throughout the night against some small area, we planned careful observation of the enemy.

In spite of the strong antiaircraft defense of the enemy and the great strain, the U-2 airplanes had very small losses throughout the period. For example, during October, the 8th Air Army flew 7,623 sorties and lost only two airplanes in combat.[9]

The operations of the night bombers from great heights (6,000 to 8,000 meters) without escort was made necessary by the lack of fighter planes for accompanying purposes. The flights for combat missions were carried out by single airplanes and by pairs of airplanes. The attacks were made against targets located not closer than five kilometers from the front line. These targets were usually concentrations of troops, railroad personnel at the stations and on the line, and sometimes enemy airdromes.

Experience showed that, in the flight of our Pe-2 bombers at great heights, the pursuit planes of the enemy (Me-109 and He-113) could attack only in the case of head-on encounters and intersecting courses. Pursuit on the tail of Pe-2 planes was usually unsuccessful—they escaped from the fighter planes of the enemy. The escape from the pursuit and attack by the enemy fighter planes was done by climbing in the direction of the sun, or when it was cloudy, the Pe-2s as a rule escaped into the clouds.

The combat support planes operated at medium altitudes in order to decrease losses caused by enemy aviation. The purpose of this measure was to improve the self-defense of the group of combat–support planes in attacks by fighter planes.

In the fighting for Stalingrad, in accordance with the data of the staff of the 8th Air Army, the overwhelming part of the losses (62 percent) of the combat–support planes resulted from the fighter planes of the enemy, even though in the first period our groups of combat–support planes were usually covered by fighter planes. Such heavy losses are to be explained by the poor planning for accompanying the combat–support planes by fighter planes and the fact that the combat–support planes themselves did not know how to conduct defensive battle. In practice, the whole group of our accompanying fighter planes engaged the fighter planes of the enemy and lost the combat–support planes that they were accompanying. When this happened, the second group of enemy fighter planes attacked them and inflicted heavy losses.

Experience showed that the most important requirements for success in the conduct of group defensive battle with the combat–support planes against the fighter planes of the enemy are a close formation and the detailing of well-trained crews for covering the tail of the group.

Groups of combat–support planes with lack of flying experience and training in groups of defensive combat could not, in hedge-hopping flights and even in flight at low altitudes, maintain a close formation. Consequently, they were unable to conduct air combat with enemy fighter planes. In case of an attack, the groups quickly broke formation because their efforts to escape combat at hedge-hopping altitudes, and they became an easy prey for enemy fighter planes.

The actions of the combat–support planes at medium altitudes enabled them to keep the close formation of the group and made it possible to get experience in conducting group combat with the fighter planes of the enemy. This does not mean, however, that group air battle is possible only at medium altitudes. In practice, there were many cases of successful conduct of air battles by our combat–support planes against enemy fighter planes at low altitudes. For example, on September 29, 1942, the fighter planes, covering the combat–support planes, were engaged in an air battle in the area of the target, and five IL-2 airplanes of the 228 Attack Air Division returned from the combat mission without cover. In the Sredne-Pogromnoe area, they were attacked by six enemy fighter Me-109 planes. The combat–support planes, having placed themselves in position in the form of the letter "S," covered the tail of each other and conducted fire against the fighter planes at each convenient opportunity. The fight lasted for 30 minutes at an altitude of 5 to 30 meters. The combat–support planes suffered no losses, and all the attacks of the enemy fighter planes were repulsed.

The essential features of the actions of the combat–support planes in the area of the target during their flights at medium altitudes were the following: the bombing was carried out from an altitude of 600 to 1,200 meters, chiefly from a dive; the firing of rocket shells was done from an altitude of 500 to 600 meters, after which the combat–support planes bombarded the target with machine guns and cannon.

Upon encounter with the fighter planes of the enemy on the flight course, the combat–support planes placed themselves in a circle drawn out along the direction of movement with intervals of 150 to 200 meters between the planes and with a bank of not over 30 degrees. The fighter planes of the covering force placed themselves in a reverse circle for intersecting the attack of the fighter planes of the enemy. In case of a group made up of a small number, when it was impossible to form a closed circle, the combat–support planes conducted defensive combat in an "S" formation, and the accompanying fighter planes devoted their chief attention to covering the tail of the group of combat–support planes.

The rise of combat–support planes to medium altitudes marked the beginning of defensive combat with the fighter planes of the enemy, as a result of which our losses decreased considerably.

We must say that the succession of heavy losses inflicted upon our aviation by enemy fighter planes could have been avoided if our air commanders and their staffs had given more serious attention to the study of the tactical methods of enemy aviation and had reacted more quickly to the changes in these tactics. The result of the lack of study of the tactical methods of the enemy was that the enemy used his different methods for a long period of time and inflicted great damage upon our aviation. For example, the flight of enemy fighter planes in two groups, one of which engaged the accompanying fighter planes in battle while the other attacked the group of combat–support planes or bombers, was not a new method. This method of the enemy and the measures for opposing it (the detailing of two groups of fighter planes—a holding group and a group for direct covering) were known from the beginning of the Great Patriotic War.

However, the enemy's method in the fighting for Stalingrad was not countered by us for a long time.[10] For example, on July 24, while six IL-2 combat–support planes were flying a combat mission, the eight LAGG-3 fighter planes accompanying them became engaged in combat with a small group of Me-109. The combat–support planes, left without cover, were attacked and destroyed by the second group of enemy fighter planes. A similar case was repeated on July 26 when seven Pe-2 planes were shot down. But even after these two cases, all necessary measures were not taken. As a result, on August 4, 11 Yak-1s covering the flight of five IL-2s were tied down by five Me-109s, and the whole group of combat–support planes were destroyed by the second group of enemy fighter planes.

Warning and guiding our fighter planes to the enemy airplanes via radio was used in the second half of October. All the work was planned in the following manner: west of the village of Burkovskii, at a distance of five to six kilometers from Stalingrad, we landed an RAF radio set and organized an observation post.[11] The observation post had the following missions:

● warning our fighter aviation of the appearance of enemy airplanes in the region of Stalingrad;
● guiding of our fighter planes to enemy airplanes; and
● controlling the air battle.

At the radio station there was always an experienced and reliable commander (commander of fighter plane aviation, his assistant, or chief of staff), who used radio to direct the action of the aviators in air battle.

For convenience in giving warning of the appearance of enemy planes, all of the area visible from the observation post was divided into sectors and each sector was given a number. The appearance of airplanes was reported in clear text to the command post of the 8th Air Army and to the airdrome of the fighter planes of the 287th Fighter Division; for example: "10 He-111s over sector no. 2."

Warning, guiding, and controlling by radio played a great part in the tactical work of fighter plane aviation on the Stalingrad front. With this measure it was possible to cover in a more effective manner the important objects in the region of Stalingrad and to conduct combat much more effectively with enemy airplanes in the air. In the second half of October alone, the radio station set up in the area of Burkovskii called fighter planes from airdromes on 95 occasions, guided our fighters to enemy bombers on 125 occasions, and by means of control by radio, 37 enemy planes were shot down.

Experience in guiding and warning by radio, gained in this period by aviation on the Stalingrad front, helped us in the following fight for Stalingrad to set up an extensive network for guiding by radio and to conduct combat with the transport airplanes of the enemy in a still more effective manner.

On the whole, during the time of the defense of Stalingrad, our aviation acquired a great deal of combat experience and greatly improved its tactics; this was one of the basic requirements for its successful action in the subsequent period ending with the crushing defeat of the Germans in the Stalingrad area.[12]

Operations of Aviation in the Period of the Destruction of the Stalingrad Group of the Enemy

The 8th, 16th, and 17th Air Armies participated in the destruction of the enemy. Participating the most actively was the 16th Air Army of the Don Front, which operated from the moment of the beginning of our ground forces' offensive up to the final liquidation of the 6th German Army.[13] The 8th and 16th Air Armies cooperated closely from the beginning of the offensive of the ground troops until the smashing of the Kotelnikovo group of the enemy trying to break through the ring of encirclement from the south, that is, up until January 1943.

The activity of the 17th Air Army was limited, however, to the period of the operational encirclement of the Stalingrad group of the enemy (November 19–23, 1942), after which it supported the offensive of the troops of the Southwestern Front along the middle Don.

Before the beginning of the offensive of the troops of the Southwestern, Don, and Stalingrad Fronts, our aviation continued to operate with its previous intensity, giving assistance and support to the defenders of Stalingrad. However, in the characteristics of its combat operations there had already appeared certain peculiarities connected with the preparation for the approaching offensive. In helping the ground troops repel all of the furious enemy attacks against Stalingrad, attacks that were still continuing, our aviation at the same time began to carry out missions in support of the approaching operations. These missions were

- covering concentrations of ground troops for the operations;
- attacking enemy aviation at its airdromes;
- acting against railroads to destroy troop transports bringing enemy reserves to Stalingrad;
- conducting careful reconnaissance of the enemy troops; and
- photographing their defenses on the sectors where our troops were planning to attack.

In addition to this, all the air units carried out a great deal of work in restoring materiel that was out of order.

As a result of the replacements in the airplane park and the repair of the defective airplanes in the units, our aviation had the following number of airplanes at the beginning of the offensive:

Number of Air Armies		Number of Airplanes					Remarks
		F	C	D	N	R	Total	
16th Air Army		114	105	—	93	3	315	Of these, up to
8th Air Army		284	273	65	122	7	751	25% were
17th Air Army		82	40	—	79	—	201	defective
	Total	480	418	65	294	10	1,267	

F = Fighters; C = Combat–Support; D = Day Bombers; N = Night Bombers;
R = Reconnaissance

For use against these forces, the Germans under the command of Colonel-General Richthofen had the 4th Air Fleet, consisting of the 4th and 5th Air Corps and the 8th Air Corps for close combat. On November 20, 1942, the Germans had up to 1,000 airplanes— 550 bombers, 350 fighter planes, and about 100 reconnaissance planes. Hence, the relative strength of air forces was, on the whole, about equal.

The first phase of the operation, which was completed by the operational encirclement of the Stalingrad group of the enemy, was carried out by the ground troops without the active participation of our aviation. The exceptionally unfavorable weather conditions made its operation almost wholly impossible.

On November 19, in the breakthrough of the defenses of the enemy northwest of Stalingrad, we carried out a total of 44 sorties against the troops of the enemy in the regions of Nizhne-Fomikhinskii and Tsumlovskii (west and south of Kletskaia).

On November 20, during the attack south of Stalingrad, aviation did not operate at all because of unbroken cloudiness. On the following days, right up to November 23, we carried out only 369 sorties (17th Air Army—83; 16th Air Army—131; 8th Air Army—155).

In this period enemy aviation was also grounded by bad weather conditions and did not fly, so that our ground forces had an opportunity to attack without the counteraction of enemy aviation. During the whole period of encirclement of the 6th Army of the enemy by our troops, that is, from November 19–23, a total of only 361 airplane sorties were observed. But we can say that from the beginning of the offensive of the Southwest, Don, and Stalingrad fronts the flight activity of the enemy decreased sharply: from November 19–30 we observed a total of only about 2,000 airplane flights. Such a decrease in the activity of enemy aviation, in comparison with the preceding months, is explained by bad weather in the first days of the offensive of our troops and by the change in base of enemy aviation from Stalingrad to the airdrome centers at Morozovskii and Tatsinskaia, which were 200 to 240 kilometers from the battlefield.

Our troops, after having carried out the encirclement, in a systematic manner started to exert pressure against the encircled 6th German Army, which passed to a rigid defense and offered stubborn resistance, making use for this purpose of every accident of the terrain and the inhabited localities. In the first period after the encirclement of the enemy, our aviation operations consisted chiefly of cooperation with our ground forces in the destruction of the encircled troops of the enemy. In the period from November 23–31, 1942 (sic—Ed.), of the 3,769 sorties flown by the 8th and 16th Air armies, about 2,500 were flown against enemy strong points and troops on the battlefield in the ring of encirclement. During this period, the command of our ground troops considered its chief mission to be the tightening of the ring of encirclement, and hence the efforts of aviation were directed at striking the 6th Army.

At the end of November, aviation was assigned a new and extremely important mission, namely, striking the transport aviation of the enemy. From then on, this mission occupied the center of attention right up to the moment of the complete liquidation of the Stalingrad group of the enemy.

During November we did not observe any intense activity on the part of enemy transport aviation, but beginning with November 26–27, we observed repeated flights of transport planes. Evidently then the exhaustion of the supplies of the encircled troops had proceeded rather quickly. Hence, in the first days of December, the transport aviation of the enemy began to operate with exceptional intensity, and after December 19, we observed up to 250 to 300 flights of transport planes a day.

By this time, our reconnaissance learned that the new 20th, 21st, and 23rd Groups of transport aviation, gathered from flying schools in the interior of Germany, had appeared in the Stalingrad direction. This was in addition to the 406th and 700th Groups of transport aviation and three squadrons of special assignment previously operating there. In accordance with the data of air reconnaissance and the statements of prisoners of war, as many as 250 planes were based on the single airdrome of Tatsinskaia on December 12, the absolute majority of which were of the JU-52 type.

In the first period (the end of November and the beginning of December), the conditions for the operation of the transport aviation of the enemy were entirely favorable. During this time, the Germans had at their disposal an extensive airdrome network, both in the immediate neighborhood of the encircled group (airdromes: Morozovskii, Tatsinskaia, Chernyshevskaia, Zimovniki, Salsk) and within the ring of encirclement (airdromes: Stalingrad, Pitomnik, Gumrak, Basargino, Bolshaia Rossoshka, Voroponovo). In addition to this, the small depth of the battle zone (40 to 60 kilometers) of our troops encircling the enemy made possible sudden flights of enemy airplanes in both directions. This made it very difficult for us to carry on combat with enemy transport aviation, which in single planes and in small groups of two to three planes made flights by day at altitudes of 1,500 to 3,000 meters without the cover of fighter planes.

The base airdromes for the landing of every transport plane were Bolshaia Rossoshka, Pitomnik, and Gumrak. These airdromes were covered by antiaircraft artillery, searchlights, and fighter planes. But in order to decrease the losses resulting from our aviation, the enemy prepared in the ring of encirclement many additional landing strips, which was facilitated to a great degree by the level relief of the locality.

Beginning December 1, the fight against enemy transport aviation became one of the basic missions of the 8th and 16th Air Armies, the first operating in the area south and southwest and the latter operating north and northwest of the encircled enemy troops. We may judge from the following figures just how important we considered the fight against enemy transport planes: out of the 4,125 sorties flown by the 16th Air Army in December, a total of 326 sorties were flown against troops, and the rest were conducted to fight enemy airplanes, with 1,021 sorties being flown against airdromes.

In the fight against enemy transport, we used all of our types of airplanes. By patrolling over our territory, over the ring of encirclement on the probable flight courses of enemy planes, and flights of airplanes, fighter planes destroyed enemy aviation in the air. Combat–support planes and day bombers, by systematic attacks against the airdromes in the ring of encirclement (Bolshaia Rossoshka, Pitomnik, Gumrak, and others), destroyed enemy airplanes on the ground, and at night our bombers blocked those airdromes of the enemy on which every transport plane made its landings.

In order to increase the effectiveness of its missions, the 8th Air Army, on November 30, 1942, rebased the 235th Fighter Plane Division and a part of the combat–support planes of the 226th Ground Attack Division on airdromes west of the Volga. Somewhat later, for this same purpose, we rebased the 220th and 283rd Fighter Divisions of the 16th Air Army on the airdromes of Peskovatka, Illarionovskii, and Buzinovka (west of the encircled troops of the enemy).

During the very first days of the operations of our aviation against enemy air transport, we obtained excellent results.[14] Between November 30 and December 1, the 16th Air Army destroyed in the ring of encirclement 28 enemy planes, the overwhelming majority of which were transport planes (JU-52). Subsequently, the number of destroyed planes increased rapidly, for example, on December 10–11, the 16th Air Army destroyed 89 enemy planes.

The great losses in airplanes forced the enemy to change the tactical methods of work of their transport aviation: instead of flights of single planes and of small groups without fighters, the enemy began to employ flights of rather large groups of airplanes, covering them with fighter planes (four to six Me-109s). In order to scatter the attention of our fighter planes and in this way to decrease their losses, the Germans began to make extensive use of flights of large groups of airplanes in waves, flying from various directions simultaneously. Usually such a "star raid" started with the flight of two or three JU-52s under cover of fighter planes, in a direction away from the intended direction of flight of the main group of transport planes.

But even this trick did not produce for the enemy the effects that they counted on. Our extensively developed radio network for warning and guiding enabled us to warn our aviation in due time of the appearance of enemy airplanes from whatever direction they might come and, if necessary, to redirect the airplanes for action where they were needed.

In addition to this, in the organization of combat with enemy transport planes, we planned for the destruction of airplanes not only on the approaches to the area of encirclement but also in the ring of encirclement itself. Our systematic aviation attacks against airdromes and blocking airdromes by day and by night created conditions under which enemy airplanes _in_ the ring of encirclement suffered heavier losses than those on the approach to it.

The counteraction to our aviation operation against the ring of encirclement was carried out chiefly by antiaircraft artillery during the first days of the operation of fighter planes. We should mention the fact that the 20 Me-109 airplanes based in the encirclement ring displayed great activity and interfered with the action of our aviation in the area of encirclement. From daylight until nightfall enemy fighter planes, flying in pairs, carried out a constant patrol of the area of encirclement; antiaircraft artillery, with its fire, directed the fighter planes to our planes. However, since this enemy fighter-plane group did not receive any replacements, it did not last long; fairly soon it was almost completely destroyed by our fighter planes.

After losing a considerable part of his transport airplanes and encountering ever-increasing resistance from our aviation, the enemy was forced in the middle of December to give up flights in the daytime and began to fly at night. The lack of transport aviation and the critical necessity of furnishing supplies to the encircled troops forced the enemy to use combat aviation (Ju-88 and He-111 airplanes) as transport planes. Our aviation attacks against the airdromes in the ring of encirclement inflicted such heavy losses upon the enemy that he gave up landing airplanes for unloading freight and began to release the freight by parachutes.

The enemy's employment of combat planes as a means of transport complicated somewhat our combat operations against these planes, but it did not lower their effectiveness. We kept operations on a high level by improving the organization of combat against transport aviation; by reinforcing the action of the fighter "hunter" planes, the widening of the radio network for warning and guiding, and the improvement of its work; and by the planning of an almost uninterrupted (by day and by night) blocking of the most important airdromes of the enemy's transport aviation.

The passing to the offensive on December 16 of the troops of our Southwestern Front and the development of a counteroffensive by the troops of the South Front (in the Kotelnikovo direction) in the second half of December deprived the enemy of a network of excellent airdromes—Morozovsk, Tatsinskaia, Salsk, Tormosin, and Verkhne-Kurmoiarskii—and forced him to rebase his aviation on the airdromes of Novocherkassk, Rostov and Stalino. This circumstance prevented the enemy from covering his transport planes with fighter planes and greatly improved for us the conditions for preventing the supplying of the encircled enemy troops at Stalingrad by air. Despite the increased difficulties, the transport planes continued to fly at night to Stalingrad, and for this purpose the Germans used the best crews from transport lines within the country, in particular from the Berlin–Paris line, and transferred them to the Stalingrad direction.

But even all of these measures could not save the encircled group of the enemy, because our aviation continued to destroy their airplanes on the ground and in the air at a steady rate. With the units of the 8th and 16th Air Armies, we destroyed in the air in December 313 enemy airplanes (of which 152 were Ju-52s) and destroyed or damaged about 440 on the airdromes.[15]

Despite the intensive work of our aviation in interrupting supplies to the encircled troops of the enemy, his transport aviation still succeeded in penetrating the area of encirclement, chiefly at night and when the weather was bad. But these were either single planes or small groups, which were not able to give much assistance to the several hundred-thousand encircled enemy troops. The disorganization of air transport was such that as early as December the losses among the enemy troops at Stalingrad as a result of hunger and cold amounted to 400 or 500 soldiers and officers a day.

In January, the fight against enemy transport planes continued with unabated effort. Even in the period of our troops' general offensive to liquidate the encircled enemy group, in which the 16th Air Army operating at Stalingrad also participated actively, the fight against German transport planes did not weaken. The great intensity of the action of our aviation for the destruction of enemy transport planes can be seen from the following table:

Date Airdromes of the enemy	4–5	7	JANUARY 1943 11	13–14	15–16 Number of airplane sorties for attacks on enemy airdromes	17–18	19–20	21	31	TOTAL
Bolshaia Rossosska	39	8	25	60	160	—	22	—	—	314
Gumrak	8	—	—	—	—	90	15	15	—	128
Pitomnik	—	—	35	43	—	—	—	—	—	78
Tsentral	—	—	—	—	—	—	—	—	—	—
Stalingradii	—	—	—	—	—	12	5	—	51	68
Drevnil Val	—	—	—	—	—	—	20	10	—	30
Stalingrad	—	—	—	—	—	—	—	—	20	20
Total	47	8	60	103	160	102	62	25	71	638

In addition to operations against airdromes from January 10–31, we carried out 1,186 airplane sorties for the destruction of enemy airplanes in the air.

We should note that with the beginning of the general offensive of our troops the effectiveness of the action of aviation increased considerably; for example, in 15 days (from December 25, 1942–January 9, 1943), we shot down 40 enemy airplanes and destroyed 87 on airdromes, while in seven days (from January 10–16), we destroyed almost the same number of enemy airplanes, or 41 shot down and 61 destroyed on airdromes.

The increase in the effectiveness of the action of our aviation in this period is explained by the improvement in all organizations of combat against enemy transport aviation and the introduction of corrections in the system of combat against enemy transport aviation. The latter expressed itself in the form of a more precise organization of cooperation between the various means of combat. All the territory over which active fighting took place was divided up into zones: an outside zone with destruction of enemy aviation in the air, a zone of fire of antiaircraft artillery and machine guns; and an inside zone with destruction of enemy aviation on airdromes in the ring of encirclement in the air.[16]

The outside zone for the destruction of airplanes in the air, with a width of 50 to 60 kilometers, embraced the area of encirclement and was the basic zone of operation of our fighter aviation for the destruction of German transport planes on the approaches to the ring of encirclement. The zone was broken into several sectors. In each sector there were fighter planes, the number of which was determined by the importance of the sector in the given concrete situation; the work of the fighter planes was directed by a reliable commander.

For the purpose of giving timely warning of the flight of enemy planes and for directing fighter planes to them, each sector had a basic and a supplementary radio network. The radio stations were on the probable flight courses of enemy planes, the radio stations of the basic network being placed closer to the outside edge of the sector and the radio stations of the supplementary network in the immediate neighborhood of the ring of encirclement. The work of the radio stations was carried on by means of a microphone, with clear text, on the same wavelength as that of the fighter planes.

The basic methods of action of fighter planes in the outside zone of destruction were patrolling on the probable direction of flight of enemy planes and sorties of duty fighter planes for interception upon receipt of radio warning signals. When patrolling fighter planes encountered a large group of transport planes under the cover of enemy fighter planes, they radioed the duty fighter planes on the airdromes for support in the area of encounter.

In the zone having a width of 8 to 10 kilometers around the ring of encirclement, enemy planes were destroyed by the fire of antiaircraft artillery and machine guns. Upon the appearance of fighter planes and the beginning of their attack, the fire of the antiaircraft guns was stopped. The fire of the antiaircraft artillery was also used as a means for guiding the fighter planes to the airplanes of the enemy. The notice of the approach of enemy planes was given by the radio warning network.

The inside zone for the destruction of aviation on the airdromes and in the air was the area occupied directly by the encircled troops of the enemy. In this area (or zone) all kinds of aviation operated—fighter planes, combat–support planes, and night bombers. Their methods of work were the following: to blocking the airdromes of transport aviation and destruction of their airplanes by means of combat–support planes and bombers. For this purpose, there were assigned in the daytime special groups of fighter planes for blocking the enemy airdrome. These fighter planes worked in pairs and were constantly over the area where the transport planes landed; upon discovery of enemy airplanes, they attacked them on the ground and in the air, chiefly the latter. Upon the discovery of the landing of a group of transport planes, one radioed for the combat–support planes and the bombers, which were constantly in state of readiness No. 2. The non-blocked airdromes and the landing strips in the area of encirclement of the enemy were under constant observation of our scouts, which, upon discovery of the landing of airplanes, also called our combat–support planes by radio.

Action at night was carried on by IL-2 and U-2 airplanes, chiefly the latter, with the mission of preventing landings and take offs of enemy planes at night in the area of encirclement. Their methods of work were the same as in the daytime, with the only difference being that upon discovery of enemy planes on the airdromes they attacked the planes themselves without calling their own aviation.

The success of the actions of our airplanes owed a great deal to the widely deployed and well-planned radio network for warning and observation and to the constant observation from the air of the enemy airdromes in the ring of encirclement. As a result of these measures, the absolute majority of the sorties of our airplanes were carried out not for a chance encounter with enemy planes but for an actual encounter.

The following is a summary of the combats with enemy transport planes: from November 23, 1942–February 2, 1943, our aviation shot down in air battles 467 enemy airplanes (of these, 250 JU-52s) and destroyed and damaged up to 590 airplanes on airdromes. It is characteristic to note that when our troops occupied the airdromes of Pitomnik and Bolshaia Rossoshka, we found on them 250 enemy airplanes destroyed or damaged by the attacks of our aviation from the air.

Hence, by the actions of our 16th and 18th Air Armies, we cut off the supplies by air to the encircled German troops at Stalingrad. This was one of the very important prerequisites for the successful conclusion of the complete liquidation of this enemy group.

The fight against German transport aviation was important, but it was not the only mission of our aviation in the course of all the period of defeating and liquidating the Stalingrad group. Parallel with the execution of this work, aviation also carried out other missions for supporting its troops.

These are shown in the following table.

From the table we can see that in this period our aviation devoted a great deal of attention to action against enemy troops in addition to action against enemy transport planes.

Missions carried out	December 1942	January 1943	Total
	Airplane Sorties		
Attacks against enemy troops	1,838	4,483	6,321
Destruction of enemy planes	4,147	2,389	6,536
Of these:			
Attacking airdromes	2,856	638	3,494
Patrolling	273	359	632
Intercepting airplanes	468	111	579
Sweeping flights	550	338	888
Blocking airdromes	—	933	933
Covering our troops	252	—	252
Accompanying combat–support planes and bombers	1,757	661	2,418
Reconnaissance	1,505	373	1,878
Action against railways	204	—	204
Other missions	756	494	1,250
Total	10,459	8,400	18,859

The operations of aviation against enemy troops were not carried out uniformly during this period; they were most active during the period of intense operations of our ground troops. These periods were the fighting of the troops of the Southern Front against the offensive of the Kotelnikovo group and the subsequent smashing of this group (from December 12–29, 1942) and the offensive of the Don Front for the purpose of liquidating the enemy encircled at Stalingrad (from January 2–February 2, 1943).

The Operation of Aviation in the Period of Combat with the Kotelnikovo Group of the Enemy

The enemy offensive starting December 12, 1942, from the area of Kotelnikovo, for the purpose of joining up with the encircled group was not unexpected at our command. Air reconnaissance discovered the approach and the concentration of enemy tanks and motorized columns a long time before the beginning of the enemy offensive. This made it possible to undertake timely countermeasures, which subsequently led to the defeat of the Kotelnikovo group of the enemy.

The offensive of the enemy from the area of Kotelnikovo was started in the period of the hardest fighting against enemy transport aviation. Hence, the 8th Air Army of the South Front, up to December 17, 1942, was obliged with a part of its forces, jointly with the 16th Air Army, to fight enemy transport planes in the area of Stalingrad.

Hence, the active operation of our aviation started in the period of the most intense fighting of the ground troops. Before this time, there operated on the Kotelnikovo direction only day bombers and the part of fighter planes that destroyed enemy troops at places of concentration and on the approaches and covered the concentration of our own troops for counterattacks.

The air situation was favorable for our aviation. The aviation of the enemy operated actively over the battlefield only in the first days of the offensive of the troops; in the subsequent period, however, the enemy was forced to shift a considerable part of his combat planes to the transportation of military supplies and food for the encircled group. The numerical ratio of forces in fighter planes 1:2 and in bombers and combat–support planes, 1.0:1.5, both in our favor.

However, the tactical work of our aviation in the course of all this period was carried out under difficult conditions due to the bad weather and the basing of the main part of our planes at a great distance from our operating troops (east of the Volga River). It was not possible to rebase our planes on the west bank of the Volga River because of the impossibility of supplying the air units with ammunition and fuel. The work of aviation became particularly complicated after the ground troops, having broken away enemy resistance, began to move forward impetuously. As early as December 27–28, the airdromes of our fighter planes and combat–support planes were at a distance of 150 to 200 kilometers from the ground troops.

The bad weather not only limited the operations of aviation, but sometimes made it almost impossible. For example, on the day of the counteroffensive of our troops in the Kotelnikovo direction (December 24, 1942), there were carried out only 27 airplane sorties.

Despite these difficult conditions, our airplanes, beginning December 17, operated very actively. During the December 17–29, 1942, they carried out 3,783 sorties, over 1,000 of which were for attacking motorized–mechanized troops of the enemy on the battlefield.

In the course of defensive fighting in the Kotelnikovo direction and the counteroffensive of our troops in this same direction, the most important missions of aviation were:

● the destruction of the motorized–mechanized groups of the enemy on the battlefield in the decisive directions of operation of our troops;
● the covering of the concentration and combat operation of our mobile troops (4th Mechanized, 4th Cavalry, and 13th Mechanized Corps); and
● action against motor highways and railways on the sector of Gremia-chii, Kotelnikovo, and Duboskoe to prevent the bringing up of enemy reserves.

Among the tactical methods employed in this operation, we should mention the pairing of combat–support and fighter aviation divisions for a long period, based on airdromes located close to each other. This facilitated mutual agreement between the combat–support planes and the fighter planes, and the prolonged period of joint work helped them to gain a knowledge of each other's characteristics, due to which cooperation in flight hours became closer. This measure not only simplified the organization of covering of combat–support planes by the fighter planes, but it also greatly improved covering oneself in flight. When combat–support planes attacked a target covered by enemy fighter planes—in addition to detailing accompanying fighter planes—we practiced sending into the area of the target a group of "sweep" planes numbering six to eight planes. This group flew into the area of operation three to five minutes ahead of the combat–support planes and engaged the fighter planes of the enemy. In the absence of the latter, it took up a jump-off combat position in three tiers at altitudes of 500 to 1,000 meters.

The Action of Aviation in the Liquidation of the Encircled Enemy Group (January 10–February 2, 1943)

The operations were carried out with our aviation in complete control of the air. Counteraction came only from antiaircraft artillery, which also weakened toward January 25.

Toward the beginning of the operation, the 16th Air Army had up to 400 planes in flying condition, about 150 of which were fighter planes. All the aviation was available in the immediate neighborhood of the front line; as a rule, the fighter planes were based at a distance of 10 to 20 kilometers from the front line and the bombers at a distance of 70 to 100 kilometers. With all the units we had good wire and radio communications.

The plan of operation for the liquidation of the encircled enemy troops in the area of Stalingrad was based on the principal of close cooperation between ground units and aviation. For operational orientation, information concerning the situation on the ground and the organization of cooperation with the ground troops were sent in to all of the armies' representatives from the air formations cooperating with them.

At the command post of the ground army operating in the main direction, there was the deputy commander of the 16th Army who exercised direct control of the operations of the aviation in accordance with the circumstances and the requirements of the ground command.

On January 10, before the beginning of the offensive of the ground troops, we delivered some powerful attacks against the large staffs of the enemy for the purpose of breaking up his command. The following staffs were attacked: the staff of the 3rd Army Corp in Bolshaia Rossoshka; the staff of the 14th Panzer Corps in Novo-Alekseevskii; and the staff of the 60th Motorized Division in Baburkin. At the beginning of the offensive, attacks were made against the strong points, personnel, and equipment of the enemy on the mainline of defense on the sector of Zapadnovka, Malaia Rossoshka, Baburkin, and Novo-Alekseevskii.

A characteristic feature of the operations of aviation throughout the time of liquidation of the Stalingrad group of the enemy was the uninterrupted attacks over a long period against enemy troops on the battlefield and especially against enemy strongholds and centers of resistance. The most important strong points were subjected to continued air attacks over a period of several days. For example, the strong points of Bolshaia Rossoshka Malaia Rossoshka were subjected to attack from January 10–15, Pitomnik from January 11–15. The intensity of the attacks was also very great; for example, the Stalingrad tractor plant, which had been converted by the Germans into a highly resistant strong point, was attacked from the air from January 26–31. During this period, we made 912 airplane sorties against it and released about 400 tons of bombs. We can readily understand that such an attack could not fail to break the resistance of the troops in it.

In the period of operations for the liquidation of the encircled German 6th Army, the 16th Air Army continued its intense activity against the transport aviation of the enemy. However, the chief task in this period was cooperation with ground troops. Of the 7,920 sorties carried out during the time of the operations (January 10–31), 4,427 sorties were against the troops of the enemy.

During the actions, for the most part over the battlefield, the chief concern of aviation was close cooperation with the ground troops. This was provided by the presence in the formations and units of combined arms of representatives from the air staffs with signal communication means, well-planned signal cooperation, basing of airplanes close to the front line, and by permanent-duty airplanes on the airdromes ready to take off upon call. As a result of these measures, the airplanes cooperating with the ground troops appeared over the battlefield at the proper time and with their fire neutralized the fire points interfering with the movement of the infantry.

In addition to action over the battlefield, aviation was very effective in the depth of the area of the encircled enemy troops. The main objectives of aviation in the depth of the enemy disposition were the concentrations of troops and material. Attacks against them were made not only for the purpose of destroying them but also for the purpose of preventing any maneuver of the same. By constant reconnaissance in the depths of the area of encirclement, we discovered in due time the concentrations of enemy troops and their displacement and at the same time made possible the carrying out of this mission.

Good planning of command made the employment of aviation very effective. In accordance with the data of the staff of the 16th Air Army for the period of preparation and the carrying out of the operations of aviation, this Air Army destroyed or disabled the following: up to 50 tanks, 1,200 motor vehicles, 30 guns, 10 mortars, 48 antiaircraft gun positions, 3 searchlights, 4 railway cars, and 20 warehouses (of these 4 had ammunition). The 16th Air Army also demolished 18 earth-and-timber pillboxes, neutralized the fire of 30 artillery and mortar batteries, and started up to 300 fires. In addition to this, it killed a large number of soldiers and officers of the enemy. The great effectiveness of the action of aviation was confirmed by the statements of German prisoners of war. Hence, in the course of all the operations, by destroying enemy personnel and material, demolishing their main strong points, and neutralizing their fire systems on all the lines of resistance, aviation rendered great assistance to the ground troops in the liquidation of the 6th German Army surrounded in Stalingrad.

The commanders of troops of combined arms had high praise for the work of our aviation. The command of the 21st Army said after the operation, "In its successful advance and excellent execution of its mission on its sector for the smashing of the enemy group encircled at Stalingrad, the 21st Army owes a great deal to the aviation cooperating with it." Similar statements concerning the operation of aviation were made by the commanders of the 66th, 65th, and 57th Armies.

The gratitude of the troops constitute a high praise for aviation and an assurance of further successes in joint operations.

Editor's Notes

1. The first Air Army was created on May 5, 1942. The intent of *Stavka* was to increase the striking power of its air units through a greater concentration of air assets. Aviation units assigned to combat duty in these formations were designated "Air (*Vozdushnaia*) Armies." Reserve units were designated as "Aviation (*Aviatsionaia*) Armies" while under *Stavka* control. By December, there were 12 Air Armies. In July, the 8th Air Army possessed about 300 aircraft. To this total could be added 150 to 200 bombers of the Long-Range Aviation and 60 *PVO* fighters. During August, the 16th Air Army was added, which possessed 110 to 180 aircraft. See I. Timokhovich, *Operativnoe iskusstvo sovetskikh VVS v Velikoi Otechestvennoi Voine* (Moscow: *Voenizdat*, 1976), p. 34. (Hereafter, Timokhovich).

2. German losses rendered this figure an abstraction. In fact, along the entire front from Norway to the Caucasus, there were only 1,134 operational aircraft on November 6, 1942. In the south, the situation was accordingly lower. On October 20, total operational strength was only 594 aircraft out of the 974 theoretically available. See *Kriegstagebuch des Oberkommando der Wehrmacht 1942, Teilband II*, pp. 912 and 1321. These figures included Allied aircraft.

3. Throughout 1942, the *Luftwaffe* continued to experience low in-commission rates, and as a result, the total German air strength remained ominously low given its many tasks. From a 39 percent in-commission rate in January 1942, it rose to 69 percent by June. However, the heavy demands of the fall and winter kept the number below this total for the rest of the year. See W. Murray, *Luftwaffe* (Baltimore: The Nautical and Aviation Publishing Co., 1985), pp. 136–37. (Hereafter, Murray).

4. Check this statement against the image of Soviet air operations alluded to in the official *Soviet History of the Red Air Force* on pages 105 and 109. See Ray Wagner, ed., *The Soviet Air Force in World War II* translated (New York: Doubleday & Co., 1973). Also see the

statements presented in G. Skorikov, "Boevoe primenenie Voenno-Vozhushnykh Sil," *Voenno istoricheskii zhurnal* No. 11, 1982. Measurements are noted but only in terms of missions flown or tonnage delivered. Nowhere in these authoritative studies do such unequivocal statements appear as in this document.

5. The Soviet emphasis on night action was not the virtue it appears in contemporary accounts. As this chapter makes clear, the necessity for night sorties rested more on German dominance of the daylight sky than on any advantage to the use of primitive aircraft conducting inaccurate night missions.

6. More is at work here than fewer Soviet aircraft. German tactical flexibility and the maintenance of the initiative by the *Wehrmacht* put Soviet air units at a distinct disadvantage. However, the appearance of radio communications provided the Red Air Force with much needed relief. This tactic had already been in use in other sectors of the front. See M. Kozhevnikov, *The Command and Staff of the Soviet Army Air Force in the Great Patriotic War 1941–1945* trans. (Washington, D.C. Government Printing Office, 1985) pp. 90 and 92. (Hereafter, Kozhevnikov). Based on past experience, a system of radio communications and ground observers was created for the 16th Air Army in September 1942.

7. This low total reveals two concurrent facts. First, the heavy strain on continuous operations coupled to the poor Soviet logistical support rendered many aircraft out of action. However, the Soviet figure of 50 percent is not much lower than the totals for the *Luftwaffe* as noted in footnotes two and three. Second, the availability of Soviet reserves and their lack of appearance at this time once again demonstrates *Stavka's* careful conservation of its resources. Interestingly, *Velakaia pobeda na Volge* p. 218, Table 12, lists 448 aircraft on the Stalingrad direction at the beginning of October.

8. There were only 62 operational *Luftwaffe* destroyer-type aircraft available on September 20 for the entire southern area of the front. A well-developed night fighter program existed in the *Luftwaffe*, but it was largely confined to the defense of the Reich.

9. This low kill ratio confirms the lack of *Luftwaffe* effort against the Soviet night raids. The U-2, being a biplane, was simply too difficult to track and destroy. It was also more of a nuisance than a weapon. Certainly *Luftwaffe* totals against western night intruders reveals a much better record of inflicting losses.

10. This was a lesson the *Luftwaffe* learned very well against Great Britain in 1940.

11. This is not a Lend-Lease item and does not refer to the Royal Air Force. The RAF radio was developed and adapted in 1939 for use at Army and Front levels.

12. The Soviet Union claims 1,400 German combat/transport aircraft were destroyed in air/ground engagements. *IVMV* vol. 5, p. 193. Murray cites different figures, albeit for the entire front.

GERMAN LOSSES JUNE 1942–JANUARY 1943

June	July	August	September	October	November	December	January
350	438	436	332	200	224	408	482

Source: Tables 25, p. 113, and 30, p. 144.

13. The commanders were 16th Air Army, Major General of Aviation S. I, Rudenko; 17th Air Army, Major General of Aviation S. A. Krasovskii; and the 8th Air Army, Major General of Aviation T. T. Khruskin. Histories of these units may be found in *Shestnadsataia vozdushnaia* (Moscow: *Voenizdat*, 1973); N. Skomorokhov, *17-ia Vozdushaia armiia v boiakh ot Stalingrada do veny* (Moscow: *Voenizdat*, 1977); and V. A. Gubin, *Vos'maia vozdushnaia* (Moscow: *Voenizdat*, 1986). A fourth Air Army, the 2nd, was attached to the Voronezh Front under the command of Major General of Aviation K. N. Smirnov and supported the counteroffensive.

14. At first, Soviet aircraft were less than successful. Novikov sent the following Directive to 16th and 8th Air Armies:

> Despite the fact that in the vicinity of the encircled enemy our aircraft have complete supremacy in the air, enemy transport planes are breaking through and landing at airfields inside the pocket. . . . Destruction of enemy transport aircraft is to be considered the main priority.

See S. Rudenko, "Above the Volga Stronghold," in *200 Days of Fire* (Moscow: Progress Publishers, 1970), p. 137.

15. Compare to 12. German records acknowledge the loss of 495 transport aircraft by February 3, 1943. See Murray, p. 150. Compare this statement to other reports in this book on Soviet tank and cavalry operations. Note Kozhevnikov's comments (pp. 100–102) about air supremacy being obtained and held after the initiation of the counterattack.

16. See Timokhovich, pp. 175–79.

Soviet Military engineers played a vital role in the battle for Stalingrad. During the defensive fighting, they constructed the enormous concentric defense lines that encompassed the positions between the Don and the Volga rivers. During the Red Army's counteroffensive, they achieved significant results in the preparation and execution of the encirclement and destruction of the German 6th Army. The detailed discussion of problems and concepts related to crossing and maintaining troops across a water barrier reflects the Stavka's *recognition that the issue would recur—Ed.*

11

Adequate Provision of Engineer Means in the Operations of the Stalingrad Front

Missions and Plans for Providing Adequate Engineer Works

The mission of the main forces of the front was to break through the enemy defense line and, jointly with the units of the Southwestern and Don Fronts, to encircle and destroy the Stalingrad group of Germans. In accordance with this, the engineer troops of the Stalingrad Front had to solve a number of missions involving a great deal of responsibility.[1]

In the preparatory period (from November 1–19, 1942) their missions were:

● to make possible an uninterrupted crossing of the troops and of all the necessary materials and technical equipment to be used in the offensive operations;
● to carry out a careful engineering reconnaissance of the forward edge and depths of the defenses of the enemy in the area of breakthrough;

258

- to organize the areas of the concentration of troops before the crossing,
- to restore, reinforce, or construct bridges anew;
- to assist the troops in occupying the areas of concentration after the crossing;
- to prepare the jump-off position for the attack of the rifle troops and artillery; to clear of mines the area before the main line of defense;
- to provide a supply of water for the troops operating in the desert steppes on the right bank of the lower Volga.

In the period of operations (November 20–December 5, 1942) their mission was to make an engineering breach: to determine and prepare passageways for the movement of the combat formations of rifle troops, tanks, and artillery through the main line of defense of the enemy in the period of the attack;

- to accompany the troops into the depths during the attack; and
- to protect reserves crossing the Volga and make possible an uninterrupted flow of supplies for the field forces.

Ten days preceding the beginning of the offensive the engineers worked out a plan for the necessary work for each army and presented it to the responsible authorities eight days before the beginning of the offensive. The engineer plans for the crossing were worked out much earlier and were turned over to the responsible authorities 20 days before the beginning of the operation.

The plan for the engineering works of the Front called for the execution of the following basic measures. For crossings the plan fixed the order of movement of the troops armament, ammunition, and food and gave the following for the crossing from the east bank of the Volga River to the west bank:

Name of the loads	In preparatory period	In operational period	Total
Men	135,000	70,000	205,000
Tanks	430	120	550
Motor vehicles	10,000	2,500	12,500
Guns	500	200	700
Horses	3,000	1,200	4,200
Vehicles	4,500	600	5,100
Ammunition (tons)	6,000	6,000	12,000
Food (tons)	4,000	4,000	8,000

In accordance with the established order for the movement of troops and their operational assignment, nine crossing sectors were fixed, three of which were basic sectors: for the *64th Army*, Lesobaza, Shchuche; for the *57th Army*, Tatianka, Svetlii and for the *51st Army*, Kenennyi Iar, Solodniki.

In view of the broad scope of the approaching crossing work and the difficulties due to the drifting ice and the stoppage of ice floes, the staff of the engineer troops of the Front worked out beforehand a plan for providing all the crossings with floating equipment, and outlined a number of measures for assuring normal conditions of operation.

For this purpose and in accordance with the orders of the Military Soviet of the Front, there were detailed from the system of departmental river organizations of the Volga basin 59 power-driven and nonpower-driven vessels: two icebreakers with a total of 1,600 horsepower; 25 tugboats with a total of 7,130 indicated horsepower; three passenger boats (560 indicated horsepower); one ferryboat (240 indicated horsepower); and 28 nonself-propelled vessels with a load capacity of 5,100 tons.

The Department of River Steam Navigation was obliged to provide all the vessels with full crews, supply rigging, tackle, and spare screw propellers and organize repair shops. The administration of the rear of the Front was to provide these workshops with motor vehicle transport. From the military flotilla we planned to assign a diver station. The supplying of the crews of the vessels and repair shops with all kinds of supplies was to be a function of the military units maintaining the crossings.

In the working out of the plan of organizational measures for the crossings, the most critical problem was supplying the vessels with fuel. The total requirements in fuel for the vessels to be used were estimated at 118 tons per day, or 3,550 tons (178 2-axle tanker cars) per month. The supplying of such a large quantity of fuel with the shortage of motor vehicles transport was very difficult; hence, the staff of the engineer troops of the Front took steps to find fuel in the immediate area. Over a period of several days a careful investigation was made of all sunken tanker vessels and vessels that had run aground. As a result, we discovered four half-submerged barges with supplies of fuel amounting to 6,000 tons. The vessels were assigned to these improvised "bases" for supplies.

When the ice began to drift, the supplying of the vessels with fuel became very complicated, because some of them failed to accomplish the trip against the current in order to get the fuel. On some occasions the vessels spent two days on such a trip, through stretches with big ice floes. In view of this, it was necessary to plan to transport the fuel by tank trucks. We organized several of such columns, but even these could not supply all the fuel needed.

In the way of engineer reconnaissance, the plan called for the following:

1. To carry out an engineer reconnaissance in the main directions of 62 kilometers of the main line of resistance to an average of 10 kilometers into the depth of the enemy defenses and to organize on this stretch 53 observation points and posts; and

2. To organize 25 engineer–reconnaissance groups and to plan jointly with the cavalry, tanks, and motorized units up to 25 deep raids into the rear of the enemy for the purpose of reconnoitering their rear lines and system of defenses.

For the covering of the areas of concentration of our troops, plans were made to provide mine reinforcements for the nine antitank centers, to lay 15 flank and switch mine fields, and to reinforce all of the existing mine fields along the main line of resistance on the sectors where the enemy was most likely to strike.

In mine clearing, the plan provided for the making of 70 passageways in our own mine fields by taking up 12,500 mines of various systems and making 38 passageways through the main line of resistance of the enemy over a total of 22 kilometers of front. For passage of tanks, artillery, and other heavy loads on the sector of the 57th Army, the plan provided for the construction of five bridges and 12 grade crossings over railway lines.

On the waterless steppes where the troops of the Stalingrad Front operated, the water supply was a very important factor in determining the combat ability of the troops. The left wing and the 28th Army, in particular, were in a serious situation. The minimum water requirements of this Army on November 1, 1942, were estimated at about 2,000 cubic meters per day. The amount supplied by all the sources on this same date amounted to about 600 cubic meters. To compensate for this water shortage, the plan provided for digging 45 new wells in the zone of the 28th and 51st Armies and the restoration of six old sources of water. In addition to this, plans were made for the restoration of wells in the towns and villages captured from the enemy.

On the whole, the plan was drawn up and presented to the troops in due time. It took into account all of the basic problems of providing adequate engineering means both in the preparatory period of the Front operations and in the period of their execution. The plan gave most consideration to problems of river crossings, since they were the most important in the operations and the most difficult to solve. The preparation of the areas of the crossings and distribution of the crossing equipment at them was carried out in accordance with the missions of the troops.

The Distribution of Forces and Means

For accomplishing this engineering plan in time, we made the proper disposition of the engineer forces of the Front. From the available forces, the following were assigned 38 battalions and three independent companies: For operating the crossings over the Volga, nine battalions (one motorized engineer and eight pontoon); for the work connected with mining/engineering entanglements, eight battalions; for the work in preparation for ice crossing, three engineer battalions; and for defensive work, 14 engineer battalions.

In reserve and for preparation of the personnel for participation in the breakthrough of enemy defenses there were left four battalions and three companies. Of the total number of engineer units of the Front, 15 battalions were assigned directly to the armies for preparatory work.[2]

At the beginning of the work of the preparatory period, the engineer units, especially the pontoon units, were far from being at full strength, having only 55 percent of the authorized personnel and only 26 percent of their motor vehicle strength. The combat engineer battalions of the divisions were in the same situation, if not worse, as to personnel strength and equipment.

The pontoon bridge units of the Front did not have any of such important engineering equipment as electric welding sets, compressors, wood saws, and diving gear. Without these, the work of lifting, repairing, and setting in place the crossing material for the construction of bridges was much slower.

Due to the losses in equipment in the preceding period, the pontoon units did not have sufficient equipment during preparation for the operation. The vessels detailed from the Department of River Transport Systems arrived very slowly. Before the beginning of the preparatory work for the crossings we received four self-propelled vessels out of the 31 called for in the plan and three nonself-propelled vessels out of the 28 which we were to have in accordance with the plan. It was only after insistent demands of the staff of the engineer troops that we suceeded in obtaining ten self-propelled vessels and one nonself-propelled, after a delay of 12 days. The motor cutters (VMK-70) made available by the Main Administration for Military Engineers did not arrive until after the crossing had been made.

To speed up the work, the staff of the engineer troops mobilized all crossing cutters, lighters, platforms, rafts, fishing boats, and pleasure boats to be found in the area of the crossing. Extensive use had to made of all these means for the arrangement of ferry crossings. In addition to this, we used armored cutters of the Volga Flotilla for the crossing of people, ammunition, and food.

The conditions under which the engineer units operated, especially at the crossings of the Volga, were exceptionally difficult. In view of the great amount of engineer work, it was not possible to place engineer units in reserve for replacements and training. All the engineer units of the Front had to be furnished replacements in the course of operations, while fighting was in progress, and these consisted of unprepared or poorly prepared personnel, the employment of which sometimes led to serious consequences. Thus, during the period of the operations, in one of the armies, 21.6 percent of the total losses of the engineer units were due to being blown up by their own mines in the demining of a jump-off line for the attack.

Work of the Engineer Units in the Preparatory Period of the Operation

Crossings

The crossings of the Volga River of troops, equipment, and ammunition, and food, as well as the evacuation of wounded and equipment to the rear, was done by ferrying on barges, pontoons, cutters, and rowboats. (The places of the crossings are given in map 8—Ed.) The crossings in the area of Stalingrad for the 62nd Army were under direct enemy bombardment by artillery, mortars, and small arms.

It was impossible to prepare bases and loading points on the left bank opposite the destination points of the vessels. The loading of the vessels was done upstream or downstream, lengthening in this way the trips of the vessels, lessening the turnover, and creating special difficulties at the beginning of the ice floes. Thus, with the approach of the enemy to the banks in the area of the "Krasnyi Oktiabr" and "Barrikadi," the use of moorings opposite the plants became difficult. By day the enemy subjected these moorings to intensive bombardment and to bombing from the air, and at night he kept them under artillery and mortar fire. The majority of the boats destroyed were knocked out at the wharves while loading and unloading and while moored in the daytime. Hence, from November 1 the main loading and unloading points and bases for the crossing equipment were moved to Verkhne Akhtuba, making the trip from 1.3 to 25 kilometers longer. Beginning on November 11, the ice floes obstructed the movement of vessels from Akhtuba and the base was transferred to Tumak.

From November 11 the crossings of the 62nd Army operated along the Tumak-Krasnyi Oktiabr march route for a distance of 22 kilometers and Tumak-Spartakovka for a distance of 32 kilometers. Throughout the month the vessels operating in the crossing of this Army were under flank artillery–mortar and machine gun fire of the enemy. Crossing was possible only at night. The supplying of replacements, ammunition, rations, and forage to one of the rifle divisions cut off from the 62nd Army was carried out along the Denezhnoi Volzhka, and in order to reach it, the armored cutters first had to neutralize the enemy fire positions on the banks.

Oftentimes the enemy released floating mines from airplanes. These

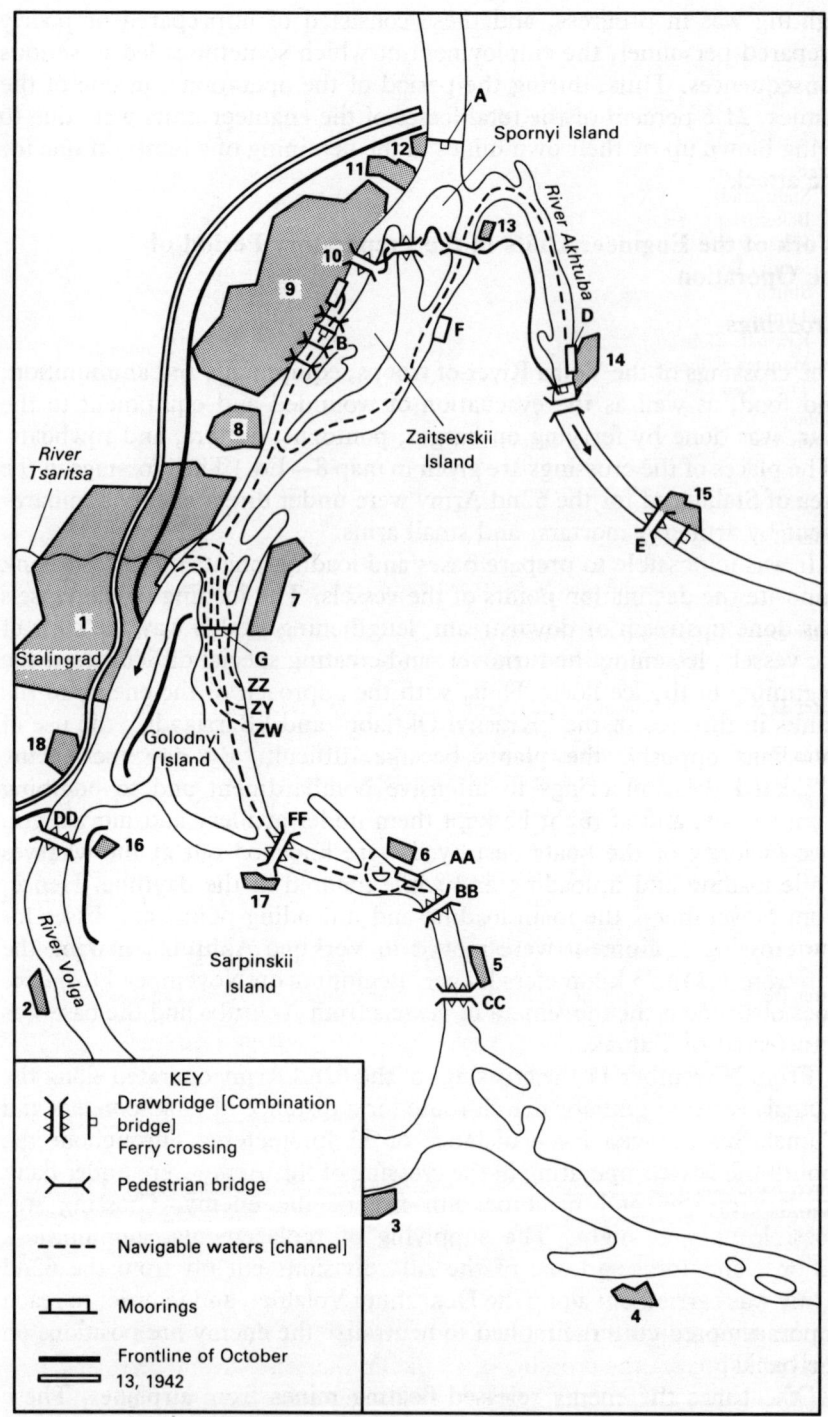

Spornyi Island

River Akhtuba

Zaitsevskii
Island

River
Tsaritsa

Stalingrad

Golodnyi
Island

Sarpinskii
Island

River Volga

KEY

Drawbridge [Combination
bridge]
Ferry crossing

Pedestrian bridge

Navigable waters [channel]

Moorings

Frontline of October
13, 1942

Source: Basic data from E.P. Egorov, ed. *Inzhenernye voiska Sovetskoi Armii, 1918-1945*
Moskva: Voenizdat, 1985. p. 362

Map Eight
"The Volga River Crossings in the Area of Stalingrad"

Cities
1. Stalingrad
2. Beketovka
3. Krasnoarmeisk
4. Svetlyi Iar
5. Shuch'e
6. Tumak
7. Krasnaia Sloboda
8. Mamaev Kurgan
9. The "Red October" Factory

10. The "Barrikady"
11. Spartakova
12. Rynok
13. Skudri
14. Verkhnaia Akhtuba
15. Srednaia Akhtuba
16. Boblyi
17. Kul'tbaza
18. Kuporosnoe

Captions

Letter A = Two ferryboats on barges and railroad crossing (until August 24, 1942). The combined length of the bridge is 1,408 meters (610 meters on pilings and master piers; 798 meters on floating supports of the DMP type). Constructed August 15 to 20, 1942; utilized until August 1942.

Letter B = Army crossing of 3 ferryboats of the N2P type, 3 type SP-19 ferryboats, 3 (towing launches) BMK type cutters, 1 launch, 6 barges, 6 tugs, 3 steamboats, a boat crossing, 3 footbridges on floats (as of August 23, 1942).

Letter D = Two N2P type ferryboats (each 16 tons), 1 ferryboat on barge (30 tons), and 1 floating bridge (8 tons). Left-bank moorage of the Army crossing. Length of the voyage is 12 km.

Letter E = A floating bridge on floats (8 tons), a wooden combination bridge with a drawbridge section (60 tons), 2 ferryboats (16 and 30 tons).

Letter F = The left bank moorage of the Army crossing. Length of the voyage is 5 km.

Letter G = Ferry crossing on pontoons of the type SP-19.

Letter ZZ = Central crossing number One, 2 barges, 2 tugs, 1 steamer. August 22 to September 13, 1942.

Letter ZY = Central crossing number two, 5 ferryboats of the type SP-19 and two cutters. August 25 to September 21, 1942.

Letter ZW = Special crossing for the wounded. Two river trams, 2 cutters. August 25 to September 20.

Letter AA = The left bank moorage of the Army crossing. Length of the voyage of 23 km.

Letter BB = Length of the bridge is 348 meters. September 21 to October 7, 1942.

Letter CC = Length of the bridge is 506 meters. September 21 to November 7, 1942.

Letter DD = The length of the bridge is 1,194 meters (1,159 meters is floating and 35 meters is trestle). Constructed August 31 through September 4, 1942, and utilized until September 8, 1942.

Letter FF = Length of the bridge is 505 meters (467 meters is floating and 38 meters of trestle for moorage). September 10 to September 20, 1942.

Source: Basic data from E.P. Egorov, ed. *Inzhenernye voiska Sovetskoi Armii, 1918-1945* Moskva: Voenizdat, 1985. p. 362.

temporarily paralyzed the movement of vessels on the separate sectors of the river. Thus, at the crossing of Kamennyi Iar on November 16 at 2:00 A.M. the barge "Kametka" struck a floating mine and was blown up;

between Kamennyi Iar and Solovniki the steamer "Altai" was also sunk by a mine. At the end of November, German aviation units mined the main stream of the Volga at Glukoi Farmstead, and this prevented the powerful ice breaker tug of the type "Dzerzhinskii" from reaching the Svetlyi Iar crossing.

The greatest hindrances to crossing were the hydrometeorological conditions; the most intense period of work coincided with the most unfavorable season of the year. At the beginning of November the level of water on the Volga rose sharply; thus, from November 1–6, the water rose to 50 centimeters and the total rise in the level of the water from the middle of October to November 13 was 196 to 220 centimeters.

Due to the rise in the level of the water, the trestles of the bridges and the moorings were flooded with water. Some of the landing places had to be raised as many as six times (the crossing at Tatianka). Since in the construction of the landing places we had not planned to raise them, this work required a great deal of time and labor. The heavy winds which we had in November made the mooring of vessels difficult and made impossible the trips of the small vessels and boats. The crossing work involved great difficulties and, at places, had to be interrupted.

On November 6–7 in the area of the Front, we had a rainy spell accompanied by winds. The waves in the river rose to 1.2 meters. On November 7, a big wave overflowed 60 pontoons of a bridge over the Sarpinskii River. The bridge was torn away from its anchorings and was carried by the current to a distance of 500 to 700 meters. This forced us to weaken the crossings of the 64th Army, by taking from them the steamer "Mikhail Vlasov."

The fall ice floes started November 10. The water continued to rise. The strong winds forced the ice first to the left side of the river and then to the right side. Near the banks there were formed unbroken belts of ice having a width of 100–600 meters and moving along slowly with the current. Under these conditions the crossing work was very complicated, because the small vessels were squeezed by the blocks of ice and had to select places that were free of ice. Crossings of small vessels were possible only in the daytime. The steering of the vessels, steamers, and boats required able and well-organized crews.

The solid belts of ice forming near the banks made it difficult for the vessels to approach the landing places. It took some of the vessels whole hours to make their way to the landing places, at times with the help of engineers who arranged passageways by blasting the ice. For these reasons the time required for a trip was greatly increased; for example, the barge "Zarnitsa," towed by the icebreaker "Dzerzhinskii" of 800 horsepower, made the trip in one day with great difficulty. Oftentimes a trip required 30 to 35 hours.

There were numerous cases in which small vessels were squeezed between the blocks of ice. Such vessels were released by stronger ones, or placed by them in a channel, the ice broken around them by hand and, farther away from the vessels, by means of explosive charges or hand grenades. The number of damaged vessels increased with the drifting of ice and this required additional work in repairing them.

Despite the unfavorable conditions (the drifting of ice, an insufficient number of crossing vessels of the ice-cutting type, a lack of pontoon units, and shelling by artillery, mortars, and light machine guns on the front of the 62nd Army), the engineer units coped with the task of preparing crossings during the preparatory period. All the units and freight arriving in November were crossed in time. During the period from November 1–20, 1942, the following were crossed:[3]

Load Designation	To Right Bank	To Left Bank	Total
Troops	114,476.0	38,109.0	149,585.0[1]
Wounded	—	10,970.0	10,970.0
Tanks	427.0	1.0	428.0
Guns	556.0	42.0	598.0
Motor vehicles	9,282.0	4,760.0	14,042.0
Tractors	136.0	51.0	187.0
Wagons	2,993.0	1,740.0	4,733.0
Horses	7,903.0	2,428.0	10,331.0
Ammunition (tons)	6,561.5	191.0	6,752.5
Class I supplies (tons)	3,759.7	190.0	3,949.7
Other loads (tons)	1,696.4	431.8	2,128.2
Large livestock	398.0	24.0	422.0
Small livestock	5,195.0	402.0	5,597.0

1. Did not total in original—Ed.

By practical work done during this period, we learned that even when there are difficult freezing conditions the use of standard and small crossing equipment, both towed and that operated by oars, is readily possible. The use of pontoons N2P or small metallic barges towed by motor launches proved to be very effective under these conditions.

Crossing in rowboats played a great part in supplying the 62nd Army and the groups cut off from it. Under the aimed fire of the enemy we crossed reinforcements, ammunition, and food. Large numbers of boats were used for the evacuation of the wounded. For example, on the night of November 28–29, 360 wounded soldiers were crossed to the left side in boats.

Engineer Reconnaissance

After we determined the direction of the main blows of our units, we organized in these areas observation posts and observation points. We arranged a total of 75 points. On an average on the shock sectors, depending upon the importance of the sector and the character of the locality, we had from one to three observation posts on each kilometer of the defense strip of the enemy. During the period when we carried on reconnaissance in force, the network of observation points on these sectors was increased two- or threefold.

The greater part of the observation points were located on the forward edge of our defenses. Each of them consisted of a heated blindage-dugout and a rifle pit with a cover for observation. Twenty-three observation points were equipped with optical devices, field glasses, and telescopes borrowed from the artillery men and the mortar crews. To each of these observation points, we assigned a group of three to four engineers under a junior officer or an educated private, whose duty it was to direct the group and keep a record of the observations. Observation was conducted on a 24-hour basis. The observation data were plotted on a map and presented each day to the unit engineer who summarized the data, put it on a general map, and in his turn gave the information each day to the higher engineer chief.   On the basis of the reconnaissance of the defense depths of the enemy from October 1–November 18, we organized and carried out in the main directions 27 engineer reconnaissance raids in the rear of the enemy for the purpose of determining their system, of antitank and antipersonnel obstacles and for finding the nature of the rear lines. On the sector of the 51st Army, this deep reconnaissance was carried out jointly with the cavalrymen and tankmen. In the area north of Stalingrad, we organized seven engineer reconnaissance groups, which went out under cover of night to a distance of five kilometers into the depths of the enemy defenses; camouflaged themselves there in haystacks, straw, or deep shell holes; and during the daytime carried on observation of the engineers and other activities of the enemy. One group consisting of three men, under the command of Sergeant Nikolenko, was within the defenses of the enemy for three days, moved over a front of 11 kilometers, and made a detailed field sketching of all the defense systems on this sector.

After the breakthrough of the enemy defenses by our troops and the capture of enemy defense lines, it was possible to study in more detail on the spot the system of engineer obstacles and the placing of the defensive installations and to compare them with the data of the engineer reconnaissance. For example, in the zone of the 57th Army, on the sector intended for the breakthrough, the engineer scouts of one Guards Division ascertained correctly the location of all the minefields of the enemy. With a fair degree of precision, the engineers on another sector ascertained the outline of the minefields over a stretch of 11 kilometers and the defensive installations consisting of barbed-wire entanglements over a stretch of 3 kilometers.

In the area of Khalkhuta, engineer reconnaissance of the 28th Army discovered a total of 37 trenches, 32 fire positions, and 10 mortar positions. In this area, we discovered a total of 45 defense positions out of a total of 102, which we found later in the system of enemy defenses. On this sector, we also discovered the location of three minefields; however, after the capture of the area, we found four additional fields not noticed by the scouts.

In the direction of the main blow of the 57th Army, in the area of Tundutovo and Balka-Tarnovaia, engineer reconnaissance obtained precise information as to the location of 35 fire positions for submachine guns, five earth-and-timber pillboxes, 12 mortar positions, and 28 artillery positions (of these five were concealed). We discovered 70 defense installations out of a total of 95 that we found to exist after the capture of the line. In these directions, at a depth of up to 3 kilometers, engineer reconnaissance correctly pointed out the defenses of the second echelon of the enemy.

Hence, in the main, engineer reconnaissance discovered the system of German–Rumanian defenses in the directions of the main attack, thus facilitating to a considerable extent the success of the breakthrough of the enemy defenses.

Among the weaknesses in the planning of engineer reconnaissance, we should mention the following: the absence of systematic duplication and checking of the reconnaissance data of the groups concerning the location of the minefields in the defense system of the enemy; and the failure to make use of such methods of reconnaissance as photography, and in certain cases, the interrogation of the prisoners.

Covering of the Areas of Concentration

From November 1–15, 1942, the Stalingrad Front carried out a regrouping and concentration of troops. The following arrived for reinforcement of the front: 15 rifle divisions, 11 tank brigades, five motorized rifle and mechanized brigades, and six cavalry regiments.

For concentrating these forces, we assigned 18 areas. In these areas, the engineer units of the front prepared large antitank obstacles. For example, in the zone of the 64th Army, on the sector of the Krasnoarmeisk–Beketovka railroad, we provided over a stretch of 8 kilometers a special fortification consisting of railway cars fastened together one after the other to form a powerful antitank barricade. In combination with minefields and natural obstacles, this barricade provided a reliable cover for the zone between the railroad and the Volga.

In the area of Kuporosnoe we constructed five antitank mine centers and three antitank switch minefields. In the zone of the 51st Army, in the area of Khargate and Zurgan, we constructed five antitank centers and laid eight switch minefields. On the sector of Malye Derbetyi, Zakharovo, and Khuslin–Ziur, we constructed three antitank centers and nine minefields in combination with barely perceptible obstacles.

In the zone of the front, we prepared minefield coverings for a total of 19 areas of troop concentration. We prepared 13 antitank centers and laid 23 minefields. We laid up to 10,000 mines of various kinds and put out more then 100 packages of barely perceptible obstacles, reinforced by landmines and booby traps. These measures enabled us to carry on concentration work without being disturbed.

For the passage of the troops from the areas of concentration to the jump-off lines, the engineer units of the Front carried out a great deal of work in the making of passageways through the engineers' mine obstacles. On the front, in the main directions, we made a total of 73 passageways having a width of 35 to 400 meters; we removed 12,405 mines of various kinds and more than 1,500 bottles with "KS" liquid fuel.

The making of passageways in minefields involved great difficulties. The work was carried out exclusively at night, oftentimes under the mortar and machine gun fire of the enemy. After rains came freezes. The upper, covering layer of earth was converted into a solid crust which froze to the mine covers. Due to the moisture the body of the "Iam-5" swelled and the cotter of the fuse froze to the side walls of the body of the mine, as a result of which the modern simplified fuses oftentimes could not be drawn out. The majority of mines had to be removed with the help of grappling-hooks or crowbars. The destruction of the mines by explosives was possible only during the time of artillery and mortar fire.

The passage of the troops to the jump-off lines, through the passageways made, was organized in the following manner. The commanders of the combat zones and the unit engineers received beforehand sketches of the minefield with the passageways indicated and got acquainted with them on the spot. For this purpose, we detailed as guides members of the engineer units who had a good knowledge of the location of the minefields and the passageways through them. From the concentration areas of the units to the minefields, we made some cross-country routes of march with signs every 50–100 meters. On these cross-country marches, we placed traffic regulation posts. The passageways themselves were marked out accurately and guarded by sentries.

The extraordinarily difficult conditions of work in the removal of mines required miners with great knowledge, skill, caution, and determination; qualities that many of them lacked because of their poor training. The unit engineers in particular were poorly trained. Despite these weaknesses, however, the engineer units of the front were still able, before the beginning of the offensive, to provide the troops the necessary safety measures.

Water Supply for the Troops

The left-flank armies operating in the Kalmuk Steppes encountered serious difficulties securing supplies of water.[4] Some of the units were at a distance of 20 to 25 kilometers from sources of water. The water in the "ponds" and lakes was salty or brackish and was unfit for drinking, preparing food, or for other purposes. The wells dug by the troops in several places, even to a depth of 8 meters, gave bitter, salt water. Deep bored wells could not be sunk because of the lack of the necessary engineering equipment. Hence, for the units far from a source of water, it was necessary to transport water in barrels and drums carried by horses or camels.

In order to provide a supply of water for the troops, we adopted the following measures:

● an inventory and investigation of all the sources of water in the armies was made;
● the army and Front engineer water supply companies began to dig wells in order to increase their supply of water;
● the 28th and 51st Armies, which were in the most unfavorable situation, were reinforced with Front specialists for the equipping of the water supply stations on the routes followed by the units; and
● in order to supply water for the military hospitals, the evacuation points, and the reserve regiments in the service area of the Front, we detailed one engineer water supply company, which, from November 1–20, repaired nine wells and dug 50 new ones.

The aforementioned measures, which were carried out by the engineer units of the Front, made it possible to supply the troops with water. The difficulty in carrying out this task was due not so much to the dryness of the region as it was to the fact that the Front was poorly supplied with the means of water supply. The Front and the army engineer water supply companies did not have their full strength of personnel and equipment. Experience has shown that in regard to the field conditions it is extremely important to have special units with equipment for boring deep wells and pumps and filters. It is also necessary to supply the front with standard reservoirs.

Work of the Engineer Troops in the Period of the Operation

Supplying Engineer Installations for the Breakthrough

In order to improve engineer preparation for breaking through the defenses of the enemy, we selected ahead of time some small engineering units to participate in the operation and assigned these to the attacking units. A total of 45 engineer companies were selected.

From the units selected, we organized 85 groups, each consisting of 10 to 25 men, depending upon the character of the mission assigned. The basic missions of these groups were surmounting the engineer–mine entanglements of the main line of enemy defenses and accompanying the attacking units through these entanglements. Each commander heading a group of engineers, jointly with the commander of the small unit attacking, studied beforehand the engineer reconnaissance data of all their combat sector, planned the route of movement, and specified in a concrete manner the missions of the engineer groups as to time and lines.

Early in the morning of November 20, 1942, several hours before our troops started their attack against the main line of enemy resistance, the engineers—under a reinforcing cover of submachine guns, light machine guns, and heavy machine guns of the rifle units—started clearing the minefields and scattered barbed-wire entanglements of the enemy. In three and one-half hours the engineers had made 64 passageways and drawn out and disarmed more than 5,000 enemy mines. Where they were not able to construct passageways, they planned 37 of the most convenient routes for bypassing the minefields.

The minefields of the enemy consisted of metallic German and Rumanian mines. The basic and most effective means for discovering them was the mine detector. However, mine detectors were used only to a limited extent because of the absence of BAS-60 batteries. The operation of searching for the mines and rendering them harmless was carried out by probes or grapplers, a method that slowed up the rate of work considerably. The engineer–mine entanglements of the enemy were overcome under exceptionally difficult circumstances and oftentimes under heavy fire.

At dawn on November 20, 1942, the troops on the front on the main sectors assumed the offensive. There was a thick fog. Before the beginning of the attack, all the passageways in the minefield and the detours of minefields were designated by markers with inscriptions on them. In the center of each passageway, in narrow trenches having a depth of 1 to $1\frac{1}{2}$ meters, there were engineer controllers, provided with signal searchlights, stakes with flags, or bunches of straw, by means of which they gave signals upon the approach of the small units.

Despite the excellent manner in which this work was planned, precise coordination between passage of the combat machines through the minefields and the discipline of movement over them was still absent on several sectors. As a result of this, we suffered unnecessary losses in equipment.

Accompanying the attacking troops

After the breakthrough of the enemy defenses, the accompanying of the tanks was entrusted to the army and front engineer units; the rifle troops and artillery, however, were accompanied by regimental and divisional engineers.[5] The mission of the accompanying forces consisted of providing a passageway through the minefields of the enemy. For accompanying the tanks, two or three engineers mounted a tank; by external signs, the engineers detected by visual examination the minefields of the enemy. When they detected a minefield, they signaled the tank to stop by a blow with the butt of their guns upon the armor. They would then demine a passageway, after which the movement continued.

In the planning for accompanying the motor–mechanized troops, the failure to provide the engineer units with transport proved to be a weakness. After passing through the minefields of the enemy, the engineers, in the course of the advance, became separated from the tanks.

The engineers accompanying the artillery and rifle troops moved with their units all the time, carrying out their missions of reconnoitering and removing entanglements, conducting reconnaissance of the rear defense lines, and participating in the blocking of the earth-and-timber pillboxes of the enemy. It was ascertained that the enemy had no defensive installations and entanglements in the rear. We discovered only separate minefields or groups of mines on the approaches to inhabited localities and near bridges.

Securing Crossings

Starting on November 18, crossing operations became more complicated, due to the sudden worsening of the ice situation and accompanied by a drop in the level of the water. The rate of drop of the level of the water on December 20 reached 17.5 centimeters per day, and by the end of December it was 26 centimeters. The ice floes in this ten-day period increased in diameter up to 40 centimeters and in thickness up to 30 to 40 centimeters. By the end of the month, the shoals on the Volga began to affect navigation.

The fall ice floes lasted longer than was predicted. In November and up to the middle of December, the hydrometeorological conditions on the Volga in the area of the front made the construction of even foot crossings impossible and created great difficulties in the operation of ferry crossings. The only foot crossing on the ice was at Astrakhan. This crossing, which had a length of 1,600 meters, started operations beginning on the morning of November 30.

Starting November 18, the drop in the level of the water of the Volga caused shoals at the landing places, a condition that was felt acutely toward the end of the month. In approaching the landing places, the vessels and barges were disabled temporarily by running on shoals and it required a great deal of work to get them off the shoals. The movement on the Volga of vessels with a large draft was limited. The abrupt drop in the level of the water required at first a lowering of the landing places, and after this—due to the formation of shoals—it was necessary to lengthen them or construct new replacements for those destroyed by the ice floes. Thus, at the Kamennyi Iar crossing, the ice destroyed 12 landing places. At this place, it was necessary to construct four new landing places for loads of 60 tons to replace those that had been torn up or rendered unfit for use by shoals. The average length of the trestles of the landing places was 350 meters.

To prevent losses of navigation material and to keep the crossings in operation, we put into effect the following measures:

● The brigades organized from the workers of the vessel repair plants, which repaired the damaged boats at the crossings themselves, made repairs up to and including the replacement of rudders and the welding of boilers.
● When it was impossible to bring the vessels up to the landing places, the loading and unloading was done on the ice itself (the Tatianka crossing had two ice-landing stages for the loading of men and freight on N2P pontoons).
● For a better utilization of the cutters and the tugs, we increased the number of pontoons so that in addition to the pontoons en route there might be pontoons loading and unloading at the same time. Such a continuous method of work made it possible for the *VMK* cutters at the crossing of Tatianka to make 12 to 19 trips during the daytime.
● Under serious ice conditions, the crossing was made on the decks of self-propelled vessels without tow barges or ferries, and the loading area was increased by removing a number of deck superstructures.

On November 28, due to the rapid formation of shoals, the crossing of wheel and caterpillar loads on barges was temporarily suspended on all sectors of the Volga, except at Kammenyi Iar. There, the shallowness was not so serious, and the ice floes were not as large as a result of the formation of obstructions upstream.

As a result of a number of organizational measures for adapting the vessels for crossing in the presence of ice, we soon put the other crossings in operation. For example, the crossing at Svetlyi Iar continued its work with the paddle-wheel tug "Krasnoflotets" and other vessels right up to the freezing of the river. Then the thickness of the ice reached 12 centimeters, and the temperature of the air went down to minus 16 degrees. Work under such conditions was carried out in the following manner: a steam icebreaker of the "Samara" type went ahead breaking a channel, and behind it came the powerful tug, "Krasnoflotets," followed by all the other small vessels. In this way, we had a caravan of vessels that moved in the ice without any special difficulty.

While providing crossing facilities in the presence of ice floes, we carried out the preparatory work for the construction of ice roads for motor vehicle transport and medium loads. For solving this problem, the engineer units at the Front did the following work:

- a reconnaissance was made of the points of crossing over the ice in the areas of Shchuche, Tatianka, Svetlyi Iar, and Krasnyi Oktiabr;
- in the area of the prospective crossing, more than 10,000 cubic meters of materials were collected for reinforcement;
- in order to provide for pedestrian traffic and the crossing of loads at the beginning period of the freezing, we started the construction of sledrope paths for loads up to 100 kilograms. By November 30, we had prepared the sleds, set up and tried out the drive wire on both banks, prepared cable, and so on; and
- carried out reconnaissance and selected a place for the construction of a low-water bridge across the Volga in the area of Tatianka for loads of 30 tons and prepared timber for this purpose in the amount of 6,000 cubic meters.

The number of loads crossed in the initial period of the operation (November 20–December 5, 1942) is shown by the following table:

Name of the Loads	To Right Bank	To Left Bank	Total
Troops	64,193	11,364	75,557
Wounded	—	14,196	14,196
Tanks	177	—	177
Guns	251	1	252
Motor Vehicles	2,363	345	2,708
Tractors	39	—	39
Wagons	766	53	819
Horses	1,589	139	1.728
Ammunition (tons)	5,331.9	51.0	5.382.9
Class I supplies (tons)	4,308.9	18.6	4.327.5
Other loads (tons)	2,403.9	87.7	2,491.6

On the basis of the crossing experience in the period of the offensive, we may draw the following conclusions:

1. Despite the extremely difficult conditions of work in the course of the operation, the Volga crossings supplied the front with everything necessary without interruptions, and in the main, they did the work within the time set by the command. However, there were gaps in their operation, as a result of which, in particular at the crossing Svetlyi Iar, the 300th Rifle Division was held up for several days.
2. Contrary to assumptions, experience showed that it was entirely possible to use paddle-wheel tug steamers in the ice floes (because broken blades could be quickly repaired on the spot) and during the

loading–unloading operations. When there were rather thick ice floes traffic was possible even when the majority of the blades were broken. These paddle-wheel tugs were shown to be superior to the screw tugs, in the case of which the repair, and all the more so the replacement, of the screw caused long interruptions in the work.

3. For urgent crossings, it was necessary to have at each place one vessel to serve as a leader—from 150 to 800 horsepower, depending upon the conditions, preferably shallow draft—and some large barges. At places where the crossings were made with large barges and tugs, the urgent crossings could be carried out satisfactorily, and where these means were not available, such crossings were hampered.

4. In crossings over wide streams in the fall and winter, it was necessary to use icebreakers (preferably with small draft).

5. The moorings and trestles of the bridges should be constructed so that they can be quickly raised and lowered, depending upon the level of the water (like the supports of the bridge RMM-2).

6. In the employment of large vessels for the crossings of loads in bulk, it was necessary to organize permanent loading–unloading crews.

7. In crossing broad streams, it is necessary to have a group of captain-instructors, familiar with the channel of the river and the area of the crossings. Jointly with them we should select the place of the crossing, the distribution of the vessels at the crossings, and the selection of routes of march to the crossing.

Command of the Engineer Troops

The staff of the engineer troops of the Front organized close and permanent signal communications with the operations and reconnaissance sections and commands of the staff of the Front and with all of the Volga crossings. For this purpose, the staff of the engineer troops created an operational group of three men. For these we provided (at the post of the operations section of the staff of the front) a shelter equipped with telephone and radio connections with all the crossings. Among the duties of the aforementioned commanders were regular information briefings to the chief of the engineer troops and the chief of staff of the engineer troops concerning all of the changes in the operational situation and the daily work of all the crossings. In certain cases, they were given the right to make independent decisions in questions pertaining to crossings.

For carrying out operational direction of a large number of crossings over the Volga, we assigned to the staff of the engineer troops a cable–pole company of signal communications with four radio stations, by means of which the staff had constant wire and radio connections with the crossings.

In the decisive directions, for rendering assistance and checking the adequacy of engineer work on the spot, we detailed responsible staff commanders. At the most important crossings, there was at all times a chief of the operations section. The chief of the engineer troops and the chief of staff of the Front also went to these places repeatedly. The command of the engineer troops was carried out chiefly through liaison officers, radio, and telephone.

Owing to close coordination of the work with the main section of the staff of the Front and commands in the presence of the operations group having technical signal communications, we assured the planning and direction of the most important sector of the work, namely, the crossings.

The absence of signal communications and coordination, with the Hydrometeorological Service, was a great handicap in getting timely predictions as to the variations in the water level. It was necessary to lose a great deal of time and labor for reequipping the moorings and even in changing, at times, the line of the crossings.

The Staffs of the Engineer Troops of the Armies

The plans for providing adequate engineer works for the operation were worked out in detail and, in the main, correctly by all the staffs of the engineer troops of the army, with the exception of the 64th Army. However, in some of the armies, the putting of the plans into the hands of the executors took place with great delay. Thus, the battalion engineers of two divisions of the 28th Army did not receive the plans from the staff of the engineer troops until November 16, and the battalion engineers of the 57th Army did not receive them until November 13–14. Before this time, the work carried out by the engineer troops in preparation for the operation was on the basis of partial instructions from the staffs.

By the beginning of the operation, the staff of the engineer troops of the 64th Army had neither an engineer plan nor a plan for material–technical supplies and limited itself to general instructions and orders. As a result of this, in the preparatory period, out of eight army and assigned front battalions, only four carried out the missions connected directly with the operations, and the rest of the battalions occupied themselves with subordinate works. The most important forms of engineer materials, such as mines, barbed wire, mine detectors, and so on, were at the beginning of the operations at the army base on the other side of the Volga. All these deficiencies had to be corrected quickly in the course of the operations.

In the control of the staffs of the engineer troops of the army, the weakest link was signal communications with the army engineer units. In view of the absence of means for technical communications and movement, signal communications with the battalions, some of which were far away, were maintained exclusively by foot messenger communications.

In view of the absence of signal communications, the staff of the engineers of the 51st Army did not know for several days the location of the two front battalions assigned to it for the time of the operation.

A weak place in the work of certain army staffs of the engineer troops was their lack of contact with the other sections of the staff of the army, in particular the operations and reconnaissance sections and rear command. As a result, they were poorly informed about the strategic situation and could not react quickly in carrying out a redistribution or regrouping of the engineer personnel or equipment.

On the whole, despite a number of weaknesses, the staffs of the engineer troops of the army, as organs of control of the chiefs of the engineers, coped in a successful manner with the work of providing adequate engineer installations for the operation. The experience gained in the operation emphasized once again the important role of the staffs of the engineer troops and, at the same time, showed the absolute necessity of improving their training and cohesion.

It is extremely necessary to provide the staffs of the engineer troops with organic means of transport; to have with the staff of the engineer troops of the army a motor vehicle platoon for the creation of mobile reserves and for the maneuverability of engineer–entanglement works; and to make adequate provision for the machines of the commanders of the armies and front engineer battalions. In order to provide for the operational direction of the army and front engineer units, it is absolutely necessary that each battalion and the staffs of the engineer troops have their own radio signal communications.

BATTALION AND BRIGADE ENGINEERS

With rare exceptions, battalion and brigade engineers directed in a concrete manner the work of the small engineer units on the battlefield itself and were always informed of the situation. However, there were cases of incorrect employment of the brigade engineers by the commanders of units of combined arms. For example, a brigade engineer of the 38th Motorized Rifle Brigade, in the period of the preparation for the offensive, was sent to the rear by the commander of the brigade for some white cloaks and, in reality, carried out the function of a quartermaster sergeant; whereas the demining work in the zone of advance of the Brigade had to be assigned to the assistant of the chief of staff of the engineer troops of the army.

A serious weakness in the work of many troop engineers was the absence of skill in planning work and the correct employment of the assigned army engineer units. In practice it turned out that the army engineer battalions assigned to the division carried out work in demining and in the main line of resistance, whereas the battalion engineers were occupied in the construction of command posts and in the repair of roads in the division and regiment service areas.

The experience of the Stalingrad operation points to the following: the necessity of teaching unit engineers the planning and organization of engineer work, the proper echeloning of engineer units, the ability to organize engineer reconnaissance, and of instilling in them the ability to work out and analyze the engineer needs pertaining to the enemy, to make engineer decisions to meet the given situation, and to utilize correctly and as effectively as possible both their own engineer equipment and that assigned to them.

General Conclusions

The combat engineer units carried out a great deal of intensive work in the offensive operations of the Stalingrad Front, especially in providing crossings over the Volga under serious natural and tactical conditions. We may judge the scope of the crossing work by the amount of freight crossed. During November, 489 echelons of military supplies were crossed, making 16 echelons a day, or 40 carloads an hour. Despite the enormous task that this represented and the difficulties of carrying it out—due to the fact that units and equipment were not up to strength and the engineer troops were not properly prepared—the missions of the command both in the crossings operations and in all other forms of necessary engineer preparations were carried out fully and on time.

The experience in the work of the engineer troops in the offensive operations of the Stalingrad Front enables us to draw a number of practical conclusions.

1. Crossings require centralized direction and the presence in the reserves of the chief of the engineer troops of the front of a powerful group of crossing equipment, which must be employed in a concentrated manner and not piecemeal.

2. Under the conditions prevailing in the crossings of a rather large river, it is absolutely necessary to have the following: repair parties supplied with the necessary tools, materials, and spare parts located at the crossings; diving parties for the repair and raising work; and a detachment of mine sweepers for demining the areas of the crossing and the channel of the river.

3. In crossing wide rivers in the fall and winter, special attention should be given to the proper organization and placing of fire guards.

4. In the areas of the crossings, it is necessary to have a supply of building materials, barges, flat boats, and rafts for the preparation of landing stages.

5. The pontoon units should be provided with transportable pile drivers, compressors, woodsaws, and so on.

6. A basic and general weakness of all of our bridge parks is the small span between the supports and the thickness of the pontoons in the line of the bridge made necessary by this. The presence of a large number of pontoons makes it easier for the enemy to knock them out with artillery, mortar, and machinegun fire.

In the presence of the thick fall ice floes, placing of the pontoon holes near the ice moving along the river is important since ice causes blocking and the consequent breaking of the bridge. It is necessary to provide long-span standard bridges on floating supports, at least for motor-and animal-drawn transport (less than 8 to 10 tons). The span structure of such a bridge could be executed in the form of a series of light metallic girders or Spengel girders. It is also possible to provide standard suspension bridges for light loads using floating supports.

7. Under all circumstances, the chief of the engineer troops should have some mobile and general reserves, capable of extensive maneuverability in carrying out demining operations on the flanks and able to render timely and effective assistance to troops in fortifying themselves on the lines reached. The mistake of such reserves again emphasizes the necessity of maximum motorization of engineer units. The Front engineer units, especially the pontoon brigades, were in a serious situation with regard to motor vehicle transport.

8. As experience in the operation has shown, the rear establishments of the army—division and brigade, whose duty it is to provide for the bringing up of all kinds of supplies—as a rule, plan last of all for the transport of engineer equipment and most often fail to transport it. In the interests of the work, it is necessary to organize independent army engineer dumps and have manual of transport at the entire disposal of the chief of the engineer troops of the army.

Editor's Notes

1. The engineer troops of the Stalingrad Front were commanded by Major General of Engineer Troops I. A. Petrov.
2. The total forces of the front included 30 engineer battalions as well as the divisional engineer battalions. See S. Aganov, "Inzhenernie Voiska" *Voenno istoricheskii zhurnal* No. 11 1982, 53. (Hereafter, Aganov). However, E. Egorov, *Inzhenernie voiska Sovetskoi Armii, 1918–1945* (Moscow: Voenizdat, 1985), p. 318, table 5, lists 29 battalions and three brigades.
3. One authoritative Soviet source lists somewhat different figures as 160,000 men; 430 tanks; 600 guns; 14,000 trucks; and 7,000 tons of ammunition. In any event, the number is representative of an impressive feat given German air superiority.
4. It was due to this fact that German forces did not expect an offensive from this area. See S. Rado, *Codename Dora* trans. (London: Abelard, 1977), p. 151.
5. Engineer units were employed to screen the flanks, and later to cover the front of the 51st Army during the defensive phase of the Kotelnikovo operation. Their tasks included building emplacement and the laying of antitank minefields.

The effort to preserve the Volga crossing points and to continue the flow of troops and supplies represents one of the major unrecognized stories of the Battle of Stalingrad. The unglamorous but necessary work of logistics receives an excellent presentation in this chapter and highlights the requirements for even the local efforts of the Stalingrad defenders. This effort to supply the Soviet troops reveals not only the underdeveloped nature of Soviet logistics at this time but serves as a guidepost for the later programs to assist the major Soviet attacks of 1943–1945.

12

Work of the Road Units at Stalingrad

In the fall and winter of 1942, the road units of the Southwestern, Don, and Stalingrad Fronts executed an enormous amount of work in providing roads for bringing supplies and for evacuation. This work was particularly intense during the period of encirclement and liquidation of the Stalingrad group of the enemy.

Below we shall give a summarized statement pertaining to the road work and the crossings on the Don and Stalingrad Fronts, which will have a certain interest for the study of the Stalingrad operations.

The Don Front

In the period of the battles for Stalingrad and the operations for the encirclement and destruction of the Stalingrad group of the enemy, the supply routes of the armies of the Don Front were based on the permanent railroad sectors of Kamyshin–Ilovlia and Frolovo–Ilovlia.

In due time before the starting of the offensive by our units, we prepared supply routes from the stations Frovlovo, Verkhne–Lipki, and Log to the crossings over the Don River in the area of Malo–Kletskii,

Kremenskaia, Kamenskaia, and Novogrigorievskaia (sketch 33). On the supply route from the aforementioned stations we constructed and repaired all the artificial structures, provided the roads with the proper markers, set up stakes, and on the sectors most subject to snowdrifts, prepared snow shields. On the roads we set up a road stage–commandant's service and prepared heating dugouts on the stage sectors where there were no inhabited localities.

During the time of the offensive on the right bank of the Don up until the completion of the encirclement of the enemy group in the area of Stalingrad, the road units, following the field units, carried out for the most part separate missions of the command in the construction of crossings (in the area of Malo-Kletskii across the Don River), the clearing of snow from the roads chiefly, the setting up of road signs, construction, and repair of artificial structures. The demining of the road in this case was carried out exclusively by the engineer units.

But despite all this, due to the conditions under which the operation was carried out, there was no stable road network during this period of the offensive operation. As before, the roads from the stations of Frolovo, Verkhne–Lipki, and Log, prepared before the start of the offensive, were still of decisive importance as basic supply routes.

After the completion of the encirclement of the enemy group in the area of Stalingrad, the front command proposed the equipment of the road to log, Ilovlinskaia, Kachalinskaia, and Kalach. The total length of the main line was 126 kilometers. In the task, we took into account the exceptionally heavy traffic (up to 5,000 motor vehicles a day) that would pass over the main line due to the fact that four armies would be dependent on it.

On the Ilovinskaia-Vertiachii sector, over which the heaviest traffic would pass, there were two independent roads: a supply road of station Ilovlia, Station Kachalino, and Vertiachii; and an evacuation route of Station Ilovlia, Ilovinskaia, Baibaev, Gnilovskii, and Vertiachii.

For this purpose, the traffic through the main inhabited localities was directed over different streets or detours were made of the inhabited localities, with the latter being the most usual. Separate traffic lines were used in the following inhabited localities: Ilovlinskaia, Kachalinskaia, Vertiachii, Peskovatka, Sokarevka, and Kalach. In addition to this, for cases of increased traffic, there were reserve roads for separate traffic on the stages of Vertiachii and Kalach. In this case, the evacuation route was to run through Vertiachii, Peskovatka, Sokarevka, and Riumino-Krasnoiarskii towards Kalach.

In view of the very heavy traffic and also the fact that a considerable part of the road was further burdened by passing into the divisional and regimental service areas, plans were made to utilize the right bank road running through Kalach, Golubinskii, Bolshenabatovskii, and Akimovskii with crossings over the Don in the areas of Peskovatka and Vertiachii.

A complete stage-commandant's service was established on the supply routes, the field routes for evacuation, and the detours of inhabited localities. The roads were provided with stakes and signs; all of the artificial structures were put in order. All places dangerous for traffic in the limits of the traveled part were sealed off, and the ravines, shell craters, ditches, and so on bordering the road were fenced off. On these roads, we adopted numerous measures for protection against snow (snow shields, preparation and distribution of means for fighting snowdrifts). On the reserve roads for evacuation, the works were limited to the setting out of signs and stakes. On the right-bank reserve road—even though to a smaller extent, as a result of the smaller number of road units on it—we also carried out road repair work and work for ensuring the passage of vehicles over it in the wintertime.

We also established a road-operating and road-commandant's service on the dirt sector; the scale of such service depended upon the length of the stretch. The conditions of operations in the wintertime made it necessary for the road-commandant's service to provide heating points, to issue warm uniforms to some of the members of the passing parties (the replacement of garrison caps with winter hats, the issue of gloves, and so on, and to arrange disinfection chambers, baths, additional supply, refueling, checking and aid stations, and points for technical assistance. For the evacuation of the wounded, points were arranged for placing the wounded on motor vehicles going in the same direction.

During the period of the offensive operations of the Don Front, the road-commandant's service did the following: provided food for 263,000 men; refueled 2,400 motor vehicles; passed 166,000 men through heating points; rendered medical assistance in 5,000 cases; and evacuated 118,000 men on passing motor vehicles.

An essential characteristic of road work in the course of the offensive operations was the organization of the work crossing the Volga River. The shifting of large reserves for the Don Front required that crossings operated continuously. The work was done during the fall seasonal rise and drop in the level of the water. Thus, by November 16, there was a noted rise of 3.5 meters; after this, by December 10, there was a drop of 4.7 meters. The rise and fall of the water reached as much as 42 centimeters per day.

For carrying out the crossing work, each point had three pairs of mooring places; of these, two pairs were always adjusted to the operating level. The mooring places were adjusted daily by two specially assigned bridge-construction battalions. In the work, special difficulties were encountered when the level of the water dropped, because in this case it was necessary to lengthen the mooring places to as much as 160 meters for reaching the minimum depth necessary for the unobstructed approach of the ferries.

From November 10 to December 20, the crossings were operated in the presence of an unbroken ice field, as a result of which we provided ahead of time three ferries of metallic barges. As tugboats we used metallic screw and paddle-wheel steamers with metallic plates. The ferryboats were accompanied by two tugs, one of which towed the vessel and the other cleared the floes from the passageway, removed the ice from the approaches to the mooring places, and assisted as a second tug at the moment of mooring.

During the offensive operation, the following were crossed: 26,000 motor vehicles; 600 tractors; 11,800 wagons; and 94,000 heads of livestock.

In addition to ferries in the limits of the Don Front from September to October, bridges were constructed across the Volga in the following areas:

● Politotdelskoe—low-water bridge with a floating unit, with the personnel and equipment of the Administration of the Motor Highway Service of the Don Front;
● Antipovka—a floating bridge, constructed by the personnel and equipment of the engineer troops of the Red Army; and
● Saratov—a floating bridge built upon orders of the Chief Administration of the Motor Highway Service of the Red Army.

The regimen of the Volga River is characterized by the great range of the floods (in the spring up to 14 meters and in the fall up to 8 meters) and by the intensive ice floes, lasting up to a month. Because of the abrupt change in the regimen of the river, up until 1942, we had not constructed a single low-water bridge across the Volga River in its lowest course, and crossing of loads was done by ferries. The situation in the area of Stalingrad required dependable crossings over the Volga at its lower course. The bridge at the village of Politotdelskoe was the first low-water bridge with a floating part constructed across the Volga.

The technical characteristics of the bridge were a rated load of passage of motor vehicles up to 8 tons and tanks up to 30 tons; clearance for two-way traffic (5.5 meters); an 80-meter long drawbridge for the passage of boats; and lengths of 1,250 meters over the main channel and 550 meters across the arms of the river.

The bridge over the main channel had a floating part with a length of 256 meters; the rest of the length of the bridge consisted of stringer trestles on pile supports (at depths of less than 4.5 meters). Because of the obliqueness of the current at the sand banks, some of the supports were set in an oblique position, and the floating part was placed along a curve having a radius of 400 meters.

The bridge was constructed in 15 days. The basic principles in the planning of the work were the following: a separate sector of the bridge was assigned to each construction unit; we drew up a schedule of work for each sector; a daily assignment was given to each unit and the unit could not leave the work site until the completion of it; and socialist emulation was used extensively.

In the construction of one running meter of bridge, the following amount of labor was used: for a trestle, 9.3 man days, and for the floating part of the bridge (with ready-prepared pontoons) 6.1 man days. And 3.25 cubic meters of timber were used.

The attempts to conserve the bridge for winter traffic were unsuccessful; the bridge was damaged by the fall seasonal rise. The experience with work on the bridges over the Volga enables us to draw a few conclusions.

The trestle bridges should be built on sand banks, which should be stable and be in the period of growth (silt deposits—Ed.). The axis of the crossing should be selected on a sector with a minimum of obliquness in the current, with as much uniformity of depth as possible, and below (on the basis of the flow of the river) the ridge of the sand bank, where there is disposition as a result of a drop in the rate of flow.

A convenient time for the employment of scaffold bridges on the Volga is the period from the beginning of July up until the middle of November. During the fall and spring floods, it is necessary to use ferries—preferably self-propelled—in view of the difficulty of steering barges by means of tugs. The bridges, due to their great length, must be designed for motor-vehicle loads and the tanks crossed on ferries (and over railroads).

The most suitable floating means have been the single-section pontoons of the Military Bridge Department of the Chief Administration of Motor Vehicle Roads of the Red Army, having dimensions of 14 x 3.30 x 1.70 meters. The employment of light pontoons of the *DMP* type for bridges across the Volga should not be allowed, especially in the period of storms. On a sector where the river has an arm, the conditions are more favorable for the planning of the work and the protection of the bridges from air attacks, especially if the bridges are not placed on the same straight line.

The Stalingrad Front

The work of the bridge-construction and road-building units of the Department of Motor Vehicle Roads of the Stalingrad Front in the preparatory period consisted of the construction of a number of ferry crossings and bridges over the Volga and the Akhtuba rivers with their numerous tributaries, as well as in the construction of an entire network of new Front and army roads under complicated and unusual natural conditions.

Both in the preparatory period and in the course of the operations, the Stalingrad Front was supplied over the Elton, Verkhnii Baskunchak, and Astrakhan branch of the Riazon-Uralsk railroad. The main motor vehicle roads were Leninski-Elton and Verkhnii Baskunchak-Leninsk, from which led a large number of dirt roads through the valley of the Volga to the crossings and farther on beyond the armies on the offensive.

The traffic conditions over the road network were unfavorable. The roads had no stone surface; the roadbed consisted, in the main, of a soft loam; a considerable part of the roads ran through the flood valleys of the Volga and Akhtuba, (subject to overflow); and the intensity of traffic amounted to 4,000 to 4,500 vehicles a day and on certain sectors to as many as 7,000 a day. Hence, in addition to the work of building roads, we also had to do a great deal of work in maintaining them. We improved a total of 175 kilometers of road and repaired 494 kilometers, using 120,000 cubic meters of repair materials, as a result of which we made possible continuous traffic over the roads.

In November, the front motor-vehicle road units also did a great amount of work in preparing the roads for traffic in the wintertime. For example, the following kinds of work were carried out: measures for snow protection; arrangement of various kinds of stations (warming, mess, dressing, refueling, checking, repair); construction of delousing chambers and baths; points for supplying warm uniforms to parties passing through; and so on.

In regard to the work on the dirt sectors of the roads of the Stalingrad Front we have data pertaining to an earlier period. For example, from August 9–October 25, 1942, 352,000 motor vehicles passed over these roads going toward the front and 336,000 coming from the front. In addition, 8,500 motor vehicles were used for wounded; 4,500 for ammunition; 311,000 men were supplied with food; medical assistance was given in 10,000 cases; technical assistance was given in 420 cases; and 2,000 motor vehicles were refueled. There is no doubt that in the period of November–December the traffic on these roads was much greater.

An essential feature of the work of providing roads during the operation was the planning of crossings over the Volga River and its tributaries. For the construction of ferry crossings over the Volga on the sector from Stalingrad to Astrakhan, we made surveys, the complexity of which was due to the short period available for the work (10 days), the great length of the sector (up to 500 kilometers), the great width of the river flood valley (up to 40 kilometers), and the fall floods, when the level of the water was 3 meters above the usual level.

We constructed a total of 28 ferry crossings, with lengths of 1.2 to 7 kilometers, one trip requiring from three to six hours; the number of mooring places at each point was from two to six pairs, and the total of the mooring places for various loads was 91 pairs. The number of ferries "surrounded by structures," varied from two to eight at each point of crossing; the total load capacity of the ferries was 34,810 tons. The crossings were served by 16 rotor and steam vessels, with a total power of 5,000 indicated horsepower.

The largest bridges, each constructed in a period of 10 days, were:

● a bridge across the Volga in the area of the tractor plant, with a combined length of 1,250 meters, single track (3.5 meters), with a load capacity of 15 tons, and a total length of two-way approach lanes of more than 12 kilometers;
● a bridge over the Volga at Kuprosnoe-Bobyli with a length of 1,250 meters, width 3.5 meters, for a capacity of 15 tons; and
● a bridge across the Staraia Volga River at Shchuchii, with a total length of 2,249 meters, a width of 5 meters, and with a load capacity of 15 tons.

In addition to the bridges across the Volga River, we built 19 bridges across the Akhtuba River, with a total running length of 2,882 meters, more than one-half of which had a load capacity up to 30 tons. The small and less important bridges had a running length of 2,748 meters, and the running length of the bridges repaired was 3,870 meters.

Such a thick network of ferry crossings and bridges made it possible to cross all of the loads without any congestion at the crossings, despite the fact that the crossings were continually knocked out by enemy aviation for long periods.

The PVO troops in the battle of Stalingrad faced the unenviable situation of being designed to combat deep incursions by enemy aircraft and yet facing the prospect of serving on the frontline. This chapter details the disruptions caused by the German advance to Stalingrad and the adaptations made in the PVO structure to accommodate the new situation. Missing are the comments about German domination of the air found in the earlier chapters, but present is a pride in having served a useful role in preserving intact the Volga crossings.

13

Means of Antiaircraft Defense in the Fight for Stalingrad

The present article is a processing of the material prepared for the press by the staff of the *PVO* defenders of the territory of the country. In reading the article we recommend that the reader uses a map with a scale of 1,000,000, sheets M–37, M–38, L–37, L–38.

In the battle for Stalingrad, the defense of the city against the heavy and almost continuous attacks from the air was provided by the antiaircraft units of the Stalingrad *PVO*.[1] A long time before the beginning of the ground battles at Stalingrad, the units of antiaircraft defense repelled repeated raids of enemy bombers trying to block the intense efforts of the city to supply the troops at the front, to destroy bases, crossings, and the most important defense plants, and to demoralize and sow panic among the inhabitants of the town. In repelling these attacks, the *PVO* units of AA defense gained a great deal of combat experience, grew stronger, and acquired combat stability and confidence in their strength.

Before the approach of the artillery of the units of combined arms, the *PVO* units for the defense of Stalingrad were the first to receive the blows of the enemy tank forces. Subsequently, in the course of the fierce battles for Stalingrad, these units, in addition to repelling the air attacks of the enemy, conducted successful battles with the enemy tanks and infantry.

288

In the period July–December, 1942, the units of the AA defense of the Stalingrad *PVO* repelled a total of 68,434 airplane raids made by enemy bombers and fighter planes, number representing 49 percent of the total of airplane sorties made by the enemy during this period over all the territory of the Soviet Union. During this same time, the units destroyed 649 airplanes, or 42 percent of the number of airplanes shot down during this period by all the *PVO* defenders of the territory of the country. They also destroyed about 2,000 aviators, 175 tanks, 8 artillery batteries, 17 field guns, 31 mortar batteries, 27 mortars, 44 machine guns, 157 motor vehicles and wagon teams loaded with troops and freight. They neutralized and/or destroyed the following: eight artillery observation points, six ammunition dumps and four covered dugouts; they also destroyed and scattered a total of 11 regiments of infantry.

The experience of the war, and particularly the fight for Stalingrad, showed in a fairly graphic manner that in battles for inhabited localities the *PVO* units can carry on in an effective manner—even though under a great strain—two missions simultaneously, namely, combat with the air enemy and combat with the ground forces, chiefly tanks. The effectiveness with which these missions are executed will be increased by careful planning of cooperation between the commanders of troops of combined arms and rifle troop commanders, who are responsible for the defense of the town (or sectors of it), and the commanders of the units of the *PVO*.[2]

The planning of cooperation and the tactical employment of the means of AA defense in the defense of an inhabited locality include the following: the drawing up of a plan for antitank point defense, closely coordinated with the *PVO* plan of defenses; the determination of the main and alternate positions, both for carrying out the missions of antitank defense and for carrying out those of AA defense; the reconnaissance and equipment of side roads, making possible maneuvers of the antiaircraft weapons; and the assignment of mobile means for maneuver by wheeled vehicles and a number of other measures designed for a more complete employment of all the power of the antiaircraft weapons for the purpose of providing a stable defense of the town.

Below we give a summary of the tactical work of the units of the *PVO* in the fight for Stalingrad. The combat experience of the units of AA defense of Stalingrad has great value not only for the commander-specialists of the troops of the *PVO* but also for the commanders of units of combined arms.

Operations of the Aviation of the Enemy

In the period June–July, 1942, the enemy carried on a systematic reconnaissance of the Stalingrad railways on the sectors of Likhaia-Stalingrad and Stalingrad-Povorino, using single airplanes. The reconnaissance was carried out chiefly with JU-88 airplanes from high altitudes.

Beginning on July 9, the activity of enemy air reconnaissance increased considerably. On this day, we recorded 20 airplane flights by single planes and groups (from two to eight airplanes). In conducting reconnaissance, the enemy dropped bombs, not limiting itself to objects on the railway but reconnoitering even the inhabited places located outside the railway (Tsymlianskaia, Serafimovich, and Vershenskaia).

During the subsequent days of July, the curve of the number of airplane flights in the Stalingrad area of antiaircraft defense rose sharply, reaching in the last days of the month as many as 200 airplane flights a day. The number of targets subjected to reconnaissance and bombing increased as each day passed.

At the end of July, with groups of 20 to 45 airplanes, at altitudes from 2,000 to 5,000 meters, the enemy carried out for the first time five converging night attacks against Stalingrad. Only single airplanes penetrated to the city through the fire of the antiaircraft artillery. Dwellings were destroyed by the bombs released; military–industrial objects were not hit. In this same period, enemy aviation began to carry out attacks against single vessels and convoys of vessels on the Volga; it also mined the channel of the river and bombed the river piers.

In the middle of August, the reconnaissance and bombing activity of aviation against the territory of Stalingrad slowed up somewhat and increased sharply in the second half of the month. We may regard August 23 as the beginning of the mass attacks of all kinds of enemy aviation against Stalingrad and the troops defending it. Beginning at this time and continuing up to the middle of November without stopping for a single day, the enemy carried out an intensive bombing of the town; field positions and antiaircraft artillery; mooring places; crossings over the Volga at Stalingrad, Kamyshin and Astrakhan; airdromes; and combat formations of troops and reserves of the Stalingrad Front.

The intensification of the military activity of enemy aviation culminated in the last 10 days of October. At this time the number of airplane sorties into the Stalingrad *PVO* of antiaircraft defense reached 9,919. This meant that the enemy carried out an average of 990 airplane sorties each day.

The straining of the resources of enemy aviation—its heavy losses from the attacks of our fighter planes and the fire of our antiaircraft artillery and the heavy losses in flight personnel—greatly relieved the situation in the air at Stalingrad. In the first 10-day period of November, the number of airplane flights decreased in comparison with the last 10-day period of October by almost one-half (5,535 instead of 9,919), and after this there was such a sharp decrease that by the end of November only solitary flights were made in the course of the day. We must say that the weather conditions also played a part in the decrease in the air activity of the enemy, but this factor was not the decisive one. There were days with decent flying weather even in November, and the situation called for active operation of enemy planes but none were observed. For example, the attempted offensive of the enemy ground forces during November 13–15, in the area of the "Krasnyi Oktyabr" and "Barrikady" plants, received very little air support.

In the last days of November and December, the flights of military aviation in the area of Stalingrad were made by single planes. But on the other hand, there was an increase in the number of flights of transport planes of the type JU-52 and Hamburg-142, (*sic*, Ed.) for the transport of Class 1 supplies and ammunition to the enemy group surrounded at Stalingrad.

During the long period of raids against Stalingrad, the enemy did not observe any patterns in their tactics of combat employment of aviation. The methods of action of their bombing and fighter aviation depended upon the circumstances and relative strength in personnel and equipment of his aviation and our antiaircraft defense. At the end of July and in August, the enemy, faced by the powerful system of antiaircraft defenses of the city, and having relatively fresh air forces, tried by simultaneous mass attacks with a large number of airplanes to neutralize, demoralize, and break up the antiaircraft defense system of Stalingrad. Raids against Stalingrad, Beketovka, and Krasnoarmeisk were carried out by groups of 15 to 280 airplanes at a time. The daily number of airplane flights each day varied from 300 to 1,200. As a rule enemy aviation displayed the greatest activity beginning with dawn, and in the second half of the day, from 3:00 P.M. to 4:00 P.M. until sundown.

In September and the following months, the enemy changed his tactics as a result of the effectiveness of antiaircraft fire and the losses sustained and began to make radio contact with small groups of three to six planes.[3] Besides, the distance between the groups of JU-87 and JU-88 airplanes was kept at two to three to five minutes, and between the airplanes in the group the distance was kept at 200 meters. At the same time, the He-111 airplanes flew bombing missions in combat flights, with intervals between the flights of one to two minutes. Such an echelon arrangement of the combat formations of bomber aviation enabled the enemy to keep the AA defense system under combat stress for 2 to 12 hours and in this way tire it out and weaken the effectiveness of its fire. We must bear in mind that by this time a considerable part of AA artillery was forced to shift to antitank defense, and the losses in personnel and equipment and the withdrawal of the posts of the Aircraft Warning Service aggravated still further the serious situation of the units.[4] Taking advantage of the proximity of the airdromes, the enemy employed the same airplanes for a large number of sorties during the day. Enemy aviation, as a rule, did not carry out night raids against objectives in the town and the troops.

There appeared over the town simultaneously a large number of enemy airplanes, which separated in groups of 6 to 9 to 18 airplanes for bombing separate objectives. The airplanes tried to approach the objectives without being seen, from the side of the sun or by utilizing cloudiness, coming from behind clouds directly on target. The bombing was carried out in waves from horizontal flight at altitudes of 4,000 to 5,000 meters and sometimes even at 7,000 meters. Upon coming under fire of the antiaircraft artillery, the enemy airplanes employed the antiaircraft artillery maneuver, continually changing course, speed, and altitude. After beginning to bomb from altitudes of 7,000 to 5,000 meters, they completed the operation and left the objective at altitudes of 3,000 to 2,000 meters. Leaving the target was executed by making a sharp turn into a cloud and, in the absence of cloudiness, by gaining or losing flight altitude.

In bombing troops on the front line, the bombing was done by groups of up to 30 airplanes. On the narrow sectors of our defense, up to 5 kilometers in width and 10 to 15 kilometers in length, the enemy employed several hundred airplanes, which for a period of 10 to 12 hours carried out continuous raids. The bombers made the approach to the objectives in trail formation. The bombing was done from a dive. Each airplane made five to seven runs in releasing its bombs on the target. A group of airplanes would keep our troops in the area of the bombing under pressure for a long period of time. As a rule, the release of bombs was carried out from a dive, from an altitude of 4,000 to 5,000 meters, at an angle of dive of 70 degrees and coming out of the dive at altitudes of 1,000 to 600 meters. If by reconnaissance the enemy learned that the troops or objectives had no means of antiaircraft defense (or that they were weakly covered), the bombing was carried out by groups of 3-30 airplanes from altitudes of 1,500 to 2,000 meters. The airplanes, arranged in trailing formation, got over the target in a circle and by single planes or pairs dived to altitudes of 500 to 300 meters, releasing the bombs in two or three runs. After releasing all the bombs, the airplanes switched on the sirens, again placed themselves in a circle, and dived to feint additional attacks.[5] This method of false attack against our personnel was intended to tie our troops to the ground by the moral effect and enable the German infantry to pass to the attack.

In bombing raids against troops, the enemy used not only airplanes of the type JU-87 and JU-88 but also Me-109 fighter planes, the latter being used for releasing small fragmentation bombs weighing from 2 to 5 kilograms and for machine gun-cannon bombardment from low altitudes. For neutralization of batteries of antiaircraft artillery, the enemy used chiefly JU-87, He-123, and Me-109 airplanes. Bomber raids against fire positions of antiaircraft batteries were always preceded by a careful reconnaissance. The bombing of fire positions of antiaircraft artillery was carried out from dives. The transitions into the dive was effected from an abrupt left turn. The bombs were released in series from altitudes of 4,000 to 3,500 meters, and the planes came out of the dive at altitudes of 2,000 to 1,500 meters. The sharp turn in a curvilinear course before the release of the bombs was to render the fire of the antiaircraft batteries more difficult and to decrease the time that the airplanes were under their fire.

Enemy fighter aviation in the Stalingrad operation had in its armament an improved variant of the Me-109.[6] The crews of the fighter planes were selected from the best flyers of the *Luftwaffe*. In the initial period of the operation, elite German fighter pilots, operating alone, in pairs, and sometimes even in large groups of six to eight airplanes, were assigned the task of destroying the best units of our fighter planes, in particular the destruction of the Yak-1 airplanes. This mission was carried out by air ambushes of our paired patrols and single airplanes, chiefly after the relief of patrols in the air and upon their return to the airdrome, when the attention of the aviators was relaxed and the supply of fuel was about exhausted. Since they were numerically superior, the German fighters employed tactics of blocking the airdromes of our fighter aviation, but they did not always succeed in doing this, because the antiaircraft artillery and machine guns used for the defense of airdromes forced them to raise the blockade.

In cooperating with bomber aviation, the fighters of the enemy appeared over the objectives to be bombed. They attracted to themselves the fire of our antiaircraft artillery and drew to themselves our pursuit planes, joining battle with them. In this way, our fighters were drawn to the side, enabling the German bombers to release their bombs without reaction from our fighter planes.

Tactical Employment of the Means of Antiaircraft Defense

Fighter Aviation

The 102nd Fighter Division, forming a part of the antiaircraft defense of Stalingrad, carried on a hard fight with the fighter and bomber aviation of the enemy. In the latter part of July, August, and September of 1942, the division fought 276 single and group battles and shot down 324 airplanes of the enemy, losing 128 of its own planes.[7]

The majority of the battles were fought with enemy bombers operating under a strong cover of fighter planes, which, possessing the best equipment and flyers with a great amount of combat experience, boldly joined battle with our fighters. Operating in groups of six to eight airplanes, the enemy often held the initiative in their hands.

The losses of the 102nd Fighter Division were chiefly the result of the fact that, in the first days of battle, our aviators—not yet having sufficient experience and faced with a numerically superior enemy air force—held to defensive tactics and also as a result of a lack of caution on the part of the flying personnel in the air. Later on, when the flight personnel began to acquire more combat experience and their actions began to take on a bold offensive character, our losses began to drop sharply.

Before the beginning of the combat operations at Stalingrad antiaircraft artillery was organized into seven combat sectors. The division command points and the command points of the sectors were located as a rule in the center of the combat formations of our regiments and smaller units. The signal communications of the antiaircraft defense of Stalingrad with the command posts of the sectors and between the sectors was by telephone and duplicated by radio. The fire position of the batteries of medium caliber antiaircraft artillery were placed 3 to 4 kilometers from each other, and in the outer zone they were placed at 5 or 6 kilometers from each other. The nearest fire positions of the medium-caliber antiaircraft artillery were placed at a distance of 1 to 2 kilometers from the object to be defended. The outer zone of antiaircraft artillery was 8 to 12 kilometers from the basic military–industrial objects of the point. Such a drawing out of the combat formation of antiaircraft artillery in the outer zone into two combat sectors did not furnish an opportunity for opening concentrated surprise fire against airplanes. When the airplanes of the enemy came under fire of one battery, they employed the antiaircraft artillery maneuver and in this way made more difficult the conduct of fire by adjacent batteries.

The small-caliber antiaircraft artillery and the antiaircraft machine guns occupied fire positions by preferences in the plant sectors of the town, and had as their mission the covering of military–industrial objects from the attacks of diving airplanes and combat–support planes.

For reconnaissance and observation of the enemy in the air the units of antiaircraft artillery had, up to August 23, 1942, a total of 26 observation posts established at a distance of 12 to 14 kilometers from the outer limits of their zone of fire. The presence of such a number of observation posts offered full protection for the points of antiaircraft defenses as a whole from sudden attacks of enemy aviation, but for target designation, tracking of targets at the batteries, and for the opening of fire, this number of observation posts was insufficient. For timely opening of fire and reliable target designation it was necessary to have at least two observation posts at each battery connected with the latter by direct telephone or radio.

The drawing near of the front and the continuous changing of the situation necessitated frequent changes both in the organization of the system of antiaircraft defense of Stalingrad as well as in its combat formation. For combating the tanks and infantry of the enemy we organized mobile maneuver groups, one of six batteries and the other of five. The groups, organized from the batteries of different regiments, were well provided with transport means and were shifted from one sector to the other.

Owing to the continuous attacks by enemy aviation against the communications of the Stalingrad Front—the basin of the Volga River and the Riazan–Uralsk Railroad—there was urgent need of covering them against air attacks. For this purpose there were created two antiaircraft groups: one for the antiaircraft defense of the Volga River on the sector Astrakhan/Saratov, detailed from the units of the antiaircraft defense of Stalingrad and consisting of 22 guns of small-caliber antiaircraft artillery and 82 aircraft machine guns; the second group was created for covering the Riazan–Uralsk Railroad on the sector Stalingrad/Pallasovka, consisting of seven armored trains of the antiaircraft defense, three battalions of medium caliber, and one battalion of small-caliber antiaircraft artillery. This same sector was also covered by the 102nd Fighter Air Division.[8]

In addition to this, with the beginning of operations on the approaches to Stalingrad, a change was made in the combat formation of the antiaircraft artillery, chiefly by shifting small-caliber antiaircraft artillery for reinforcement of the defense of the crossings over the Volga and the supply routes, and also for reinforcement of the western sectors at the expense of the eastern and southern sectors.

During the first days of the battle for Stalingrad, as a result of the absence of our troops on the approaches to the city from the west, the chief attention of the batteries of the front line was given to combating the ground forces of the enemy.

For the covering of the combat formations of the batteries of antiaircraft artillery from the ground and from the air, we used antiaircraft machine guns, small-caliber antiaircraft cannon and 76 mm field guns received from the Stalingrad Front. With these weapons we organized 13 field batteries, which, in addition to the mission of protecting the combat formations of the antiaircraft artillery, were assigned by the chiefs of the sectors independent missions for combating enemy tanks and motorized infantry.

From the beginning of the battles on the approaches to the city the antiaircraft batteries had to fight the aviation and the ground forces of the enemy at the same time. In these cases, when the fire positions of the batteries were subjected to attack simultaneously from the air and from the ground, one or two of the guns of the battery conducted fire against the airplanes and the rest against the ground targets.

In the latter part of September and in October, the main part of the antiaircraft artillery of the Stalingrad *PVO* antiaircraft defense zone was transferred to the left bank and to the islands of Sarpinskii, Golodnyi, and Zaitseveskii. To this group we assigned the mission of covering the crossings and military formations of the troops stationed on the right bank. The covering of the ground troops of the Stalingrad Front, which were on the front line, and the crossings to the right bank of the Volga was provided by one regiment of small caliber antiaircraft artillery and by a group of antiaircraft artillery comprising five batteries of medium caliber.

For the covering of the combat formations of the units of antiaircraft artillery placed on the right bank of the Volga, we formed from the free personnel of the antiaircraft units a destroyer battalion made up of 400 men, armed with antitank rifles, machine guns, submachine guns, and rifles.

Two regiments of medium-caliber antiaircraft artillery and one regiment of small-caliber antiaircraft artillery covered from their old positions the objects and troops of the front south of Stalingrad in the area of Beketovka/Krasnoarmeisk.

In November, for covering the concentration of our troops, airdromes, crossings, and army dumps, a part of the antiaircraft weapons were shifted to the area of Svetlyi Iar, Raigorod, and Solovniki Kamennyi Iar. The means of antiaircraft defense of the Riazan–Uralsk Railway were also reinforced.

The limited means of the auto–tractor park hindered the maneuver of antiaircraft artillery by means of vehicles. However, practice showed that with good organization the combination of various small units into antiaircraft artillery groups was readily possible even with comparatively few motor vehicles. In these cases, the maneuver was realized by alternate shifting both of the batteries to new positions and the supplying of all the groups with ammunition.

In defense of Stalingrad with antiaircraft artillery, we used almost all forms of fire and they proved to be effective. In the battles for Stalingrad, enemy aviation operated chiefly in the daytime and, hence, the units of antiaircraft artillery employed scarcely any barrage fire.

The medium-caliber antiaircraft artillery conducted fire chiefly by the tracking method, which was the basic and secondary method, and fired against diving airplanes. Against single airplanes, reconnaissance planes and bombers, tracking fire was conducted by two or three batteries; against a group of airplanes it was concluded simultaneously by several battalions. Fire against enemy fighter planes was conducted only in exceptional cases, chiefly to prevent them from blockading our airdromes, because fire or destruction against fighter planes proved to be lacking in effectiveness due to their great maneuverability in the zone of fire of antiaircraft artillery.

Fire with antiaircraft directors was used rarely, because the enemy airplanes in the bombing of combat formations of the troops and the fire positions of the batteries approached the targets from a circle, changing altitude and speed of flight in an abrupt manner. Often releasing the bombs from a circle formation with a sharp antiaircraft maneuver was the result of the fact that the enemy considered the possibilities of our antiaircraft directors and tried to make fire difficult for the batteries in order to lessen their losses from the fire of our antiaircraft artillery.

The fire of medium-caliber antiaircraft artillery against diving airplanes as one might expect, was not very effective, chiefly for two reasons: first, because the commanding personnel and crews of the batteries were not trained sufficiently in this method of fire; second, because the batteries, as a rule were located far from the objects against which the attacks were made.

Against airplanes of the enemy diving upon the battery, fire was conducted by direct fire pieces, because in the majority of cases the dive was carried out simultaneously by several airplanes from different directions. As experience showed, in firing medium-caliber antiaircraft artillery at diving airplanes, it is advantageous to lay down a curtain when the airplane is at two points—at the point of going into the dive and at the point of coming out of the dive. By such a method the 2nd Battery of the 267th Independent Antiaircraft Artillery Battalion shot down two JU-87s in one raid.

In the fight against diving airplanes, the mutual assistance given by the batteries was very important. For example, when several dive bombers attacked one battery, three batteries of the same regiment supported it with their fire, and as a result of this the enemy, after losing one He-123 and one Me-109, stopped the attack from the air against this battery and did not dive again in the zone of its fire. For mutual fire support by batteries, it is necessary that their positions be placed at intervals of not more than 2.5 to 3 kilometers, and in the instructions pertaining to fire and in the assignments, each battery must know what battery it is to support with fire in repelling the attack of divers.

Hardly a single battery succeeded in conducting fire with all of its weapons simultaneously at one target and this, of course, will often be the case in combat practice or antiaircraft artillery. On a narrow sector of the front it was necessary to repel simultaneously the attacks of enemy bombers, tanks, and submachine guns. Thus, during the day of September 7, 17 JU-87s made continuous dive attacks against the 4th Battery of the 1079th Antiaircraft Artillery Regiment, and at the same time the battery was fired upon by mortar and was subjected to attacks by enemy infantry. The battery conducted fire with one or two guns against the dive bombers, and with the rest of the weapons against ground targets. All the attacks of the dive bombers and the attacks of the enemy infantry were repelled. The rest of the batteries had to fight enemy tanks, infantry, and aviation under the same conditions.

The raids of enemy aviation against large separate objectives or groups of objectives, covered by some regiment or other, were sometimes carried out for several days in succession. In these cases, and especially in repelling converging raids, a great role was played by the control of fire from the command post of the regiment. The timely warnings of the battalions' rapid and precise target designation, and the correct distribution of the fire of the batteries against the targets gave excellent results. Under the combat conditions prevailing during the battle of Stalingrad the commander and staff of the regiment had to be ready to repel not only the separate episodic raids but also to repel air attacks following one after the other almost continually. Under these conditions the correct disposition and mobilization of all the weapons and the forces for the security of the combat operations of the regiment over a long period acquired enormous importance.

During the period of the night raids by enemy aviation, the airplanes were very rarely illuminated by searchlights, and even when caught in the rays of the searchlights, they were in them only for a few seconds and this was not sufficient for conducting fire against an invisible target. Fire with the help of sound locator apparatus and with mass employment of antiaircraft artillery, did not justify itself, because after the very first volleys the sound observers lost their bearings and could not determine the coordinates of the target. Hence, in night raids the majority of the batteries had to lay down barrage fire, which, even though it led to a great consumption of ammunition, still did some good, because only separate planes broke through the antiaircraft fire to the objective. At night the batteries connected with "SON-2" apparatus conducted fire through tracking and barrage fire, which was sufficiently effective.

The small-caliber antiaircraft artillery, in combating enemy dive-bombing during the battle of Stalingrad, proved exceptionally effective. It passed fire against the leading dive-bomber from a distance of 2,400 meters with target angles greater than zero and from a distance of 3,000 meters with a target angle of zero. When the airplane came out of the dive, fire against it was interrupted and shifted to the next airplane. When airplanes dived on a battery (platoon), all the personnel had to stand firm, because JU-87 and He-123 airplanes oftentimes dove point blank utilizing steep dive angles, descending to low altitudes and coming out from the dive in a hedgehog flight. When the crews stood firm, the enemy divers, upon encountering an intensive fire aimed point blank, frequently did not persist, but released their bombs at random, pulled out and withdrew. For example, on September 16 a platoon of the 1st battery of a independent antiaircraft artillery battalion was attacked by 10 JU-87s, each of which made three runs for a dive but none of which succeeded in releasing its bombs. As a result of accurate fire by one of the guns, two JU-87s were shot down.

For fire against diving airplanes we placed in each clip of the 37 mm guns, one or two armor-piercing shells, in addition to the fragmentation-tracer shells.

With the 20 mm gun it is necessary to conduct fire against enemy airplanes from a distance of not more than 1,500 meters, and it is also necessary to place in each of the guns an armor-piercing shell after each one or two tracer shells. On September 5 and 7, with such a ratio of tracer and armor-piercing shells, the 20 mm guns of the 3rd Battery of the 93rd Independent Antiaircraft Artillery Battalion shot down one Me-109 and one JU-88.

Under the combat conditions prevailing during the fight for Stalingrad, the antiaircraft artillery of medium caliber had great need for small-caliber antiaircraft artillery for covering its fire positions. There were times when up to 50 airplanes dove against one antiaircraft battery of medium caliber, and in addition to this it still had to repel the attacks of tanks and submachine guns.

The fight with enemy ground units

The first violent pressure of enemy tanks and infantry against the direct approach to Stalingrad had to be resisted by means of antiaircraft artillery after the Germans broke through our front in the area of Kachalinskaia, when the powerful battering-ram attacks of the German Panzer divisions moved toward Stalingrad from the northwest. All the *PVO* system of antiaircraft defense was made ready for combat. The batteries were prepared to conduct fire against tanks and infantry. The lines were fired upon for adjustment, and all the critical lanes of Panzer approach were studied by careful reconnaissance. With the personnel of small units not having any equipment of their own, and in general with all persons who had no combat duty, we created tank destroyer parties and groups for covering batteries, armed with submachine guns and rifles. The intervals between the batteries were occupied by numerically small rifle troop units.

The few examples cited below give us an idea of the intensity and effectiveness of the action which the antiaircraft artillery carried out against the air enemy and the ground enemy at the same time.

At 3:00 P.M. on August 28, four columns of enemy tanks and motorized infantry coming from the northwest under cover of German airplanes, appeared opposite the sector of the 1007th Antiaircraft Regiment. The first to go into battle was the 5th Battery opposite a column of tanks and motorized infantry having a total strength of 80 machines. In repelling the attacks of the airplanes, tanks, and submachine guns, the battery destroyed seven tanks, crippled eight, and destroyed a platoon of submachine gunners. The 6th Battery was attacked by 50 tanks. As a result of the fighting the battery destroyed 18 tanks, three motor vehicles with infantry and ammunition, and shot down three enemy airplanes. The 4th Battery of this same regiment was attacked by tanks with submachine guns and at the same time its position was subjected to bombing by up to 20 diving planes. As a result of the battle the battery destroyed six tanks and crippled 12; it destroyed eight motor vehicles with infantry and supplies and one light machine, up to 70 soldiers and officers, and shot down two enemy airplanes. The 3rd Battery defended the bridge across the Mechetka River and, repelling all the attacks of the enemy, held the line until the approach of our rifle troops.

Toward evening on September 6 the enemy concentrated up to 150 tanks and up to two motorized divisions for the purpose of capturing the central airdrome. The antitank defense of the airdrome we had assigned from the composition of the units of the antiaircraft defense of Stalingrad—five antiaircraft batteries of medium-caliber artillery. Throughout the day of September 7 the batteries repelled fierce infantry attacks supported by groups of 30 to 50 tanks and up to 50 airplanes of various types. During this time the batteries destroyed the following: six tanks, two armored cars, six mortar batteries, two machine gun positions, and up to three battalions of infantry. We lost six guns destroyed and two were disabled, but the personnel were still able to remove them.

Antiaircraft artillery was very often used for supporting the counterattacks of rifle troops and tanks. The calls for fire were made through the observation and command posts of the antiaircraft artillery, which were connected with the sector commanders of units of combined arms and tanks. In these cases the observation posts performed the role of a signal communication staff section with rifle troops and tanks.

The good camouflage of the fire positions against the ground and air observation of the enemy made it possible for the batteries to conduct fire without being discovered for a long time. In the period of the approach of the main line of resistance to the positions of antiaircraft artillery, the batteries were necessarily subjected to bombardment by diving groups of three to 30 JU-88s or JU-87s. The batteries which knew how to change their fire positions after the first dive attack and to equip a dummy position in the place of the old one were not subjected to enemy action, because the dummy positions were subjected to bombing and to bombardment by mortar fire. Usually, the engineer work provided the personnel with good protection but not the guns, which in the majority of cases had damaged counterrecoil mechanisms, caused by fragments of shells and aerial bombs.

In the period of the battle for Stalingrad the antiaircraft/machine gun units of the Stalingrad *PVO* provided defensive cover fire from air attack for the large plants, the railroad stations, crossings, vessels on the Volga River (from Saratov to Astrakhan), and for the combat formations of the antiaircraft artillery. In their armament the units had the most varied kinds of machine gun systems: DShk, BK, compound four-barrel mounts, tripod and single-leg PV-1, coaxial pedestal mount Model 1939, coaxial "Colt-Browning," single-leg system Maxim, and others.

In all, the antiaircraft machine gun units on the vessels of the Volga basin, in the areas of Kalach, Kotluban, and Stalingrad shot down 26 airplanes. In addition to this, the antiaircraft machine guns were used successfully against the ground forces of the enemy. With machine guns they dispersed and destroyed several companies of enemy infantry in the areas of Kotluban and Orlovka.

The experience of the fighting at Stalingrad showed that the covering of large objects with antiaircraft machine guns is not expedient when the forces defending these objects have antiaircraft artillery of medium and small calibers, because bombs are released upon such objects from altitudes beyond the range of effective fire of antiaircraft machine guns.

The searchlight units gained a great deal of combat experience during the battle for Stalingrad, making it possible to draw a number of valuable practical conclusions.

Night raids against the city were started at the same time as the day raids. A characteristic feature was that the raids were carried out chiefly on moonlit nights. As a rule, the airplanes came from the direction of the moon toward the center of the fires started in the daytime. They came singly or in small groups, spaced in time and altitude. The majority of the raids took place at altitudes from 2,500 to 5,000 meters. The searchlights had to operate on moonlit nights and oftentimes with broken cloudiness, making it possible for the airplanes to escape behind clouds. Operation in the area of the town itself was particularly difficult. The haze from the dust raised by the bombing, and the thick smoke of fires hanging sometimes in a continuous curtain over the town often made it impossible for the searchlights to operate. Taking this into account, the enemy frequently approached the town after the release of bombs, covering themselves with a belt of smoke stretching toward the town, in this way avoiding illumination by searchlights.

The bombers tried to cross the main zone of searchlight protection with muffled motors in order to render more difficult the work of the sound observers. The main difficulty in catching the airplanes lay in the tracking, because the searchlights were not sufficient in number. Here at first we made the searches with a wide beam. This method of searching was effective, and in combat the units were convinced of the advantage of its employment. An enemy airplane caught in the beam generally tried to deceive the searchlight operators by signalling with rockets "I am your own plane"—a method which at first succeeded—or they tried to escape into the clouds, after bombarding their target or the station. The stations were subjected to ground shelling and bombardment from the air even in the daytime, when the front line was close to the forward edge of light protection. This made it necessary to move back certain stations in the daytime and place them under cover, moving them back into their positions again at night. When the front came up close to the forward searchlights, the latter were placed on the line of the artillery batteries where they were assigned two missions: to operate against enemy airplanes and tanks. In reality they mostly carried out only the first mission, but here and there the searchlight crews, jointly with the artillerymen, covered the batteries from enemy submachine guns.

As the Germans moved toward the city and intensified night bombing of the railway running along the Akhtuba River, a part of the searchlights were shifted beyond the Volga for protection of the railroad and crossings over the Akhtuba River and the Volga. Since the enemy airplanes did not expect the searchlights here, they at first did not take countermeasures —they flew in ordinary formations at low altitudes. Hence, on the first few nights the work of the searchlights was such that they caught large numbers of airplanes in their beams. After this the flights were made at higher altitudes and the numbers caught fell sharply.

At about this time, our aviation started to carry out large night raids against the combat formations of the Germans. The searchlights, illuminating their own bombers by mistake, began to interfere with the work of our aviation, and for this reason the operation of the searchlights was stopped.

Searchlights were used with great effectiveness for illuminating the opposite banks of the Volga occupied by the Germans and subjected to bombing by our aviation; they were also used effectively as beacons for our own aviation and for target designation. The searchlights were used as beacons in the following manner: At a certain time the beams were projected into the zenith, immediately sloped in the given direction by 12 to 15 degrees and then extinquished in this position; after 10 to 15 seconds the whole process was repeated. Target designation was carried out by two searchlights, using the method of crossing the beams over the object to be bombed in the enemy dispositions or by direct illumination from behind the Volga of the place where the Germans were located.

Heavy night bombing of the German combat formations forced the latter to move many searchlights up to their front line. At night one could sometimes observe the so-called rivalry between our searchlights and those of the Germans, when our searchlights interrupted the Heinkels and the Junkers on their way to bomb our rear, at the same time that they were mistakenly illuminated by the Germans themselves.

The Aircraft Warning Service protected both the equipment of antiaircraft defense and aviation and that of the commanders of units of combined arms.

The reports from the observation posts were transmitted over the existing lines of the People's Commissariat of Signal Communication, and during the period when the front was still far from Stalingrad, these reports, as a rule reached, the Main Post of the Stalingrad *PVO* in due time. The Main Post was able, in doubtful cases, to check the reports by making inquiries of its airdromes, and in this way determine the nationality of the planes. As the front drew nearer, however, the problem of warning suddenly grew worse. The separate sectors of interurban and local communications of the People's Commissariat of Signal Communications, used by the posts of the Aircraft Warning Service, were taken over by the unit and army commanders of signal communications without any agreement with the command of antiaircraft defense.

The signal communication lines running along the banks of the Volga were taken over for army telegraph communications. Later on, and only upon agreement with the Chief of Signal Communications of the Front, the disconnected antiaircraft warning posts were connected with phonic sets. Without any warning, the posts of the Aircraft Warning Service were switched off, their lines being overloaded by special communication of the NKVD.[9] In the majority of cases, the attempts of the workers of the *PVO* corps area defense failed to come to an agreement with the workers of special communications of the NKVD concerning the method of using the signal communications, which were also used jointly by the units of Aircraft Warning Service and the staffs of the Army; thus it was not always possible to transmit air reports, because during this time the lines were busy with operational conversations between the staffs of the units.

The result of such a situation in signal communications was that even during fighting on the distant approaches to Stalingrad, reports from the posts of the Aircraft Warning Service often did not come in at all. This led to a delay in the warning of the antiaircraft artillery, fighter aviation, and the population of the town about the raids of enemy airplanes, which would then appear by surprise over the town and encounter the proper resistance by means of antiaircraft defense.

The antiaircraft artillery, machine guns, and searchlights were warned from the Main Post of the Antiaircraft Warning Service. In addition to this, the antiaircraft artillery had the usual observation posts for its immediate warning. From the moment the enemy came into the immediate area of the fire positions of antiaircraft artillery, the reports of the Antiaircraft Warning System ceased to have an essential importance, because its weapons were always in combat readiness and conducted battle against the enemy in the air and on the ground.

The airdromes of fighter aviation were warned by nearby reconnaissance posts and observation posts of the Aircraft Warning Service, with simultaneous and parallel reports to the main post of the Aircraft Warning Service. Special installations of the Aircraft Warning Service known as "Pegmatite" were stationed in the area of the airdromes, operated for aviation, and simultaneously transmitted reports to the Main Post. When aviation was rebased, the location of these installations was also changed.

Target indication and the guiding of our fighter aviation to the airplanes of the enemy were carried out from special posts of target designation. The posts for the daytime work had the ordinary fabric streamers; for the night work special light indicators were provided. In the first period, when signal communications with the observation posts still operated effectively, target indication was carried out upon command from the Main Post of the Aircraft Warning Service or by visual signals. However, when interruptions began to occur in signal communications, the guiding of fighter aviation was turned over to the posts of target indication themselves. During the mass raids, the posts could not cope with their task. Later on, target designation posts were organized only with the operational groups of the command of fighter aviation.

In the scheme of warning for the Main Post of the Aircraft Warning Service, we included the staff of the front, the staff of the 8th Air Army, and the staff of the Volga Military Flotilla. The troop unit staffs were warned through the company posts or even through the observation posts of the Aircraft Warning Service.

In addition to observation of the air, there was also observation of the action of the enemy on the ground. From the battalions of the Aircraft Warning Service we sent out special reconnaissance groups from the makeup of the company posts with the mission of observing the movements of the enemy and reconnoitering the place of concentration of enemy troops and their actions. For example, a reconnaissance unit of the Aircraft Warning Service discovered the precise location of the staff of the enemy and the place of concentration of his tanks. The data concerning the enemy ground forces obtained by the reconnaissance groups and posts were transmitted to the staff of the 8th Air Army. There were cases when the posts of the Aircraft Warning Service happened to be in the rear of the advancing enemy troops, but, despite this, observation was conducted continuously and the reports were transmitted until signal communications were interrupted.

With the approach of the troops of the enemy to the edges of the town, we set up additional posts in the town itself. In the period of mass raids of enemy aviation against the town, the posts of the Aircraft Warning Service located in the town carried on continuous observation. For restoring the lines of signal communications destroyed by bombing, we sent out reconstruction parties and established control posts at intervals of 1 kilometer on the line. As lines of communication, we used the existing high voltage lines and the permanent city lines and illumination network which had escaped the raids. The posts of the Aircraft Warning Service located along the banks of the Volga were moved up very close to the river itself in order that we might observe its navigable channel. When enemy airplanes dropped mines in the water, they reported that fact to the local river dispatchers and the staff of the Volga Flotilla.

Command of Antiaircraft Defense

The command of the means of antiaircraft defense of the Stalingrad *PVO*, before the beginning of combat operations in the area and on the immediate approaches to Stalingrad, was centralized in the hands of the regional commander. The commanders of the regiments of antiaircraft artillery (the chiefs of sectors) at Stalingrad and the commanders of the independent battalions, armored trains, and small antiaircraft machine gun units, defending the separate objects of the area, received instructions directly from the commanders of the area, who had direct signal communications with them. Later on, the circumstances often necessitated a change in the forms of control.

With the beginning of active operations by enemy aviation against vessels, wharves, and against the Riazan-Uralsk Railroad—when it became necessary to assign antiaircraft means for the defense of these objects—we organized operational groups from the makeup of the staff and control personnel of the commander of the area. There was one operational group for the control of the equipment assigned for accompanying the vessels and for the antiaircraft defense of the wharves, and two for this same purpose on the Riazan-Uralsk Railroad. As a result, when the Germans approached close to Stalingrad, a great part of the means of antiaircraft defense was transferred from the right bank of the Volga to the left and took up a defense front having a width of 50 to 70 kilometers from Sredne–Pogromnoe up to Kammenyi Iar. It was impossible to exercise centralized control of them over such a long distance and, hence, we created three additional operational groups.

To the operational groups we assigned commanders with initiative and good tactical preparation, capable—in case of interruptions in the functioning of signal communications—of making independent decisions and directing the tactical employment of the means entrusted to them.

For connecting the staff of the area and the operational groups with the units of antiaircraft defense, the sending out of liaison officers was practiced extensively and proved to be effective.

For convenience of control and stability the command posts of the regiments and battalions were placed in the field. Combat experience confirmed the correctness of this decision. The very first days of fighting the enemy ground forces showed that it was necessary for the antiaircraft gunners to have observation posts for the conduct of fire from covered positions against the infantry and concentrations of motor vehicle transport. Such observation posts should be placed forward on the front line of our rifle troops, have a good field of view, and reliable signal communications with the fire positions of their batteries.

Combat experience with the means of antiaircraft defense showed that the most reliable form of signal communications assuring uninterrupted control of troops is radio. As a result of continuous bombing from the air and intensive mortar and artillery fire, the permanent wire lines were quickly knocked out and their restoration was very difficult because as a result of the continuous raids against the town the poles and fittings were burned and the conductors, as a result of the heat of the flames, curled up in loops and spirals difficult to straighten out. The field cable lines laid to the side of structures and in the ravines proved to be the most stable. Such lines could be restored rather quickly by the line inspectors who were on the battlefield all the time. But still the system of wire communications was frequently interrupted and the only reliable means of signal communications left was radio.

The underestimation of the value of the radio, before the beginning of the battle for Stalingrad, resulted in adverse effects upon its operation. There was an insufficient number of radio stations. Since cadres of good radio operators had not been trained in time and the command personnel of the units and sections of signal communications of the staff of the *PVO* had little faith in the reliability of radio and did not have sufficient experience in planning and coordinating its work, the transition to radio as a basic means of signal communications involved difficulties. In particular, we had not taken into account the fact that, in view of the situation, mobile radio stations were needed. Since they were set up stationary, in dugouts, or placed in buildings, it was necessary to reinstall them on machines and this required a great deal of time and labor.

A great defect in the work of radio and wire communications was the absence of reserves of signal communications equipment. Everything had been calculated only for a single stationary position; when the situation forced a change in the command post, it was necessary to shorten the separate directions and increase the number of receivers and transmitting centers in the radio network. This resulted in an overloading of the receivers and transmitters, because one radio station worked in two radio networks. All this taken together had a harmful effect upon the continuity of command.

With the passage of the Command Post of the *PVO* to the left bank of the Volga, signal communications with the units remaining on the right bank were maintained by radio and field telephone. The field cables from the left to the right bank of the river were laid in water. It turned out that the insulation of the field cable could resist water for only 10 or 15 days, after which it was necessary to lay a new line. Despite the frequent change of cable under enemy fire, the new lines were laid across the river in due time and signal communications functioned continuously.

The lines and centers of wire communications of the automatic exchange and the trunk exchanges were operated with a high degree of efficiency during all the periods of the battle for Stalingrad, until they were completely destroyed.

The network of the automatic exchanges and the trunk exchanges were well-planned beforehand, and trained brigades specially detailed from the signal communications network of the area were always present at the automatic exchanges and the trunk exchanges and from there provided reliable signal communications.

Conclusions

The combat experience of the units of antiaircraft defense in the battle for Stalingrad enables us to draw the following conclusions:

1. In the organization of the antiaircraft defense of any point, however far it is from the front line, the arrangement of the combat formation of antiaircraft artillery should always take into account the purpose and mission of antitank defense.

2. In the defense of a point it is necessary to arrange the group of antiaircraft batteries in such a way that the most important objects will be covered by the greatest concentration of fire; the batteries should not be distributed uniformly around all of the point to be defended. At the same time, the fire positions of the batteries covering a given object should not be more than 1.5 to 2.2 kilometers from the object in question. The purpose of this is to enable the batteries to combat dive-bombers successfully and to create concentrated fire on the immediate approaches to the object and over the object itself.

3. The mutual disposition of the guns in the fire position should take into account simultaneous action against enemy airplanes, tanks, and submachine guns and not conform to a fixed pattern, obligatory in the form of a trapezium.

For combating dive-bombers and combat-support planes attempting to neutralize batteries of medium caliber, it is necessary to assign one to two small-caliber antiaircraft guns or large-caliber machine guns for the covering of each of these batteries.

4. In order to deceive the enemy as to the actual location of the fire positions, the employment of dummy positions, changing the main firing position to the alternate fire position, and the use of roving guns will be very useful.

5. For the defense of the separate objects covered by dense fire of antiaircraft artillery of medium and small caliber, it will not be advantageous to employ antiaircraft machine guns because enemy airplanes under the fire of small antiaircraft artillery rarely descend to altitudes within the range of effective fire of antiaircraft machine guns.

6. The medium-caliber batteries of antiaircraft artillery, in use for the defense of points, should be capable of rapid maneuver on wheels, and should not be converted into semi-stationary fire positions, covering the points with underground shelters and other installations. The personnel of the batteries, and foremost the commander, should be trained to select and change fire positions quickly. Transport, reconnaissance, and signal communications should always be ready. Maneuver of vehicles, just as in the case of fire maneuver, should constitute the basis of the tactical training of point antiaircraft batteries.

7. For counteraction against the aviation and the ground troops of the enemy in the direction of the main blow, it is necessary to have maneuverable groups of medium-caliber antiaircraft artillery composed of one to two battalions reinforced by small-caliber antiaircraft artillery, antiaircraft machine guns, and a detachment of tank and infantry destroyers as well as antitank riflemen, grenadethrowers, and submachine gunners.

8. Antiaircraft artillery units may constitute reliable means for combating enemy ground forces, including armored units. In planning the antitank point defense, defended by antiaircraft artillery, we should—in case we do not have sufficient special antitank artillery—make provisions for including antiaircraft artillery in the system of antitank defense.

In a complicated situation the antiaircraft artillery may, even though it places a great strain upon the personnel, perform two missions simultaneously: repel attacks from the air and engage the ground forces of the enemy.

For antitank defense the batteries should not be split up by detailing separate guns, but we should employ them as a whole from one main position or from positions specially equipped for antitank defense and located not far from the main position.

9. In anticipation of a direct clash with enemy ground forces, it is necessary to have intervals between the fire positions of the batteries, in agreement with the command of troops of combined areas, to supplement the infantry and antitank means. With the troops and commanders of small line units not required to execute combat missions and not having at the time any material; we should organize, on the scale of a battalion up to a regiment, groups of submachine gunners and tank chasers and use them, depending upon the circumstances, at the place where they are needed.

10. The success of fire is determined by the quality of preparation of the

first volley of the batteries and the concentration of fire of all the batteries which may conduct fire against the given target. Volley fire, in comparison with continuous fire, produces the best effect in fire by the basic and supplementary methods.

We should remember that the great deviations of the bursts from the target after the first three or four volleys occurred when the target made some kind of maneuver, and if there were great deviations of the bursts in the first volley, it was the result of poor previous on-the-spot training of the battery and the gunner in opening fire.

11. Fire against ground targets should be conducted with careful observation of its results. In fire onslaughts against concentrations of enemy troops on the basis of target data determined on the map, we should conduct fire with three range settings: a measured one and two differing by 200 meters on the over side and on the short side, taking into account the ballistic and meteorological conditions of fire.

12. In the control of fighter aviation in the air, it was found that the staffs of the air units did not have sufficient training for the utilization of the radio installations "Pigmatit," "Redoubt," and radio.[10]

13. There has been confirmation of the necessity of better selection and training of chiefs of searchlight stations and a more careful checking of the equipment of these stations before the combat work. The training should develop initiative and give excellent technical and tactical ability.

The employment of searchlights for target designation to assist our own aviation and for blinding tanks in night tanks attacks was found to be feasible and advantageous.

14. In order that the staff of the area may not lose contact with the units, and so that the latter may not lose contact with the smaller units, it is necessary to depend first of all on radio as the basic means of signal communications under the conditions of intense combat activity.

Editor's Notes

1. The Stalingrad *PVO* region was created by an order of the People's Commissariat of Defense, No. 0071 of April 20, 1942. It consisted of nine antiaircraft artillery regiments, twelve antiaircraft artillery battalions, two antiaircraft machine gun battalions, and 25 antitank machine gun companies and platoons. Also available were seven battalions and three companies of the Aircraft Warning Service, one searchlight battalion and one searchlight regiment, one division of barrage balloons, six armored antiaircraft trains, and the 102nd *PVO* Interceptor Division. See Rokossovskii, *Velikaia pobeda na Volge*, p. 58.
2. The Commander of the Stalingrad *PVO* was Colonel Ia. A. Raynin.
3. Unmentioned is that three new air regiments and additional antiaircraft guns were transferred in August from the Moscow *PVO*.
4. The Aircraft Warning Service, *VNOS*, was relocated within the city and across the Volga River. This obviously cut warning time severely.
5. German JU 87 dive-bombers carried sirens to increase the morale effect of their attacks.
6. This was the Me-109 G model.
7. Rokossovskii, *Velikaia pobeda ne Volge*, p. 58, indicates 85 aircraft at the beginning of the struggle. However, S. Romanov, "Voiska protivovozdushnoi oborony strany" in *Voenno istorichestkii zhurnal* 11(1982): 29, lists only 60 fighters. (Hereafter Romanov, *VIZ*).

8. *PVO* units from as far away as Voronezh, Borisoglebsk, Saratov, Balashov, and Penza were utilized to cover the railroads. These included 70 fighters, 570 antiaircraft guns, 226 machine guns, and 59 searchlights. See Romanov, *VIZ*, p. 33

9. An interesting comment on the friction between the NKVD and the armed forces. Certainly it is not a comment that can be found in modern works or in even a fraction of the works previously published.

10. "Redoubt" was a gun-laying radar. "Pigmatit" was a new detection and guidance radar.

14

Editor's Appendix

Selected Biographies of the Authors

Arkhadii Petrovich Alekseev (–1985)

Retired Major General and former Chief of Staff of Engineer Troops at Front level. Member of the Communist Party since 1939. Awarded Order of the Fatherland War 1st Class in 1945.

Zelik Solomonovich Al'shits (–present)

Began the war as the Chief of Intelligence of the 6th Rifle Corps. Awarded the Order of the Red Star in 1944 while a Lieutenant Colonel. After the war, was an instructor at the Frunze Military Academy. Promoted to Colonel.

Fodor Gerasimovich Barskii (–present)

Colonel and author during the war. Awarded the Order of the Red Banner in 1945; the Order of Kutuzov 3rd Class in 1944; and the Order of the Fatherland War 1st Class in 1944.

Mikhail L'vovich Cherniavskii (–1983)

Retired Lieutenant General of Tank Troops. Member of the Communist Party since 1917 and veteran of the Civil War. By 1940, Chief of the M.V. Frunze Armored School and later Commander of the 1st Mechanized Corps. In 1942, Deputy Commander of the 3rd Tank Army. In 1944–45, Commander of Armored and Mechanized Troops of the 2nd Baltic and 2nd Belorussian Fronts.

Pavel Grigorivich Esalov (–present)

In 1944, promoted to Major General. Served as Commander of 68th Mechanized Brigade.

311

Aleksandr Alekseevich Matianov (–present)

Promoted Major General in 1940. Service branch was the Cavalry. By February 1944, possibly Chief of the Cavalry Staff of the Red Army.

Leonid Vasilievich Onianov (1898–1966)

Retired Lieutenant General. Member of the Communist Party since 1919. Fought in the Civil War. Post-Civil War, served in command and instructor positions. In World War II, worked on the General Staff in compiling data on enemy strength and organizations. Late World War II, served as Chief of the Directorate of Agents in Enemy Armies of the *GRU*. Last position was as a faculty chief at the Frunze Military Academy. Many orders and medals.

Arsenii Petrovich Penchevskii (1903–1952)

Promoted to Major General in 1945. Member of the Communist Party since 1941. In World War II, served on the staffs of several (70th, 33rd) field armies. Continued service after war on staffs of Central Ministry of Defense apparatus. Awarded the Order of Lenin, four Orders of the Red Banner, the Order of Suvorov 2nd Class, the Order of the Red Star, and many medals.

N. G. Pavlenko (–present)

Retired as Lieutenant General of Reserves. Doctor of Historical Sciences and Professor. Served on the General Staff during World War II. In 1964, Chief Editor of *Voenno istoricheskii zhurnal*. From 1967–71 Chief, History of War and Military Sciences *kefedra* at the General Staff Academy. By 1971, Chairman of *DOSAAF* Joint Committee of Central Directives and Institutions of the Ministry of Defense. Prolific author of books and articles.

Fodor Aleksandrovich Samsanov (1901–1980)

Retired Colonel General of Artillery. Graduate of the Frunze and General Staff Academies. Member of the Communist Party since 1921. Started in political–party work in the 1920s. Pre-World War II, served as Chief of the Rostov Artillery School. In 1941 served as Chief of Artillery of the 28th Army. From December 1941–46, served as Chief of Staff of Artillery of the Soviet Army. Later (1959–64), Editor in Chief, editorial board of *Voenno istoricheskii zhurnal*. Published numerous articles and served as editor of *Artilleriia i artilleriskoie snabzhenie v*

Otechestvennoi Voine 1941–1945 (1964). Awarded many orders including the Order of Lenin, three Orders of the Red Banner, Orders of Suvorov 1st and 2nd Class, and many others as well as many medals.

Nikolai Aleksandrovich Talenskii (1901–1967)

Retired Major General and Doctor of Military Science and Professor. Specialty was military history. Member of Communist Party since 1922. Veteran of the Civil War. Post-Civil War, served in staff jobs. From 1930s to World War II, Chief of the Scientific Research Department of the Frunze Military Academy. From 1940–50, Chief of the Military History Department (later Directorate) of the General Staff. From 1943–45, Editor in Chief of *Krasnaia zvezda*. Post-World War II, consultant on military–scientific matters. From 1960–67, Chief, Sector of History for Disarmament Problems, Institute of History, USSR Academy of Science. Over 70 scientific works on military matters and over 100 newspapers and journal articles on military subjects. Many awards.

Mikail Viktorovich Savin (–1959)

Major General and Docent. Member of the Communist Party since 1941. Served in the Civil War. Post-Civil War, served as an instructor. In World War II, served in the Ministry of Defense apparatus. Author of several military historical works. Awarded Order of Lenin, two Orders of the Red Banner, Order of the Fatherland War 1st Class, and the Order of the Red Star. Many medals.

Aleksandr Danilovich Tsirlin (1902–1976)

Retired Colonel General of Engineer Troops and Doctor of Military Science and Professor. In 1948, graduate of the General Staff Academy and in 1956 awarded Doctorate. Member of the Communist Party since 1924. In 1940 was Chief of the Leningrad Military Engineer School. In World War II, in the central apparatus and with field armies. Served as Deputy Chief of Staff of Engineer Troops, later chief of Engineer Troops of the Red Army of several (Steppe, 2nd Ukrainian, Transbaikal) Fronts. After war served on General Staff and as Chief of the Kuibishev Military Engineer School. Some publications. Awarded State Prize (1967), two Orders of Lenin, four Orders of the Red Banner, two Orders of Kutuzov 1st Class, Order of Suvorov 2nd Class, Order of Kutuzov 2nd Class, and many others.

Vladimir Dmitriievich Utkin (–1980)

Retired Major General. Member of the Communist Party since 1930. Former senior instructor at the General Staff Academy. Awarded the Order of the Red Banner in 1944.

Piotr Panteleimonovich Vechnii (1891–1957)

Retired Lieutenant General and candidate Military Science Docent. Member of the Communist Party since 1939. Civil War veteran and military adviser to the Spanish Army. In 1941–42, served in staff positions in southern USSR. From 1942–44, served as Chief of the General Staff group to study war experiences. In 1946, at the Frunze Military Academy. Editor of *Voennaia Misi*. Many publications and awards.

Mikhail Petrovich Vorobev (1896–1957)

Marshal of Engineer Troops and Docent. Member of the Communist Party since 1919. Fought in the Civil War. Post-Civil War, command positions in Engineer Troops. From 1936–40, Chief of the Zhdanov Military Engineer School at Leningrad. In 1940, Inspector General of Engineer Troops. In 1941 with field forces. In 1942, Chief of Engineer Troops of Western Front and Commander of 1st Sapper Army. From 1942–46, Chief of Engineer Troops of the Ministry of Defense. From 1946–52, Chief of Engineer Troops, Ground Forces. Later Chief of Engineer Troops of various Military Districts and senior posts. Awarded two Orders of Lenin, three Orders of the Red Banner, Order of Suvorov 1st Class, Order of the Fatherland War 1st Class, and Order of the Red Banner of Labor (1948).

Nikolai Mikhailovich Zamiatin (1896–1951)

Major General and Candidate of Military Science. Graduate of the Frunze Military Academy. Fought in the Civil War. In World War II, served in scientific research work as well as Instructor in the Military History Department of the General Staff Academy. Many publications. Awarded the Order of Lenin, two Orders of the Red Banner, Order of Kutuzov 2nd Class, two Orders of the Red Star, and seven medals.

Nikolai Akimovich Zhuravlev (1895–1960)

Lieutenant General of Aviation. Fought in World War I and the Civil War. Post-Civil War in Border Troops. Transferred to the Air Force and by 1940 was an instructor at the Zhukovskii Air Force Academy. In 1942,

served on staff at General Staff Academy. Several publications and awards including the Order of Lenin, two Orders of the Red Banner, Order of Suvorov 2nd Class, Order of Kutuzov 2nd Class, Order of the Fatherland War 1st Class, and medals.
Source: The information contained in these brief biographies comes from the extensive collection of material in the possession of Mr. Albert Graham and Mr. Frank Lyons. The planned multi-volume series, tentatively entitled *Soviet Officer Biographies* was made available to assist in the completion of this work.

TABLE A.1. Planned and Actual Scope of Operation "Uranus" (November–December)

| | Depth of Operation (kms) | | Duration of Operation (days) | | Average Daily Rates of Advance (kms) | |
| | | | | | Planned | Actual |
Front	Planned	Actual	Planned	Actual	Rifle/Mobile Formation	Rifle/Mobile Formation
Southwestern	140	140–160	3	5	20–25/40–45	15–20/28–35
Don	60	30–60	3	5	15–20/20	6–12/6–12
Stalingrad	90	85	2	4	10–15/45	12–15/20–35

Source: "Kontrnastuplenie pod Stalingradom v tsifrakh (operatsiia 'Uran')" *Voenno istorichestkii zhurnal* 3 (1968): 64, Table 1.

TABLE A.2. Strength of the Soviet Forces of the Three Fronts on November 20, 1942

	Southwest Front[1]		Don Front		Stalingrad Front[2]		In Three Fronts[3]	
	Total	In Combat Units	Total	In Combat Units	Total	In Combat Units	Total	In Combat Units
Men	338,631	275,504	292,707	185,565	383,961	258,633	1,015,299	719,702
Rifles	191,020	166,234	159,330	124,846	176,957	142,867	527,307	433,947
Submachine guns	27,081	25,634	29,902	18,144	37,799	35,366	84,782	79,144
Machine Guns								
Light	5,143	4,791	4,160	3,647	5,587	5,037	14,890	13,475
Heavy	1,802	1,741	1,843	1,756	2,264	2,203	5,909	5,700
Heavy caliber	622	581	374	348	463	395	1,459	1,324
Total	**7,567**	**7,113**	**6,377**	**5,751**	**8,314**	**7,635**	**22,258**	**20,499**
Antitank Rifles	6,280	6,195	5,733	5,545	5,649	5,037	17,662	16,777
Artillery								
45 mm Antitank guns*	740	728	581	532	986	945	2,307	2,205
76 mm Field	974	963	838	829	1,185	1,141	2,997	2,933
107 mm & up	487	486	419	412	372	368	1,278	1,266
Total	**2,201**	**2,177**	**1,838**	**1,773**	**2,543**	**2,454**	**6,582**	**6,404**
Mortars								
120 mm	541	532	444	418	624	599	1,609	1,549
82 mm	1,828	1,793	2,010	1,885	1,506	1,449	5,344	5,127
50 mm	1,932	1,846	1,483	1,336	1,178	1,077	4,593	4,259
Total	**4,301**	**4,171**	**3,937**	**3,639**	**3,308**	**3,125**	**11,546**	**10,935**
Antiaircraft guns								
76–85 mm	45	45	53	53	245	245	343	343
25–37 mm	278	276	133	133	287	273	698	682
Total	**323**	**321**	**186**	**186**	**532**	**518**	**1,041**	**1,025**
Guards Mortars								
BM-8/BM-13	148	148	147	147	145	145	440	440
M-30	480	480	288	288	192	192	960	960

	628	628	435	435	337	337	1,400	1,400
Total	628	628	435	435	337	337	1,400	1,400
Tanks								
Heavy	145	145	43	42	49	49	237	236
Medium	318	316	67	65	357	354	742	735
Light	267	262	70	59	244	218	581	539
Total	730	723	180	166	650	621	1,560	1,510
Armored cars	99	93	38	20	181	164	381	277
Vehicles	14,529	8,599	12,003	4,383	14,881	7,750	41,413	20,732
Tractors	792	477	864	498	1,001	626	2,657	1,601
Horses	69,003	62,752	44,915	28,078	55,691	39,398	169,609	130,228

1. Excluded are 4th and 6th Guards Rifle Corps (35th, 38th, 41st, 44th Guards and 195th Rifle divisions, and 40th and 42nd Guards Artillery Regiments, which did not start to arrive with the 1st Guards Army until after November 21, 1942.

2. In the composition of the Stalingrad Front are included all men and arms available on November 20, including the forces of the 28th Army around Astrakhan, the 300th Rifle Division in the reserves of the front, and the 77th, 115th, and 156th Fortified Regions, which were deployed on the small islands and left bank of the Volga. Also included are the forces of the Stalingrad *PVO*. Omitted from the totals are the forces of the Volga River Flotilla because in November 1942, only two gunboats—"Usyskin" and "Chapaev"—were operational, as the rest had been stored for the winter on November 1. Also not included were the 87th and 315th Rifle Division's, which did not arrive until November 23–24.

3. In general, the number of tanks for the three fronts includes all models that were in good repair (heavy KV, medium T–34, light T–60, and T–70) as well as older model tanks (BT–7, T–26, T–37, and T–38). In the composition of the Southwestern Front are indicated 113 medium and 50 light tanks of the 1st Guards Mechanized Corps, which were in the reserves of the front and thus did not take part in the November offensive. In the composition of the Stalingrad Front are included tanks of the 28th Army (70 units) and also the recently returned 85th Tank Brigade and the 35th and 166th Independent Tank Regiments (125 units), which were all in the reserves of the front on November 20. In some works the number of tanks in the composition of the three fronts is given as 984. This figure does not include light T–60 tanks, older models (BT and T–26), and tanks of the 28th Army, the 85th Tank Brigade, and the 35th and 166th Independent Tank regiments of the Stalingrad Front and the 1st Guards Mechanized Corps of the Southwestern Front.

Source: "Kontrnastuplenie pod Stalingradom v tsifrakh (operatsiia 'Uran')," *Voenno istoricheskii zhurnal* 3 (1968): 67, table 2.

Battle for Stalingrad

TABLE A.3. Composition of Southwestern, Don, and Stalingrad Fronts (November 20 and December 1, 1942)

	November 20, 1942				December 1, 1942			
	Southwestern	Don	Stalingrad	Total	Southwestern	Don	Stalingrad	Total
Armies								
Combined arms	2	3	5	10	1	4	5	10
Tank	1	—	—	1	1	—	—	1
Air Army	2	1	1	4	2	1	1	4
Flotillas	—	—	1	1	—	—	1	1
Corps								
Rifle	—	—	1	1	3	—	1	4
Cavalry	2	—	1	3	2	—	1	3
Mechanized	1	—	1	2	2	—	1	3
Tank	3	1	1	5	2	3	1	6
PVO Corps	—	—	1	1	—	—	1	1
Divisions								
Rifle	18	24	24	66	20	27	26	73
Cavalry	6	—	2	8	6	—	2	8
Artillery	1	—	—	1	1	2	1	4
Antiaircraft	2	1	—	3	1	3	1	5
UR[2]	—	2	7	9	—	2	7	9
Independent Brigades								
Rifle	—	—	15	15	1	—	15	16
Motor rifle	1	—	1	2	1	—	1	2
Tank Destroyer[3]	1	—	1	2	1	—	1	2
Tank	1	6	8	15	2	6	7	15
Engineers	2	2	3	7	3	3	5	11
Independent Regiments								
Rifle	—	—	1	1	—	—	1	1
Cavalry	3	—	1	4	4	—	6	10
Tank	1	—	2	3	1	—	—	1
Motorcycle	1	—	—	1	1	8	—	9
Artillery	12	13	14	39	8	9	8	25
Tank Destroyer[2]	20	4	18	42	12	7	16	35

Mortar	8	2	3	13	5	5	3	13
Guards Mortars	7	12	14	33	4	15	14	33
Antiaircraft	12	9	14	35	4	11	7	22
Engineer	—	1	—	1	1	—	1	2
Independent Battalions								
Tank	2	—	1	3	2	—	1	3
Armored train	—	4	4	8	—	4	4	8
Heavy artillery	—	—	1	1	15	—	—	—
Guards Mortars	13	13	—	14	5	—	1	16
Antiaircraft	6	2	5	13	5	5	—	10

1. Until January 9, 1943, the 13th Corps was considered a tank corps, although in reality it was organized like a mechanized corps (three mechanized brigades).
2. UR = Fortified Region.
3. Tank Destroyer = Destroyer.

Source: "Kontrnastuplenie pod Stalingom v tsifrakh (Operatsiia 'Uran')" *Voenno istoricheskii zhurnal* Number 3 (1968): p 68, table 3.

TABLE A.4. Composition and Strength of the Soviet Air Force (November 20, 1942)

Formations	17th Air Army Southwestern Front	2nd Air Army Voronezh Front	16th Air Army Don Front	8th Air Army Stalingrad Front	102d PVO Fighter Division	Total
Mixed air corp	1	—	—	1	—	2
Air divisions	5	4	5	10	1	25
Bomber	1	—	—	1	—	2
Ground attack	1	1	2	2	—	6
Mixed	—	—	—	2	—	2
Night bomber	1	1	1	1	—	4
Fighter	2	2	2	4	1	11
Regiments	18	12	22	47	4	103
Bomber	3	—	1	4	—	8
Ground attack	5	4	7	14	—	30
Reconnaissance	—	1	—	1	—	2
Fighter	6	4	8	17	4	39
Night bomber	4	3	6	6	—	19
Mixed	—	—	—	5	—	5

Aircraft	SW Front Total	Op	Voronezh Front Total	Op	Don Front Total	Op	Stalingrad Front Total	Op	PVO Total	Op	Total	Op
Bomber	57	46	7	4	20	11	68	29	—	—	152	90
Ground attack	133	118	64	57	103	68	255	177	—	—	555	420
Fighter	169	147	31	23	107	81	408	235	88	23	803	509
Reconnaissance	6	6	15	12	3	2	15	3	—	—	39	23
Night bombers	76	71	54	48	116	98	121	91	—	—	367	308
Total	441	388	171	144	349	260	867	535	88	23	1,916	1,350

*Op=Operational

Source: "Kontrnastuplenie pod Stalingradom v tsifrakh (Operatsiia 'Uran')," *Voenno istoricheskii zhurnal* 3 (1968): 69, table 4.

TABLE A.5. Attack Frontage and Density of Soviet Forces (November 20, 1942)

	Frontage (km)			Total					Attack Zone				Bkth¹ Sectors				Average Density (km Div)		
	Tot	Atk Zone	Bkth¹ Sect	Corps	Div	Bde	FA	Div² Equ	Corps	Div	Bde	Div Equ	Corps	Div	Bde	Div Equ	Total	Atk Zone	Bkth¹ Sect
Southwestern Front																			
1st Guards Army	175	10.0	—	—	6	1	—	6.5	—	2	—	2.0	—	—	—	—	26.9	5.0	—
5th Tank Army	35	27.0	10.0	3	9	—	—	9.0	3	9	—	9.0	2	4	1	4	3.9	3.0	2.5
21st Army	40	19.0	12.0	2	9	1	—	9.5	2	9	—	9.0	2	8	—	8	4.2	2.1	1.5
Front Reserve	—	—	—	1	—	—	—	—	—	—	—	—	—	—	—	—	—	—	—
TOTAL	250	56.0	22.0	6	24	2	—	25.0	5	20	—	20.0	4	12	—	12	10.0	2.8	1.8
Don Front																			
65th Front Army	80	16.0	6.0	1	9	—	—	9.0	1	5	—	5.0	1	4	—	4	8.9	3.2	1.5
24th Army	40	4.5	4.5	—	9	—	1	10.0	—	4	—	4.0	—	4	—	4	4.0	1.1	1.1
66th Army	30	—	—	—	6	—	—	6.0	—	—	—	—	—	—	—	—	5.0	—	—
Front Reserve	—	—	—	1	—	—	1	1.0	—	—	—	—	—	—	—	—	—	—	—
TOTAL	150	20.5	10.5	1	24	—	2	26.0	1	9	—	9.0	1	8	—	8	5.8	2.3	1.3
Stalingrad Front																			
62nd Army	40	—	—	—	10	6	—	13.0	—	—	—	—	—	—	—	—	3.0	—	—
64th Army	35	12.0	12.0	—	5	6	1	9.0	—	4	—	4.0	—	4	—	4	3.9	3.0	3.0
57th Army	35	16.0	16.0	1	2	1	—	2.5	1	2	1	2.5	1	2	1	2.5	14.0	6.4	6.4
51st Army	130	12.0	12.0	2	6	1	1	7.5	2	5	—	5.0	2	5	—	5	17.3	2.4	2.4
28th Army	210	—	—	—	2	3	3	5.5	—	—	—	—	—	—	—	—	38.2	—	—
Front Reserve	—	—	—	—	1	—	—	4.0	—	—	—	—	—	—	—	—	—	—	—
TOTAL	450	40.0	40.0	3	26	17	7	41.5	3	11	1	11.5	3	11	1	11.5	10.8	3.5	3.5
TOTAL	850	115.5	72.5	10	74	19	9	92.5	9	40	1	40.5	8	31	1	31.5	9.2	2.9	2.3

1. Bkth Sect = Breakthrough Sector

2. In the table, two brigades (rifle, motorized rifle, or engineer) are equivalent to one division. One fortified region is equivalent to one division.

Source: "Kontrnastuplenie pod Stalingradom v tsifrakh (Operatsiia 'Uran')" in *Voenno istoricheskii zhurnal* 3 (1968): 72, table 7.

TABLE A.6. Operational Density of Artillery and Tanks in the Counterattack at
Stalingrad (November Operations)

	Fronts		
	Southwestern	Don	Stalingrad
Frontage (km)			
Total	250.0	150.0	450.0
Attack zone	56.0	10.5	40.0
Breakthrough sector	22.0	10.5	40.0
Guns and Mortars[1]			
Front	4,320.0 [2]	4,076.0	4,502.0
Total	17.3	27.2	10.0
Per km			
Attack zone			
Total	3,508.0	735.0	1,320.0
Per km	62.4	70.0	33.0
Breakthrough sector			
Total	1,452.0	735.0	1,320.0
Per km	66.0	70.0	33.0
Guards Mortars[1]			
BM–13 and BM–8			
Front total	148.0	147.0	145.0
Per km	0.6	1.0	0.3
Attack zone/breakthrough sector	134.0	105.0	90.0
Per km	2.4	10.0	2.2
M–30			
Front total	480.0	288.0	192.0
Per km	2.0	1.9	0.4
Attack zone/breakthrough sector	480.0	288.0	192.0
Per km	8.6	27.4	4.8
Tanks[1]			
Front			
Total	560.0 [2]	166.0	621.0
Per km	2.2	1.1	1.4
Attack zone			
Total	560.0	161.0	397.0
Per km	10.0	15.3	9.9
Breakthrough sector			
Total	560.0	161.0	397.0
Per km	25.4	15.3	9.9

1. Antiaircraft guns, tanks, and 50 mm mortars are not included.
2. 182 guns and mortars and 163 tanks of the 1st Guards Mechanized Corps in the forces of the
   Southwestern Front that were not involved in the initial counteroffensive phase are not
   included.

Source: "Kontrnastuplenie pod Stalingradom v tsifrakh (Operatsiia 'Uran')" *Voenno istoricheskii
zhurnal* 3 (1968): 73, table 8.

TABLE A.7. Soviet Order of Battle on November 20, 1942

Southwestern Front

1st Guards Army	1st, 153rd, 197th, 203rd, 266th, 278th Rifle Divisions; 1st Guards Mechanized Corps (1st, 2nd, 3rd Guards Mechanized Brigades and 16th, 17th Guards Tank Regiments)[1], 22nd Motorized Rifle Brigade
5th Tank Army	14th, 47th, 50th Guards Rifle Divisions; 119th, 159th, 346th Rifle Divisions; 8th Cavalry Corps (21st, 55th, 112th Cavalry Divisions); 1st Tank Corps (89th, 117th, 159th Tank Brigades and 44th Motorized Rifle Brigade); 26th Tank Corps (19th, 157th, 216th Tank Brigades and 14th Motorized Rifle Brigade); 8th Guards Tank Brigade; 8th Motorcycle Regiment; 510th, 511th Independent Tank Battalions
21st Army	63rd, 76th, 96th, 277th, 293rd, 333rd Rifle Divisions; 3rd Guards Cavalry Corps (5th and 6th Guards Cavalry and 32nd Cavalry Divisions); 5th Independent Engineer Brigade; 1st, 21st, 60th, 99th Independent Antitank Battalions; 4th Tank Corps (45th, 69th, 122nd Tank Brigades and 4th Motorized Rifle Brigade); 1st, 2nd, 4th Guards Independent Tank Regiments
17th Air Army	
2nd Air Army	(From the Voronezh Front)

[1]The 1st Guards Mechanized Corps was not fully concentrated on November 20.

TOTALS

Rifle Divisions	18	Cavalry Corps	2
Tank Corps	3	Motorcycle Regiments	1
Motorized Rifle Brigade	1	Cavalry Divisions	6
Independent Tank Brigades	1	Independent Tank Battalions	2
Independent Rifle Brigades	1	Mechanized Corps	1
Independent Tank Regiments	3		

Combat Forces of the Don Front

24th Army	49th, 84th, 120th, 173rd, 214th, 233rd, 260th, 273rd, 298th Rifle Divisions; 54th Fortified Region (UR); 58th, 61st Guards Independent Antitank Battalions; 16th Tank Corps (107th, 109th, 164th Tank Brigades; 15th Motorized Rifle Brigade); 10th Tank Brigade; 134th, 224th, 229th Independent Heavy Tank Battalions
65th Army	4th, 27th, 40th Guard Rifle Divisions; 23rd, 24th, 252nd, 258th, 304th, 321st Rifle Divisions; 54th, 64th Independent Antitank Battalions; 59th, 121st Tank Brigades; 59th Independent Heavy Tank Regiment
66th Army	64th, 99th, 116th, 226th, 299th, 343rd Rifle Divisions; 63rd Independent Antitank Battalion; 58th Tank Brigade
16th Air Army	
Formations Attached to the Front	159th Fortified Region (UR); 65th, 66th, 97th, 98th, 99th, 100th, 101st, 102nd Independent Antitank Battalions; 64th 148th Tank Brigades; 39th, 40th, 377th Independent Antiaircraft Armored Regiments

TOTALS

Rifle Divisions	24
Fortified Regions (UR)	2
Tank Corps	1
Independent Tank Brigades	6
Independent Heavy Tank Regiments	6

Combat Forces of the Stalingrad Front

28th Army	34th Guards; 248th Rifle Division; 52nd, 152nd, 159th Rifle Brigades; 78th, 116th Fortified Regions (UR); Independent Cavalry Regiment

	(without number); 6th Guards Tank Brigade; 565th Independent Tank Battalion; 35th Independent Heavy Tank Battalion; 30th, 33rd, 46th Independent Heavy Tank Regiment
51st Army	15th Guards; 91st, 126th, 302nd Rifle Divisions; 76th Fortified Region (UR); 4th Cavalry Corps (61st, 81st); 4th Mechanized Corps (36th, 59th, 60th Mechanized Brigades and 55th 158th Tank Regiments); 38th Motorized Rifle Brigade; 254th Tank Brigade
57th Army	169th, 422nd Rifle Divisions; 143rd Rifle Brigade; 45th, 172nd, 177th Independent Machinegun Artillery Battalions (76 UR); 13th Tank Corps (17th, 61st, 62nd Mechanized Brigades)[1], 90th, 235th Tank Brigades; 156th Independent Naval Infantry Battalion
62nd Army	13th, 37th, 39th Guards Rifle; 45th, 95th, 112th, 131st, 138th, 193rd, 284th, 308th Rifle Divisions; 42nd, 92nd, 115th, 124th, 149th, 160th Rifle Brigades; 84th Tank Brigade; 506th Independent Tank Battalion (235th Tank Brigade)
64th Army	7th Rifle Corps (93rd, 96th, 97th Rifle Brigade); 36th Guards; 29th, 38th, 157th, 204th Rifle Divisions; 66th, 154th Naval Infantry Brigades; 20th Independent Engineer Brigade; Composite cadet regiment; 118th Fortified Region (UR); 13th, 56th Tank Brigades
8th Air Army	——
Stalingrad *PVO*	——
Volga Flotilla	——
Formations	300th Rifle Divisions; 77th, 115th, 156th Fortified Region (UR); 85th
Attached to Front	Tank Brigade; 166th Independent Tank Regiment

TOTALS

Rifle Corps	1	Cavalry Divisions	2
Rifle Divisions	24	Tank Corps	1
Rifle Brigades	15	Mechanized Corps	1
Motorized Rifle Brigades	1	Independent Tank Brigades	8
Independent Engineer Brigade	1	Independent Tank Regiments	2
UR	7	Independent Tank Battalions	1
Independent Rifle/Cavalry Regiments	2	Independent Heavy Tank Regiments	4
Cavalry Corps	1		

Source: A. Samsonov, *Stalingradskaia bitva*, Moscow: *Nauka*, 1968) pp. 561–64, Appendix 11.
Note 1. 13th Tank Corps is, as previously noted, more appropriately identified as the 13th Mechanized Corps. On November 20, it was still called the 13th Tank Corps—Ed.

TABLE A.8   Combat Forces of the Don Front on January 1, 1943

21st Army	51st, 52nd Guards Rifle Divisions; 96th, 20th, 252nd, 277th, 293rd, 298th Rifle Divisions; 1st 21st, 99th Independent Ski Battalions; 1st Guard Independent Tank Regiment
24th Army	49th, 84th, 260th, 273rd Rifle Divisions; 54th Fortified Region (UR); 8th, 9th Guard Independent Tank Regiments
57th Army	15th Guards Division; 38th, 422nd Rifle Divisions; 20th Independent Engineer Brigade; 115th Fortified Region; 235th, 254th Tank Brigades; 234th Independent Tank Regiment; 156th Independent Motorized Rifle Brigade
62nd Army	13th, 39th Guards Rifle Divisions; 45th, 95th, 138th, 284th Rifle Divisions; 92nd, 124th, 149th Rifle Brigades; 156th Fortified Regions; 198th Independent Tank Regiment
64th Army	7th Rifle Corps (93rd, 96th, 97th Rifle Brigades); 36th Guard; 29th, 157th, 169th, 204th Rifle Divisions; 66th, 154th Naval Infantry Brigades; 77th, 118th Fortified Regions; 90th Tank Brigade; 38th

	Motorized Rifle Brigade; 35th, 166th Independent Tank Regiment; 28th Armored Train
65th Army	27th Guard Rifle Divisions; 23rd, 24th, 173rd, 214th, 233rd, 304th Rifle Divisions; 91st Tank Brigade; 5th, 10th Guard Independent Tank Regiment
66th Army	64th, 99th, 116th, 226th, 299th, 343rd Rifle Divisions; 7th Guard Independent Tank Regiment
16th Air Army	——
Stalingrad *PVO*	——
Front Troops	159th Fortified Region: 121st Tank Brigade: 2nd, 4th, 6th, 15th Guards Independent Tank Regiment; 512th Independent Tank Battalion; 48th, 49th, 52nd Barrage Battalion; 39th, 59th, 377th Antiaircraft Independent Armored Train

TOTALS			
Rifle Corps	1	Independent Tank Brigades	5
Rifle Divisions	39	Independent Motorized Rifle Brigade	1
Rifle Brigades	9	Independent Tank Regiments	14
Independent Rifle Brigades	1	Independent Tank Battalions	1
UR	6	Barrage Battalions	3
Ski Battalions	3	Armored Trains	4

Source: A. Samsonov *Stalingradskaia bitva*, (Moscow: *Nauka*, 1968), pp. 565–66, Appendix 12.

About the Editor

Louis Rotundo received his undergraduate and graduate degrees from the University of Central Florida. He has been an advanced research fellow of the U.S. Army War College Foundation and a consultant and lecturer for the Central Intelligence Agency and the U.S. Army Command and Staff College at Fort Leavenworth. A former staff assistant to U.S. Senator Lawton Chiles and a special assistant to the president of the University of Central Florida, Rotundo is now the president of Rotundo and Associates in Orlando, Florida. Currently serving on the editorial board for the *Journal of Soviet Military Studies*, Rotundo has written numerous articles on Soviet military history and current defense policy such as "The Creation of Soviet Reserves and the 1941 Campaign," *Military Affairs Journal* (January 1986); "War Plans and the 1941 Kremlin Wargame," *Journal of Strategic Studies* (March 1987); "The Road to Stalingrad Revisited," *Journal of the Royal United Services Institute* (June 1987); and the forthcoming "Stalin and the Outbreak of War in 1941," *Journal of Contemporary History*.

Name Index

Aganov, S. 280
Alekseev, A. P. 11, 310
Alshits, Z. A. 11, 310
Antonescu, I. 95, 132
Barskii, F. G. 11, 30
Batov, P. I. 4, 9, 95
Baumstein, V. G. 187, 198
Belogorskii, A. I. 197
Biriuzov, S. S. 4, 9
Bock, F. V. 20, 25
Bogdanov, S. I. 133
Borisov, M. I. 197
Budennyi, S. M. 20
Butkov, V. V. 113

Chalenko, I. T. 197
Chepurkin, N. S. 197
Cherniavskii, M. L. 11, 310
Chistiakov, I. M. 95
Chuikov, V. I. 4, 9, 51, 67, 95

Danilov, A. I. 67, 173
Dmitriev, M. P. 228
Dokuchev, M. S. 197

Egorov, E. P. 265, 280
Eremenko, A. I. 3, 48, 67, 95, 119, 126
Esalov, P. G. 11, 310

Fillipov, G. N. 108, 113

Galinin, I. V. 68, 95
Gerasimenko, V. F. 95
Golikov, F. I. 67
Gordov, V. N. 67
Graham, A. 314
Grechko, A. A. 4, 9
Gromov, G. A. 9
Gromov, I. E. 11

Gubin, V. A. 256

Halder, F. 20, 40
Halperin, M. 197
Hitler, A. 38, 40, 95, 132
Hoth, H. 27

Kantor, A. 197
Katzenbach, E. 197
Kazakov, V. I. 3, 228
Kehrig, M. 20, 94, 132, 133, 137
Khasin, A. M. 68
Khruskin, T. T. 256
Kluge, H. V. 25, 26
Kolomiets, T. K. 67
Kolpatchi, V. Ia. 66, 67
Koshelev, V. v. 68
Kozhevnikov, M. N. 256
Kozlov, D. T. 68
Krasovskii, S. A. 256
Kravchenko, A. G. 228
Kruchenkin, V. D. 67
Khrushchev, N. S. 2, 3, 4, 8, 67
Krylov, N. I. 4, 9
Kuchler, G. v. 25
Kuliev, Ia. K. 198
Kulovsky, Col. v. (von Kunowski) 34, 138, 158
Kuznetsov, N. G. 20
Kuznetsov, V. I. 67

Laiok, V. M. 67
Larionov, V. V. 9
Lasker, General 30
Leliushenko, D. D. 4, 9
List, W. v. 25, 37, 40
Litvinov, G. V. 11
Lizukov, A. I. 20
Lopatin, A. I. 67
Lyons, F. 314

Malenkov, G. M. 2

Malinin, M. S. 158
Malinovskii, R. Ia. 68, 132
Maliukov, G. F. 197
Manstein, E. v. 114, 116, 139, 198
Martianov, A. A. 11, 311
Maslov, A. G. 228
Matveev, V. N. 228
Mazalov, M. R. 11
Mazarini, General 30
Mazurkevich, R. 113
Mellenthin, F. W. 158
Molotov, V. M. 20
Moskalenko, K. S. 4, 9, 67, 68
Muller-Hillebrand, B. 39, 40
Murray, W. 255, 256, 257

Nikishev, D. N. 67
Novikov, A. A. 3, 256

Onianov, L. V. 11, 311

Paulus, F. 17, 26, 36, 39, 67, 114, 134,
    139, 149, 152, 154
Pavlenko, N. G. 11, 311
Pavlov, P. P. 113
Penchevskii, A. P. 11, 311
Peshekhontsev, V. P. 11
Petrov, I. A. 280
Pliev, I. A. 197
Plotnikov, Iu. V. 113
Plotnikov, Y. 20
Popov, A. F. 68
Popov, M. M. 133
Pospelov, P. N. 9
Pushkin, E. G. 68

Radio, S. 20, 280
Radzievskii, A. I. 113
Raynin, Ia. A. 309
Reichel, Major 40
Rodin, A. G. 113
Rokossovskii, K. K. 3, 4, 5, 44, 67, 75,
    84, 95, 132, 133, 137, 149, 158, 309
Romanenko, P. L. 95, 113
Romanov, S. 309
Rotmistrov, P. A. 132
Rudenko, S. I. 256

Safranov, S. 20
Samsanov, F. A. 11, 311
Samsonov, A. M. 5, 20, 68, 132, 323,
    324

Saraev, A. A. 68
Savin, M. V. 11, 312
Seaton, A. 39, 40
Sevrugov, S. N. 11
Seydlitz-Kurzbach, W. v. 40
Shaimuratov, M. M. 197
Shapkin, T. T. 197
Shaposhnikov, B. M. 20
Shumilov, M. S. 95
Skoromorokhov, N. 256
Skorikov, G. 255
Slomin, V. 67
Smirnov, K. N. 256
Soshnikov, A. I. 197
Stalin, J. V. 2, 3, 6, 7, 20, 21, 22, 39,
    68, 95
Stenescu, Brig. General 30

Talenskii, N. A. 11, 312
Tanaschishin, T. I. 132
Telegin, K. F. 158
Terekin, Colonel 187
Timokhovich, I. V. 197, 255, 257
Timoshenko, S. K. 20
Tolbulkhin, F. I. 95
Trufanov, N. I. 67, 95
Tsirlin, A. D. 11, 312
Tsvetaev, V. D. 133
Tumanian, G. L. 113
Turbin, Commissar 187

Utkin, V. D. 11, 312

Vasilevskii, A. M. 2, 3, 8, 20, 67, 92,
    95, 144, 153, 158
Vatutin, N. F. 4, 9, 95
Vechnyi, P. P. 1, 11, 313
Vladimirov, S. A. 11
Volskii, V. T. 132
Vorobev, F. D. 11
Vorobev, M. P. 11, 313
Voronov, N. N. 3, 20, 92, 149, 228
Voroshilov, K. E. 20

Wagner, R. 197, 255
Wiechs, M. v. 39

Zakharov, G. F. 67
Zakharov, Iu. D. 9
Zakharov, M. V. 5, 9
Zamiatin, N. M. 11, 313
Zhadov, A. S. 4, 9
Zhukov, G. K. 2, 3, 8, 15, 20, 68, 92
Zhuralev, N. A. 11, 313
Ziemke, E. F. 20

Subject Index

Order of Battle

Romanian Formations

ARMIES
3rd 17, 23, 25, 26, 28, 29, 31, 38, 41, 45, 69, 70, 75, 83, 101, 106, 109, 110, 132
4th 69, 83

CORPS
1st 29, 70, 83
2nd 29, 70, 77, 83
4th 70, 83
4th Cavalry 89
5th 29, 30, 70, 77, 83, 105
6th 23, 24, 25, 27, 29, 31, 38, 41, 49, 50, 53, 56, 71, 75, 78, 83, 89, 178
7th 83

DIVISIONS
Cavalry
1st 29, 31, 32, 33, 34, 70, 75, 83, 86, 137, 138, 172, 173
5th 29, 32, 33, 71, 83, 116, 119, 179
7th 29, 30, 32, 75, 83, 102, 106, 209
8th 29, 31, 32, 33, 71, 83, 116, 119, 180
Infantry
1st 27, 28, 29, 31, 32, 43, 56, 71, 75, 83, 88, 116, 119, 128, 178, 179, 182, 189
2nd 27, 28, 29, 31, 32, 43, 56, 71, 75, 79, 83, 88, 119
4th 27, 28, 29, 32, 33, 44, 56, 71, 83, 116, 119, 128, 129, 179
5th 29, 30, 31, 32, 70, 75, 79, 83, 85, 101, 105, 106, 161, 209
6th 29, 30, 31, 32, 70, 75, 83, 85, 209
7th 29, 32, 70, 75, 83, 161, 163, 166, 167, 170, 191, 210
9th 29, 30, 32, 70, 75, 79, 83, 85, 101, 161, 163, 166, 191
11th 29, 32, 70, 83, 161, 210
13th 29, 30, 31, 32, 70, 75, 83, 85, 170, 209
14th 29, 30, 32, 70, 75, 79, 83, 85, 101, 105, 106, 161, 163, 166, 167, 191, 209
15th 29, 30, 31, 32, 70, 75, 83, 85, 106, 170, 209
17th 51
18th 29, 31, 32, 70, 75, 83, 88, 116, 119
20th 88, 138, 219
Panzer
1st 29, 30, 32, 40, 75, 83, 85, 94, 102, 106, 107, 110, 163, 164, 191, 194

REGIMENTS
Cavalry
2nd/1st Cav. Div. 170
2nd/8th Cav. Div. 180, 189

3rd/8th Cav. Div.   180, 189
4th/8th Cav. Div.   180, 189
Infantry
1st/15th Inf. Div.   75
2nd/15th Inf. Div.   75
3rd/15th Inf. Div.   75
5th Jaegar/1st Inf. Div.   178, 189
17th/1st Inf. Div.   183
85th/1st Inf. Div.   183, 189
93rd/1st Inf. Div.   178, 182, 183, 189
Artillery
3rd   189
38th   183

BATTALIONS
7th Infantry Assault   170
4th Engineers   167

Italian Formations

ARMIES
8th   17, 23, 25, 26, 27, 31, 38, 41, 55, 69, 70, 83, 132

CORPS
2nd   70
35   70
Expeditionary   38

DIVISIONS
2nd Inf.   55, 83
9th Inf.   55, 83

BRIGADES
"January" Blackshirt   83

Hungarian Formations

ARMIES
2nd   23, 25, 26, 38, 41

German Formations

ARMY GROUPS
"A"   24, 25, 26, 37, 40
"B"   24, 25, 26, 38
North   24, 25
Center   24, 25
South   40
Don   132

ARMIES
2nd   24, 25, 26, 38

4th   25
6th   13, 17, 19, 23, 25, 26, 27, 28, 29, 31, 33, 34, 36, 37, 39, 40, 43 45, 49, 55, 59, 64, 69, 75, 83, 87, 92, 94, 114, 116, 117, 119, 123, 130, 132, 134, 137, 138, 149, 152, 154, 158, 170, 188, 244, 254, 258
9th   25
11th   24, 25, 26, 40
16th   25
17th   25, 26, 38
18th   25
20th   24, 25
"Lapland"   24
1st Panzer   13, 23, 25, 26, 38, 41
2nd Panzer   25
3rd Panzer   25
4th Panzer   13, 25, 26, 27, 29, 31, 33, 37, 38, 39, 41, 44, 49, 56, 57, 58, 59, 64, 69, 75, 83, 119, 134, 138, 149

CORPS
4th   27, 29, 30, 33, 83, 136, 138
7th   93
8th   26, 28, 29, 33, 83, 136, 137, 138
11th   26, 29, 33, 83, 137, 138
29th   31, 70, 210
51st   26, 29, 33, 83, 137, 138
14th Panzer   26, 27, 28, 29, 33, 83, 136, 138, 253
48th Panzer   27, 29, 75, 83, 94, 95
57th Panzer   132, 133

DIVISIONS
Infantry
3rd Mountain   24
5th Mountain   24
7th Mountain   24
7th Luftwaffe Field   32
41st   43
44th   27, 29, 32, 33, 34, 49, 55, 70, 75, 83, 86, 136, 138
62nd   31, 49, 83
71st   27, 28, 29, 33, 34, 43, 49, 70, 75, 83, 136, 138
76th   27, 28, 29, 33, 34, 43, 55, 70, 75, 83, 136, 138
79th   26, 28, 29, 33, 34, 49, 55, 70, 75, 83, 138
94th   27, 28, 29, 33, 34, 44, 56, 70, 75, 83, 138
100th Jaegar   27, 28, 29, 33, 34, 49, 55, 70, 75, 83, 86, 136, 138
113th   26, 29, 33, 34, 49, 55, 70, 75, 83, 136, 138
271st   49
294th   31, 49, 55
295th   27, 28, 29, 33, 34, 43, 56, 70, 75, 83, 137, 138
297th   27, 28, 29, 33, 34, 36, 43, 44, 49, 56, 75, 83, 136, 138
305th   27, 28, 29, 33, 34, 43, 49, 55, 70, 75, 83, 137, 138
336th   32
371st   27, 28, 29, 33, 34, 44, 56, 70, 75, 83, 136, 138
376th   27, 29, 31, 32, 33, 34, 49, 55, 70, 75, 83, 86, 136, 138
384th   27, 29, 32, 33, 34, 43, 49, 55, 70, 75, 83, 86, 138
389th   27, 28, 29, 33, 43, 55, 70, 75, 83, 137, 138
Motorized
3rd   27, 29, 31, 33, 34, 44, 49, 55, 57, 70, 75, 83, 86, 136, 138, 140, 170, 174
16th   49, 79
29th   27, 28, 29, 32, 33, 34, 43, 44, 49, 56, 70, 75, 83, 88, 89, 136, 138

60th   27, 29, 33, 34, 44, 49, 55, 57, 70, 75, 83, 137, 138, 253
Panzer
3rd   26
6th   32, 33, 37, 115, 116, 119, 123, 127, 132, 184, 187, 189, 198
9th   26, 40
11th   26, 32, 40
13th   26
14th   26, 27, 28, 29, 30, 31, 32, 33, 34, 40, 43, 49, 56, 70, 75, 83, 86, 137, 138,
    170, 173, 175, 209
16th   26, 27, 29, 33, 34, 44, 49, 55, 57, 70, 75, 83, 137, 138, 174, 175
17th   32, 33, 37, 119, 122, 127, 128, 133, 198
22nd   22, 26, 27, 29, 30, 31, 32, 40, 49, 55, 75, 83, 85, 94, 102, 106, 107, 109, 110,
    111, 164, 167, 191, 194, 209
23rd   22, 26, 32, 33, 37, 40, 116, 119, 121, 122, 127, 128, 198
24th   22, 26, 27, 28, 29, 33, 34, 43, 49, 56, 70, 75, 83, 86, 89, 137, 138

REGIMENTS
114th Motorized   184, 189
11th Panzer   189

LUFTWAFFE
4th Air Fleet   243
9th Flak Division   40
52nd Fighter Group   233
20th Transport Group   245
21st Transport Group   245
23rd Transport Group   245
406th Transport Group   245
700th Transport Group   245

Finnish Formations

ARMIES
Northern   25
Karelian   25

Soviet Formations

FRONTS
Don   15, 16, 17, 18, 33, 62, 65, 69, 71, 74, 76, 78, 84, 87, 89, 95, 130, 134, 137,
    138, 139, 140, 143, 144, 145, 146, 147, 148, 149, 150, 151, 152, 153, 154, 155,
    156, 158, 159, 160, 199, 201, 209, 210, 211, 212, 221, 228, 242, 243, 244, 251,
    258, 281, 283, 314, 315, 317, 319, 320, 321, 322, 323
Karelian   24
North Causasus   51
Northwestern   24
Southeastern   14, 52, 53, 54, 56, 58, 59, 60, 61, 66, 67
Southern   3, 44, 66, 149, 247, 251
Southwestern   13, 15, 16, 17, 44, 62, 66, 67, 76, 77, 78, 79, 84, 89, 95, 100, 101,
    112, 114, 123, 134, 159, 160, 199, 200, 205, 210, 211, 218, 228, 242, 243, 244,
    247, 258, 281, 314, 315, 316, 317, 319, 320, 321, 322
Stalingrad   13, 14, 15, 18, 22, 45, 49, 51, 52, 54, 55, 57, 58, 59, 62, 65, 66, 67, 71,
    74, 75, 76, 78, 83, 84, 86, 87, 89, 92, 100, 101, 102, 114, 121, 124, 132, 134,
    144, 153, 159, 160, 178, 192, 199, 200, 209, 217, 218, 228, 243, 244, 258, 259,
    260, 261, 262, 266, 269, 270, 271, 276, 279, 280, 281, 285, 314, 315, 316, 317,
    319, 320, 321, 322

Volkhov 24
Voronezh 201, 322

ARMIES
1st Guards 14, 44, 54, 55, 60, 61, 68, 84, 101, 107, 163, 166, 191, 199, 200, 201,
203, 209, 210, 316, 320, 321, 322
2nd Guards 119, 121, 122, 123, 124, 126, 127, 129, 130, 131, 132, 139, 144, 188
5th Shock 124, 133, 139, 144
1st Tank 49, 50, 67, 68, 96
4th Tank 44, 49, 50, 52, 54, 57, 58, 60, 62, 67, 96
5th Tank 20, 74, 75, 76, 79, 84, 85, 95, 96, 100, 101, 102, 103, 104, 106, 107, 108,
110, 113, 161, 162, 163, 166, 167, 190, 191, 192, 193, 194, 195, 200, 201, 203,
204, 205, 206, 209, 210, 228, 320, 322
1st Reserve 67
2nd Reserve 68
5th Reserve 66
7th Reserve 66
8th Reserve 68
9th Reserve 68
21st 44, 45, 50, 52, 54, 55, 60, 62, 67, 74, 76, 77, 84, 85, 86, 89, 95, 101, 106,
107, 109, 110, 111, 113, 137, 140, 144, 145, 150, 151, 154, 168, 169, 170, 171,
173, 177, 189, 190, 191, 192, 194, 195, 199, 200, 202, 203, 204, 206, 209, 210,
255, 320, 322, 323
24th 60, 61, 62, 68, 74, 78, 84, 86, 87, 95, 137, 140, 144, 145, 151, 155, 211, 212,
215, 320, 322, 323
28th 67, 79, 83, 95, 114, 144, 261, 269, 271, 277, 316, 320, 322
38th 67
51st 17, 44, 45, 51, 53, 67, 74, 78, 79, 83, 87, 88, 95, 114, 115, 116, 120, 121, 122,
124, 126, 127, 129, 130, 131, 144, 178, 179, 180, 182, 183, 185, 186, 188, 193,
195, 217, 218, 219, 220, 221, 226, 260, 261, 268, 271, 278, 280, 320, 323
57th 49, 53, 56, 74, 78, 79, 83, 87, 88, 92, 95, 119, 137, 144, 146, 150, 151, 154,
155, 178, 217, 218, 219, 221, 255, 260, 268, 320, 323
61st 14
62nd 44, 45, 46, 48, 50, 52, 53, 55, 57, 58, 64, 66, 67, 74, 78, 84, 89, 90, 95, 137,
140, 143, 144, 151, 232, 263, 267, 320, 323
63rd 14, 45, 49, 52, 54, 55, 60, 62, 64, 66, 76, 85, 101, 168
64th 44, 46, 49, 51, 52, 53, 56, 58, 67, 74, 78, 83, 87, 95, 119, 122, 137, 143, 144,
146, 150, 217, 220, 221, 259, 269, 277, 320, 323
65th 74, 78, 84, 86, 87, 89, 95, 137, 140, 144, 145, 150, 151, 155, 169, 170, 189,
211, 213, 255, 320, 322, 324
66th 68, 74, 84, 89, 137, 140, 146, 155, 211, 212, 217, 255, 320, 322, 324
Air Force
2nd Air 256, 319, 322
8th Air 230, 234, 237, 239, 242, 244, 245, 247, 250, 251, 255, 256, 319, 323
16th Air 230, 234, 242, 244, 245, 246, 247, 248, 250, 251, 253, 254, 255, 256, 319,
322, 324
17th Air 242, 244, 256, 319, 322

CORPS
Cavalry
3rd Guards 74, 75, 84, 85, 92, 159, 160, 168, 169, 170, 171, 172, 173, 175, 177,
189, 190, 191, 192, 193, 194, 195, 196, 197, 207, 208, 212, 322
4th 17, 74, 79, 83, 88, 114, 115, 120, 121, 122, 123, 126, 127, 130, 159, 160, 177,
178, 179, 180, 181, 182, 183, 185, 186, 187, 188, 189, 191, 192, 193, 194, 197,
218, 222, 223, 252, 323
7th Guards 168, 197
8th 74, 75, 84, 101, 102, 103, 106, 107, 109, 110, 111, 159, 160, 161, 162, 163,
164, 165, 166, 167, 168, 190, 191, 192, 193, 194, 195, 197, 205, 207, 322

Rifle
7th   74, 83, 137, 323
1st Guards   121, 122, 126, 128
4th Guards   316
6th Guards   316
13th Guards   121, 122, 124, 126, 128
Mechanized
1st Guards   316, 321, 322
2nd Guards   121, 122, 123, 124, 126, 127, 128
3rd Guards   123, 126, 128, 129, 131, 133
4th   74, 75, 79, 83, 85, 88, 92, 119, 121, 122, 132, 133, 178, 179, 190, 218, 220, 222, 223, 225, 252, 323
6th   126, 127, 128, 129, 131, 133
13th   44, 74, 75, 78, 79, 88, 92, 115, 119, 121, 126, 127, 128, 129, 132, 218, 252, 318, 323
Tank
1st   74, 75, 77, 84, 85, 101, 103, 105, 106, 107, 108, 110, 111, 113, 161, 162, 163, 177, 190, 193, 195, 205, 207, 322
2nd   44
4th   74, 75, 84, 85, 92, 169, 170, 171, 177, 189, 194, 195, 207, 208, 209, 212, 228, 322
7th   119, 122, 123, 124, 126, 127, 128, 131, 132
13th   67, 83, 132, 318, 323
16th   74, 84, 211, 228, 322
23rd   44, 57, 68
25th   112, 113
26th   74, 75, 77, 84, 85, 101, 102, 103, 105, 106, 108, 109, 110, 111, 113, 205, 207, 209, 212, 322
28th   67

DIVISIONS
Cavalry
5th Guards   159, 169, 170, 172, 173, 174, 176, 177, 194, 197, 322
6th Guards   159, 169, 170, 172, 173, 174, 175, 176, 177, 191, 197, 322
21st   109, 159, 163, 166, 168, 190, 191, 197, 322
32nd   159, 168, 171, 172, 173, 174, 175, 176, 177, 197, 322
55th   159, 161, 162, 163, 164, 165, 166, 168, 193, 195, 197, 322
61st   115, 119, 120, 159, 179, 180, 181, 183, 184, 185, 186, 188, 191, 192, 198, 226, 323
81st   115, 116, 119, 120, 154, 159, 179, 180, 181, 182, 183, 184, 185, 186, 187, 191, 192, 193, 194, 198, 226, 323
112th   159, 161, 162, 163, 164, 165, 166, 168, 193, 195, 197, 322
Rifle
3rd Guards   122, 126, 127
4th Guards   84, 322
13th Guards   84, 126, 137, 323
14th Guards   84, 103, 105, 113, 161, 209, 322
15th Guards   44, 83, 137, 224, 323
24th Guards   124, 128
26th Guards   44
27th Guards   84, 137, 322, 324
33rd Guards   44, 49, 126
34th Guards   322
35th Guards   44, 57, 316
36th Guards   44, 83, 137, 323
37th Guards   84, 323
38th Guards   122, 316
39th Guards   84, 137, 323

40th Guards 84, 166, 322
41st Guards 316
44th Guards 316
47th Guards 84, 103, 106, 109, 110, 113, 161, 167, 195, 322
49th Guards 124, 126, 127
50th Guards 322
51st Guards 323
52nd Guards 137, 323
53rd Guards 137
10th NKVD 44, 68
1st 322
20th 323
23rd 84, 137, 322, 324
24th 84, 126, 137, 322, 324
29th 44, 51, 83, 137, 323
38th 44, 83, 119, 126, 137, 323
45th 84, 137, 323
49th 84, 137, 322, 323
63rd 84, 322
64th 84, 137, 322, 324
76th 84, 169, 172, 173, 175, 176, 322
84th 84, 137, 322, 323
87th 57, 119, 121, 122, 123, 126, 127, 129, 316
91st 83, 119, 120, 121, 126, 129, 178, 180, 182, 192, 226, 323
93rd 84
95th 84, 137, 323
96th 84, 137, 322, 323
98th 122, 124, 128
99th 83, 137, 322, 324
112th 44, 83, 323
116th 84, 137, 322, 324
118th 44
119th 84, 103, 107, 109, 110, 113, 322
120th 84, 137, 322
124th 84, 107, 109, 110, 113, 137
126th 44, 51, 83, 119, 120, 121, 126, 129, 131, 179, 180, 181, 182, 183, 184, 185,
        186, 188, 222, 226, 323
131st 44, 323
138th 44, 51, 84, 137, 323
153rd 322
157th 44, 51, 56, 84, 137, 323
159th 109, 110, 113, 322
169th 84, 137, 323
173rd 84, 137, 322, 324
184th 49
187th 44
193rd 83, 323
195th 316
196th 44
197th 84, 322
198th 44
203rd 84, 201, 209, 322
204th 44, 83, 137, 323
208th 51
214th 84, 137, 322, 324
226th 83, 137, 322, 324
233rd 84, 137, 322, 324
244th 44

248th   322
252nd   84, 137, 322, 323
258th   84, 322
260th   84, 137, 322, 323
266th   322
273rd   84, 137, 322, 323
277th   84, 137, 177, 322, 323
278th   84, 322
284th   84, 137, 323
293rd   137, 169, 172, 322, 323
298th   84, 137, 322, 323
299th   84, 137, 322, 324
300th   119, 121, 122, 126, 127, 188, 275, 316, 323
302nd   83, 115, 117, 119, 121, 126, 127, 182, 184, 185, 186, 188, 194, 222, 226,
         323
304th   84, 137, 322, 324
308th   84, 323
315th   57, 119, 316
321st   84, 322
333rd   84, 322
343rd   84, 137, 322, 324
346th   84, 109, 110, 113, 322
387th   126, 127
422nd   44, 83, 137, 323
Air Defense
3rd PVO AA   169, 171
120th PVO Fighter   293, 294, 309, 319
Air Force
220th Fighter   246
226th Ground Attack   246
228th Attack   240
235th Fighter   246
283rd Fighter   246
287th Fighter   242
Fortified Regions
54th   137, 322, 323
76th   83, 121, 126, 127, 128, 226, 322, 323
77th   137, 316, 323
113th   137
115th   137, 316, 323
116th   322
118th   323
156th   137, 316, 323
159th   137, 322, 324

BRIGADES
Artillery
5th Tank Destroyer   169, 171, 207, 208
20th Tank Destroyer   122
Engineer
5th Independent   322
20th   44, 323
Mechanized
1st Guards   322
2nd Guards   322
3rd Guards   322
17th   120, 323
36th   323

59th   323
60th   323
61st   132, 323
62nd   120, 130, 323
Motorized
   4th Motorized Rifle   322
   14th Motorized Rifle   108, 322
   15th Motorized Rifle   322
   20th Motorized Rifle   44
   22nd Motorized Rifle   322
   38th Motorized Rifle   44, 137, 278, 323, 324
   44th Motorized Rifle   105, 322
   66th Motorized Rifle   44, 56
   154th Motorized Rifle   44
   156th Independent Motorized Rifle   137, 323
Rifle
   15th Naval   51
   66th Naval   83, 137, 323
   154th Naval   83, 137, 323
   42nd   84, 323
   52nd   322
   92nd   84, 137, 323
   93rd   137, 323
   96th   137, 323
   97th   137, 323
   115th   84, 323
   124th   84, 323
   143rd   83, 137, 323
   149th   84, 137, 323
   152nd   322
   159th   322
   160th   84, 323
Tank
   6th Guards   323
   8th Guards   101, 109, 110, 322
   10th   322
   13th   120, 127, 128, 323
   19th   106, 107, 108, 111, 32ℓ
   29th Independent   119
   26th   44
   45th   322
   56th   323
   58th   322
   59th   322
   64th   322
   69th   322
   78th   44
   84th   323
   85th   120, 185, 186, 187, 190, 316, 323
   89th   105, 322
   90th   137, 323
   91st   137, 324
   107th   322
   109th   322
   117th   105, 322
   121st   322, 324
   122nd   322
   138th   44

148th 322
157th 108, 322
159th 105, 322
164th 322
216th 102, 103, 322
235th 119, 137, 323
254th 126, 137, 323

REGIMENTS
Artillery
5th Guards 214, 216
33rd Tank Destroyer 105, 207
40th Guards 316
42nd Guards 316
43rd Gun 224
70th Guards 218
85th Guards Howitzer 218, 223, 224
148th Mortar 161
149th Tank Destroyer 178, 179, 180, 181, 183, 185
152nd Mortar 170, 171
152nd Howitzer 190, 207
174th Tank Destroyer 161, 162, 164, 190, 207
179th 161, 163, 164, 190, 207
213 Gun 201
266th Gun 218
312 Gun 202
331st Howitzer 207, 208
296th Gun 201
481st Tank Destroyer 207, 208
491st Tank Destroyer 218
492nd 218
518th Gun 210
565th Tank Destroyer 122, 218
648th Gun 202
765th Tank Destroyer 217
1092nd Gun 202
1104th Gun 218
1105th Gun 222
1107th Gun 202
1111th Gun 218
1159th Gun 218
1166th Gun 202
1168th Gun 202
1241st Tank Destroyer 207, 208
1249th Tank Destroyer 201
1250th Tank Destroyer 169, 170
1180th Tank Destroyer 207, 208
21st Guard Mortar 169, 170, 172, 202
35th Guard Mortar 161, 163, 164, 190, 202
62nd Guard Mortar 202
66th Guard Mortar 224
75th Guard Mortar 202
80th Guard Mortar 224
85th Guard Mortar 202
86th Guard Mortar 202
88th Guard Mortar 202
90th Guard Mortar 122, 224
91st Guard Mortar 122

125th Guard Mortar   218
140th Guard Mortar   218
39th PVO   322, 324
40th PVO   322
59th PVO   324
113th PVO   187
377th PVO   322, 324
586th PVO   161, 162, 163, 190, 191
1113th PVO   218
1170th PVO   218
1079th PVO   297
Cavalry
   Independent   323
Mechanized
   125th   222, 223
Motorcycle
   8th   75, 101, 102, 106, 109, 162, 205, 207, 208, 322
Rifle
   Composite cadet   323
   378th   123
   832nd   115
   971st   137
   1026th   137
   1028th   137
   1030th   137
   1034th   215
Tank
   1st Guards   137, 176, 322, 323
   2nd Guards   176, 322, 324
   4th Guards   170, 172, 176, 322, 324
   5th Guards   137, 324
   6th Guards   324
   7th Guards   137, 324
   8th Guards   137, 323
   9th Guards   137, 323
   10th Guards   137, 324
   14th Guards   137
   15th Guards   137, 324
   16th Guards   322
   17th Guards   322
   47th Guards   137
   30th Independent Heavy   323
   33rd Independent Heavy   323
   35th Independent   137, 316
   41st   120
   46th Independent Heavy   323
   55th   323
   59th Independent Heavy   322
   158th   323
   166th Independent   137, 316, 323, 324
   189th   137
   198th Independent   323
   234th Independent   137, 323

BATTALIONS
Artillery
   1st Tank Destroyer   322
   3rd Guards Independent Tank Destroyer   171

4th Tank Destroyer   181
8th Independent Tank Destroyer   162, 163
8th Independent Horse   171
13th Independent Horse   180
21st Tank Destroyer   322
1/21 Mortar   170
2/21 Mortar   170
45th Machinegun-Artillery   83
60th Tank Destroyer   322
63rd Independent Tank Destroyer   322
64th Independent Tank Destroyer   322
65th Independent Tank Destroyer   322
66th Independent Tank Destroyer   322
97th Independent Tank Destroyer   322
98th Independent Tank Destroyer   322
99th Independent Tank Destroyer   322
100th Independent Tank Destroyer   322
101st Independent Tank Destroyer   322
102nd Independent Tank Destroyer   322
1/152 Mortar   170
157th Independent   44
160th Independent   44
172nd Independent Machinegun-Artillery   323
177th Independent Machinegun-Artillery   83, 323
263rd Independent Horse   162
348th   137
400th Independent   137
416th Independent   137
267th Independent PVO   297
1007th PVO   299
Rifle
1st Independent Ski   323
15th Reconnaissance   108
21st Independent Ski   323
99th Independent Ski   323
156th Independent Naval   323
Tank
35th Independent Heavy   323
506th Independent   323
510th Independent Flamethrower Tank   103, 190, 322
511th Independent Flamethrower Tank   103, 161, 162, 163, 164, 190, 322
512th Independent   324
565th Independent   323

BATTERIES
See 222